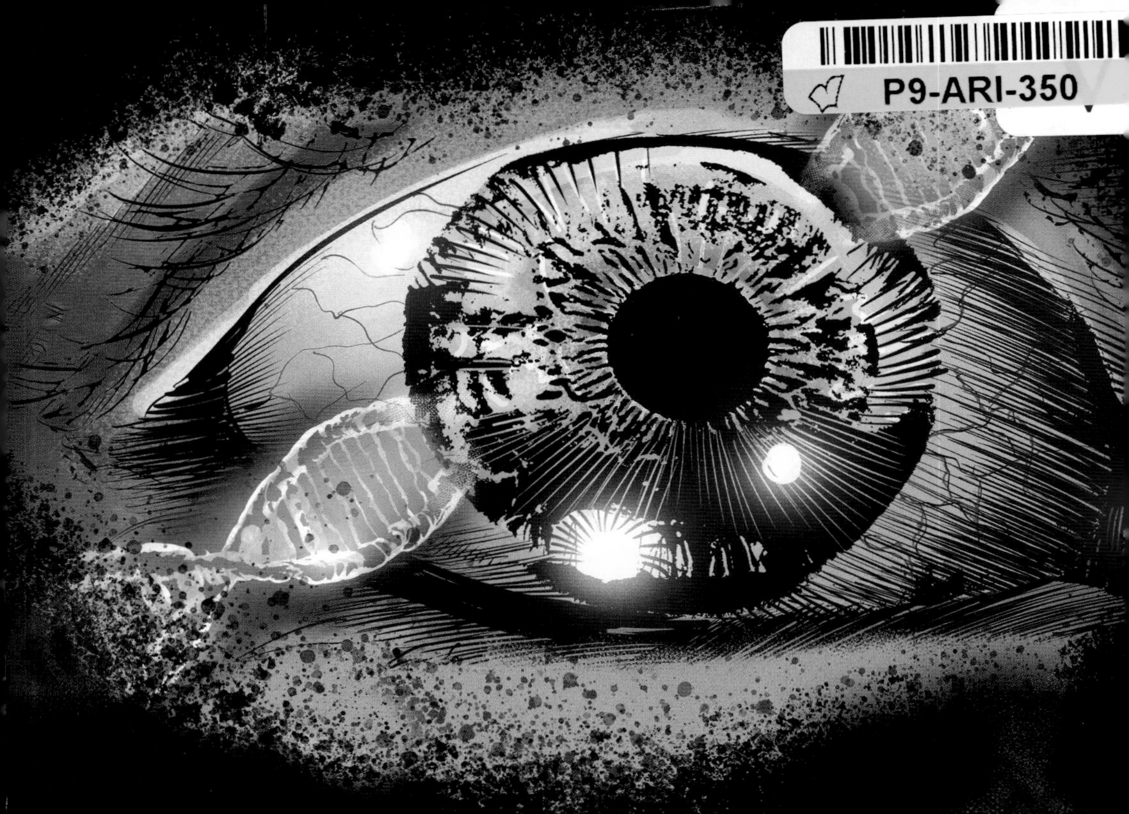

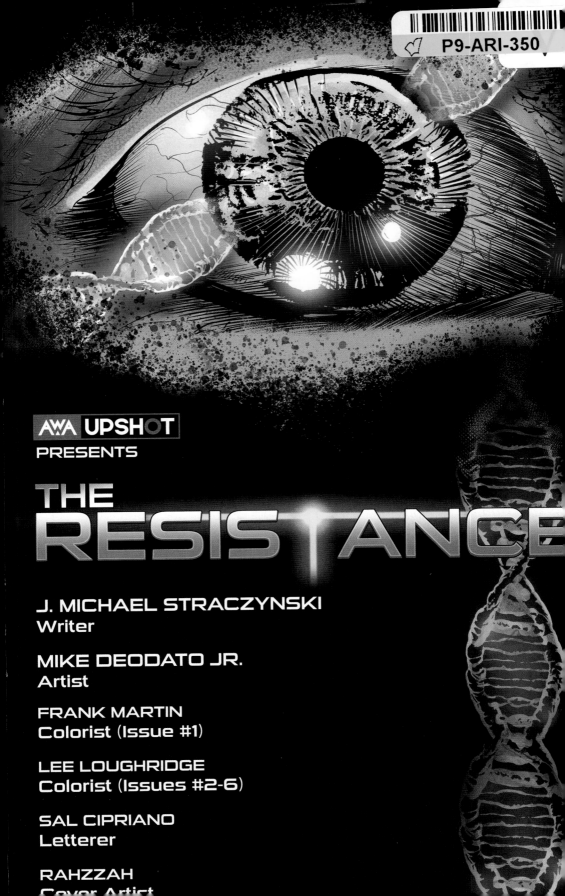

AWA UPSHOT
PRESENTS

THE RESISTANCE

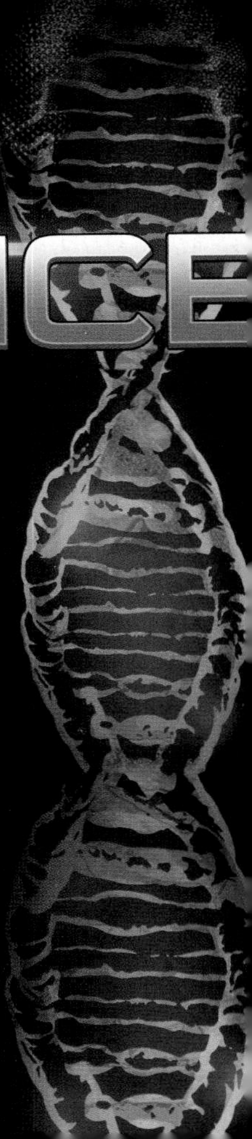

J. MICHAEL STRACZYNSKI
Writer

MIKE DEODATO JR.
Artist

FRANK MARTIN
Colorist (Issue #1)

LEE LOUGHRIDGE
Colorist (Issues #2-6)

SAL CIPRIANO
Letterer

RAHZZAH
Cover Artist

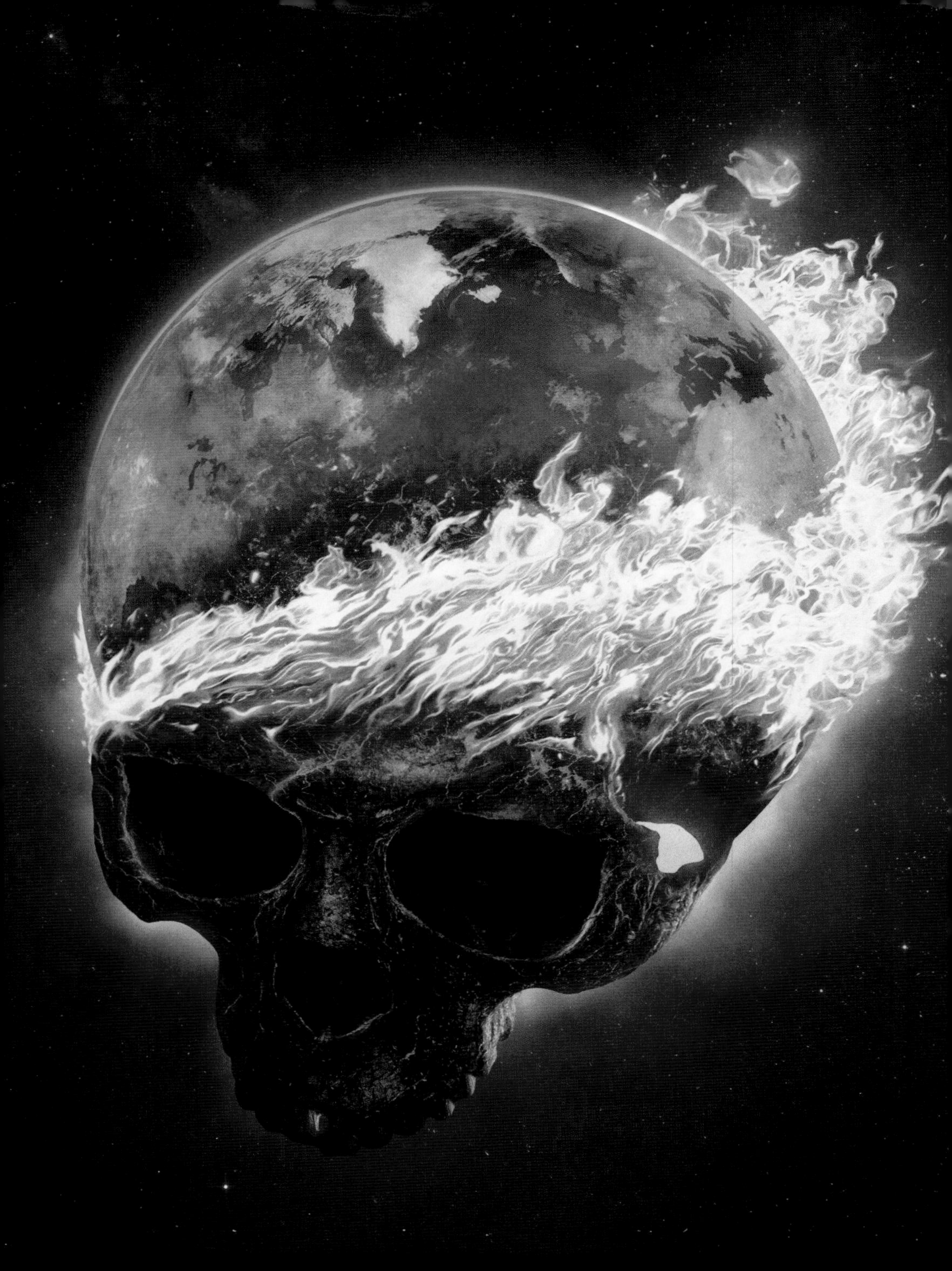

AWA UPSHOT AWA_studios AWAstudiosofficial UPSHOT_studios UPSHOTstudiosofficial

xel Alonso Chief Creative Officer
hris Burns Production Editor
an Chou Art Director, Logo Designer
ichael Coast Senior Editor
ime Coyne Associate Editor
ank Fochetta Senior Consultant, Sales & Distribution
illiam Graves Managing Editor
ll Jemas CEO & Publisher

Amy Kim Events & Sales Associate
Bosung Kim Production & Design Assistant
Allison Mase Executive Assistant
Dulce Montoya Associate Editor
Kevin Park Associate General Counsel
Maureen Sullivan Controller
Lisa Y. Wu Marketing Manager

HE RESISTANCE, VOLUME 1. October 2020. Published by Artists Writers & Artisans, Inc. Office of publication: 1359 Broadway, Suite 800, New York, NY

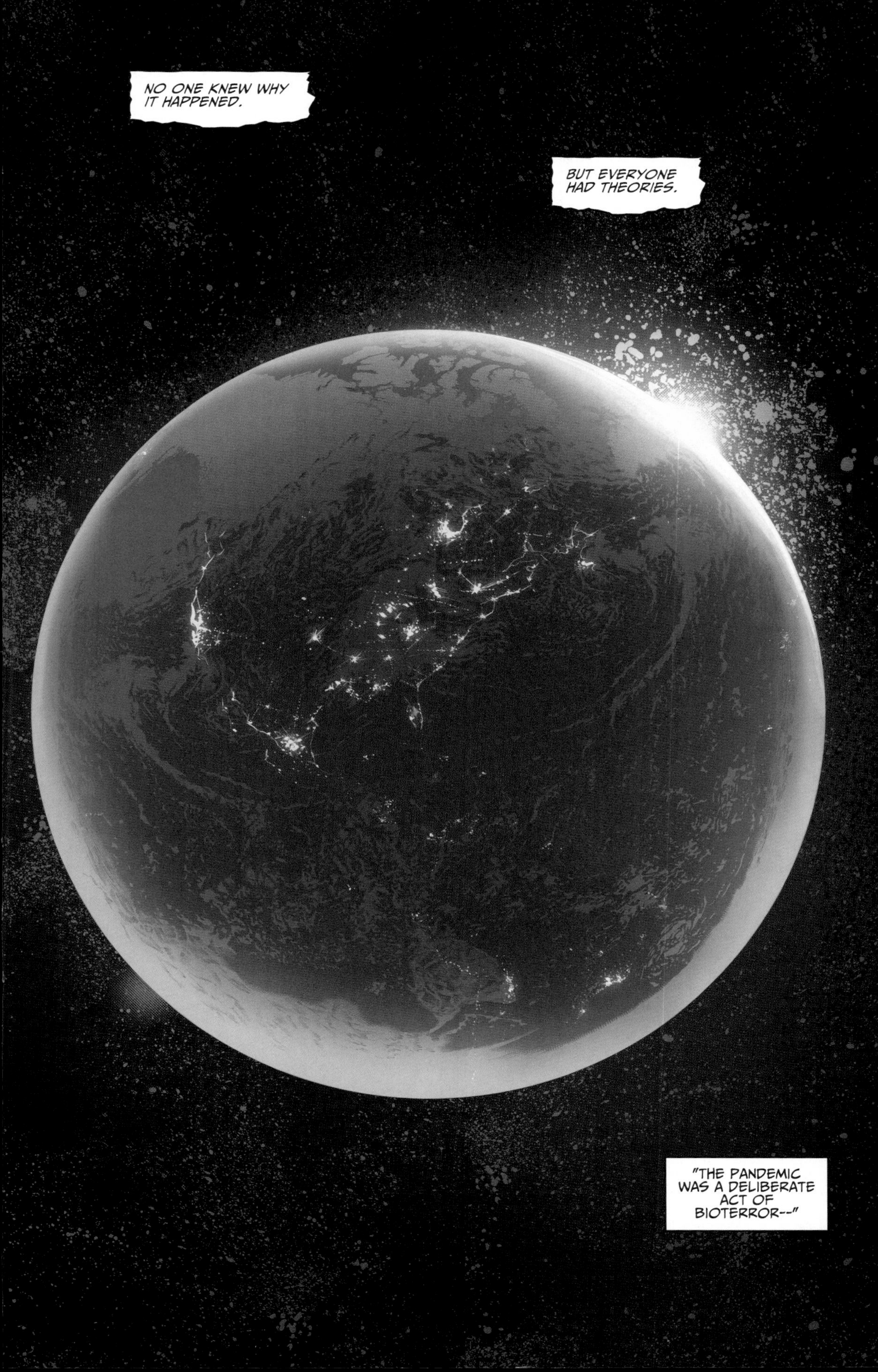
NO ONE KNEW WHY IT HAPPENED.
BUT EVERYONE HAD THEORIES.
"THE PANDEMIC WAS A DELIBERATE ACT OF BIOTERROR--"

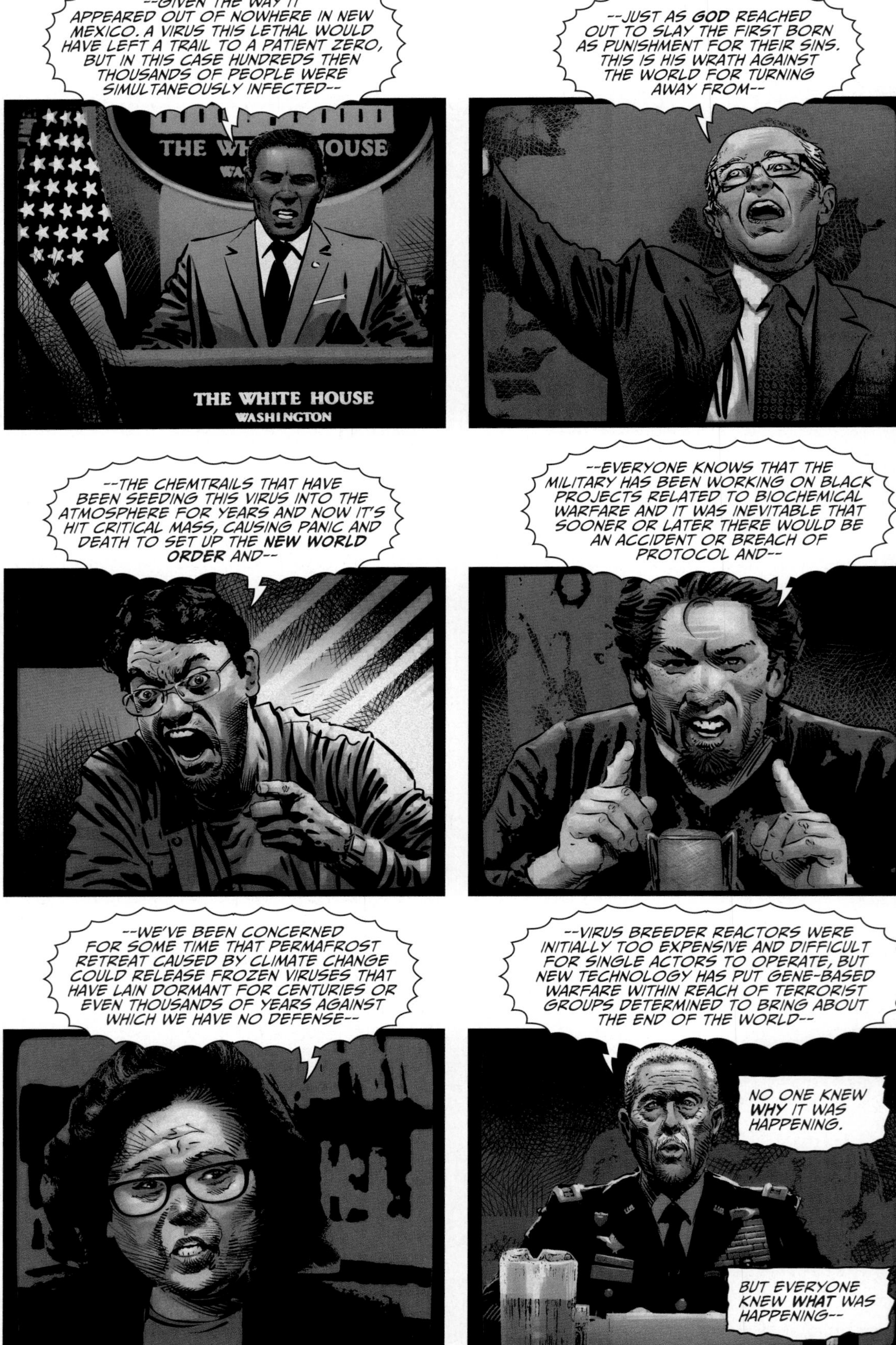
--GIVEN THE WAY IT APPEARED OUT OF NOWHERE IN NEW MEXICO. A VIRUS THIS LETHAL WOULD HAVE LEFT A TRAIL TO A PATIENT ZERO, BUT IN THIS CASE HUNDREDS THEN THOUSANDS OF PEOPLE WERE SIMULTANEOUSLY INFECTED--
THE WHITE HOUSE
WASHINGTON
--JUST AS GOD REACHED OUT TO SLAY THE FIRST BORN AS PUNISHMENT FOR THEIR SINS. THIS IS HIS WRATH AGAINST THE WORLD FOR TURNING AWAY FROM--
--THE CHEMTRAILS THAT HAVE BEEN SEEDING THIS VIRUS INTO THE ATMOSPHERE FOR YEARS AND NOW IT'S HIT CRITICAL MASS, CAUSING PANIC AND DEATH TO SET UP THE NEW WORLD ORDER AND--
--EVERYONE KNOWS THAT THE MILITARY HAS BEEN WORKING ON BLACK PROJECTS RELATED TO BIOCHEMICAL WARFARE AND IT WAS INEVITABLE THAT SOONER OR LATER THERE WOULD BE AN ACCIDENT OR BREACH OF PROTOCOL AND--
--WE'VE BEEN CONCERNED FOR SOME TIME THAT PERMAFROST RETREAT CAUSED BY CLIMATE CHANGE COULD RELEASE FROZEN VIRUSES THAT HAVE LAIN DORMANT FOR CENTURIES OR EVEN THOUSANDS OF YEARS AGAINST WHICH WE HAVE NO DEFENSE--
--VIRUS BREEDER REACTORS WERE INITIALLY TOO EXPENSIVE AND DIFFICULT FOR SINGLE ACTORS TO OPERATE, BUT NEW TECHNOLOGY HAS PUT GENE-BASED WARFARE WITHIN REACH OF TERRORIST GROUPS DETERMINED TO BRING ABOUT THE END OF THE WORLD--
NO ONE KNEW WHY IT WAS HAPPENING.
BUT EVERYONE KNEW WHAT WAS HAPPENING--

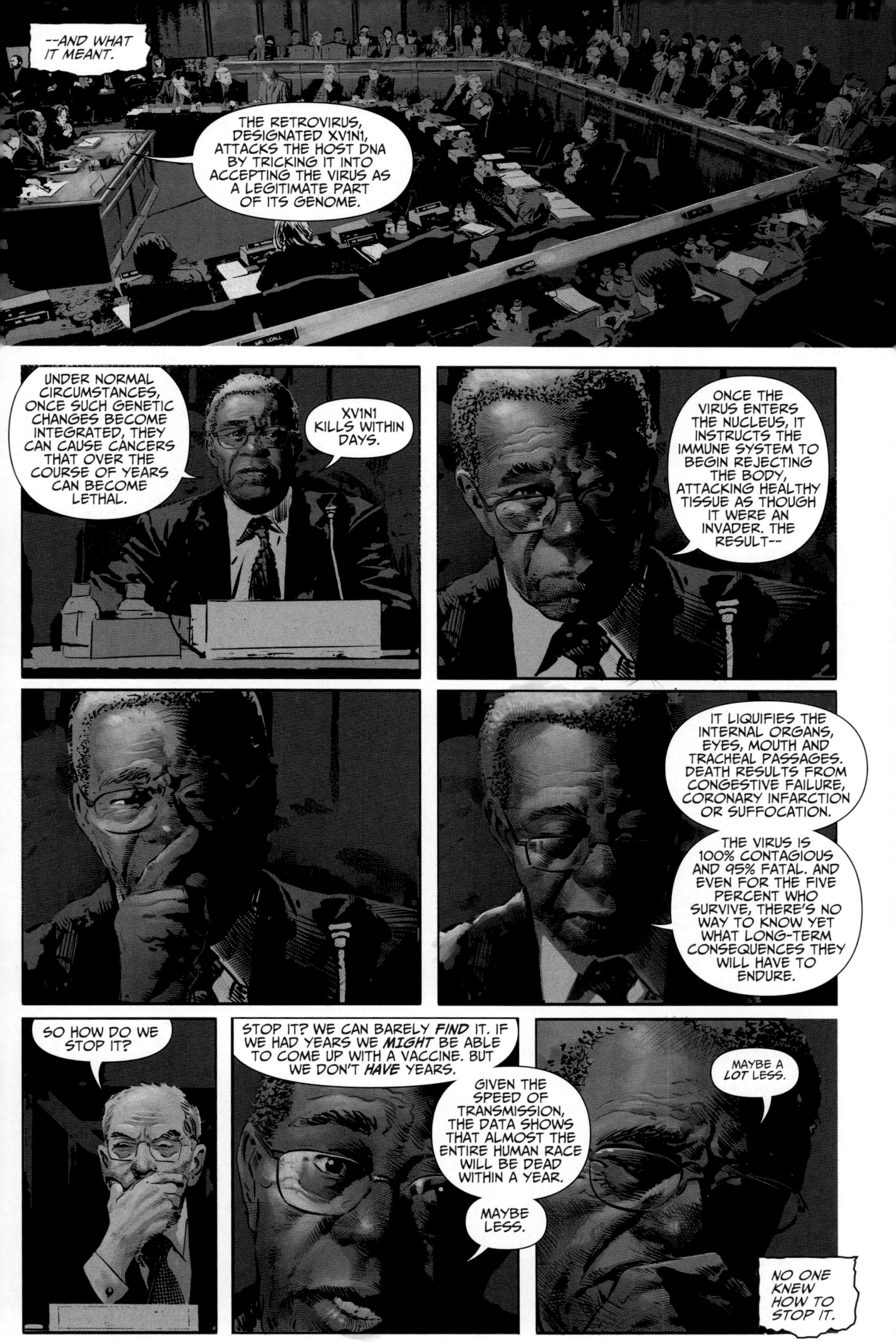
--AND WHAT IT MEANT.
THE RETROVIRUS, DESIGNATED XV1N1, ATTACKS THE HOST DNA BY TRICKING IT INTO ACCEPTING THE VIRUS AS A LEGITIMATE PART OF ITS GENOME.
UNDER NORMAL CIRCUMSTANCES, ONCE SUCH GENETIC CHANGES BECOME INTEGRATED, THEY CAN CAUSE CANCERS THAT OVER THE COURSE OF YEARS CAN BECOME LETHAL.
XV1N1 KILLS WITHIN DAYS.
ONCE THE VIRUS ENTERS THE NUCLEUS, IT INSTRUCTS THE IMMUNE SYSTEM TO BEGIN REJECTING THE BODY, ATTACKING HEALTHY TISSUE AS THOUGH IT WERE AN INVADER. THE RESULT--
IT LIQUIFIES THE INTERNAL ORGANS, EYES, MOUTH AND TRACHEAL PASSAGES. DEATH RESULTS FROM CONGESTIVE FAILURE, CORONARY INFARCTION OR SUFFOCATION.
THE VIRUS IS 100% CONTAGIOUS AND 95% FATAL. AND EVEN FOR THE FIVE PERCENT WHO SURVIVE, THERE'S NO WAY TO KNOW YET WHAT LONG-TERM CONSEQUENCES THEY WILL HAVE TO ENDURE.
SO HOW DO WE STOP IT?
STOP IT? WE CAN BARELY *FIND* IT. IF WE HAD YEARS WE *MIGHT* BE ABLE TO COME UP WITH A VACCINE. BUT WE DON'T *HAVE* YEARS.
GIVEN THE SPEED OF TRANSMISSION, THE DATA SHOWS THAT ALMOST THE ENTIRE HUMAN RACE WILL BE DEAD WITHIN A YEAR.
MAYBE LESS.
MAYBE A *LOT* LESS.
NO ONE KNEW HOW TO STOP IT.

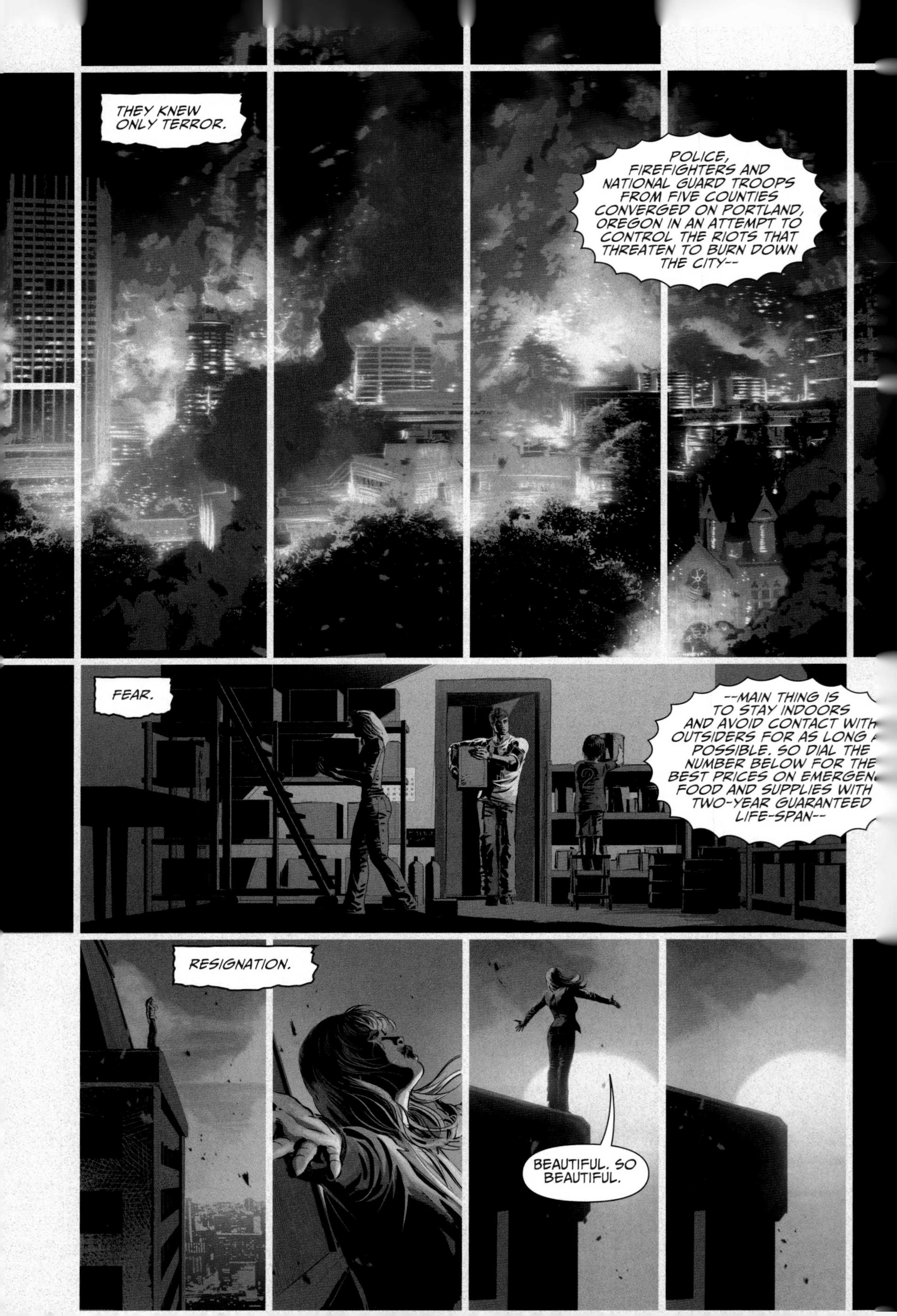
THEY KNEW ONLY TERROR.
POLICE, FIREFIGHTERS AND NATIONAL GUARD TROOPS FROM FIVE COUNTIES CONVERGED ON PORTLAND, OREGON IN AN ATTEMPT TO CONTROL THE RIOTS THAT THREATEN TO BURN DOWN THE CITY--
FEAR.
--MAIN THING IS TO STAY INDOORS AND AVOID CONTACT WITH OUTSIDERS FOR AS LONG POSSIBLE. SO DIAL THE NUMBER BELOW FOR THE BEST PRICES ON EMERGEN FOOD AND SUPPLIES WITH TWO-YEAR GUARANTEED LIFE-SPAN--
RESIGNATION.
BEAUTIFUL. SO BEAUTIFUL.

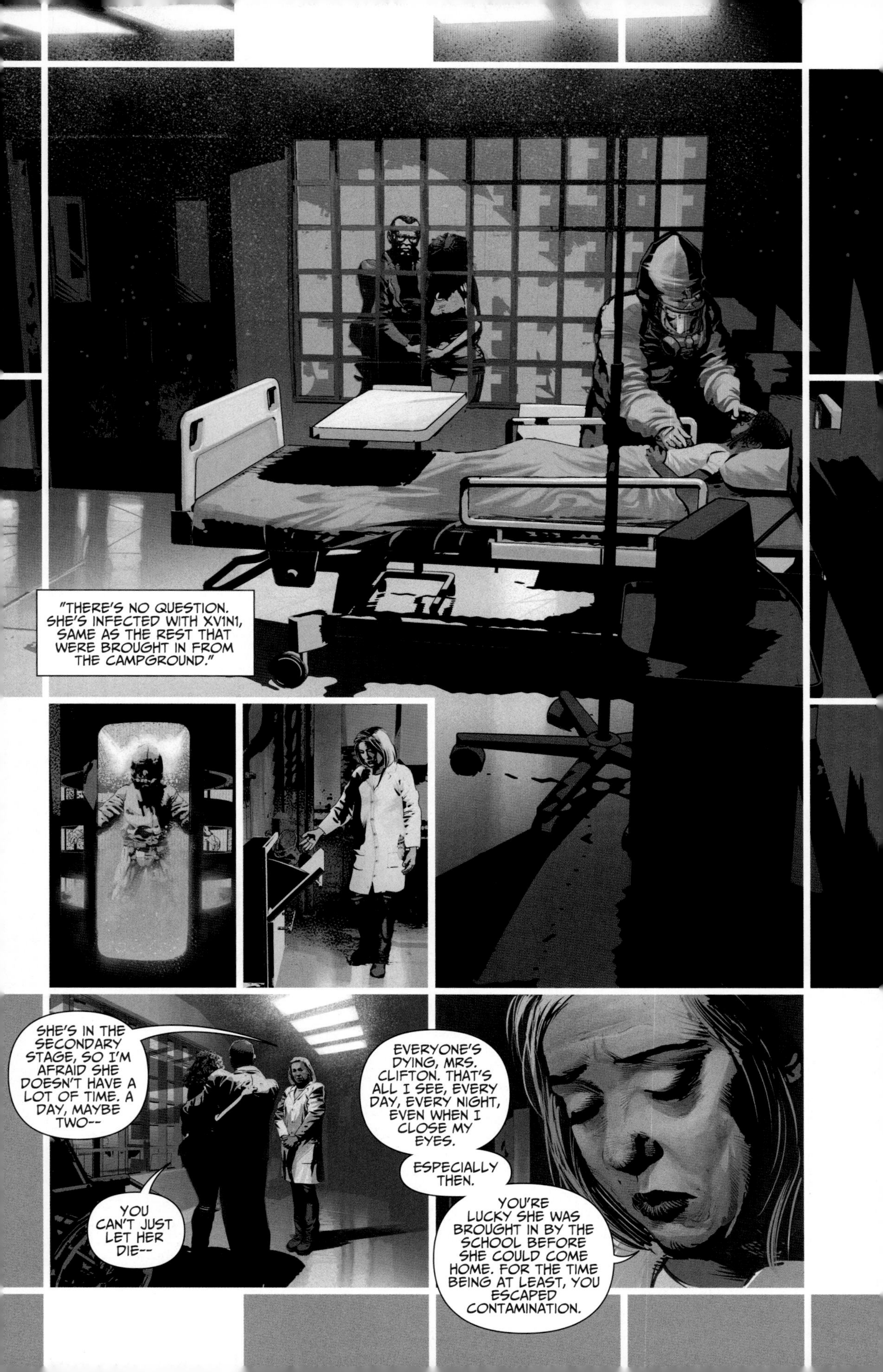
"THERE'S NO QUESTION. SHE'S INFECTED WITH XV1N1, SAME AS THE REST THAT WERE BROUGHT IN FROM THE CAMPGROUND."
SHE'S IN THE SECONDARY STAGE, SO I'M AFRAID SHE DOESN'T HAVE A LOT OF TIME. A DAY, MAYBE TWO--
YOU CAN'T JUST LET HER DIE--
EVERYONE'S DYING, MRS. CLIFTON. THAT'S ALL I SEE, EVERY DAY, EVERY NIGHT, EVEN WHEN I CLOSE MY EYES.
ESPECIALLY THEN.
YOU'RE LUCKY SHE WAS BROUGHT IN BY THE SCHOOL BEFORE SHE COULD COME HOME. FOR THE TIME BEING AT LEAST, YOU ESCAPED CONTAMINATION.

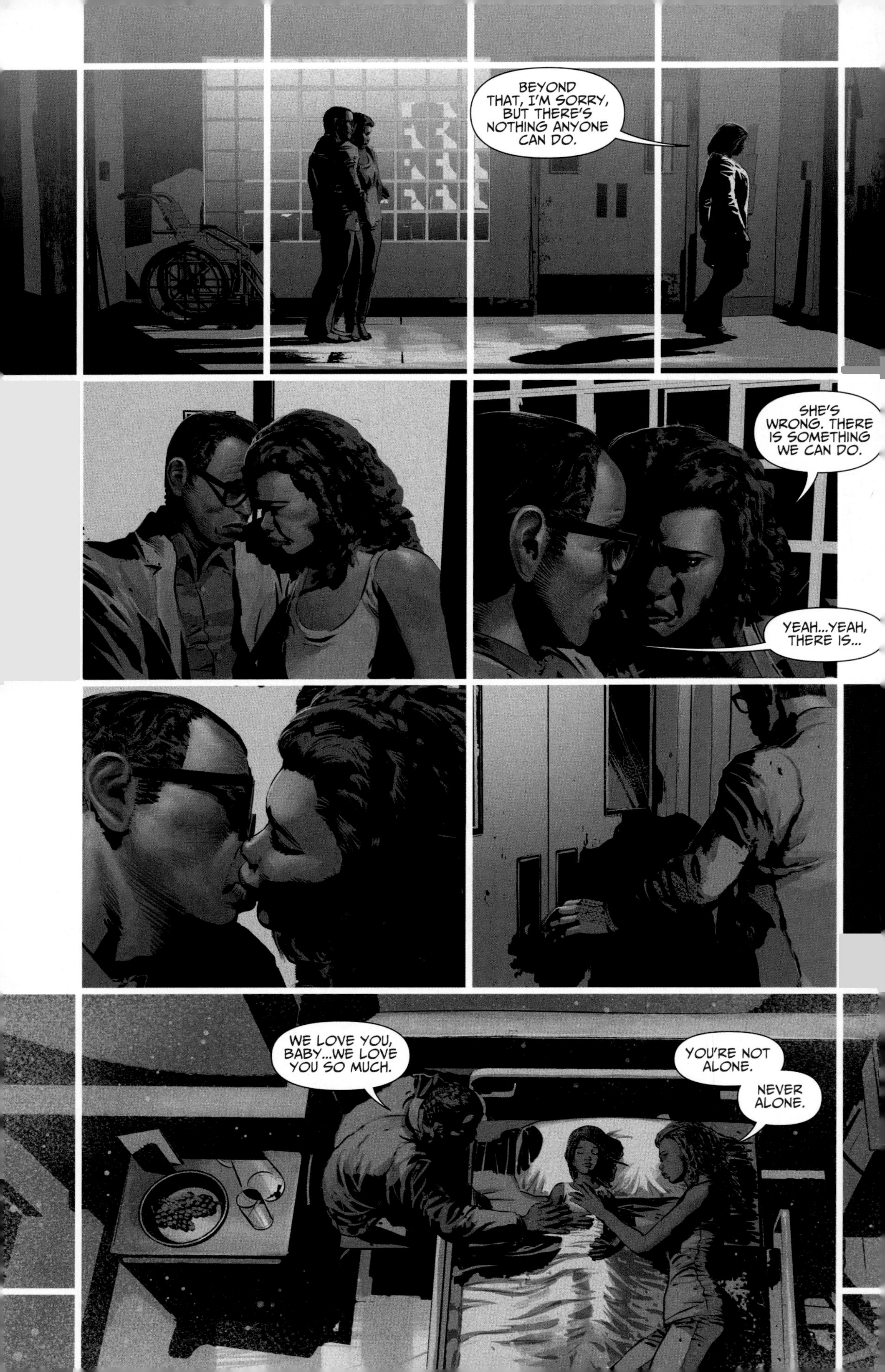
BEYOND THAT, I'M SORRY, BUT THERE'S NOTHING ANYONE CAN DO.
SHE'S WRONG. THERE IS SOMETHING WE CAN DO.
YEAH...YEAH, THERE IS...
WE LOVE YOU, BABY...WE LOVE YOU SO MUCH.
YOU'RE NOT ALONE.
NEVER ALONE.

THE NATIONS OF THE WORLD, ONCE DIVIDED BY FEAR, NOW FOUND THEMSELVES UNITED BY IT.

"THE BLOCKADES AND CURFEWS ARE NOT WORKING, PRESIDENT VOLKOV."

PEOPLE STILL HAVE TO EAT, THAT MEANS GOING INTO SHOPPING AREAS AND TOUCHING FOOD THAT HAS BEEN--

THEN SHUT DOWN THE MARKETPLACES.

THEN THE PEOPLE WILL STARVE.

THEN THEY WILL STARVE.

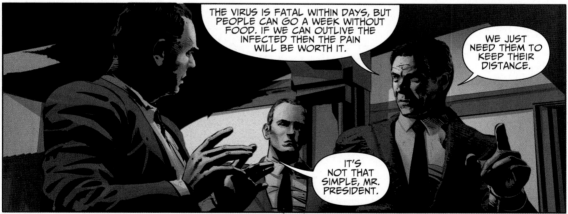

THE VIRUS IS FATAL WITHIN DAYS, BUT PEOPLE CAN GO A WEEK WITHOUT FOOD. IF WE CAN OUTLIVE THE INFECTED THEN THE PAIN WILL BE WORTH IT.

WE JUST NEED THEM TO KEEP THEIR DISTANCE.

IT'S NOT THAT SIMPLE, MR. PRESIDENT.

ONE OF THE LAST RECORDED CASES OF SMALLPOX WAS IN 1970. THE PATIENT WAS KEPT IN COMPLETE ISOLATION IN AN OTHERWISE EMPTY HOSPITAL WING IN MESCHEDE, WEST GERMANY.

DESPITE THIS, A PATIENT ON THE FLOOR *ABOVE* HIM, WHO NEVER HAD ANY CONTACT WITH THIS INDIVIDUAL, *ALSO* CAME DOWN WITH SMALLPOX.

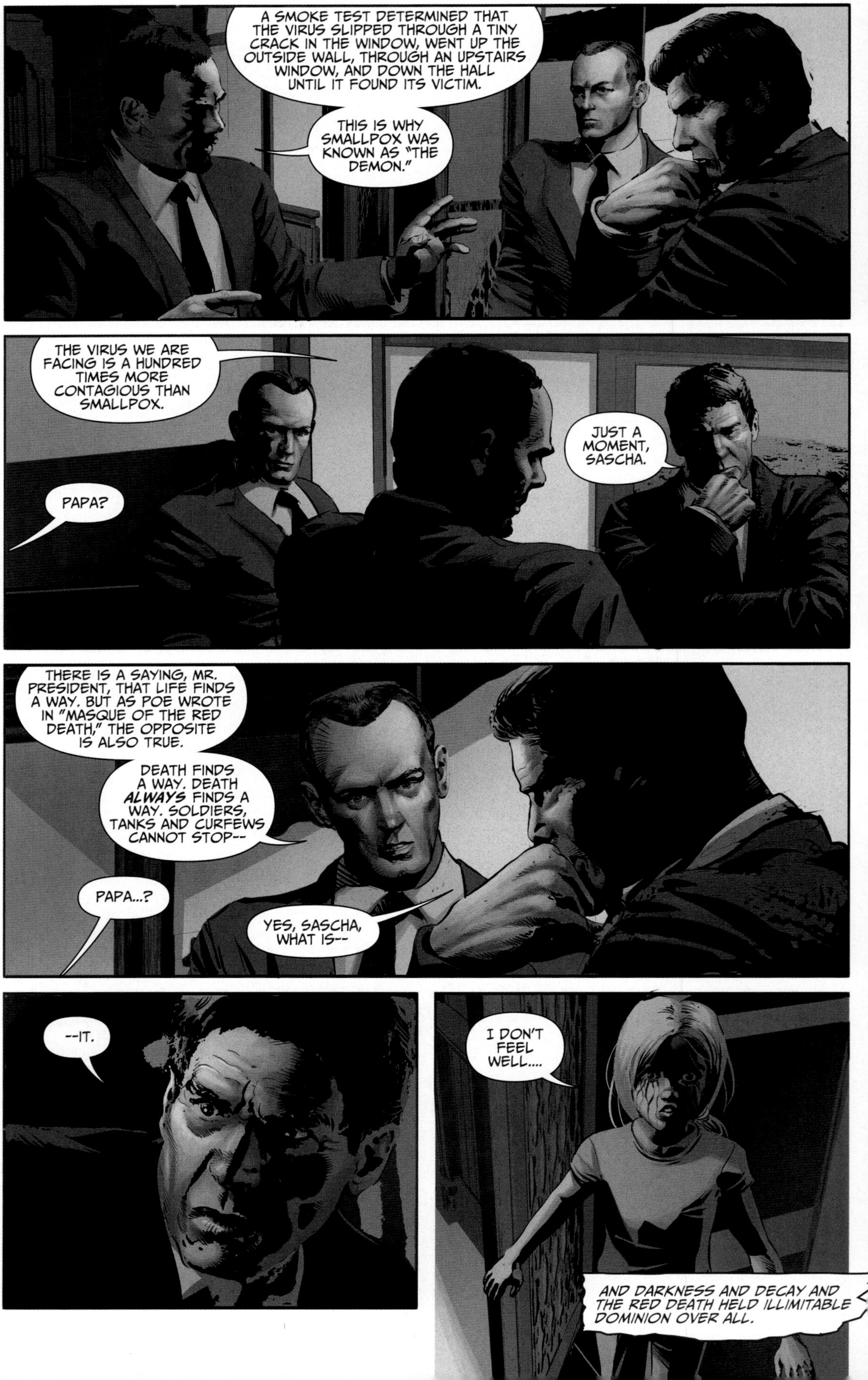
A SMOKE TEST DETERMINED THAT THE VIRUS SLIPPED THROUGH A TINY CRACK IN THE WINDOW, WENT UP THE OUTSIDE WALL, THROUGH AN UPSTAIRS WINDOW, AND DOWN THE HALL UNTIL IT FOUND ITS VICTIM.
THIS IS WHY SMALLPOX WAS KNOWN AS "THE DEMON."
THE VIRUS WE ARE FACING IS A HUNDRED TIMES MORE CONTAGIOUS THAN SMALLPOX.
PAPA?
JUST A MOMENT, SASCHA.
THERE IS A SAYING, MR. PRESIDENT, THAT LIFE FINDS A WAY. BUT AS POE WROTE IN "MASQUE OF THE RED DEATH," THE OPPOSITE IS ALSO TRUE.
DEATH FINDS A WAY. DEATH *ALWAYS* FINDS A WAY. SOLDIERS, TANKS AND CURFEWS CANNOT STOP--
PAPA...?
YES, SASCHA, WHAT IS--
--IT.
I DON'T FEEL WELL....
AND DARKNESS AND DECAY AND THE RED DEATH HELD ILLIMITABLE DOMINION OVER ALL.

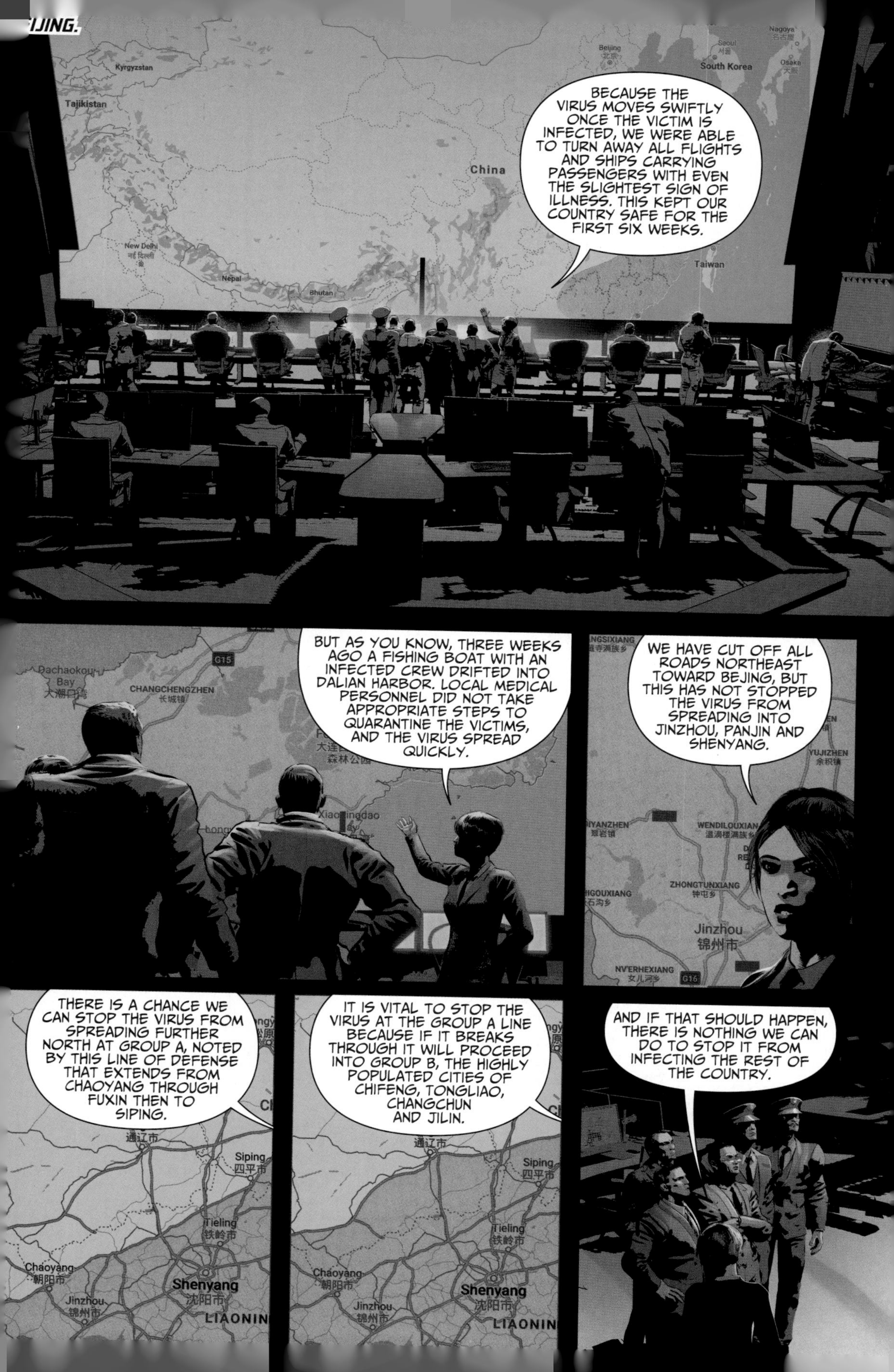
IJING.
BECAUSE THE VIRUS MOVES SWIFTLY ONCE THE VICTIM IS INFECTED, WE WERE ABLE TO TURN AWAY ALL FLIGHTS AND SHIPS CARRYING PASSENGERS WITH EVEN THE SLIGHTEST SIGN OF ILLNESS. THIS KEPT OUR COUNTRY SAFE FOR THE FIRST SIX WEEKS.
BUT AS YOU KNOW, THREE WEEKS AGO A FISHING BOAT WITH AN INFECTED CREW DRIFTED INTO DALIAN HARBOR. LOCAL MEDICAL PERSONNEL DID NOT TAKE APPROPRIATE STEPS TO QUARANTINE THE VICTIMS, AND THE VIRUS SPREAD QUICKLY.
WE HAVE CUT OFF ALL ROADS NORTHEAST TOWARD BEJING, BUT THIS HAS NOT STOPPED THE VIRUS FROM SPREADING INTO JINZHOU, PANJIN AND SHENYANG.
THERE IS A CHANCE WE CAN STOP THE VIRUS FROM SPREADING FURTHER NORTH AT GROUP A, NOTED BY THIS LINE OF DEFENSE THAT EXTENDS FROM CHAOYANG THROUGH FUXIN THEN TO SIPING.
IT IS VITAL TO STOP THE VIRUS AT THE GROUP A LINE BECAUSE IF IT BREAKS THROUGH IT WILL PROCEED INTO GROUP B, THE HIGHLY POPULATED CITIES OF CHIFENG, TONGLIAO, CHANGCHUN AND JILIN.
AND IF THAT SHOULD HAPPEN, THERE IS NOTHING WE CAN DO TO STOP IT FROM INFECTING THE REST OF THE COUNTRY.

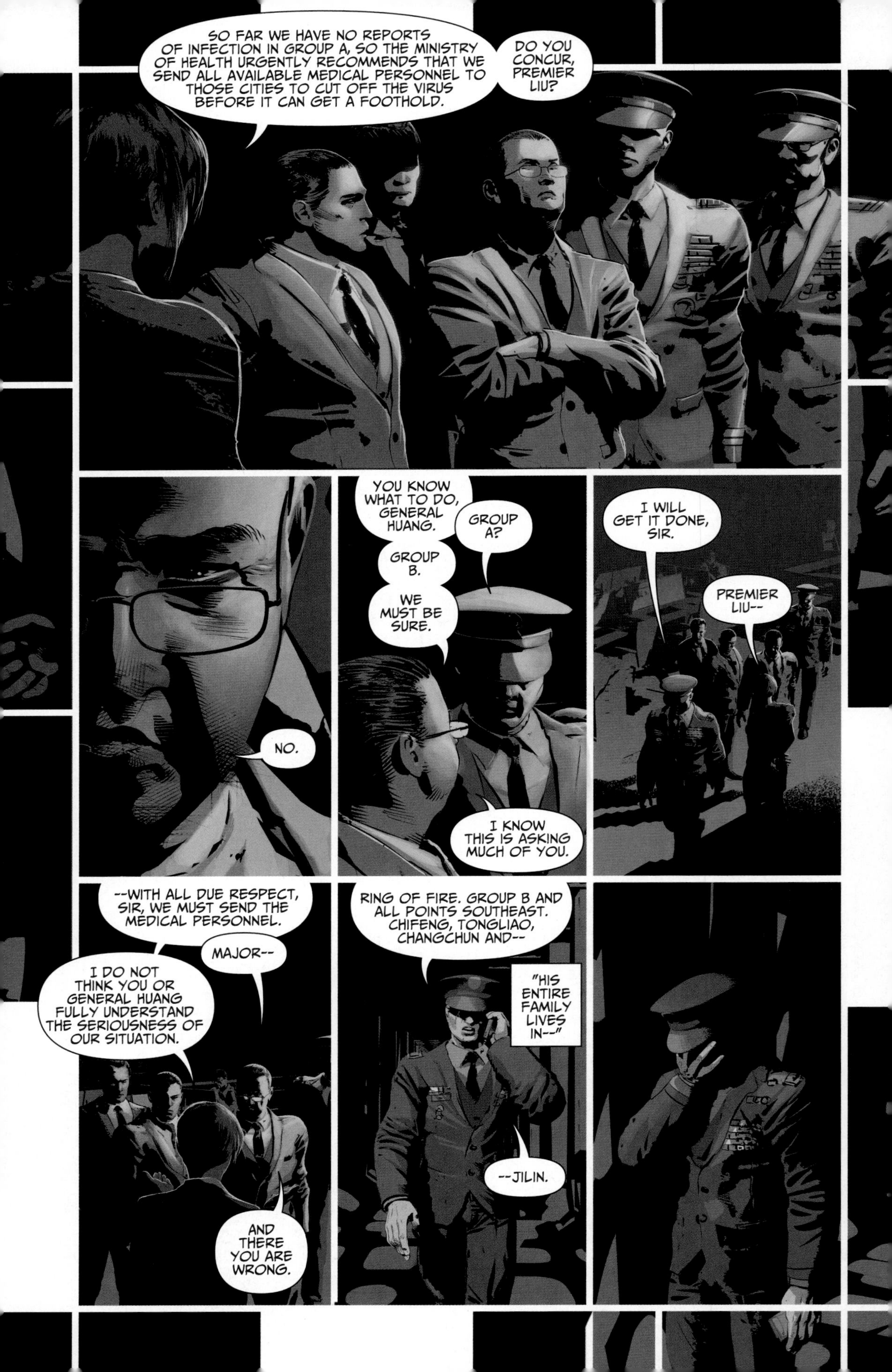
SO FAR WE HAVE NO REPORTS OF INFECTION IN GROUP A, SO THE MINISTRY OF HEALTH URGENTLY RECOMMENDS THAT WE SEND ALL AVAILABLE MEDICAL PERSONNEL TO THOSE CITIES TO CUT OFF THE VIRUS BEFORE IT CAN GET A FOOTHOLD.
DO YOU CONCUR, PREMIER LIU?
NO.
YOU KNOW WHAT TO DO, GENERAL HUANG.
GROUP A?
GROUP B.
WE MUST BE SURE.
I KNOW THIS IS ASKING MUCH OF YOU.
I WILL GET IT DONE, SIR.
PREMIER LIU--
--WITH ALL DUE RESPECT, SIR, WE MUST SEND THE MEDICAL PERSONNEL.
MAJOR--
I DO NOT THINK YOU OR GENERAL HUANG FULLY UNDERSTAND THE SERIOUSNESS OF OUR SITUATION.
AND THERE YOU ARE WRONG.
RING OF FIRE. GROUP B AND ALL POINTS SOUTHEAST. CHIFENG, TONGLIAO, CHANGCHUN AND--
"HIS ENTIRE FAMILY LIVES IN--"
--JILIN.

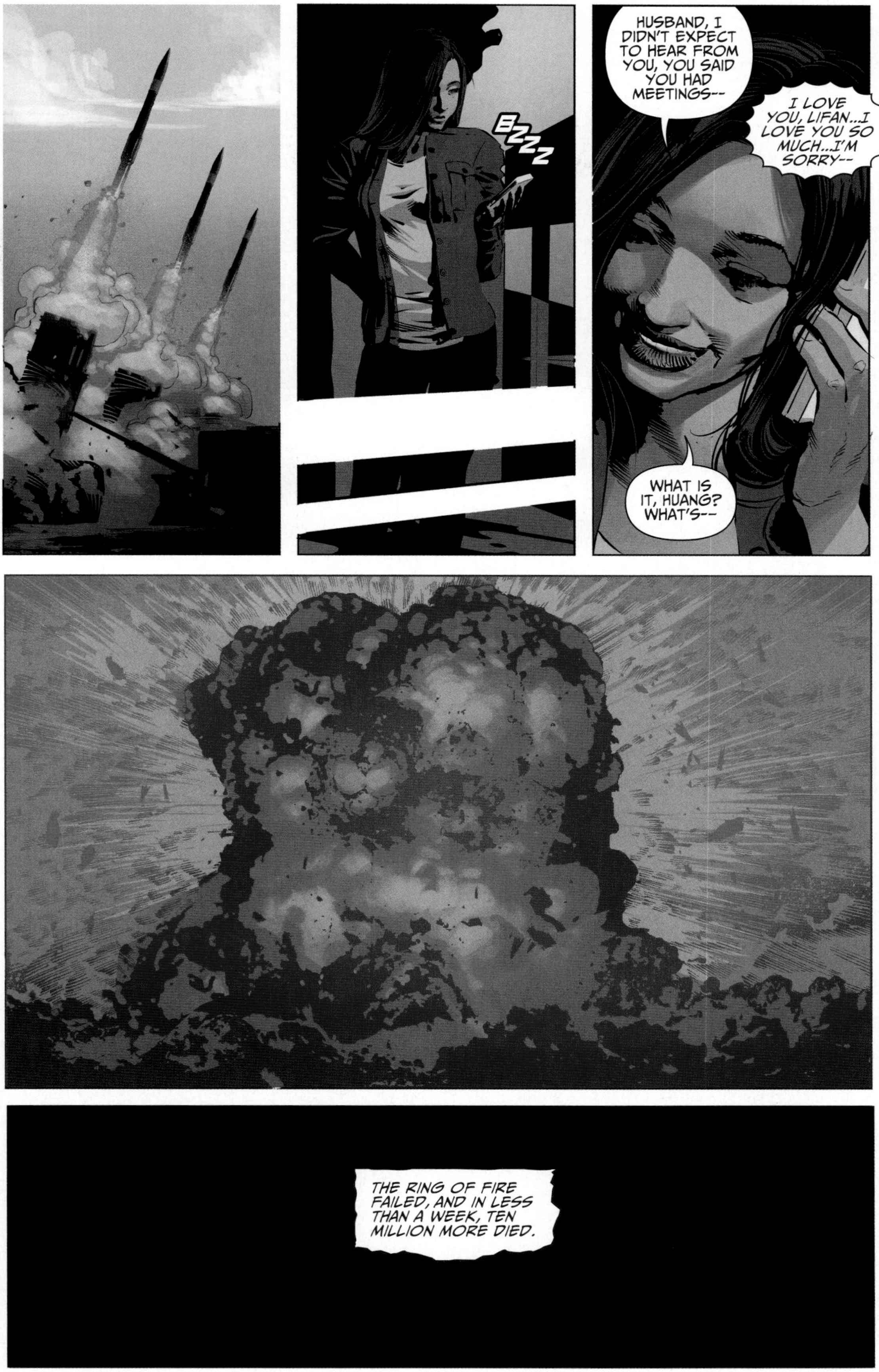
BZZZ
HUSBAND, I DIDN'T EXPECT TO HEAR FROM YOU, YOU SAID YOU HAD MEETINGS--
I LOVE YOU, LIFAN...I LOVE YOU SO MUCH...I'M SORRY--
WHAT IS IT, HUANG? WHAT'S--
THE RING OF FIRE FAILED, AND IN LESS THAN A WEEK, TEN MILLION MORE DIED.

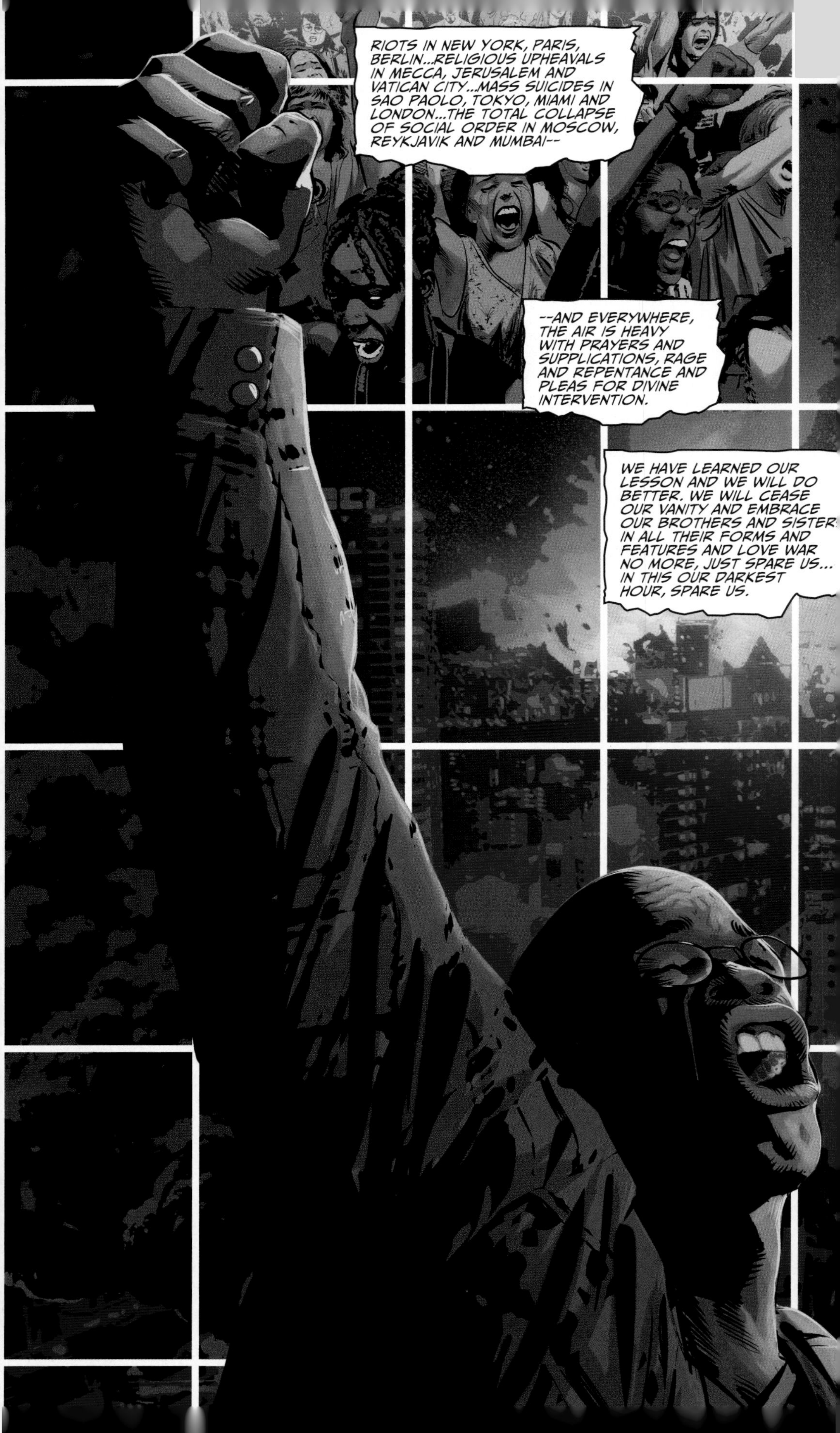
RIOTS IN NEW YORK, PARIS, BERLIN...RELIGIOUS UPHEAVALS IN MECCA, JERUSALEM AND VATICAN CITY...MASS SUICIDES IN SAO PAOLO, TOKYO, MIAMI AND LONDON...THE TOTAL COLLAPSE OF SOCIAL ORDER IN MOSCOW, REYKJAVIK AND MUMBAI--
--AND EVERYWHERE, THE AIR IS HEAVY WITH PRAYERS AND SUPPLICATIONS, RAGE AND REPENTANCE AND PLEAS FOR DIVINE INTERVENTION.
WE HAVE LEARNED OUR LESSON AND WE WILL DO BETTER. WE WILL CEASE OUR VANITY AND EMBRACE OUR BROTHERS AND SISTER IN ALL THEIR FORMS AND FEATURES AND LOVE WAR NO MORE, JUST SPARE US... IN THIS OUR DARKEST HOUR, SPARE US.

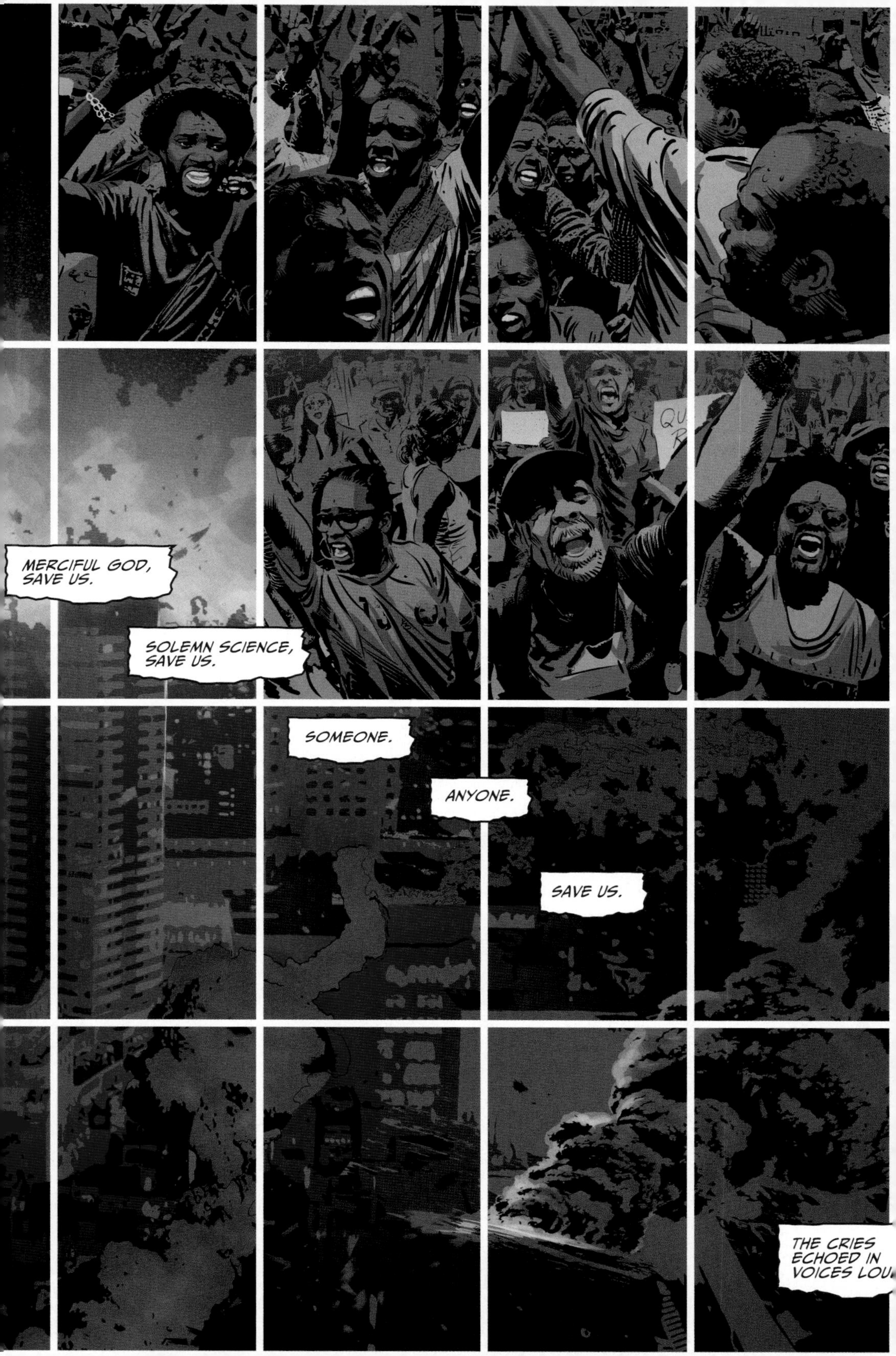
MERCIFUL GOD, SAVE US.
SOLEMN SCIENCE, SAVE US.
SOMEONE.
ANYONE.
SAVE US.
THE CRIES ECHOED IN VOICES LOU

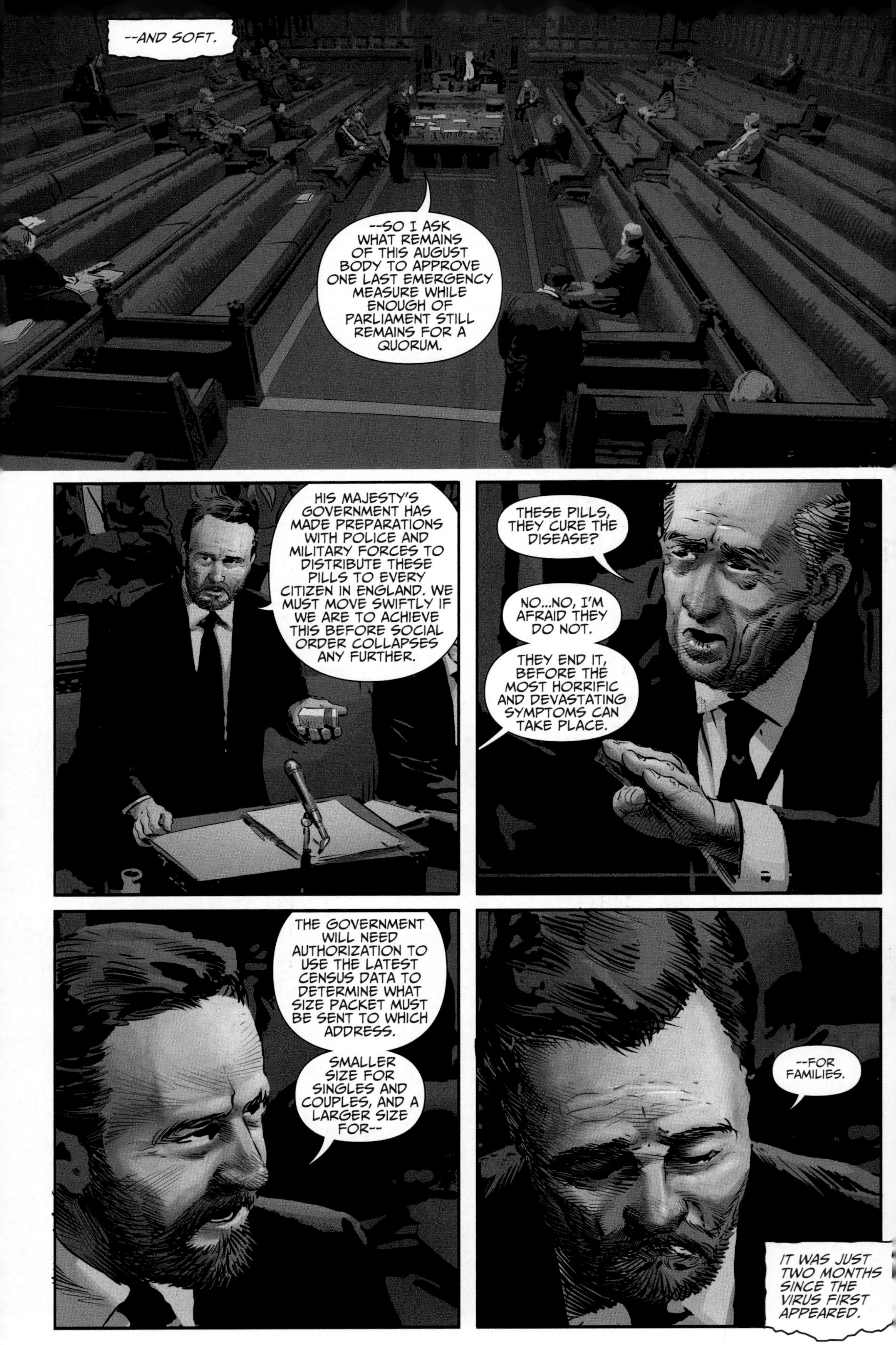
--AND SOFT.
--SO I ASK WHAT REMAINS OF THIS AUGUST BODY TO APPROVE ONE LAST EMERGENCY MEASURE WHILE ENOUGH OF PARLIAMENT STILL REMAINS FOR A QUORUM.
HIS MAJESTY'S GOVERNMENT HAS MADE PREPARATIONS WITH POLICE AND MILITARY FORCES TO DISTRIBUTE THESE PILLS TO EVERY CITIZEN IN ENGLAND. WE MUST MOVE SWIFTLY IF WE ARE TO ACHIEVE THIS BEFORE SOCIAL ORDER COLLAPSES ANY FURTHER.
THESE PILLS, THEY CURE THE DISEASE?
NO...NO, I'M AFRAID THEY DO NOT.
THEY END IT, BEFORE THE MOST HORRIFIC AND DEVASTATING SYMPTOMS CAN TAKE PLACE.
THE GOVERNMENT WILL NEED AUTHORIZATION TO USE THE LATEST CENSUS DATA TO DETERMINE WHAT SIZE PACKET MUST BE SENT TO WHICH ADDRESS.
SMALLER SIZE FOR SINGLES AND COUPLES, AND A LARGER SIZE FOR--
--FOR FAMILIES.
IT WAS JUST TWO MONTHS SINCE THE VIRUS FIRST APPEARED.

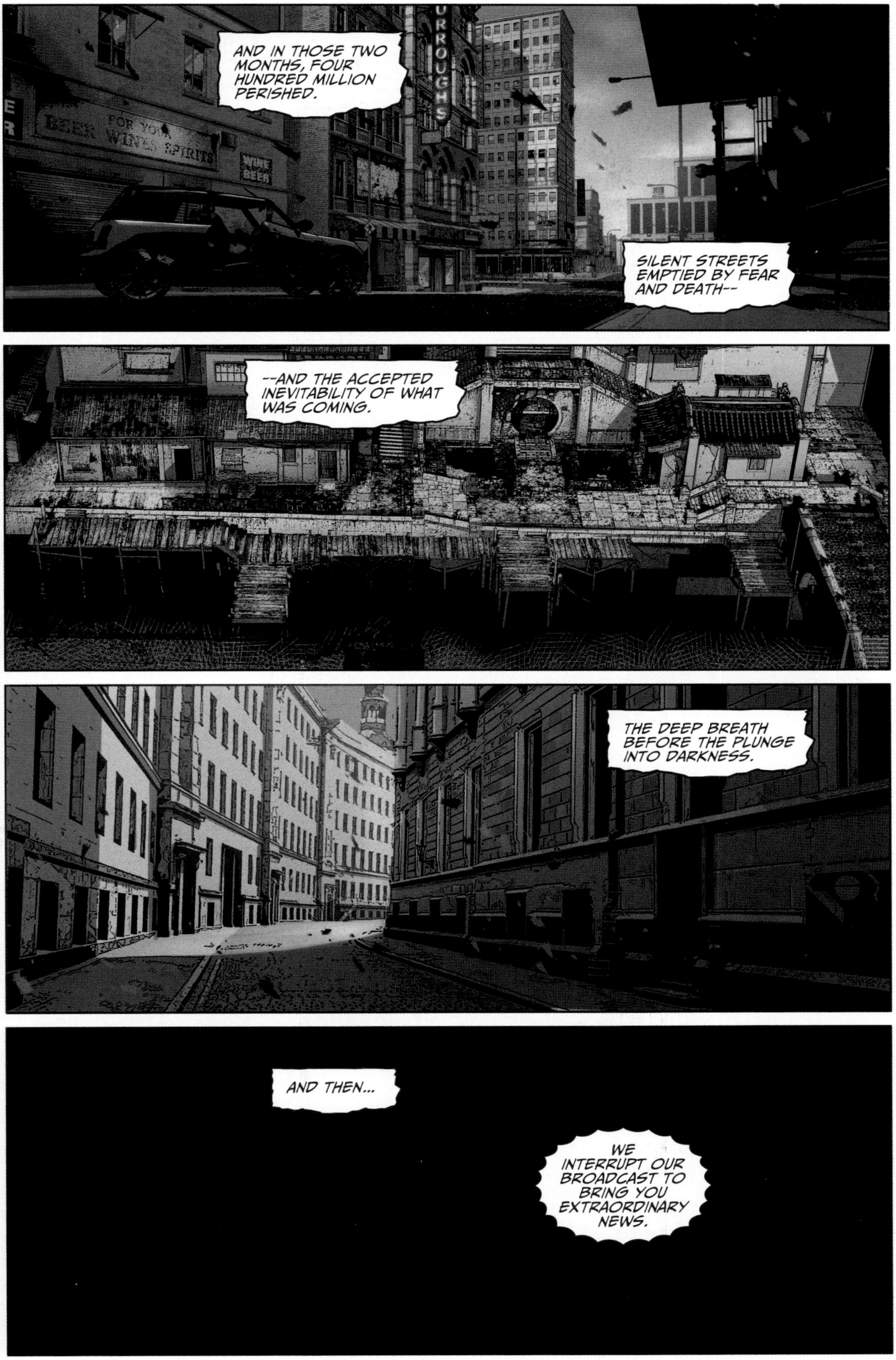
AND IN THOSE TWO MONTHS, FOUR HUNDRED MILLION PERISHED.
SILENT STREETS EMPTIED BY FEAR AND DEATH--
--AND THE ACCEPTED INEVITABILITY OF WHAT WAS COMING.
THE DEEP BREATH BEFORE THE PLUNGE INTO DARKNESS.
AND THEN...
WE INTERRUPT OUR BROADCAST TO BRING YOU EXTRAORDINARY NEWS.

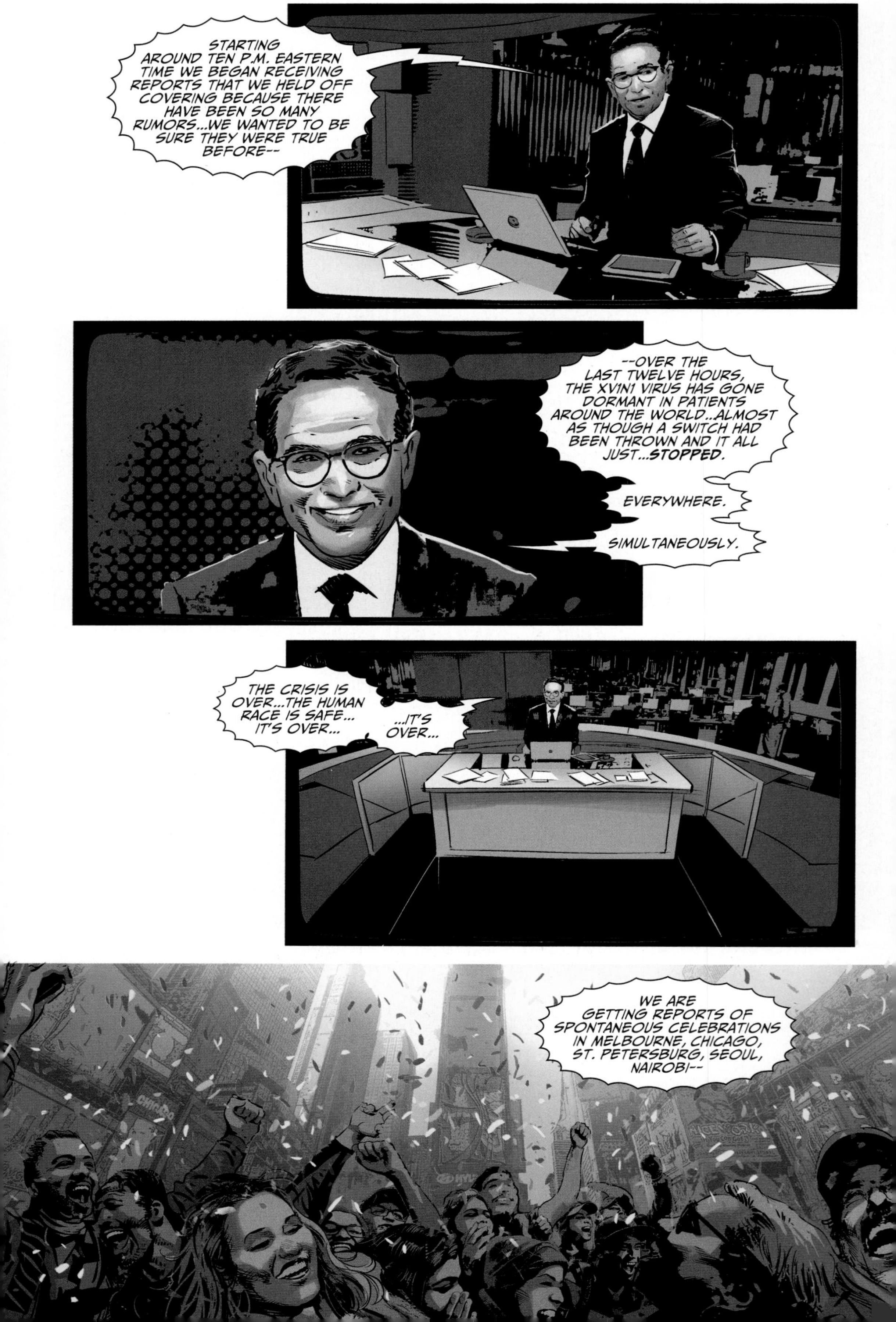
STARTING AROUND TEN P.M. EASTERN TIME WE BEGAN RECEIVING REPORTS THAT WE HELD OFF COVERING BECAUSE THERE HAVE BEEN SO MANY RUMORS...WE WANTED TO BE SURE THEY WERE TRUE BEFORE--
--OVER THE LAST TWELVE HOURS, THE XV1N1 VIRUS HAS GONE DORMANT IN PATIENTS AROUND THE WORLD...ALMOST AS THOUGH A SWITCH HAD BEEN THROWN AND IT ALL JUST...**STOPPED.**
EVERYWHERE.
SIMULTANEOUSLY.
THE CRISIS IS OVER...THE HUMAN RACE IS SAFE... IT'S OVER...
...IT'S OVER...
WE ARE GETTING REPORTS OF SPONTANEOUS CELEBRATIONS IN MELBOURNE, CHICAGO, ST. PETERSBURG, SEOUL, NAIROBI--

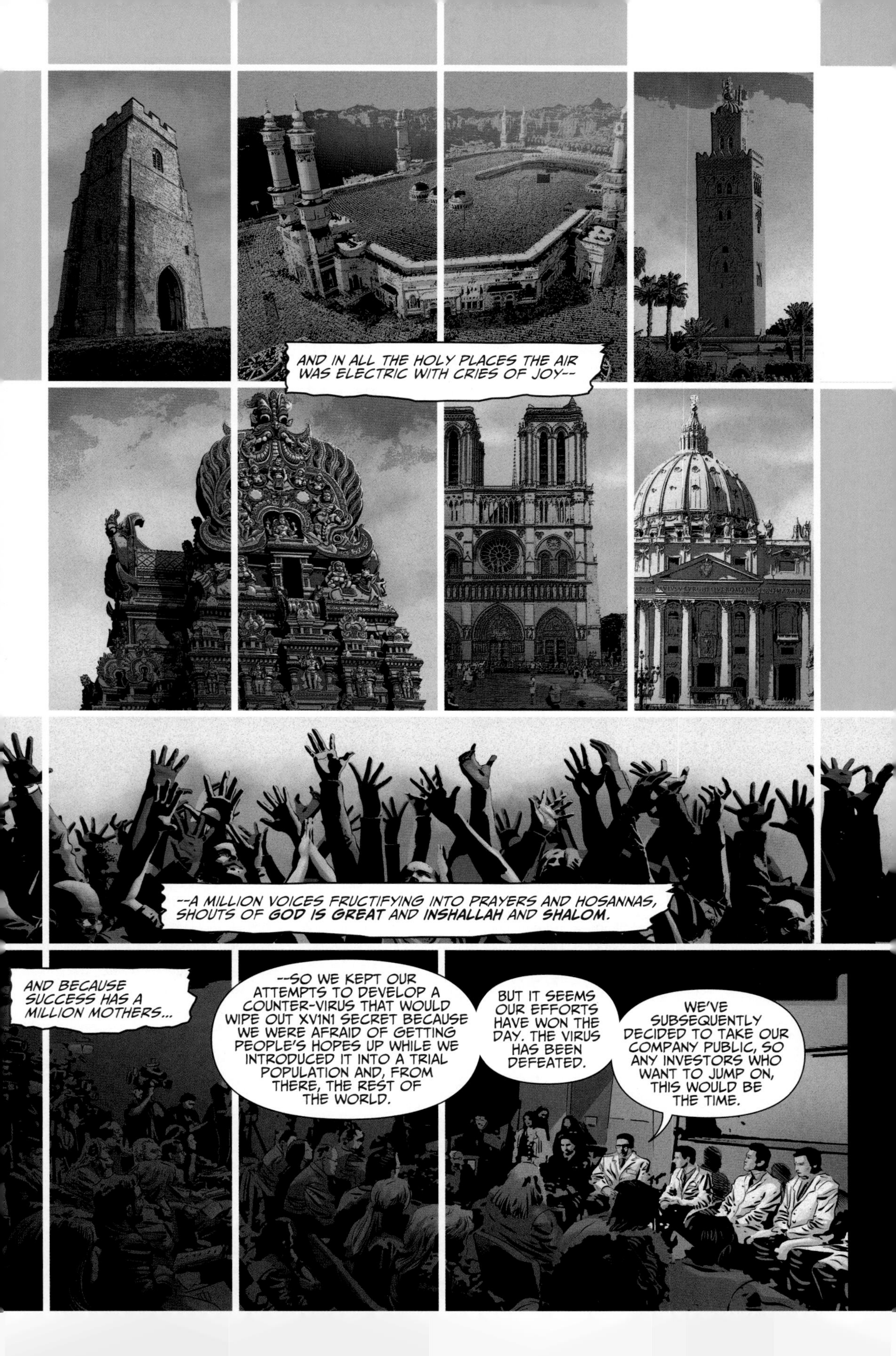
AND IN ALL THE HOLY PLACES THE AIR WAS ELECTRIC WITH CRIES OF JOY--
--A MILLION VOICES FRUCTIFYING INTO PRAYERS AND HOSANNAS, SHOUTS OF **GOD IS GREAT** AND **INSHALLAH** AND **SHALOM**.
AND BECAUSE SUCCESS HAS A MILLION MOTHERS...
--SO WE KEPT OUR ATTEMPTS TO DEVELOP A COUNTER-VIRUS THAT WOULD WIPE OUT XV1N1 SECRET BECAUSE WE WERE AFRAID OF GETTING PEOPLE'S HOPES UP WHILE WE INTRODUCED IT INTO A TRIAL POPULATION AND, FROM THERE, THE REST OF THE WORLD.
BUT IT SEEMS OUR EFFORTS HAVE WON THE DAY. THE VIRUS HAS BEEN DEFEATED.
WE'VE SUBSEQUENTLY DECIDED TO TAKE OUR COMPANY PUBLIC, SO ANY INVESTORS WHO WANT TO JUMP ON, THIS WOULD BE THE TIME.

IT SEEMED *EVERYONE* HAD THEORIES AS TO WHY THE VIRUS HAD SIMPLY...STOPPED.

--A RESISTANCE MOVEMENT INSIDE THE ORGANIZATION THAT UNLEASHED THIS VIRUS TO CREATE A NEW WORLD ORDER WERE ABLE TO TURN IT OFF. IT'S THE ONLY WAY TO EXPLAIN HOW IT HAPPENED ALL AT ONCE--

THE WHOLE THING WAS JUST A FALSE FLAG TO COVER GENOCIDE--

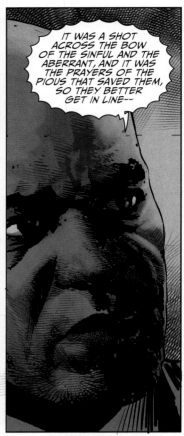

IT WAS A SHOT ACROSS THE BOW OF THE SINFUL AND THE ABERRANT, AND IT WAS THE PRAYERS OF THE PIOUS THAT SAVED THEM, SO THEY BETTER GET IN LINE--

I DON'T WANT TO RAIN ON ANYBODY'S PARADE BUT SOMEONE SHOULD POINT OUT THAT THE VIRUS IS STILL THERE, IT'S JUST DORMANT--

THE QUESTION NOW IS WHAT DO WE DO ABOUT THOSE WHO SURVIVED THE VIRUS, AND ARE DEALING WITH AFTER-EFFECTS THAT RANGE FROM THE MINIMAL TO THE HORRIFIC TO THE UNKNOWN--

I DON'T CARE ABOUT ANY OF THAT! WHAT MATTERS IS THAT I'M ALIVE, MY WHOLE FAMILY IS ALIVE AND *BEING ALIVE IS AMAZING!*

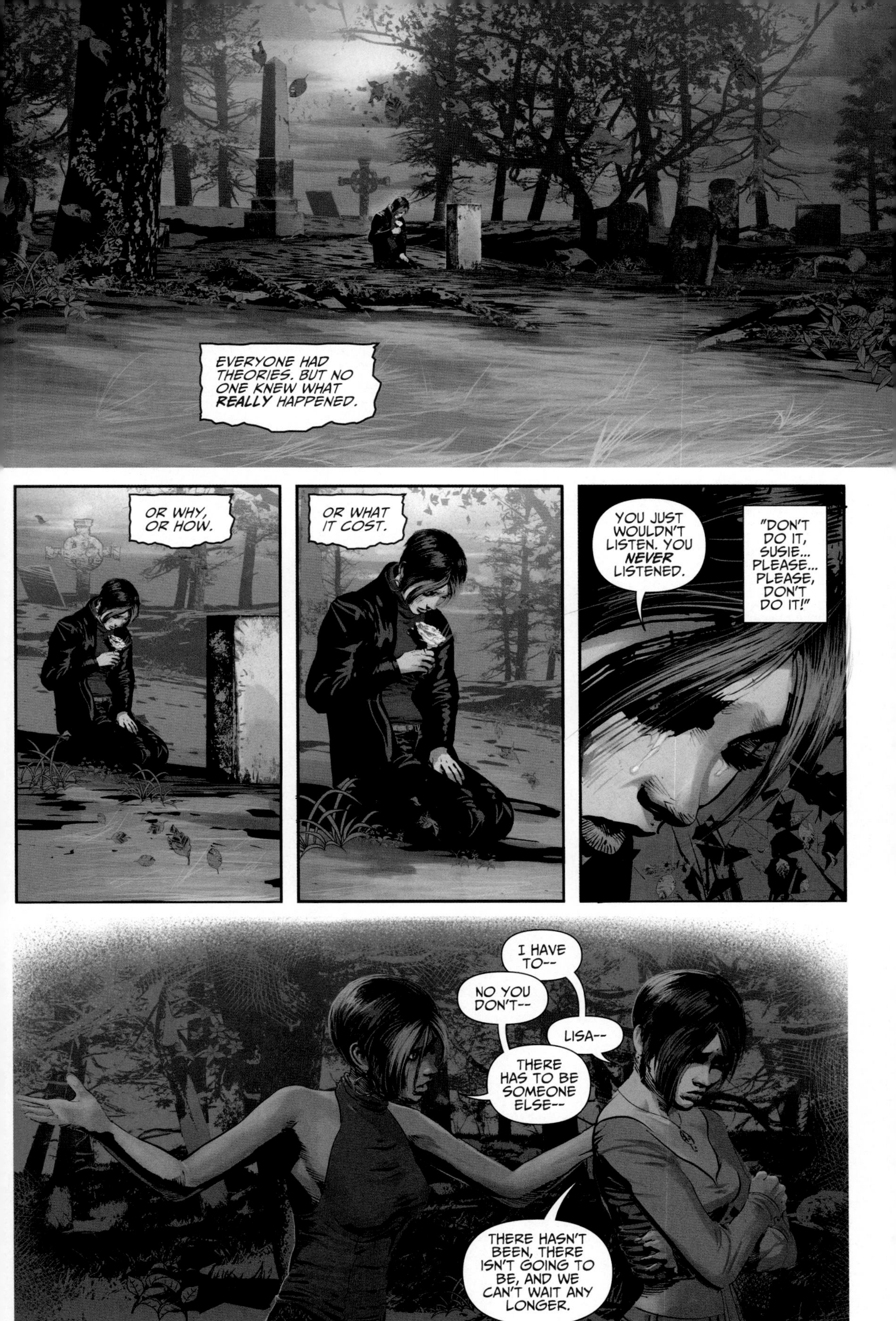
EVERYONE HAD THEORIES. BUT NO ONE KNEW WHAT **REALLY** HAPPENED.
OR WHY, OR HOW.
OR WHAT IT COST.
YOU JUST WOULDN'T LISTEN. YOU **NEVER** LISTENED.
"DON'T DO IT, SUSIE... PLEASE... PLEASE, DON'T DO IT!"
I HAVE TO--
NO YOU DON'T--
LISA--
THERE HAS TO BE SOMEONE ELSE--
THERE HASN'T BEEN, THERE ISN'T GOING TO BE, AND WE CAN'T WAIT ANY LONGER.

WHEN WE SURVIVED THE VIRUS... WHEN WE WERE PART OF THAT IMPOSSIBLY LUCKY FIVE PERCENT... I THOUGHT IT WAS A MIRACLE. WE *BOTH* DID.

THEN AFTERWARD, WHEN WE LEARNED WHAT WE COULD *DO*... IT BECAME EVEN *MORE* OF A MIRACLE.

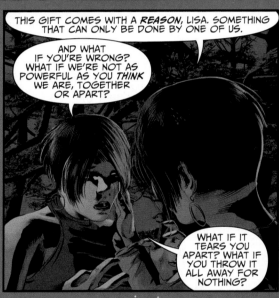

THIS GIFT COMES WITH A *REASON*, LISA. SOMETHING THAT CAN ONLY BE DONE BY ONE OF US.

AND WHAT IF YOU'RE WRONG? WHAT IF WE'RE NOT AS POWERFUL AS YOU *THINK* WE ARE, TOGETHER OR APART?

WHAT IF IT TEARS YOU APART? WHAT IF YOU THROW IT ALL AWAY FOR NOTHING?

THEN I'LL KNOW I TRIED.

I TRIED TO SAVE THE WORLD.

HOW MANY CAN SAY THAT?

GOODBYE, LITTLE SISTER.

NO... DON'T...PLEASE, SUSIE...DON'T LEAVE ME...

GOODBYE... GOODBYE MY BETTER SELF, MY BEAUTIFUL REFLECTION...

...GOODBYE...

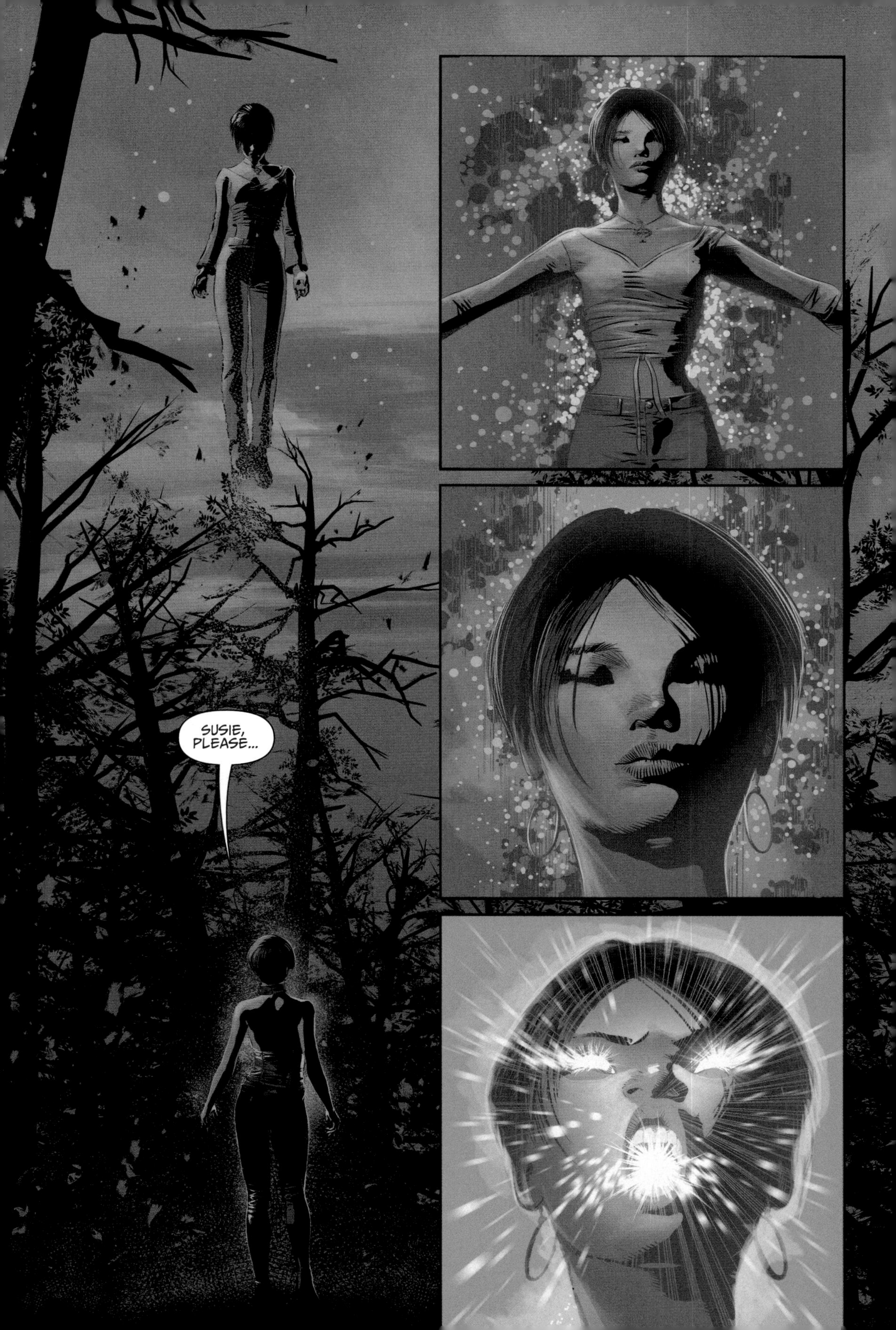
SUSIE, PLEASE...

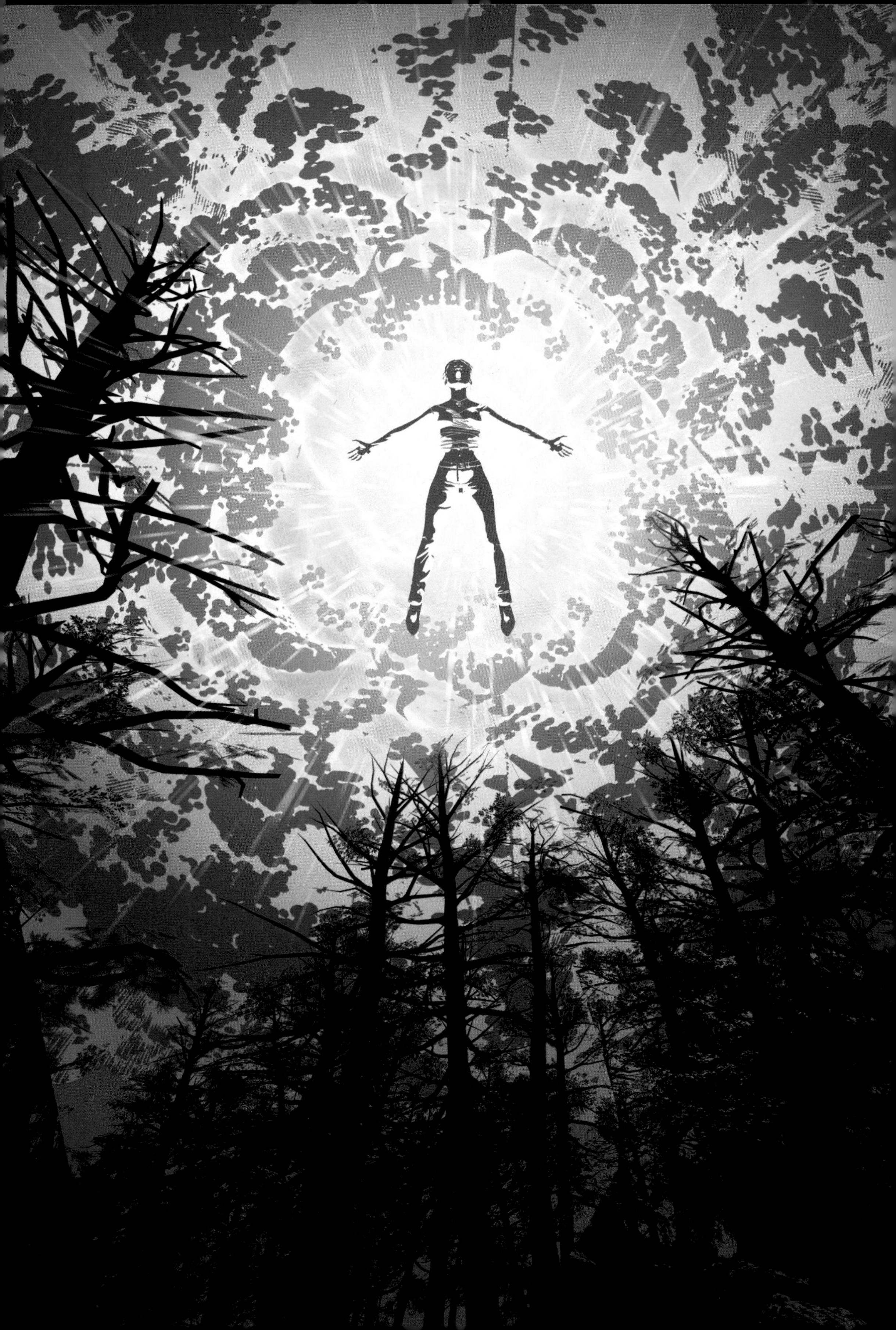

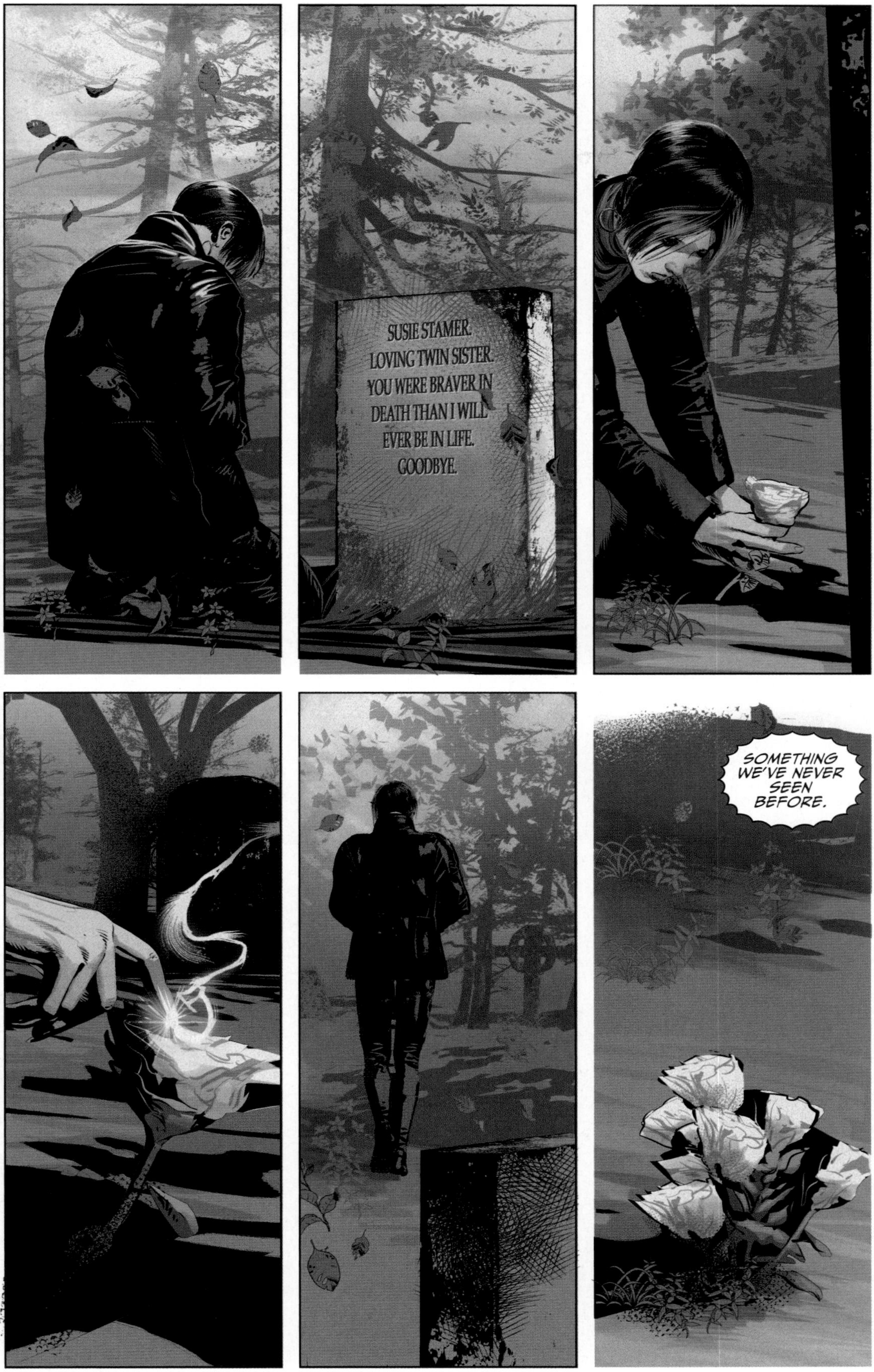
SUSIE STAMER.
LOVING TWIN SISTER.
YOU WERE BRAVER IN
DEATH THAN I WILL
EVER BE IN LIFE.
GOODBYE.
SOMETHING WE'VE NEVER SEEN BEFORE.

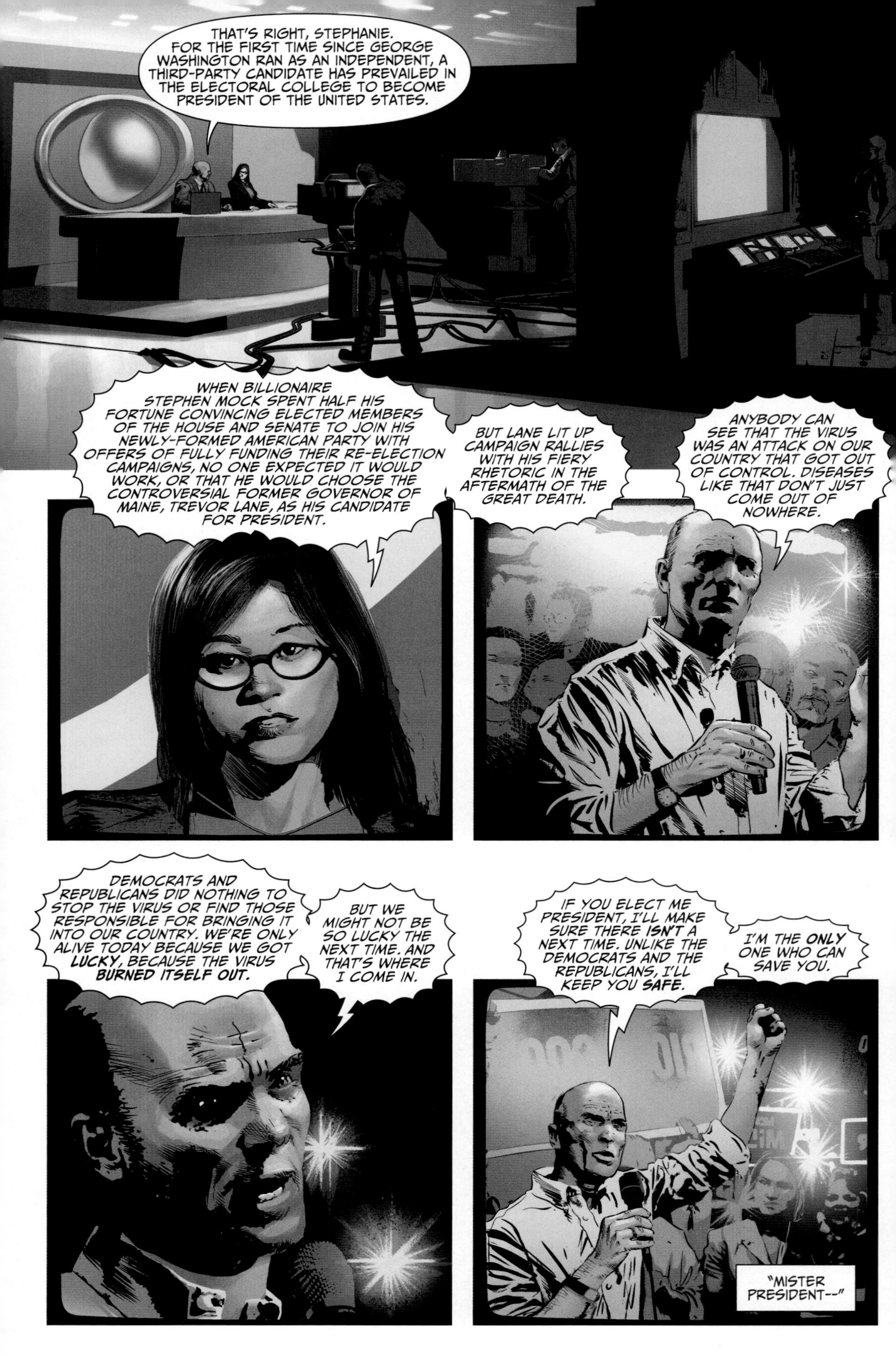
THAT'S RIGHT, STEPHANIE. FOR THE FIRST TIME SINCE GEORGE WASHINGTON RAN AS AN INDEPENDENT, A THIRD-PARTY CANDIDATE HAS PREVAILED IN THE ELECTORAL COLLEGE TO BECOME PRESIDENT OF THE UNITED STATES.
WHEN BILLIONAIRE STEPHEN MOCK SPENT HALF HIS FORTUNE CONVINCING ELECTED MEMBERS OF THE HOUSE AND SENATE TO JOIN HIS NEWLY-FORMED AMERICAN PARTY WITH OFFERS OF FULLY FUNDING THEIR RE-ELECTION CAMPAIGNS, NO ONE EXPECTED IT WOULD WORK, OR THAT HE WOULD CHOOSE THE CONTROVERSIAL FORMER GOVERNOR OF MAINE, TREVOR LANE, AS HIS CANDIDATE FOR PRESIDENT.
BUT LANE LIT UP CAMPAIGN RALLIES WITH HIS FIERY RHETORIC IN THE AFTERMATH OF THE GREAT DEATH.
ANYBODY CAN SEE THAT THE VIRUS WAS AN ATTACK ON OUR COUNTRY THAT GOT OUT OF CONTROL. DISEASES LIKE THAT DON'T JUST COME OUT OF NOWHERE.
DEMOCRATS AND REPUBLICANS DID NOTHING TO STOP THE VIRUS OR FIND THOSE RESPONSIBLE FOR BRINGING IT INTO OUR COUNTRY. WE'RE ONLY ALIVE TODAY BECAUSE WE GOT **LUCKY**, BECAUSE THE VIRUS **BURNED ITSELF OUT.**
BUT WE MIGHT NOT BE SO LUCKY THE NEXT TIME. AND THAT'S WHERE I COME IN.
IF YOU ELECT ME PRESIDENT, I'LL MAKE SURE THERE **ISN'T** A NEXT TIME. UNLIKE THE DEMOCRATS AND THE REPUBLICANS, I'LL KEEP YOU **SAFE**.
I'M THE **ONLY** ONE WHO CAN SAVE YOU.
"MISTER PRESIDENT--"

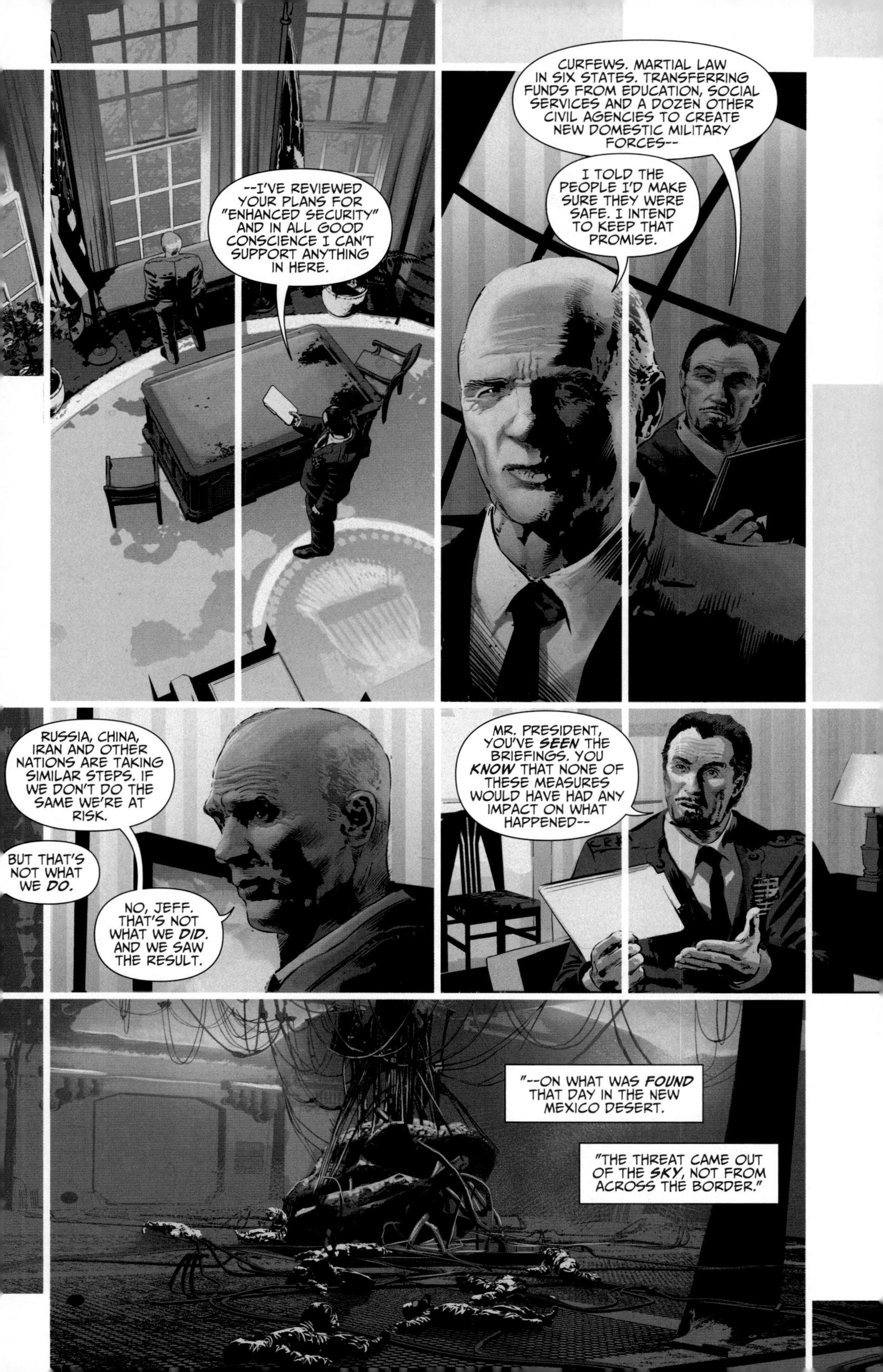
--I'VE REVIEWED YOUR PLANS FOR "ENHANCED SECURITY" AND IN ALL GOOD CONSCIENCE I CAN'T SUPPORT ANYTHING IN HERE.
CURFEWS. MARTIAL LAW IN SIX STATES. TRANSFERRING FUNDS FROM EDUCATION, SOCIAL SERVICES AND A DOZEN OTHER CIVIL AGENCIES TO CREATE NEW DOMESTIC MILITARY FORCES--
I TOLD THE PEOPLE I'D MAKE SURE THEY WERE SAFE. I INTEND TO KEEP THAT PROMISE.
RUSSIA, CHINA, IRAN AND OTHER NATIONS ARE TAKING SIMILAR STEPS. IF WE DON'T DO THE SAME WE'RE AT RISK.
BUT THAT'S NOT WHAT WE *DO*.
NO, JEFF. THAT'S NOT WHAT WE *DID*. AND WE SAW THE RESULT.
MR. PRESIDENT, YOU'VE *SEEN* THE BRIEFINGS. YOU *KNOW* THAT NONE OF THESE MEASURES WOULD HAVE HAD ANY IMPACT ON WHAT HAPPENED--
"--ON WHAT WAS *FOUND* THAT DAY IN THE NEW MEXICO DESERT.
"THE THREAT CAME OUT OF THE *SKY*, NOT FROM ACROSS THE BORDER."

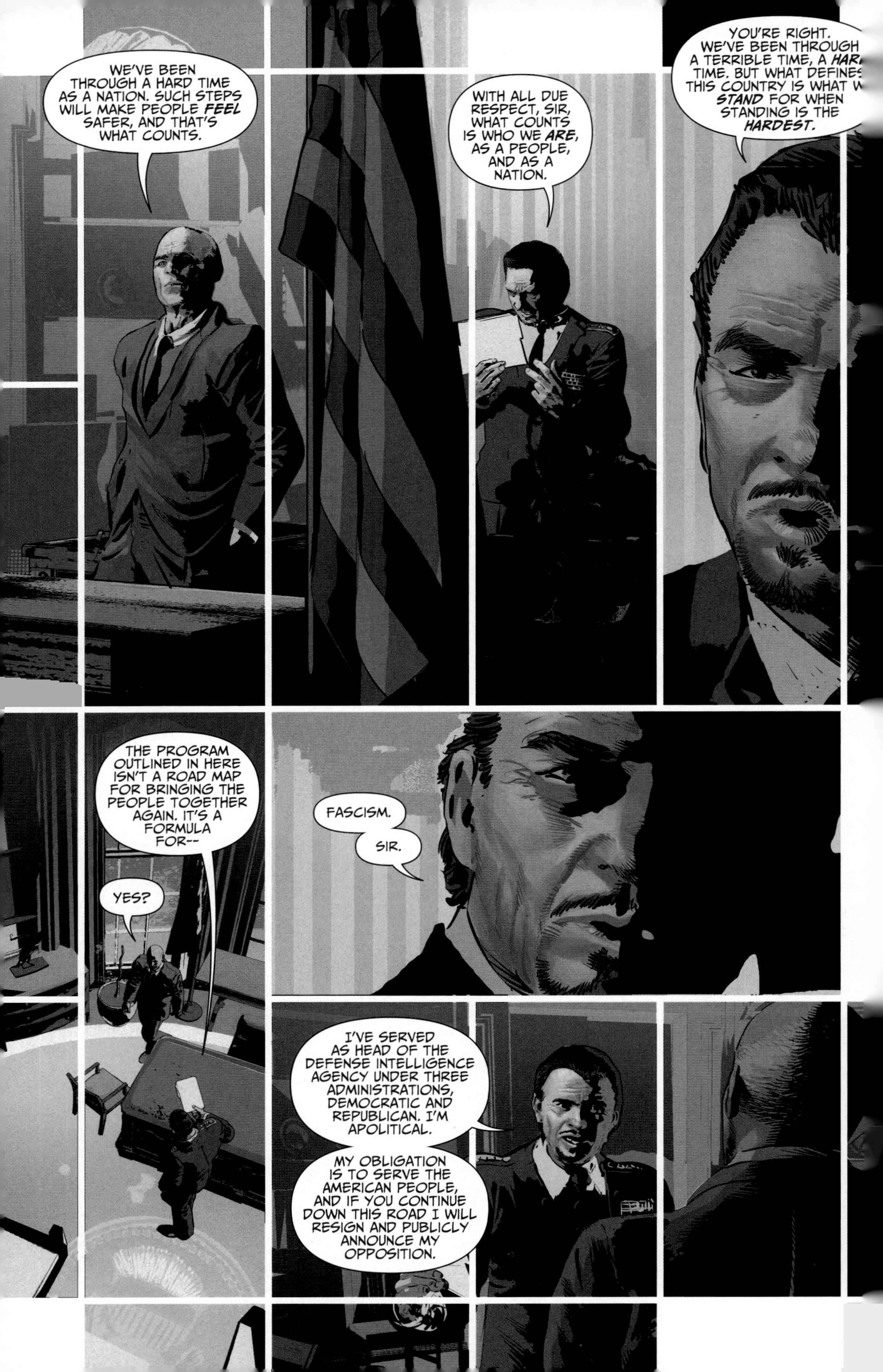
WE'VE BEEN THROUGH A HARD TIME AS A NATION. SUCH STEPS WILL MAKE PEOPLE *FEEL* SAFER, AND THAT'S WHAT COUNTS.
WITH ALL DUE RESPECT, SIR, WHAT COUNTS IS WHO WE *ARE*, AS A PEOPLE, AND AS A NATION.
YOU'RE RIGHT. WE'VE BEEN THROUGH A TERRIBLE TIME, A *HAR* TIME. BUT WHAT DEFINES THIS COUNTRY IS WHAT W *STAND* FOR WHEN STANDING IS THE *HARDEST.*
THE PROGRAM OUTLINED IN HERE ISN'T A ROAD MAP FOR BRINGING THE PEOPLE TOGETHER AGAIN. IT'S A FORMULA FOR--
YES?
FASCISM.
SIR.
I'VE SERVED AS HEAD OF THE DEFENSE INTELLIGENCE AGENCY UNDER THREE ADMINISTRATIONS, DEMOCRATIC AND REPUBLICAN. I'M APOLITICAL.
MY OBLIGATION IS TO SERVE THE AMERICAN PEOPLE, AND IF YOU CONTINUE DOWN THIS ROAD I WILL RESIGN AND PUBLICLY ANNOUNCE MY OPPOSITION.

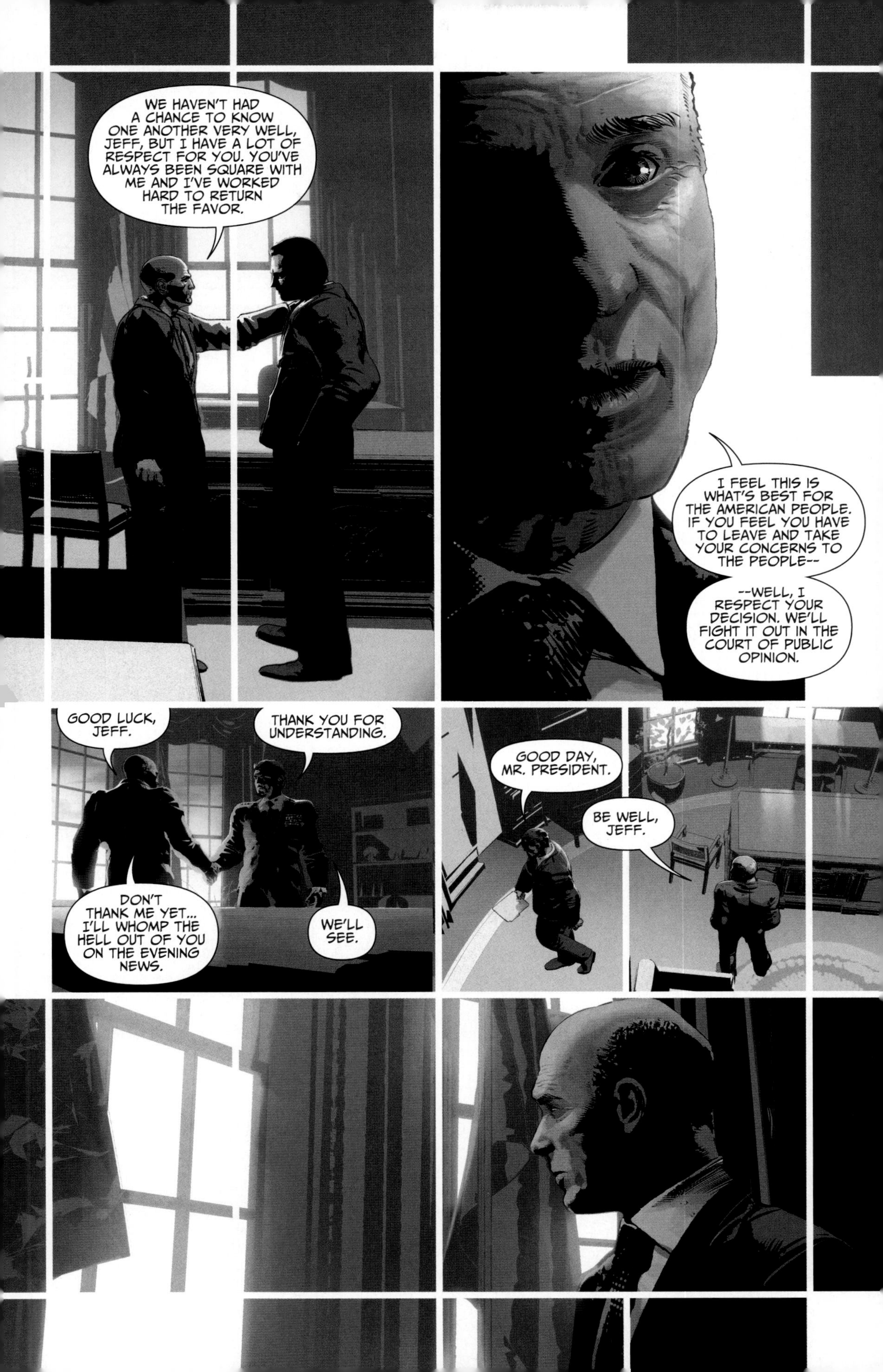
WE HAVEN'T HAD A CHANCE TO KNOW ONE ANOTHER VERY WELL, JEFF, BUT I HAVE A LOT OF RESPECT FOR YOU. YOU'VE ALWAYS BEEN SQUARE WITH ME AND I'VE WORKED HARD TO RETURN THE FAVOR.
I FEEL THIS IS WHAT'S BEST FOR THE AMERICAN PEOPLE. IF YOU FEEL YOU HAVE TO LEAVE AND TAKE YOUR CONCERNS TO THE PEOPLE--
--WELL, I RESPECT YOUR DECISION. WE'LL FIGHT IT OUT IN THE COURT OF PUBLIC OPINION.
GOOD LUCK, JEFF.
THANK YOU FOR UNDERSTANDING.
DON'T THANK ME YET... I'LL WHOMP THE HELL OUT OF YOU ON THE EVENING NEWS.
WE'LL SEE.
GOOD DAY, MR. PRESIDENT.
BE WELL, JEFF.

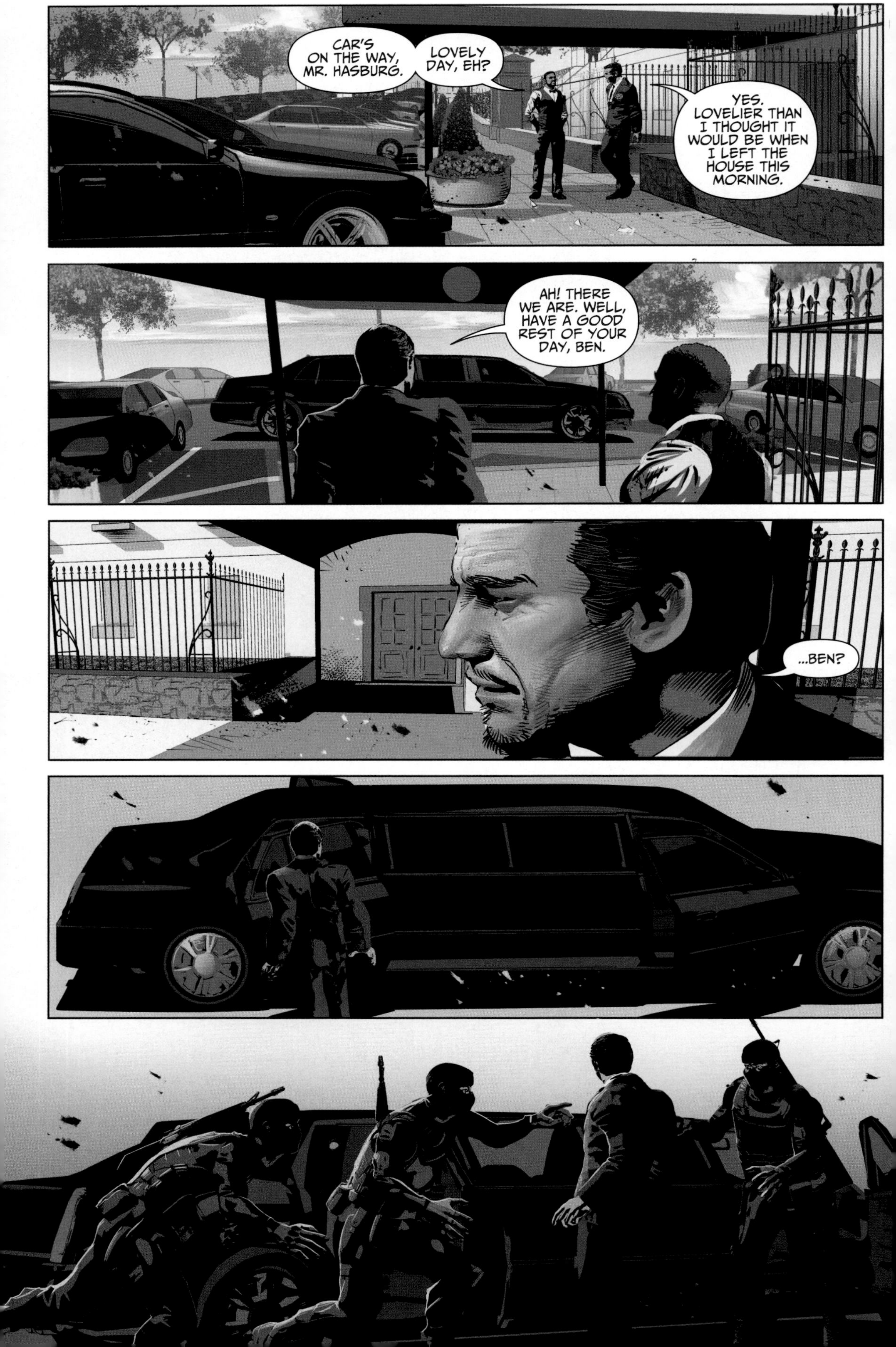
CAR'S ON THE WAY, MR. HASBURG.
LOVELY DAY, EH?
YES. LOVELIER THAN I THOUGHT IT WOULD BE WHEN I LEFT THE HOUSE THIS MORNING.
AH! THERE WE ARE. WELL, HAVE A GOOD REST OF YOUR DAY, BEN.
...BEN?

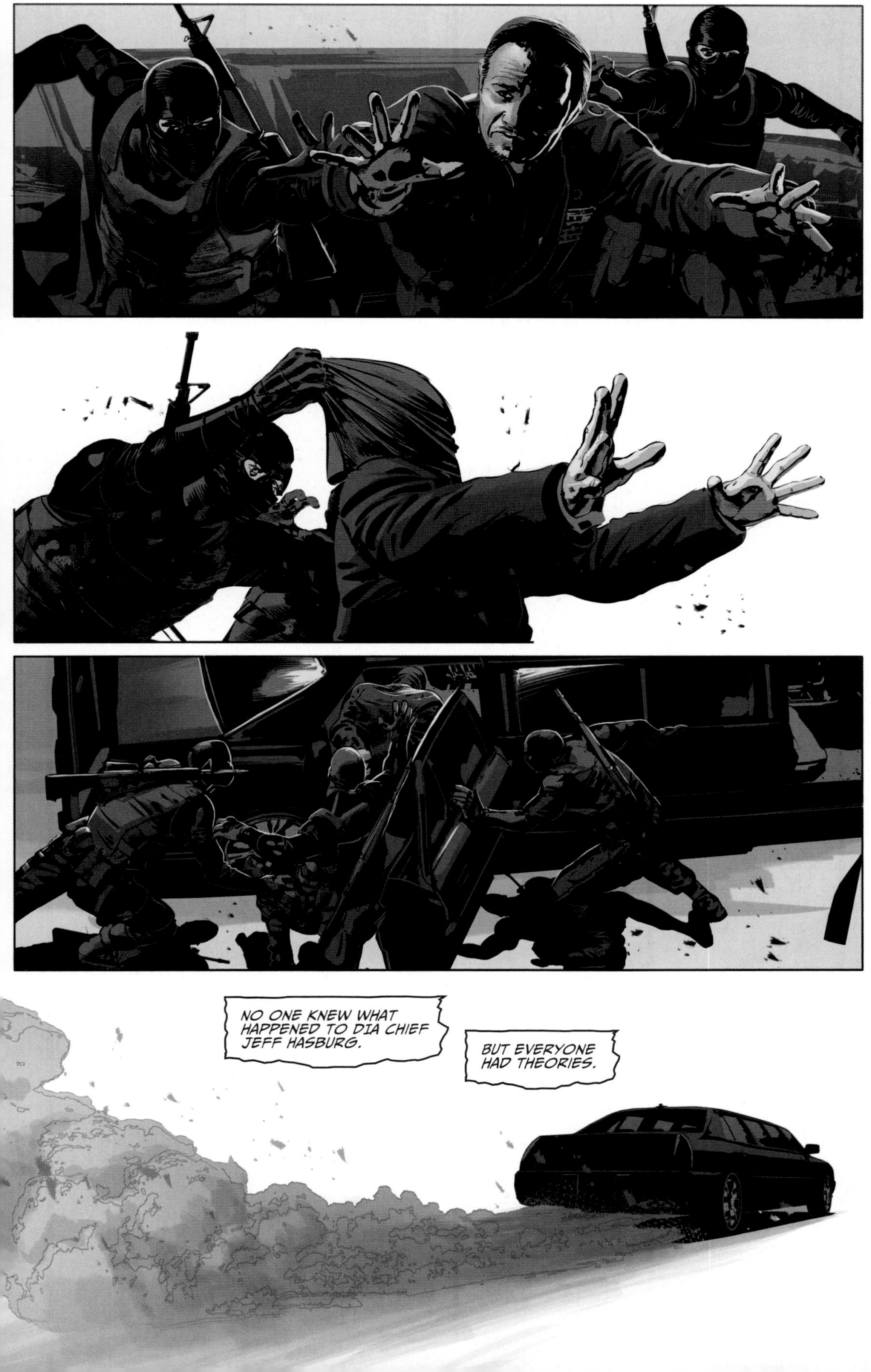
NO ONE KNEW WHAT HAPPENED TO DIA CHIEF JEFF HASBURG.
BUT EVERYONE HAD THEORIES.

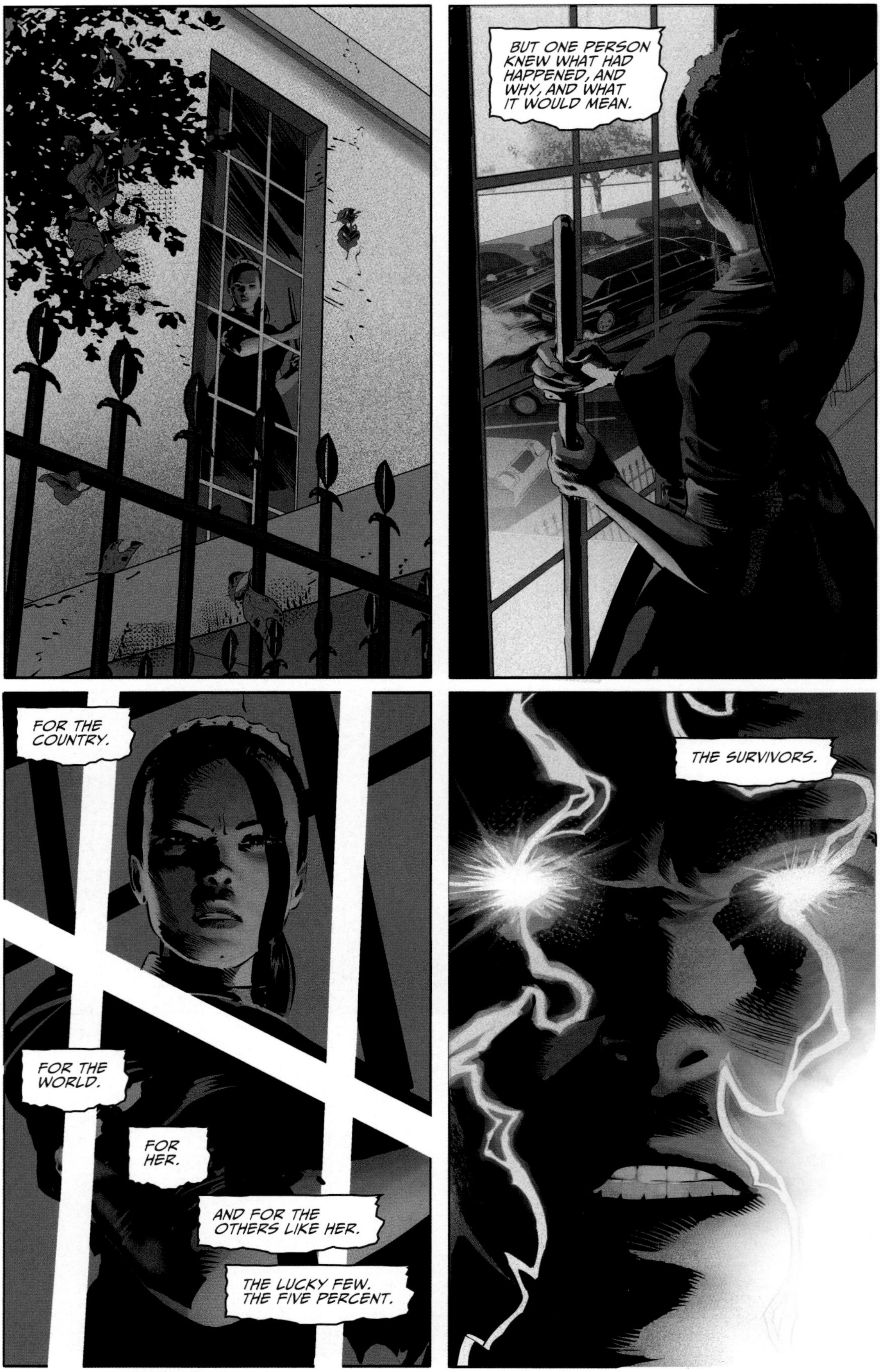
BUT ONE PERSON KNEW WHAT HAD HAPPENED, AND WHY, AND WHAT IT WOULD MEAN.
FOR THE COUNTRY.
FOR THE WORLD.
FOR HER.
AND FOR THE OTHERS LIKE HER.
THE LUCKY FEW. THE FIVE PERCENT.
THE SURVIVORS.

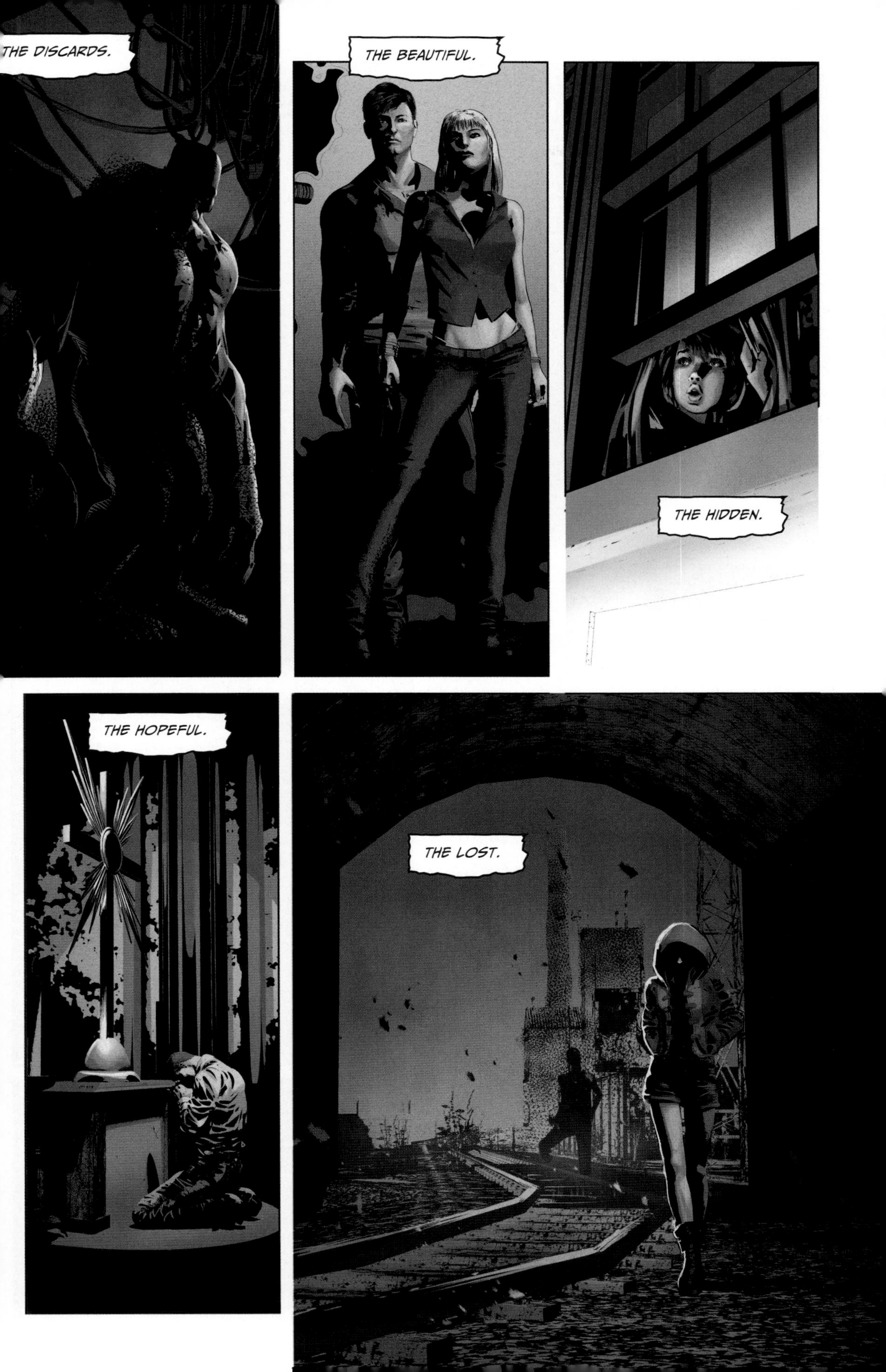
THE DISCARDS.
THE BEAUTIFUL.
THE HIDDEN.
THE HOPEFUL.
THE LOST.

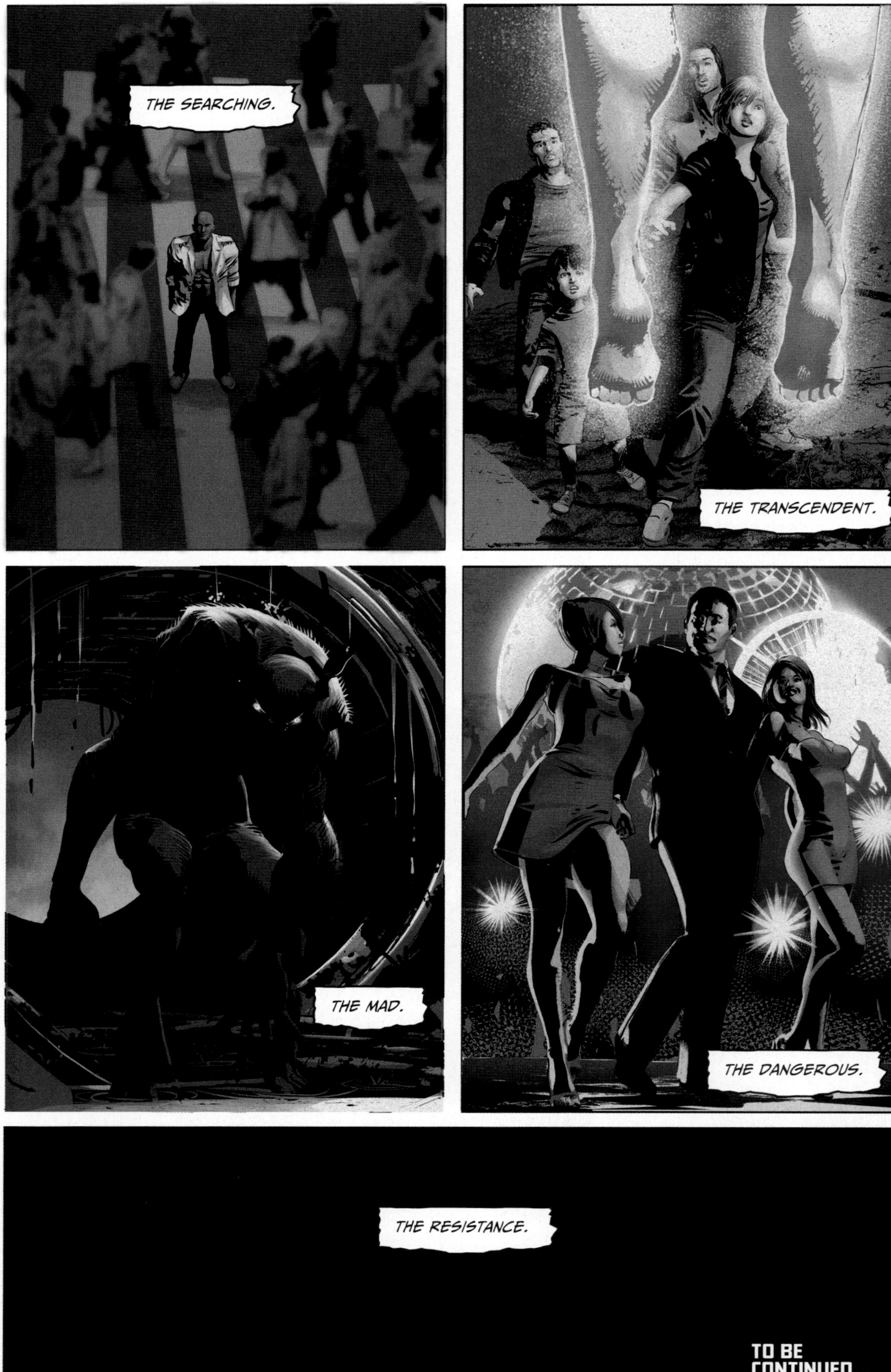
THE SEARCHING.
THE TRANSCENDENT.
THE MAD.
THE DANGEROUS.
THE RESISTANCE.
TO BE CONTINUED...

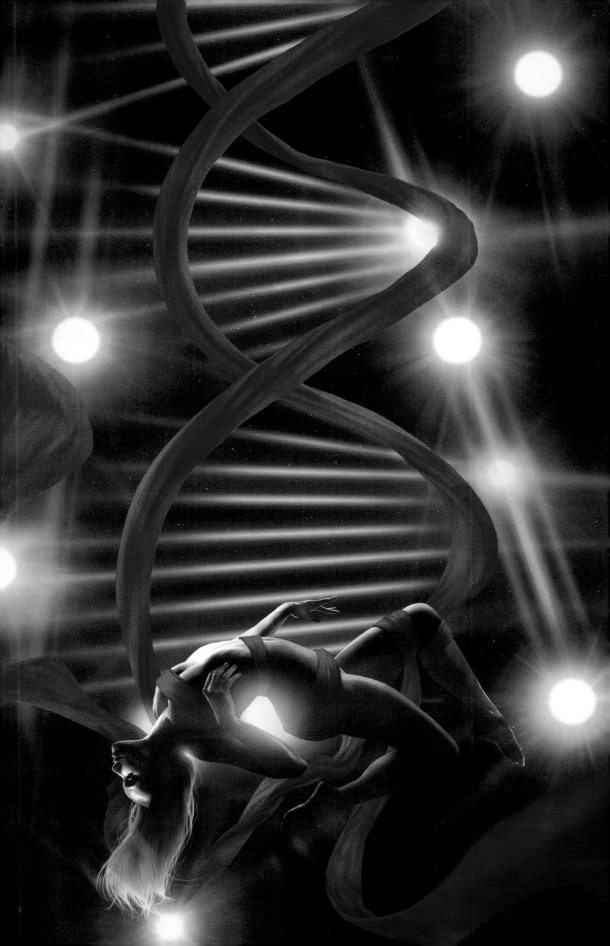

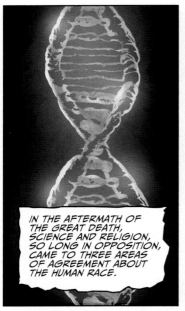

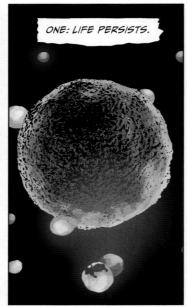

ONE: LIFE PERSISTS.

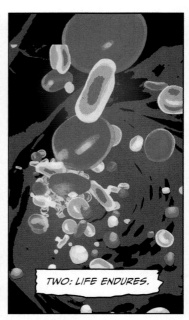

IN THE AFTERMATH OF THE GREAT DEATH, SCIENCE AND RELIGION, SO LONG IN OPPOSITION, CAME TO THREE AREAS OF AGREEMENT ABOUT THE HUMAN RACE.

TWO: LIFE ENDURES.

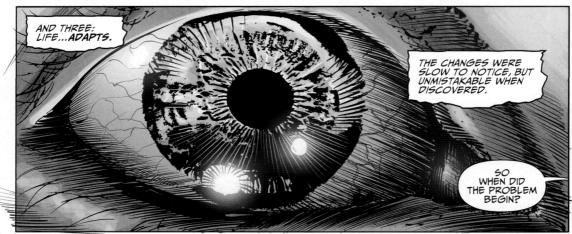

AND THREE: LIFE...ADAPTS.

THE CHANGES WERE SLOW TO NOTICE, BUT UNMISTAKABLE WHEN DISCOVERED.

SO WHEN DID THE PROBLEM BEGIN?

PORTLAND, OREGON.

ABOUT TWO WEEKS AGO. ONCE THE TRAVEL BAN WAS DROPPED I FLEW IN FROM FLORIDA TO BRING HIM HOME TO STAY WITH ME AND HIS UNCLE.

SOLE SURVIVOR?

YES. PARENTS, SISTERS, BROTHERS... ALL GONE.

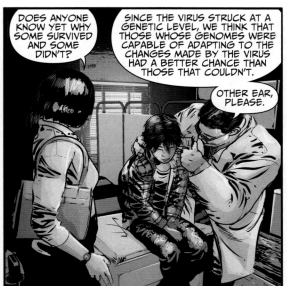

DOES ANYONE KNOW YET WHY SOME SURVIVED AND SOME DIDN'T?

SINCE THE VIRUS STRUCK AT A GENETIC LEVEL, WE THINK THAT THOSE WHOSE GENOMES WERE CAPABLE OF ADAPTING TO THE CHANGES MADE BY THE VIRUS HAD A BETTER CHANCE THAN THOSE THAT COULDN'T.

OTHER EAR, PLEASE.

FOR SOME SURVIVORS, THE PHYSICAL CHANGES WERE FAIRLY SMALL. FOR OTHERS, IT'S--

--PROBABLY BEST NOT TO TALK ABOUT IT IN FRONT OF THE BOY. I'M SURE HE HAS NIGHTMARES ENOUGH AS IT IS.

YOUR EARS LOOK FINE, SON.

THEN WHY DO I KEEP HEARING VOICES?

WELL, SOMETIMES EXPERIENCING GREAT SHOCK OR TRAUMA CAN AFFECT THE BRAIN IN WAYS THAT CAN CREATE THE *ILLUSION* OF VOICES THAT AREN'T ACTUALLY THERE. THE LOSS OF YOUR FAMILY COULD CERTAINLY HAVE TRIGGERED IT.

SO I'D LIKE TO SEND YOU ON TO ANOTHER KIND OF DOCTOR, ONE WHO CAN--

I'M *NOT* MAKING THEM UP--

NO ONE SAID YOU WERE--

THEY'RE *REAL*.

ALL RIGHT, THEN...SO ARE YOU HEARING THEM NOW?

YES.

AND WHAT ARE THEY SAYING?

RATHER THAN BEING A SINGLE AND THEREFORE MORE EASILY TREATABLE DISORDER, GLAUCOMA IS ACTUALLY A GROUP OF EYE CONDITIONS THAT CAN DAMAGE THE OPTIC NERVE THAT IS NECESSARY FOR GOOD VISION.

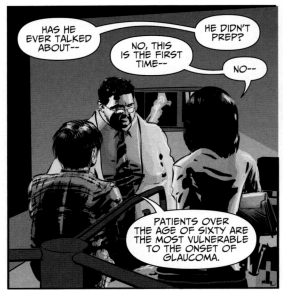

HAS HE EVER TALKED ABOUT--

NO, THIS IS THE FIRST TIME--

HE DIDN'T PREP?

NO--

PATIENTS OVER THE AGE OF SIXTY ARE THE MOST VULNERABLE TO THE ONSET OF GLAUCOMA.

WAIT A MINUTE, I JUST REMEMBERED--

BUT DEPENDING ON THE TYPE OF GLAUCOMA IT'S POSSIBLE FOR SOME PATIENTS TO SEE INSTANCES OF EARLY-ONSET SYMPTOMS.

THAT'S ME CALLING YOUR NUMBER. KEEP THE LINE OPEN.

BUT--

STAY ON THE SPEAKER!

BECAUSE GLAUCOMA HAS FEW IMMEDIATE SYMPTOMS, IT'S OFTEN POSSIBLE TO IGNORE THE ONSET UNTIL THE CONDITION BECOMES QUITE ADVANCED.

DR. CYNTHIA RHODES. TOPIC: GLAUCOMA. 3:00.

THE TWO MAIN CATEGORIES OF GLAUCOMA--

THE TWO MAIN CATEGORIES OF GLAUCOMA--

--ARE OPEN-ANGLE GLAUCOMA, AND ACUTE ANGLE-CLOSURE GLAUCOMA--

--ARE OPEN-ANGLE GLAUCOMA, AND ACUTE ANGLE-CLOSURE GLAUCOMA--

...OH MY GOD...

"YOU *MESSED* WITH MY FRIEND."

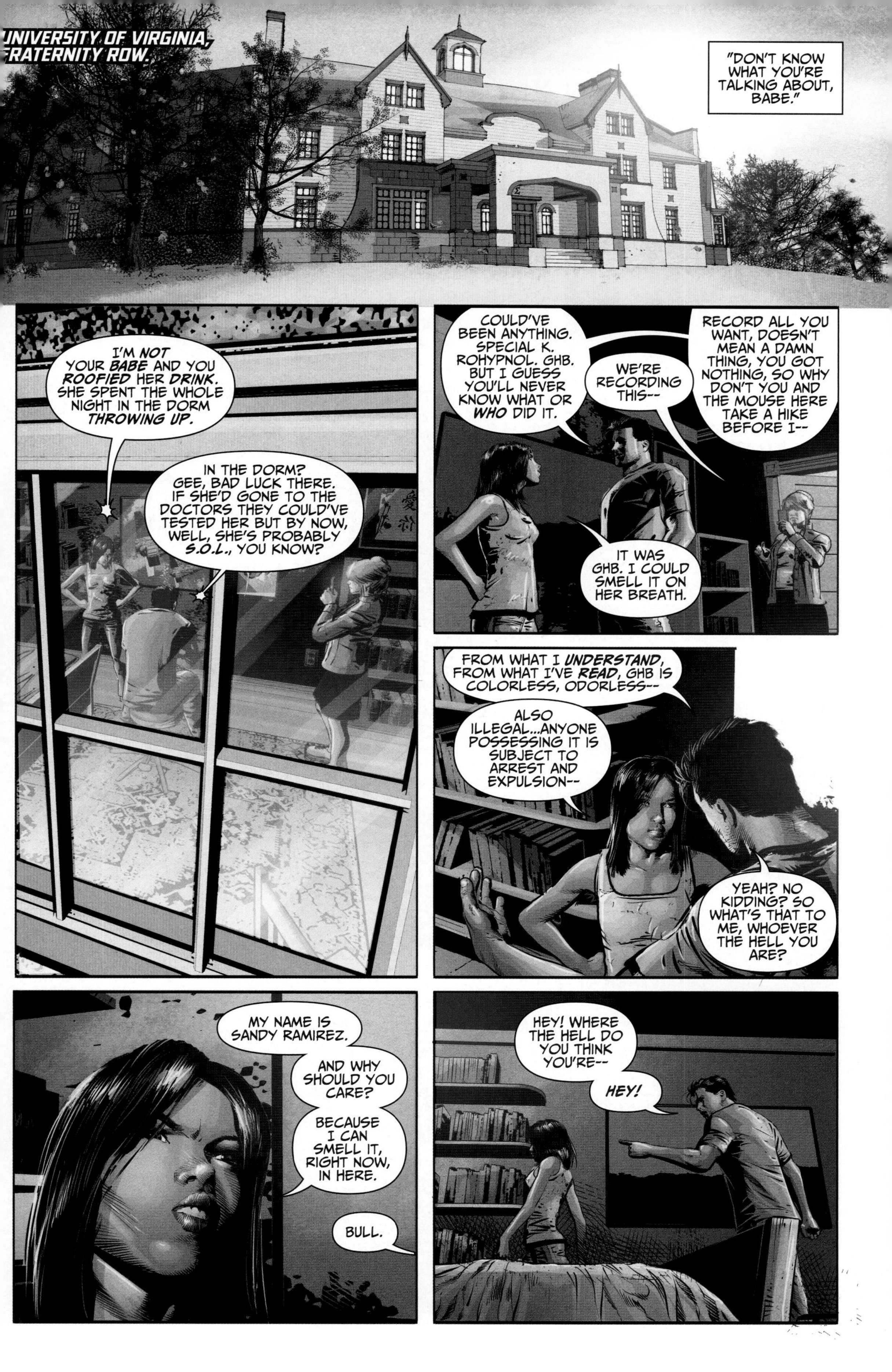
UNIVERSITY OF VIRGINIA, FRATERNITY ROW.
"DON'T KNOW WHAT YOU'RE TALKING ABOUT, BABE."
I'M NOT YOUR BABE AND YOU ROOFIED HER DRINK. SHE SPENT THE WHOLE NIGHT IN THE DORM THROWING UP.
IN THE DORM? GEE, BAD LUCK THERE. IF SHE'D GONE TO THE DOCTORS THEY COULD'VE TESTED HER BUT BY NOW, WELL, SHE'S PROBABLY S.O.L., YOU KNOW?
COULD'VE BEEN ANYTHING. SPECIAL K. ROHYPNOL. GHB. BUT I GUESS YOU'LL NEVER KNOW WHAT OR WHO DID IT.
WE'RE RECORDING THIS--
RECORD ALL YOU WANT, DOESN'T MEAN A DAMN THING, YOU GOT NOTHING, SO WHY DON'T YOU AND THE MOUSE HERE TAKE A HIKE BEFORE I--
IT WAS GHB. I COULD SMELL IT ON HER BREATH.
FROM WHAT I UNDERSTAND, FROM WHAT I'VE READ, GHB IS COLORLESS, ODORLESS--
ALSO ILLEGAL...ANYONE POSSESSING IT IS SUBJECT TO ARREST AND EXPULSION--
YEAH? NO KIDDING? SO WHAT'S THAT TO ME, WHOEVER THE HELL YOU ARE?
MY NAME IS SANDY RAMIREZ.
AND WHY SHOULD YOU CARE?
BECAUSE I CAN SMELL IT, RIGHT NOW, IN HERE.
BULL.
HEY! WHERE THE HELL DO YOU THINK YOU'RE--
HEY!

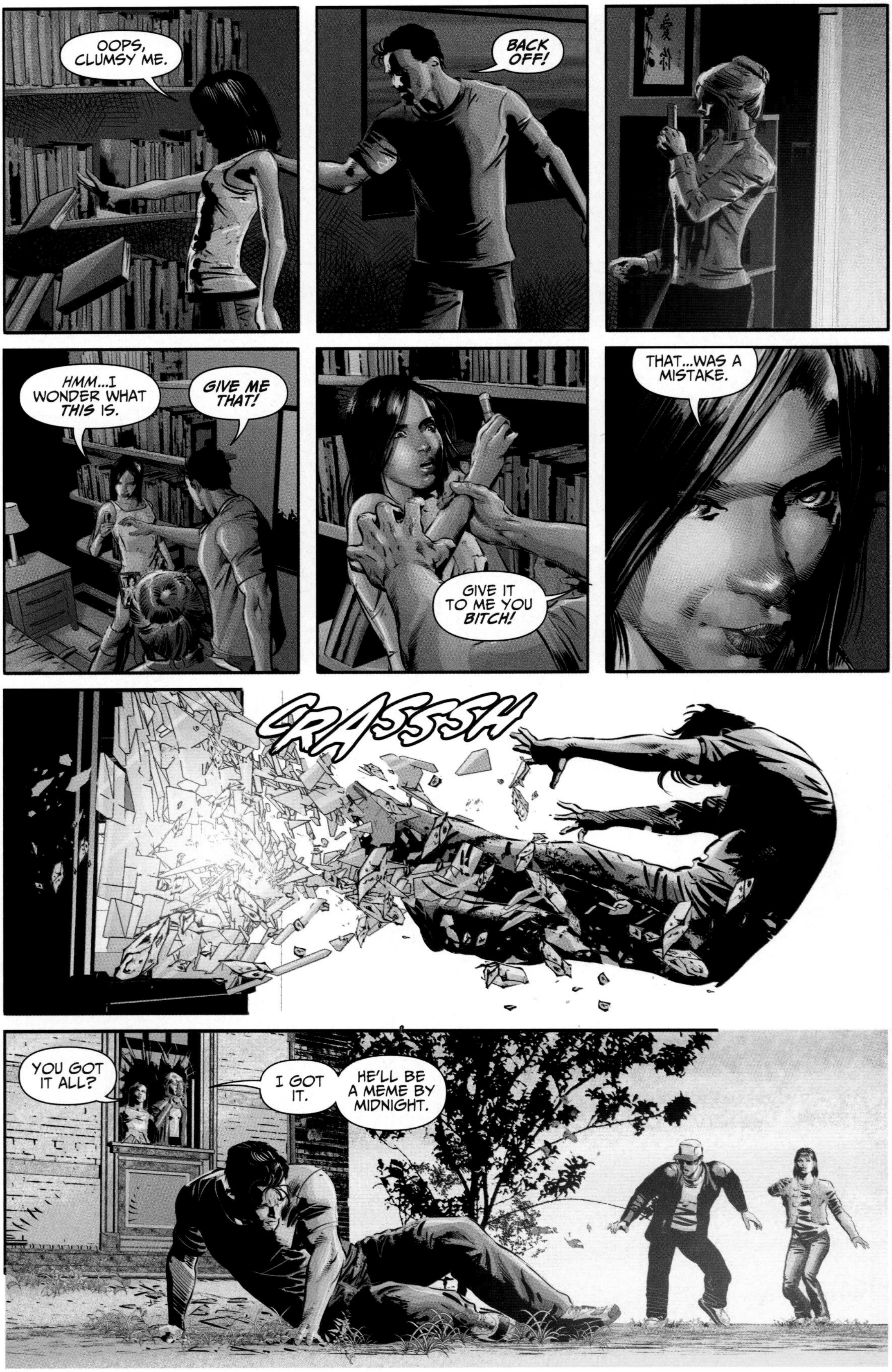
OOPS, CLUMSY ME.
BACK OFF!
HMM...I WONDER WHAT THIS IS.
GIVE ME THAT!
GIVE IT TO ME YOU BITCH!
THAT...WAS A MISTAKE.
CRASSSH
YOU GOT IT ALL?
I GOT IT.
HE'LL BE A MEME BY MIDNIGHT.

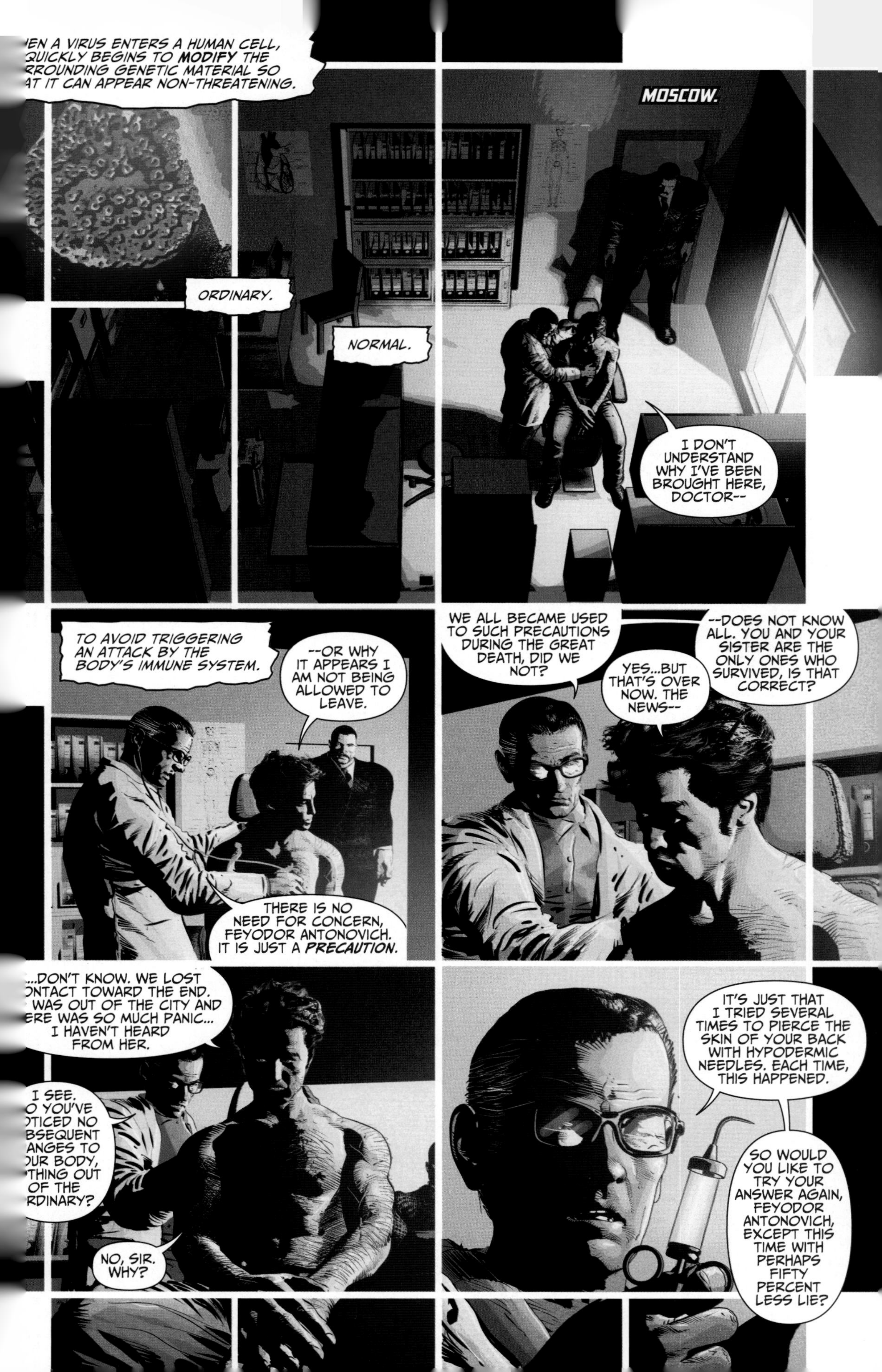

HEN A VIRUS ENTERS A HUMAN CELL, QUICKLY BEGINS TO MODIFY THE RROUNDING GENETIC MATERIAL SO AT IT CAN APPEAR NON-THREATENING.
MOSCOW.
ORDINARY.
NORMAL.
I DON'T UNDERSTAND WHY I'VE BEEN BROUGHT HERE, DOCTOR--
TO AVOID TRIGGERING AN ATTACK BY THE BODY'S IMMUNE SYSTEM.
--OR WHY IT APPEARS I AM NOT BEING ALLOWED TO LEAVE.
THERE IS NO NEED FOR CONCERN, FEYODOR ANTONOVICH. IT IS JUST A PRECAUTION.
WE ALL BECAME USED TO SUCH PRECAUTIONS DURING THE GREAT DEATH, DID WE NOT?
YES...BUT THAT'S OVER NOW. THE NEWS--
--DOES NOT KNOW ALL. YOU AND YOUR SISTER ARE THE ONLY ONES WHO SURVIVED, IS THAT CORRECT?
...DON'T KNOW. WE LOST ONTACT TOWARD THE END. WAS OUT OF THE CITY AND ERE WAS SO MUCH PANIC... I HAVEN'T HEARD FROM HER.
I SEE. O YOU'VE OTICED NO BSEQUENT ANGES TO OUR BODY, OTHING OUT OF THE RDINARY?
NO, SIR. WHY?
IT'S JUST THAT I TRIED SEVERAL TIMES TO PIERCE THE SKIN OF YOUR BACK WITH HYPODERMIC NEEDLES. EACH TIME, THIS HAPPENED.
SO WOULD YOU LIKE TO TRY YOUR ANSWER AGAIN, FEYODOR ANTONOVICH, EXCEPT THIS TIME WITH PERHAPS FIFTY PERCENT LESS LIE?

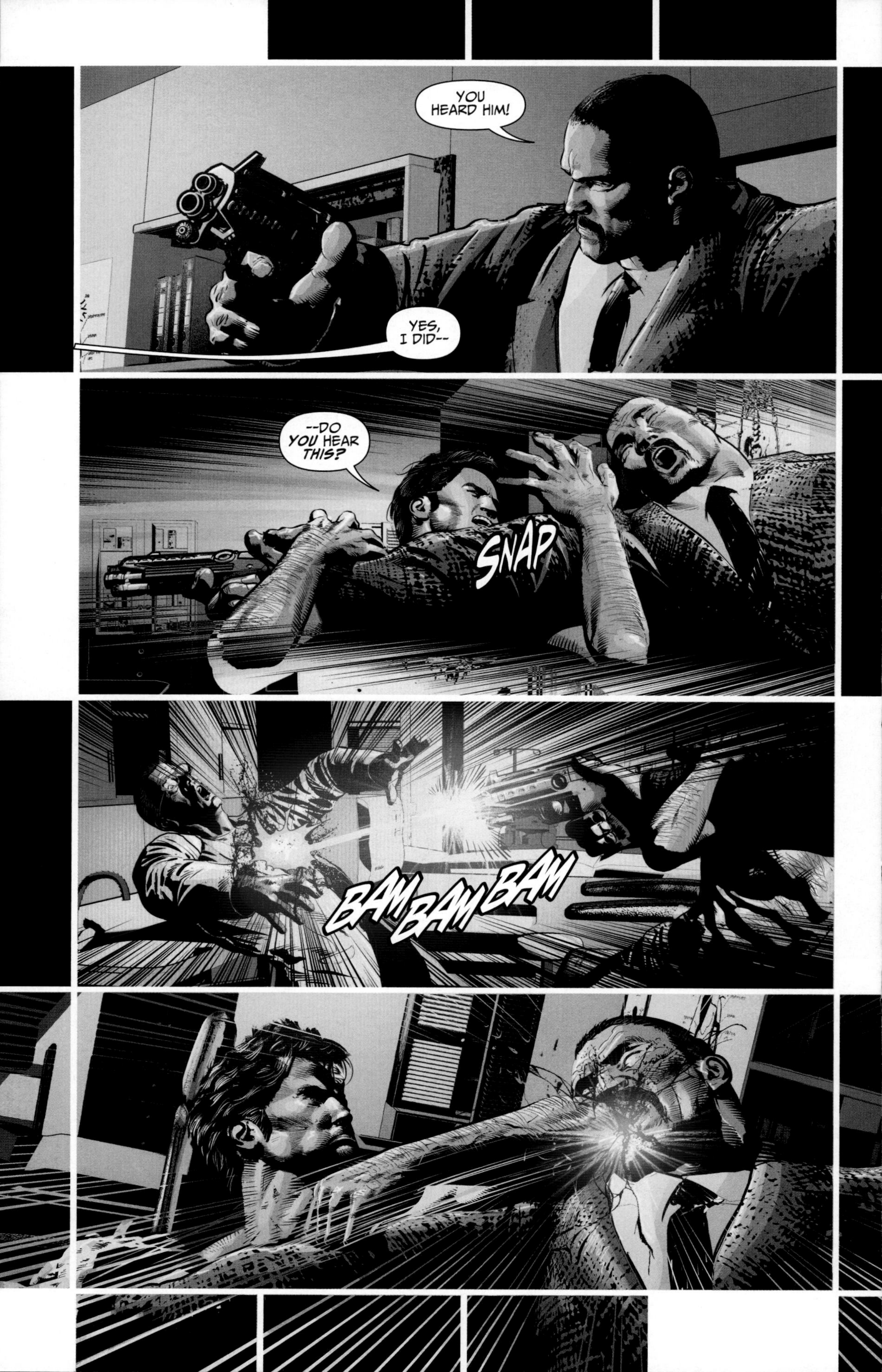

YOU HEARD HIM!
YES, I DID--
--DO YOU HEAR THIS?
SNAP
BAM BAM BAM

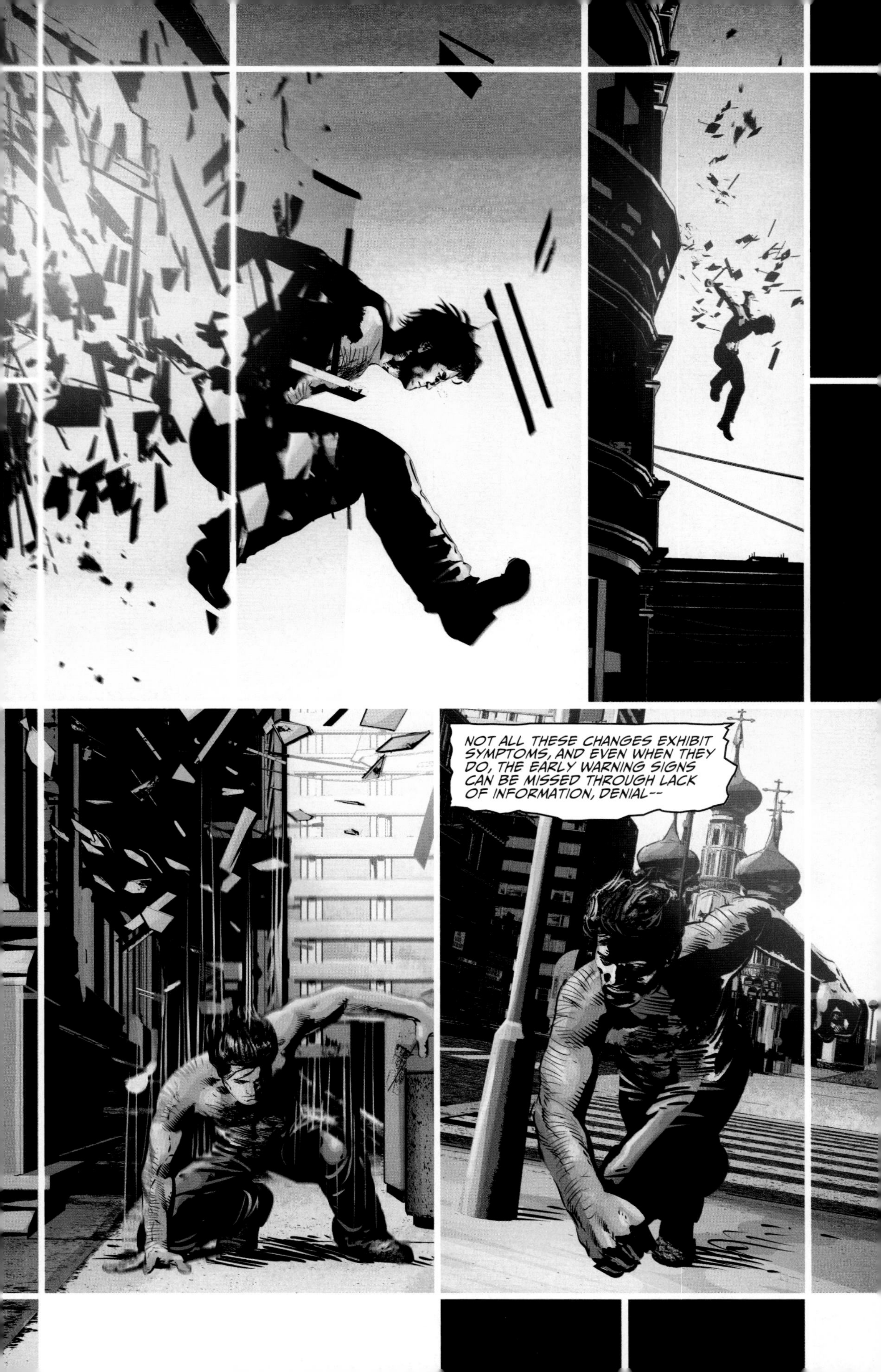
NOT ALL THESE CHANGES EXHIBIT SYMPTOMS, AND EVEN WHEN THEY DO, THE EARLY WARNING SIGNS CAN BE MISSED THROUGH LACK OF INFORMATION, DENIAL--

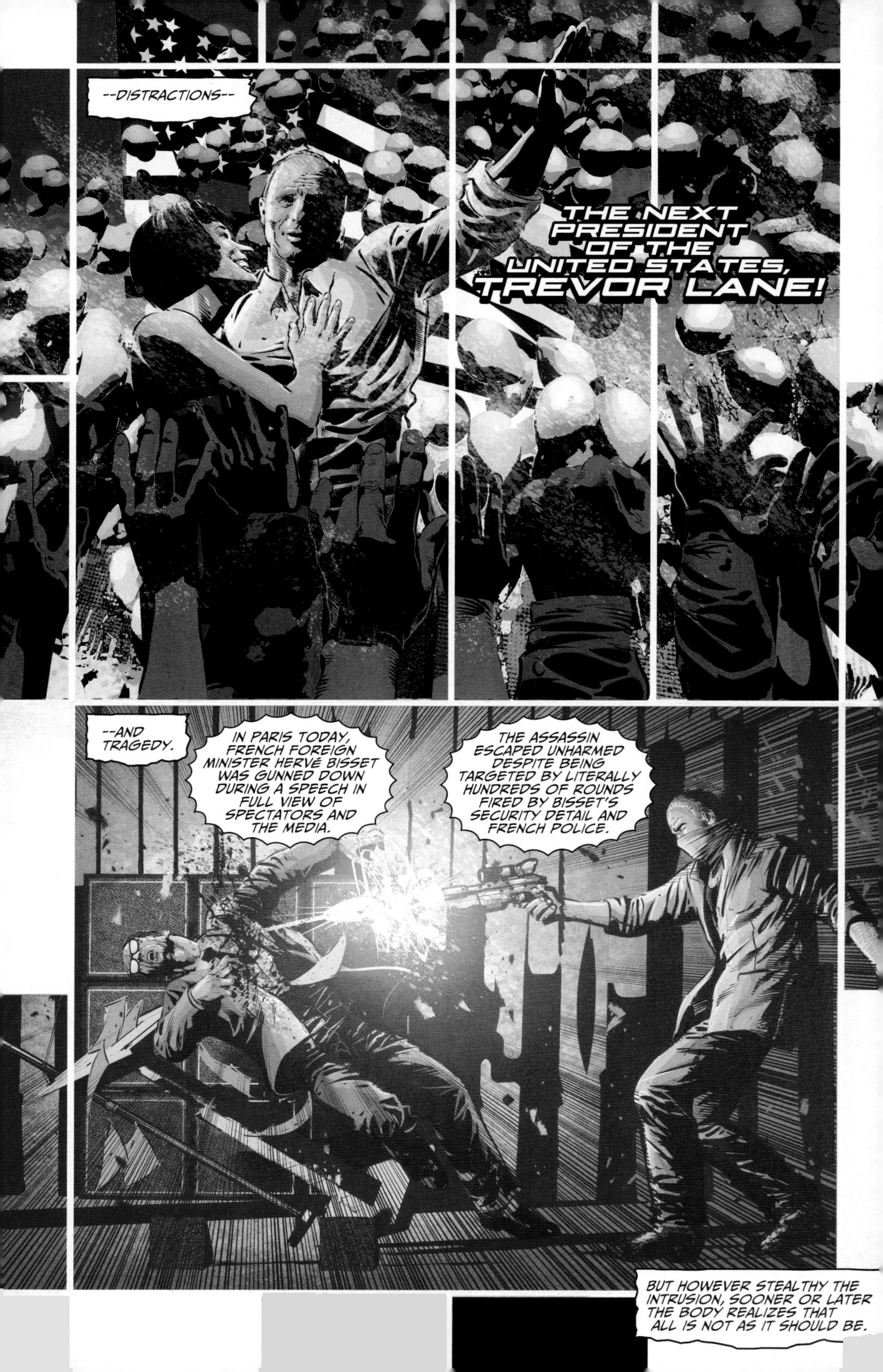
--DISTRACTIONS--
THE NEXT PRESIDENT OF THE UNITED STATES, TREVOR LANE!
--AND TRAGEDY.
IN PARIS TODAY, FRENCH FOREIGN MINISTER HERVÉ BISSET WAS GUNNED DOWN DURING A SPEECH IN FULL VIEW OF SPECTATORS AND THE MEDIA.
THE ASSASSIN ESCAPED UNHARMED DESPITE BEING TARGETED BY LITERALLY HUNDREDS OF ROUNDS FIRED BY BISSET'S SECURITY DETAIL AND FRENCH POLICE.
BUT HOWEVER STEALTHY THE INTRUSION, SOONER OR LATER THE BODY REALIZES THAT ALL IS NOT AS IT SHOULD BE.

ISED, HIGH-SECURITY INTELLIGENCE BRIEFING FOR THE UNITED NATIONS SECURITY COUNCIL.

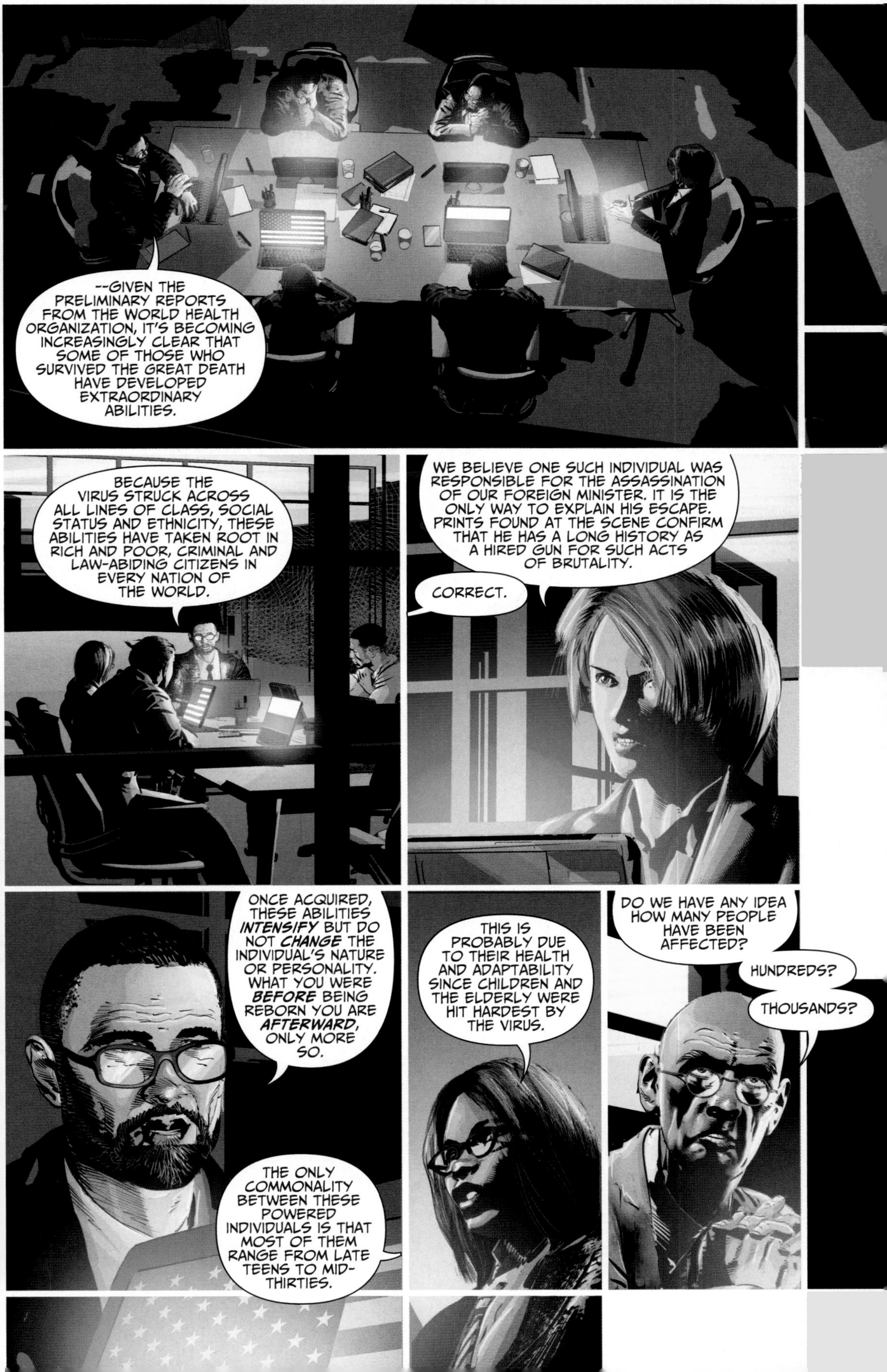
--GIVEN THE PRELIMINARY REPORTS FROM THE WORLD HEALTH ORGANIZATION, IT'S BECOMING INCREASINGLY CLEAR THAT SOME OF THOSE WHO SURVIVED THE GREAT DEATH HAVE DEVELOPED EXTRAORDINARY ABILITIES.
BECAUSE THE VIRUS STRUCK ACROSS ALL LINES OF CLASS, SOCIAL STATUS AND ETHNICITY, THESE ABILITIES HAVE TAKEN ROOT IN RICH AND POOR, CRIMINAL AND LAW-ABIDING CITIZENS IN EVERY NATION OF THE WORLD.
WE BELIEVE ONE SUCH INDIVIDUAL WAS RESPONSIBLE FOR THE ASSASSINATION OF OUR FOREIGN MINISTER. IT IS THE ONLY WAY TO EXPLAIN HIS ESCAPE. PRINTS FOUND AT THE SCENE CONFIRM THAT HE HAS A LONG HISTORY AS A HIRED GUN FOR SUCH ACTS OF BRUTALITY.
CORRECT.
ONCE ACQUIRED, THESE ABILITIES *INTENSIFY* BUT DO NOT *CHANGE* THE INDIVIDUAL'S NATURE OR PERSONALITY. WHAT YOU WERE *BEFORE* BEING REBORN YOU ARE *AFTERWARD*, ONLY MORE SO.
THE ONLY COMMONALITY BETWEEN THESE POWERED INDIVIDUALS IS THAT MOST OF THEM RANGE FROM LATE TEENS TO MID-THIRTIES.
THIS IS PROBABLY DUE TO THEIR HEALTH AND ADAPTABILITY SINCE CHILDREN AND THE ELDERLY WERE HIT HARDEST BY THE VIRUS.
DO WE HAVE ANY IDEA HOW MANY PEOPLE HAVE BEEN AFFECTED?
HUNDREDS?
THOUSANDS?

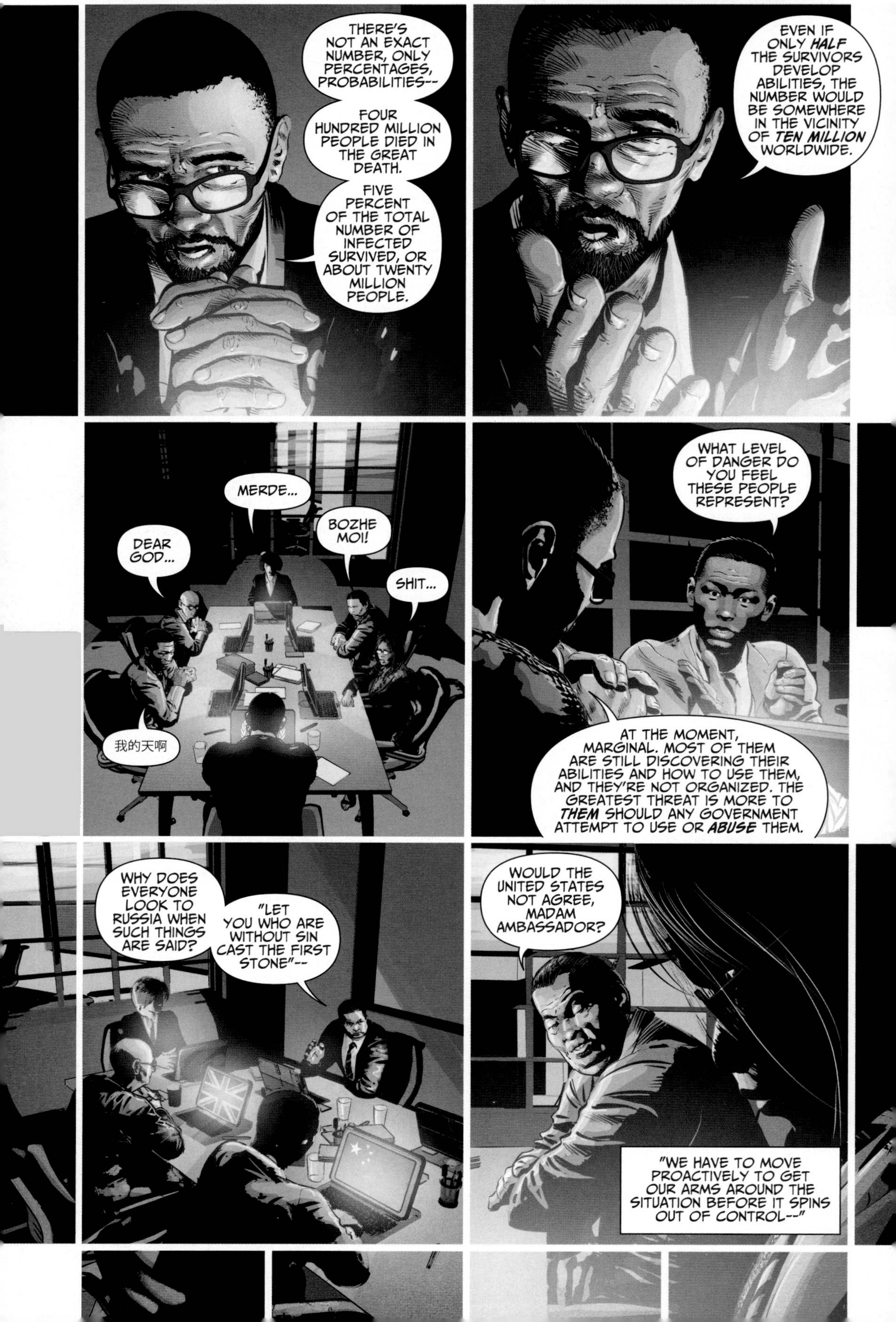
THERE'S NOT AN EXACT NUMBER, ONLY PERCENTAGES, PROBABILITIES--
FOUR HUNDRED MILLION PEOPLE DIED IN THE GREAT DEATH.
FIVE PERCENT OF THE TOTAL NUMBER OF INFECTED SURVIVED, OR ABOUT TWENTY MILLION PEOPLE.
EVEN IF ONLY HALF THE SURVIVORS DEVELOP ABILITIES, THE NUMBER WOULD BE SOMEWHERE IN THE VICINITY OF TEN MILLION WORLDWIDE.
MERDE...
BOZHE MOI!
DEAR GOD...
SHIT...
我的天啊
WHAT LEVEL OF DANGER DO YOU FEEL THESE PEOPLE REPRESENT?
AT THE MOMENT, MARGINAL. MOST OF THEM ARE STILL DISCOVERING THEIR ABILITIES AND HOW TO USE THEM, AND THEY'RE NOT ORGANIZED. THE GREATEST THREAT IS MORE TO THEM SHOULD ANY GOVERNMENT ATTEMPT TO USE OR ABUSE THEM.
WHY DOES EVERYONE LOOK TO RUSSIA WHEN SUCH THINGS ARE SAID?
"LET YOU WHO ARE WITHOUT SIN CAST THE FIRST STONE"--
WOULD THE UNITED STATES NOT AGREE, MADAM AMBASSADOR?
"WE HAVE TO MOVE PROACTIVELY TO GET OUR ARMS AROUND THE SITUATION BEFORE IT SPINS OUT OF CONTROL--"

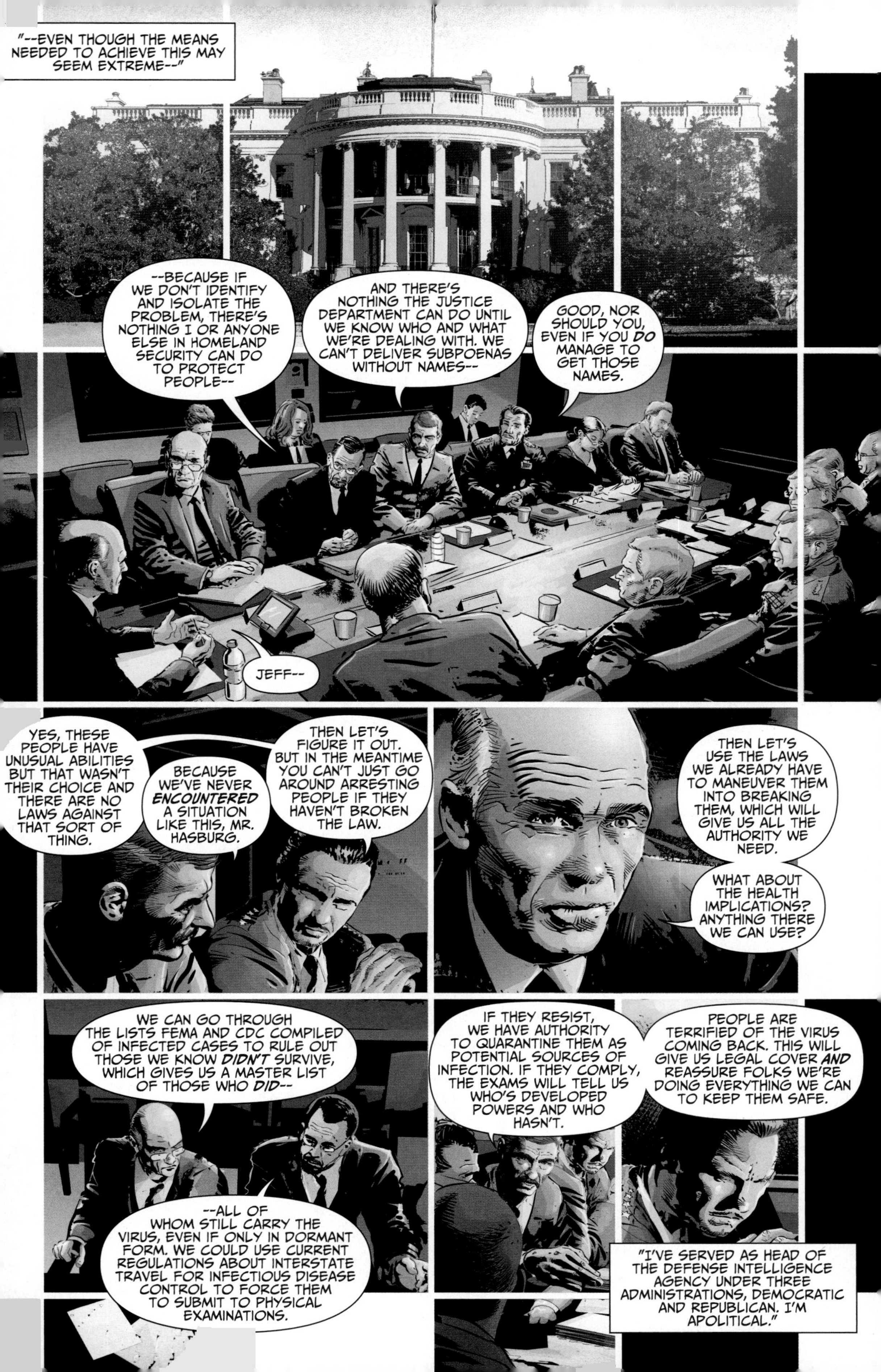
"--EVEN THOUGH THE MEANS NEEDED TO ACHIEVE THIS MAY SEEM EXTREME--"
--BECAUSE IF WE DON'T IDENTIFY AND ISOLATE THE PROBLEM, THERE'S NOTHING I OR ANYONE ELSE IN HOMELAND SECURITY CAN DO TO PROTECT PEOPLE--
AND THERE'S NOTHING THE JUSTICE DEPARTMENT CAN DO UNTIL WE KNOW WHO AND WHAT WE'RE DEALING WITH. WE CAN'T DELIVER SUBPOENAS WITHOUT NAMES--
GOOD, NOR SHOULD YOU, EVEN IF YOU DO MANAGE TO GET THOSE NAMES.
JEFF--
YES, THESE PEOPLE HAVE UNUSUAL ABILITIES BUT THAT WASN'T THEIR CHOICE AND THERE ARE NO LAWS AGAINST THAT SORT OF THING.
BECAUSE WE'VE NEVER ENCOUNTERED A SITUATION LIKE THIS, MR. HASBURG.
THEN LET'S FIGURE IT OUT. BUT IN THE MEANTIME YOU CAN'T JUST GO AROUND ARRESTING PEOPLE IF THEY HAVEN'T BROKEN THE LAW.
THEN LET'S USE THE LAWS WE ALREADY HAVE TO MANEUVER THEM INTO BREAKING THEM, WHICH WILL GIVE US ALL THE AUTHORITY WE NEED.
WHAT ABOUT THE HEALTH IMPLICATIONS? ANYTHING THERE WE CAN USE?
WE CAN GO THROUGH THE LISTS FEMA AND CDC COMPILED OF INFECTED CASES TO RULE OUT THOSE WE KNOW DIDN'T SURVIVE, WHICH GIVES US A MASTER LIST OF THOSE WHO DID--
--ALL OF WHOM STILL CARRY THE VIRUS, EVEN IF ONLY IN DORMANT FORM. WE COULD USE CURRENT REGULATIONS ABOUT INTERSTATE TRAVEL FOR INFECTIOUS DISEASE CONTROL TO FORCE THEM TO SUBMIT TO PHYSICAL EXAMINATIONS.
IF THEY RESIST, WE HAVE AUTHORITY TO QUARANTINE THEM AS POTENTIAL SOURCES OF INFECTION. IF THEY COMPLY, THE EXAMS WILL TELL US WHO'S DEVELOPED POWERS AND WHO HASN'T.
PEOPLE ARE TERRIFIED OF THE VIRUS COMING BACK. THIS WILL GIVE US LEGAL COVER AND REASSURE FOLKS WE'RE DOING EVERYTHING WE CAN TO KEEP THEM SAFE.
"I'VE SERVED AS HEAD OF THE DEFENSE INTELLIGENCE AGENCY UNDER THREE ADMINISTRATIONS, DEMOCRATIC AND REPUBLICAN. I'M APOLITICAL."

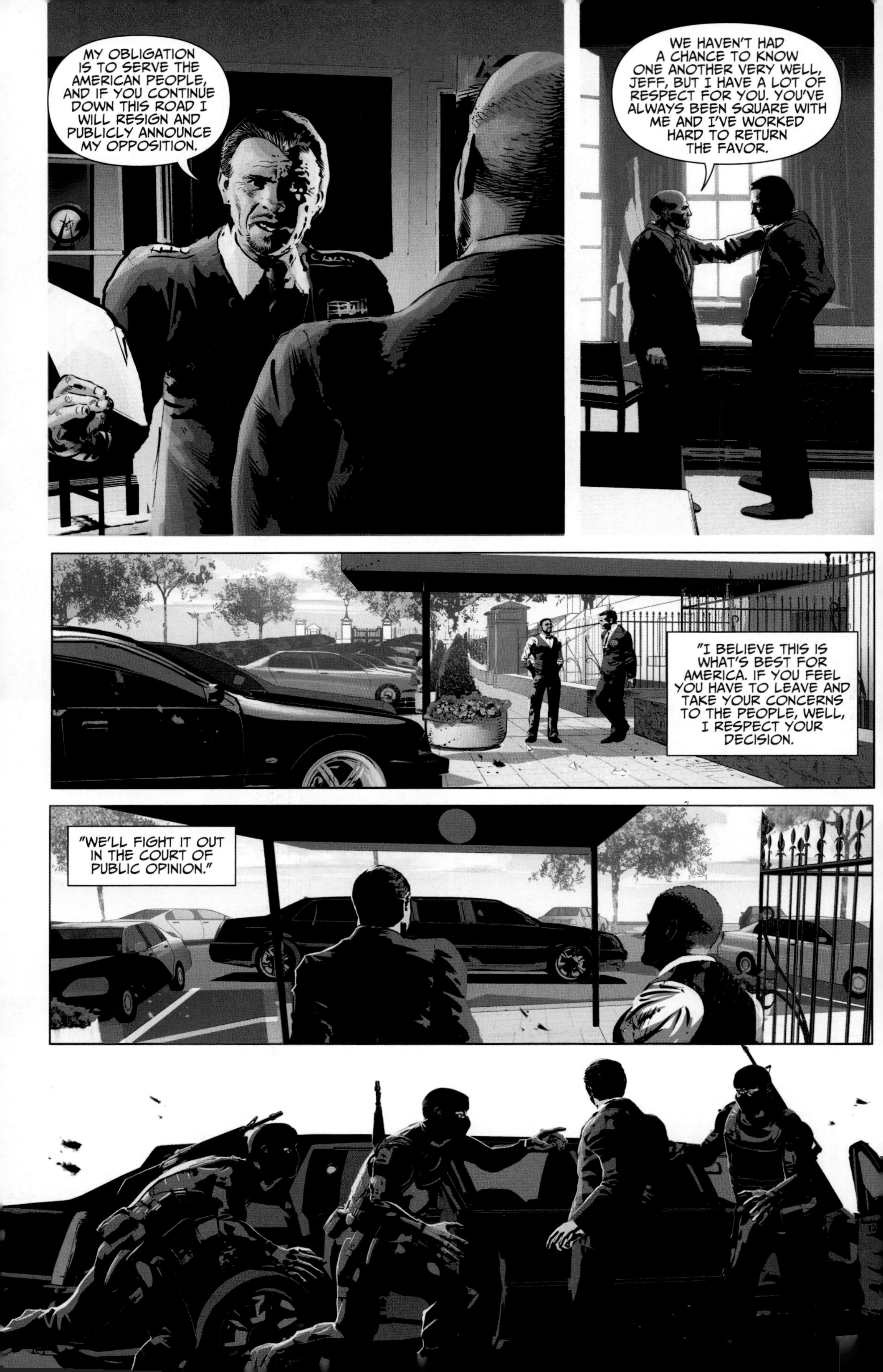
MY OBLIGATION IS TO SERVE THE AMERICAN PEOPLE, AND IF YOU CONTINUE DOWN THIS ROAD I WILL RESIGN AND PUBLICLY ANNOUNCE MY OPPOSITION.
WE HAVEN'T HAD A CHANCE TO KNOW ONE ANOTHER VERY WELL, JEFF, BUT I HAVE A LOT OF RESPECT FOR YOU. YOU'VE ALWAYS BEEN SQUARE WITH ME AND I'VE WORKED HARD TO RETURN THE FAVOR.
"I BELIEVE THIS IS WHAT'S BEST FOR AMERICA. IF YOU FEEL YOU HAVE TO LEAVE AND TAKE YOUR CONCERNS TO THE PEOPLE, WELL, I RESPECT YOUR DECISION.
"WE'LL FIGHT IT OUT IN THE COURT OF PUBLIC OPINION."

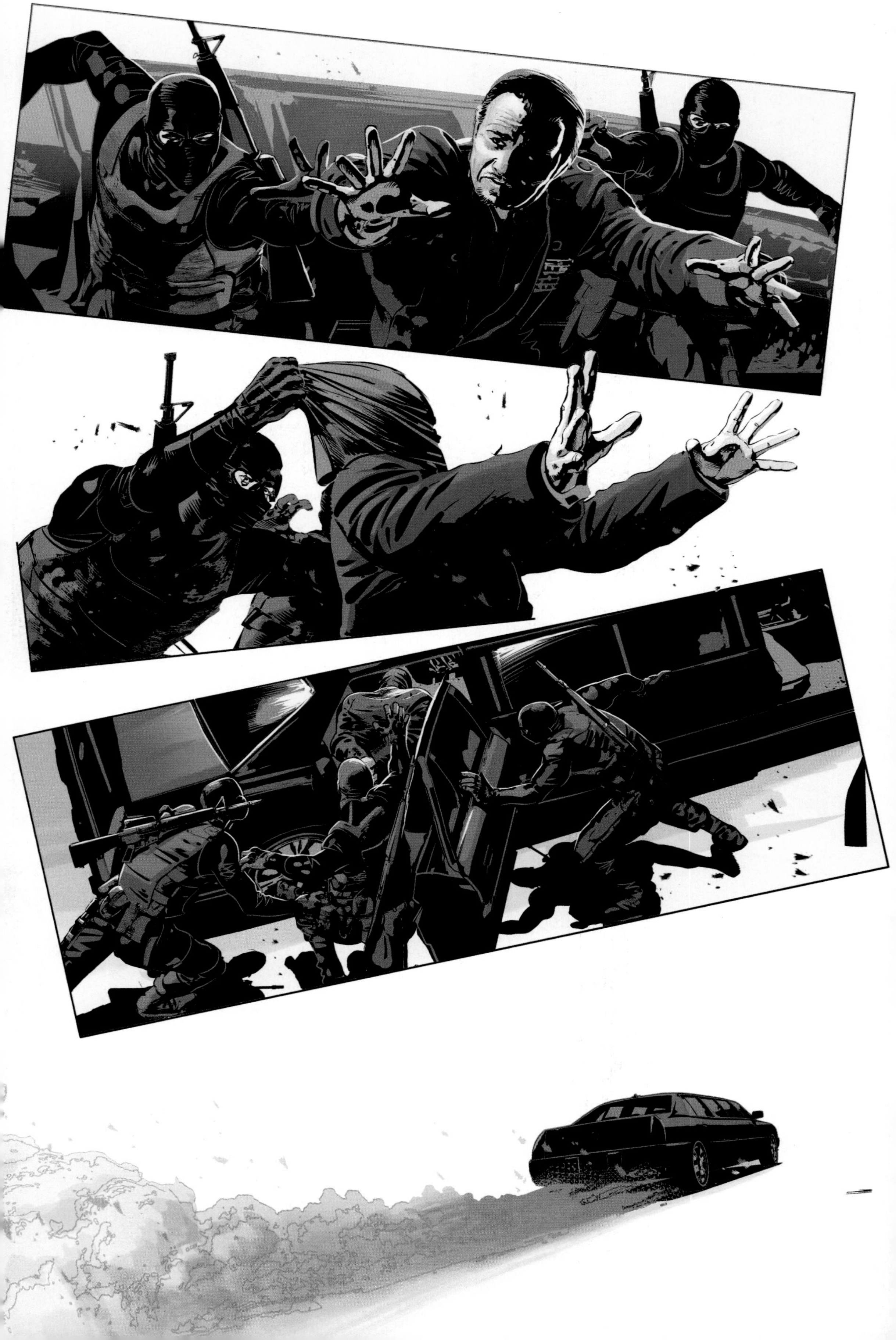

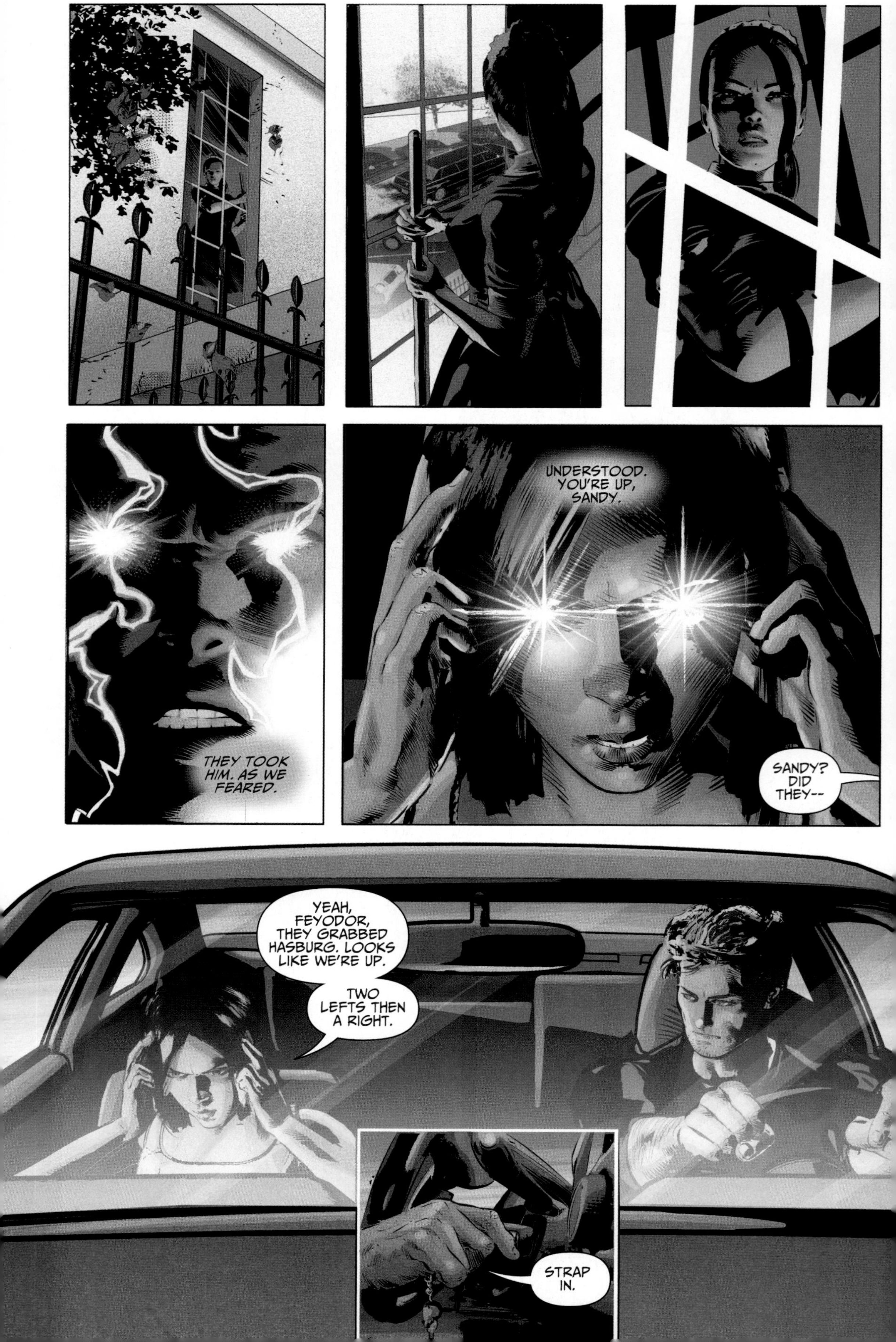
THEY TOOK HIM. AS WE FEARED.
UNDERSTOOD. YOU'RE UP, SANDY.
SANDY? DID THEY--
YEAH, FEYODOR, THEY GRABBED HASBURG. LOOKS LIKE WE'RE UP.
TWO LEFTS THEN A RIGHT.
STRAP IN.

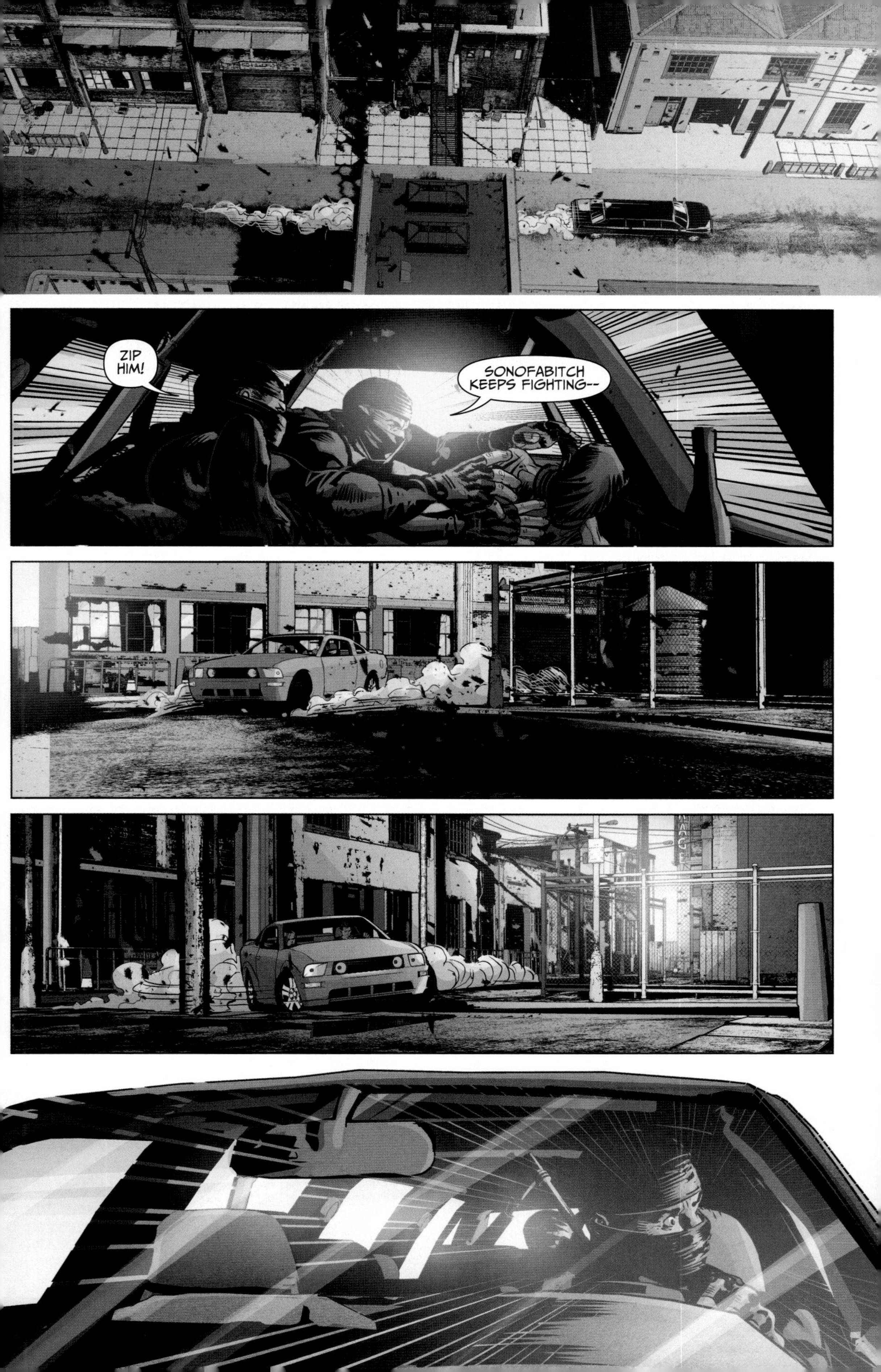
ZIP HIM!
SONOFABITCH KEEPS FIGHTING--

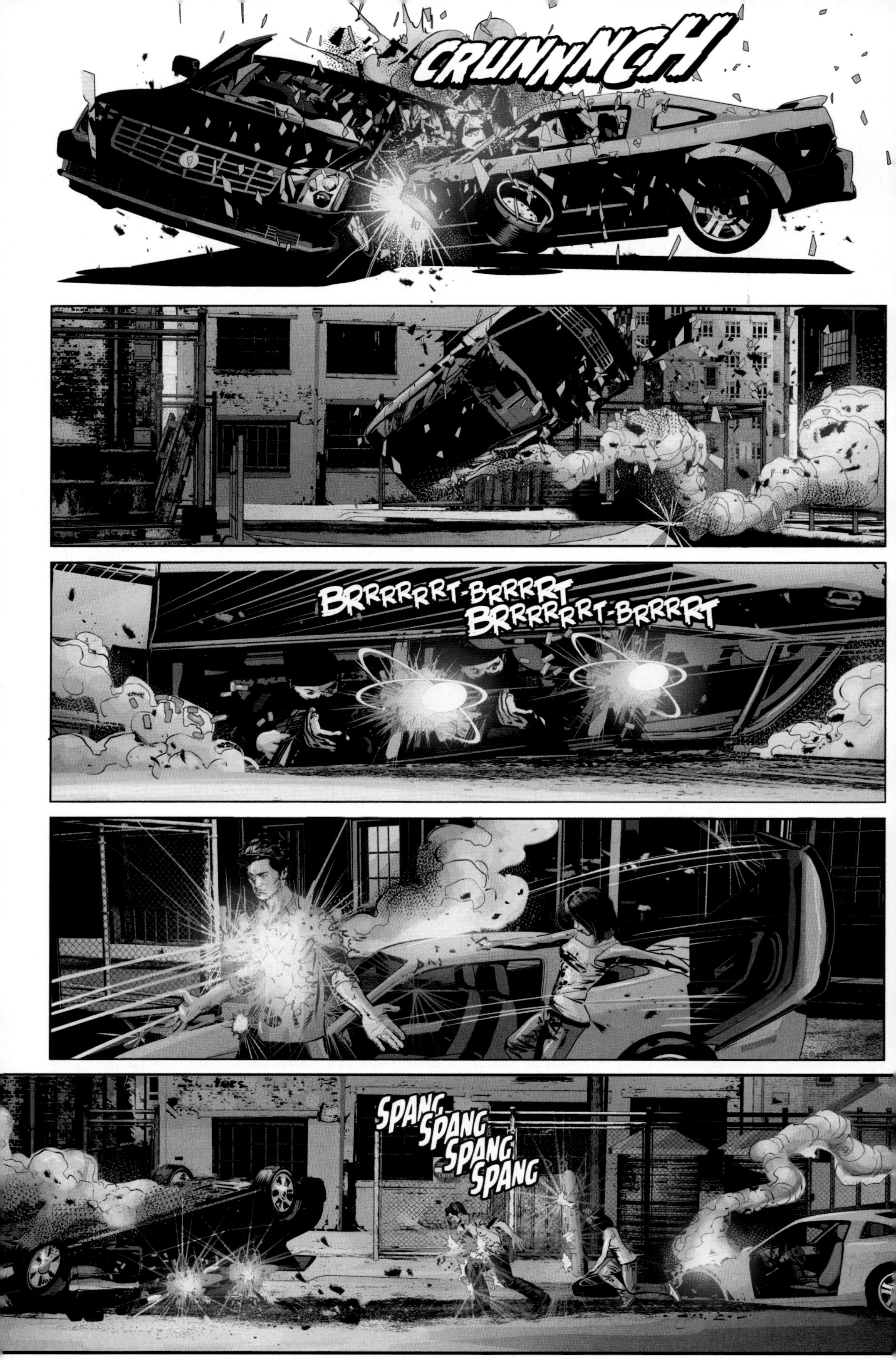
CRUNNNCH
BRRRRRT-BRRRRT
BRRRRRT-BRRRRT
SPANG
SPANG
SPANG
SPANG

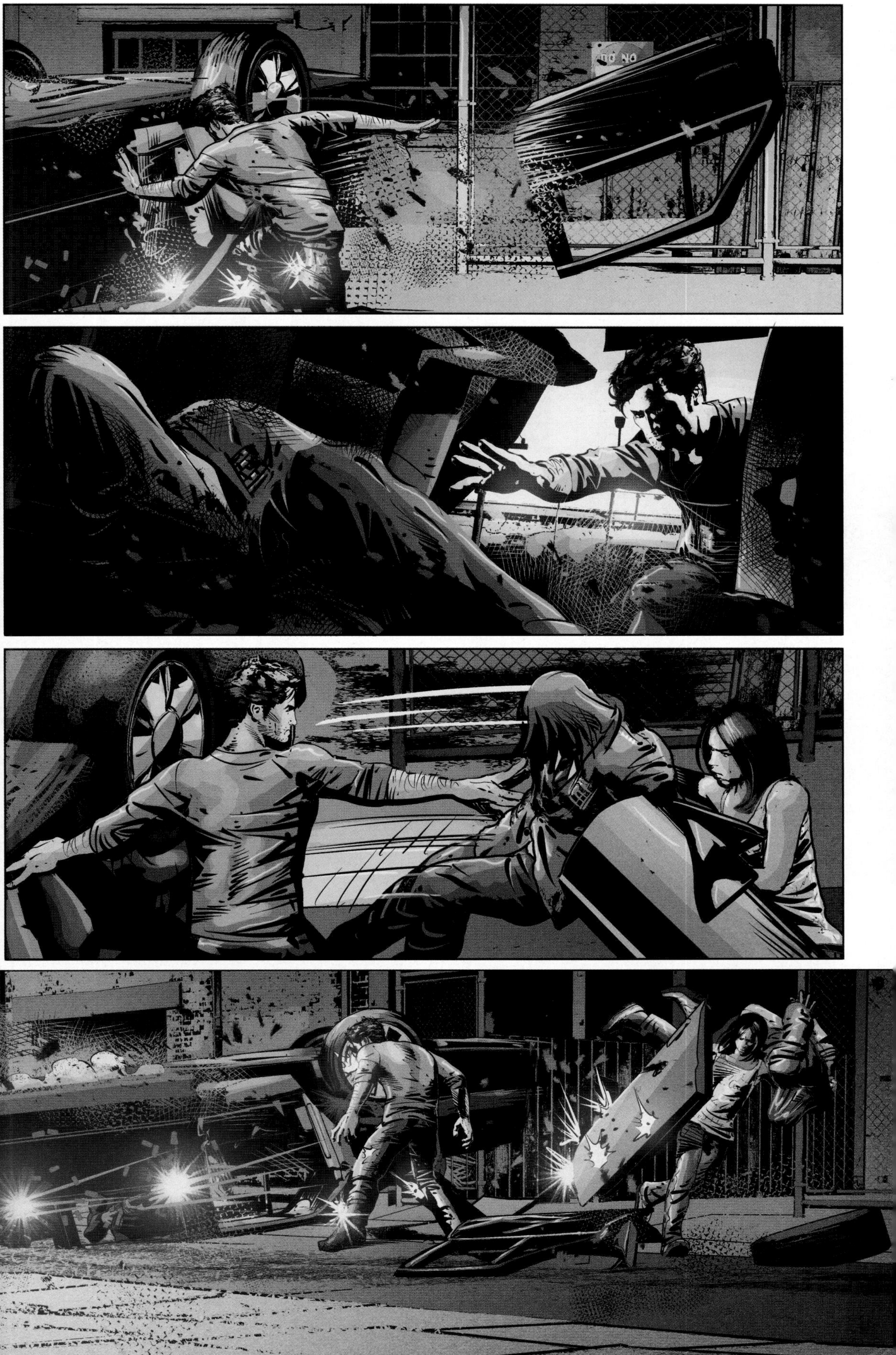
DO NO

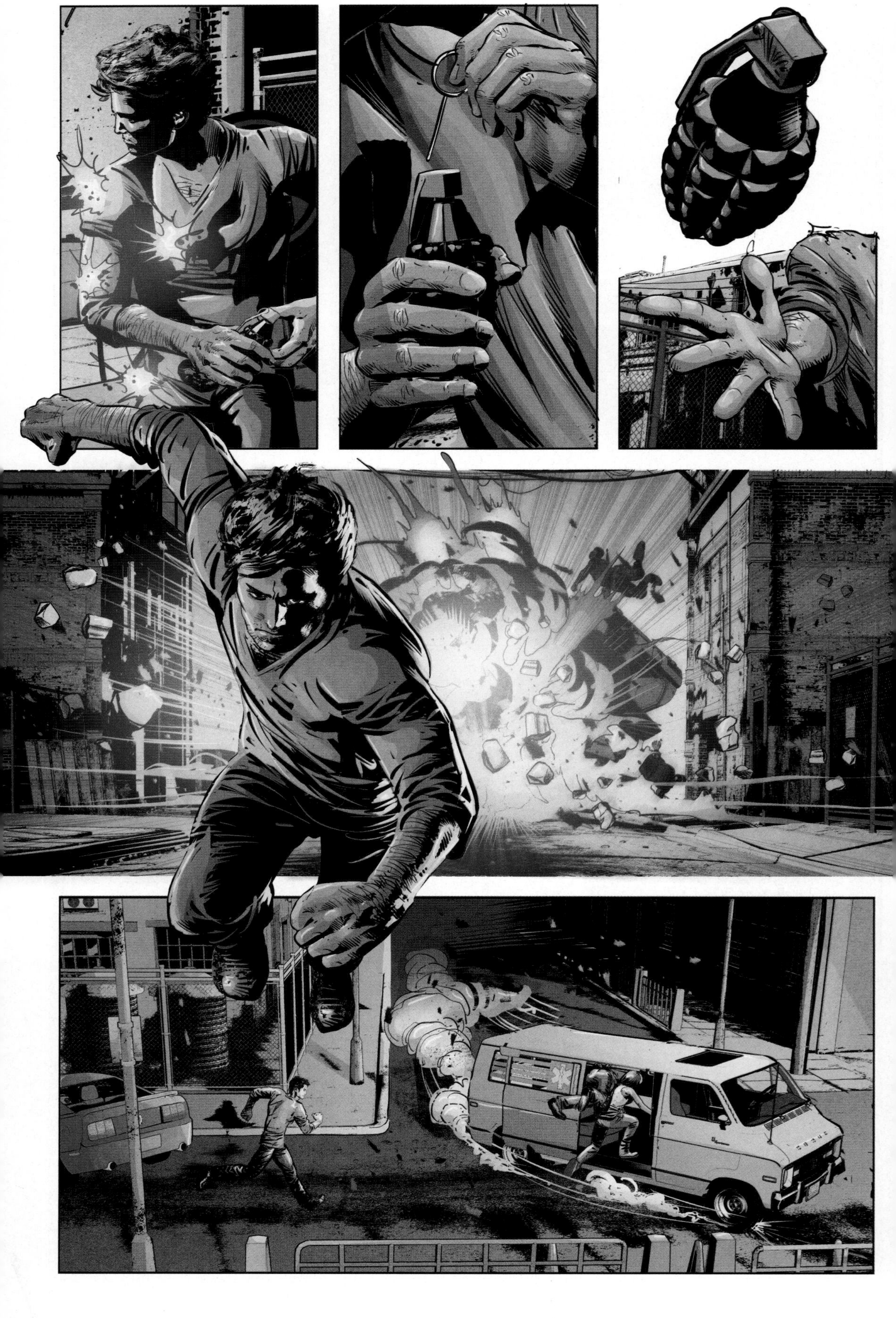

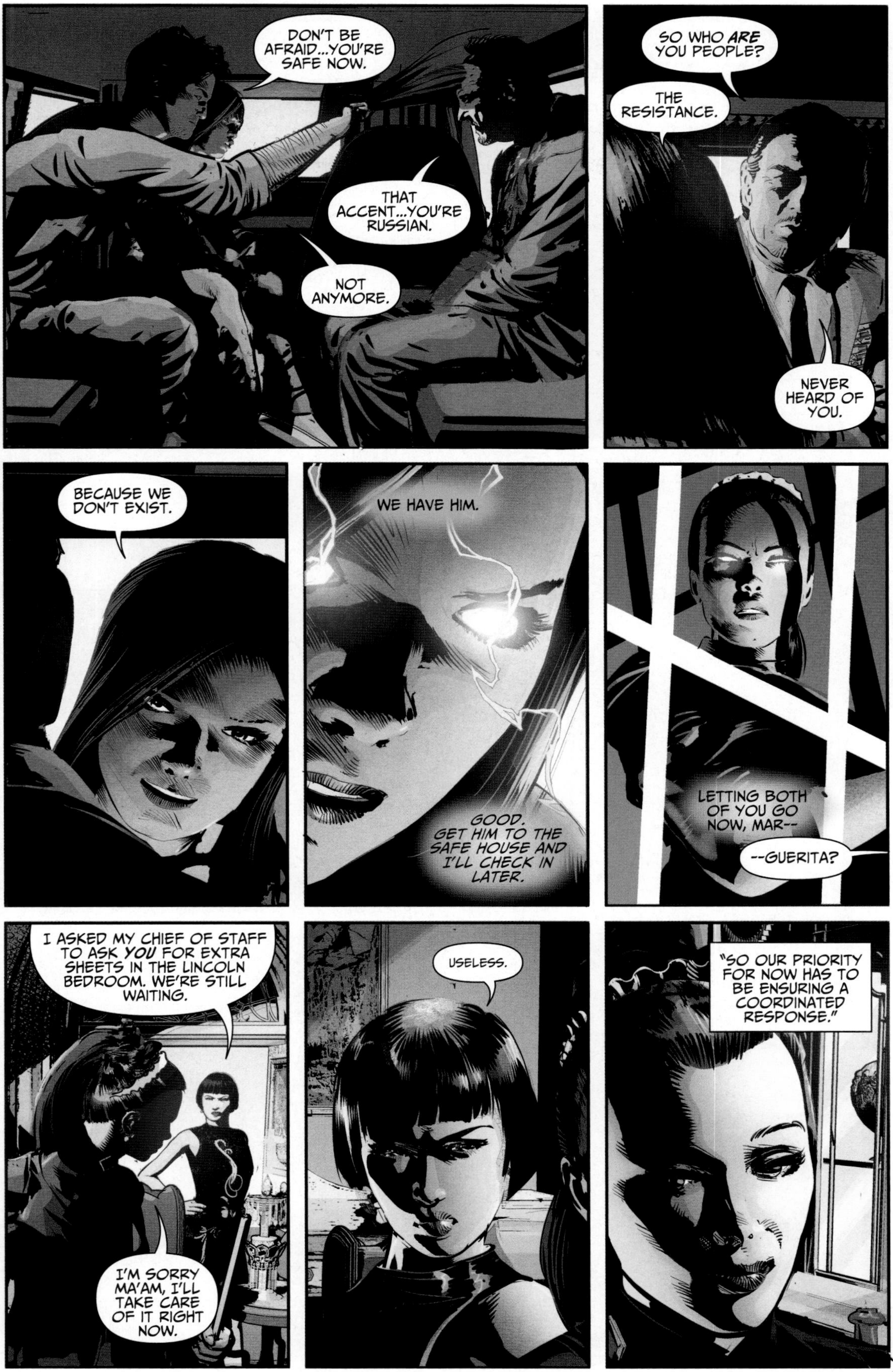
DON'T BE AFRAID...YOU'RE SAFE NOW.
THAT ACCENT...YOU'RE RUSSIAN.
NOT ANYMORE.
SO WHO ARE YOU PEOPLE?
THE RESISTANCE.
NEVER HEARD OF YOU.
BECAUSE WE DON'T EXIST.
WE HAVE HIM.
GOOD. GET HIM TO THE SAFE HOUSE AND I'LL CHECK IN LATER.
LETTING BOTH OF YOU GO NOW, MAR--
--GUERITA?
I ASKED MY CHIEF OF STAFF TO ASK YOU FOR EXTRA SHEETS IN THE LINCOLN BEDROOM. WE'RE STILL WAITING.
I'M SORRY MA'AM, I'LL TAKE CARE OF IT RIGHT NOW.
USELESS.
"SO OUR PRIORITY FOR NOW HAS TO BE ENSURING A COORDINATED RESPONSE."

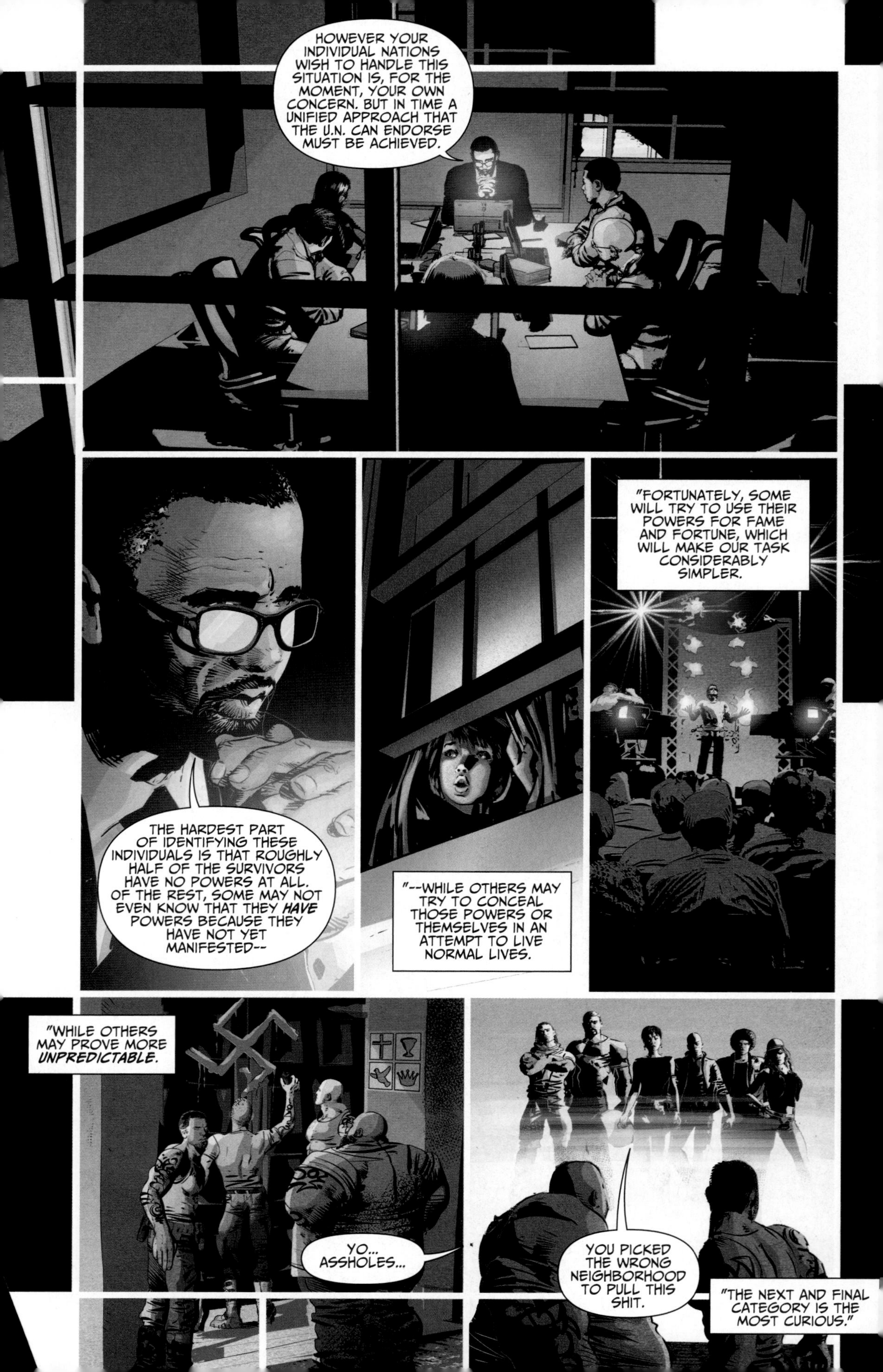
HOWEVER YOUR INDIVIDUAL NATIONS WISH TO HANDLE THIS SITUATION IS, FOR THE MOMENT, YOUR OWN CONCERN. BUT IN TIME A UNIFIED APPROACH THAT THE U.N. CAN ENDORSE MUST BE ACHIEVED.
THE HARDEST PART OF IDENTIFYING THESE INDIVIDUALS IS THAT ROUGHLY HALF OF THE SURVIVORS HAVE NO POWERS AT ALL. OF THE REST, SOME MAY NOT EVEN KNOW THAT THEY *HAVE* POWERS BECAUSE THEY HAVE NOT YET MANIFESTED--
"--WHILE OTHERS MAY TRY TO CONCEAL THOSE POWERS OR THEMSELVES IN AN ATTEMPT TO LIVE NORMAL LIVES.
"FORTUNATELY, SOME WILL TRY TO USE THEIR POWERS FOR FAME AND FORTUNE, WHICH WILL MAKE OUR TASK CONSIDERABLY SIMPLER.
"WHILE OTHERS MAY PROVE MORE ***UNPREDICTABLE***.
YO... ASSHOLES...
YOU PICKED THE WRONG NEIGHBORHOOD TO PULL THIS SHIT.
"THE NEXT AND FINAL CATEGORY IS THE MOST CURIOUS."

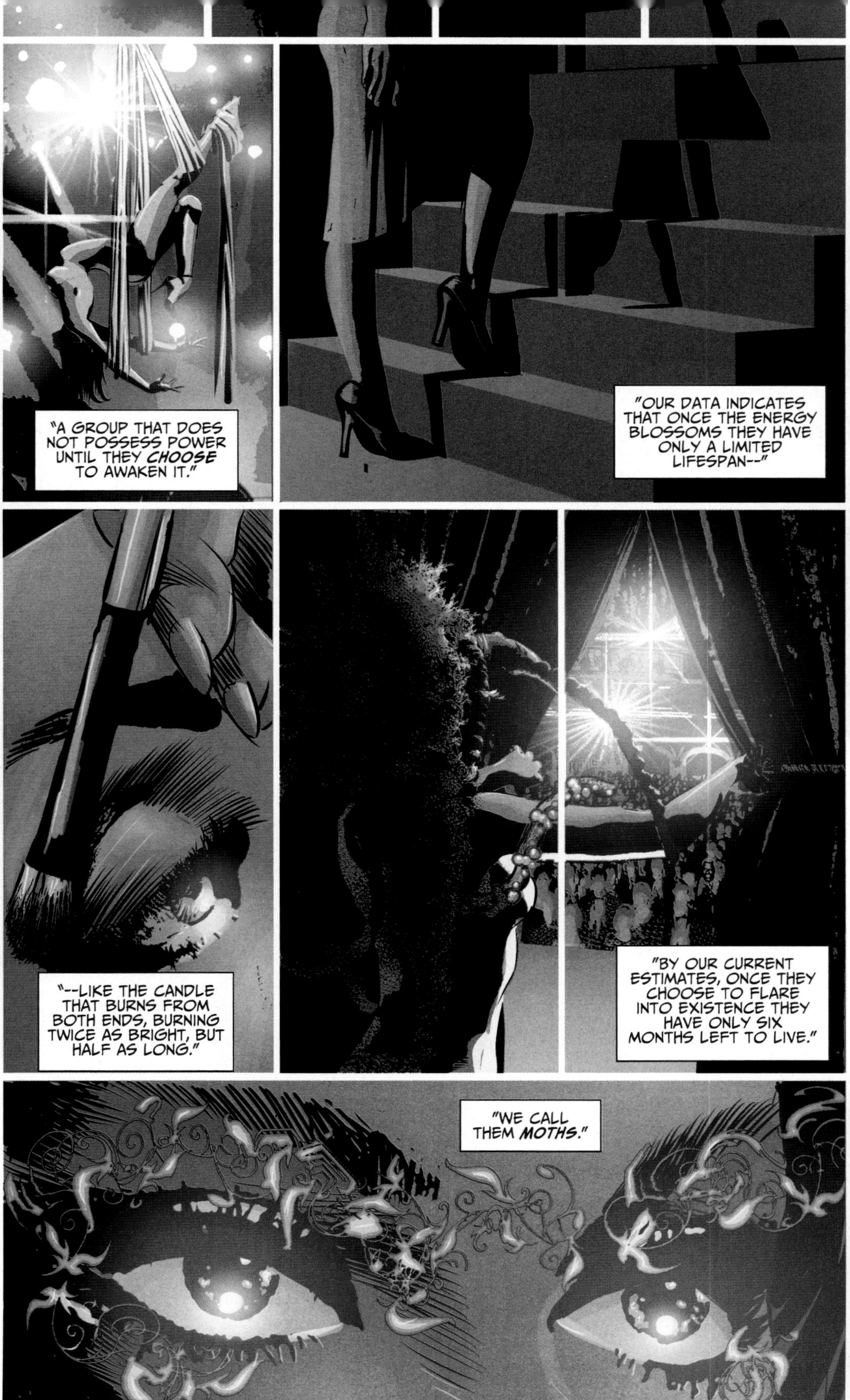
"A GROUP THAT DOES NOT POSSESS POWER UNTIL THEY *CHOOSE* TO AWAKEN IT."
"OUR DATA INDICATES THAT ONCE THE ENERGY BLOSSOMS THEY HAVE ONLY A LIMITED LIFESPAN--"
"--LIKE THE CANDLE THAT BURNS FROM BOTH ENDS, BURNING TWICE AS BRIGHT, BUT HALF AS LONG."
"BY OUR CURRENT ESTIMATES, ONCE THEY CHOOSE TO FLARE INTO EXISTENCE THEY HAVE ONLY SIX MONTHS LEFT TO LIVE."
"WE CALL THEM *MOTHS*."

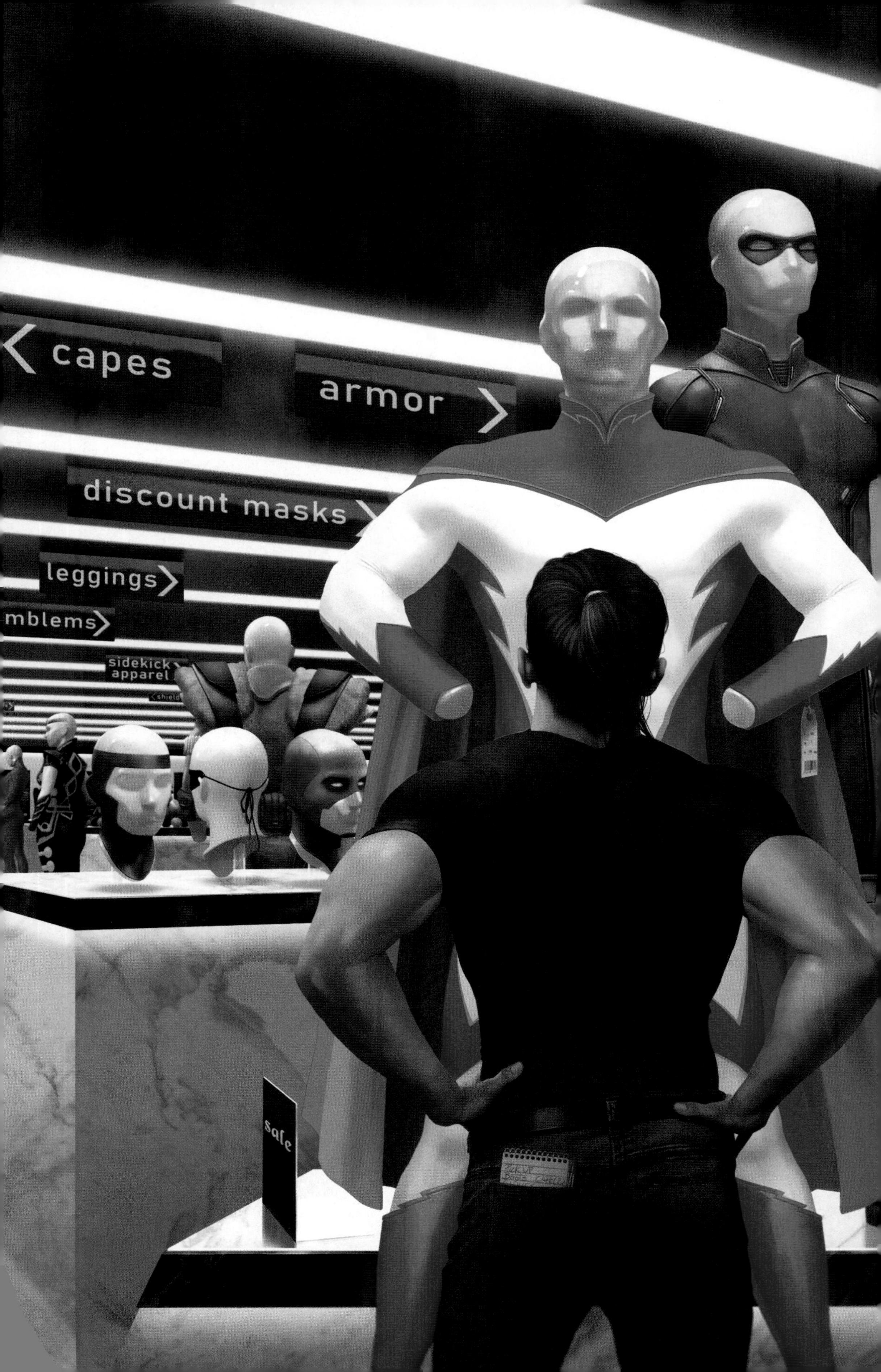
capes
armor
discount masks
leggings
mblems
sidekick apparel
sale

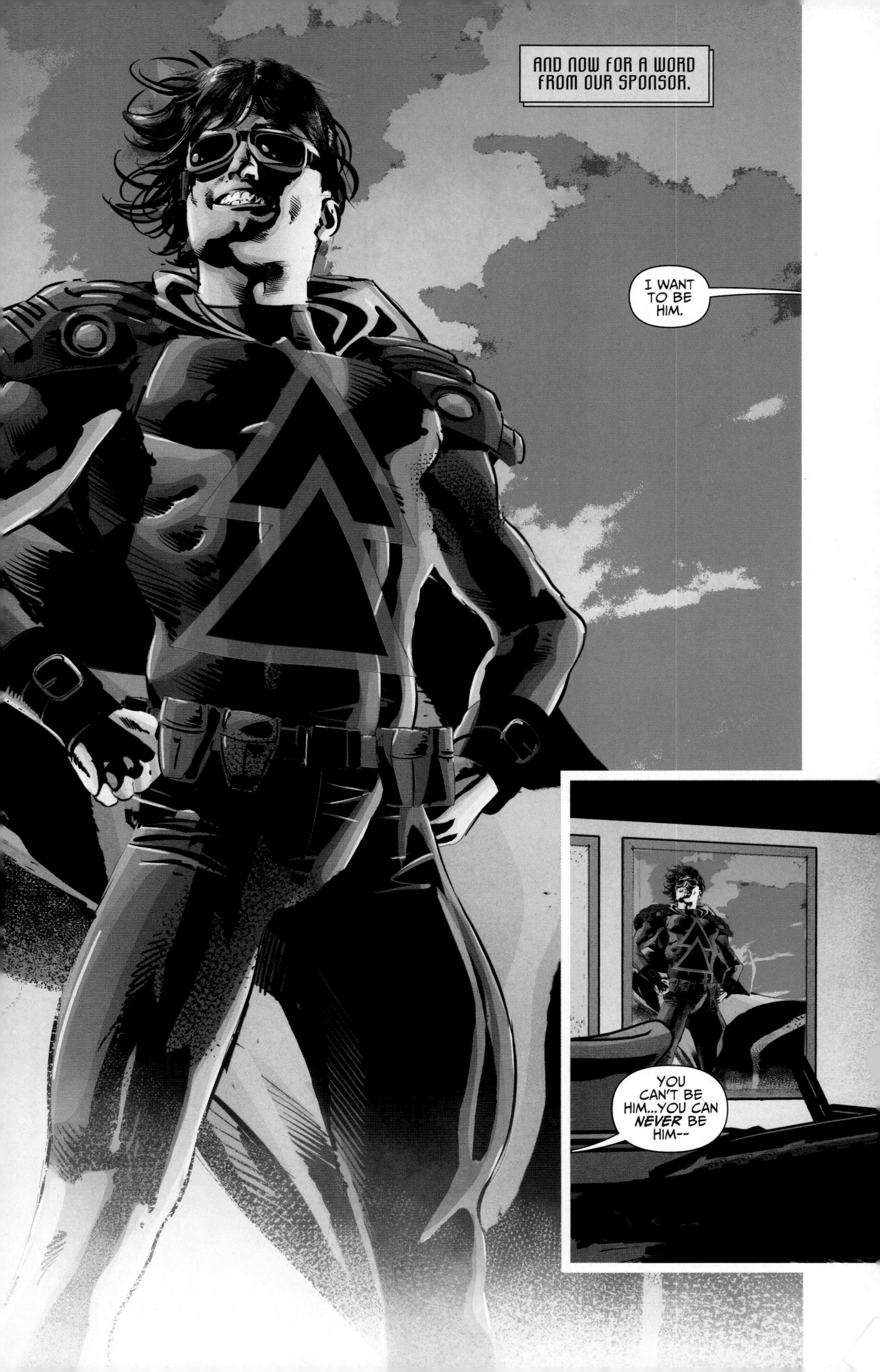
AND NOW FOR A WORD FROM OUR SPONSOR.
I WANT TO BE HIM.
YOU CAN'T BE HIM...YOU CAN *NEVER* BE HIM--

--BECAUSE THAT PARTICULAR COSTUME DESIGN AND THE *AGENT ARROW* NAME ARE ALREADY TAKEN.

SO I CAN'T GET SOMETHING THAT EVEN COMES *CLOSE*?

NO. INTERFERES WITH MARKETING. OUR CLIENTS NEED TO BE IMMEDIATELY IDENTIFIABLE AND DISTINCT FROM EACH OTHER.

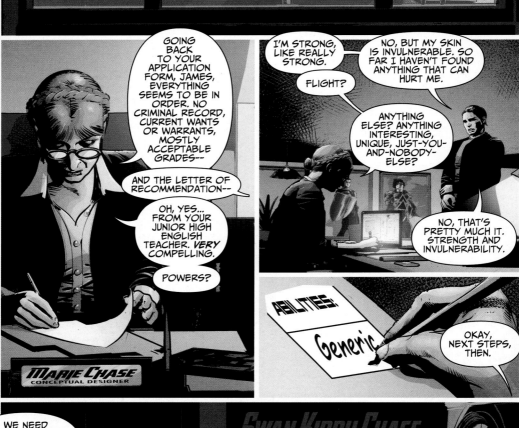

GOING BACK TO YOUR APPLICATION FORM, JAMES, EVERYTHING SEEMS TO BE IN ORDER. NO CRIMINAL RECORD, CURRENT WANTS OR WARRANTS, MOSTLY ACCEPTABLE GRADES--

AND THE LETTER OF RECOMMENDATION--

OH, YES... FROM YOUR JUNIOR HIGH ENGLISH TEACHER. *VERY* COMPELLING.

POWERS?

I'M STRONG, LIKE REALLY STRONG.

FLIGHT?

NO, BUT MY SKIN IS INVULNERABLE. SO FAR I HAVEN'T FOUND ANYTHING THAT CAN HURT ME.

ANYTHING ELSE? ANYTHING INTERESTING, UNIQUE, JUST-YOU-AND-NOBODY-ELSE?

NO, THAT'S PRETTY MUCH IT. STRENGTH AND INVULNERABILITY.

MARIE CHASE
CONCEPTUAL DESIGNER

ABILITIES:
Generic

OKAY, NEXT STEPS, THEN.

WE NEED TO KNOW WHAT WE'RE MARKETING TO BUYERS, AND THAT HAS TO COME FROM YOU--

--AT LEAST WITHIN COMPANY GUIDELINES--

--SO WE NEED TO KNOW NOT JUST WHO YOU *ARE* BUT WHO YOU *WANT* TO BE BEFORE WE CAN FINALIZE THE CONTRACT.

SWAN KIRBY CHASE
POWERS PLACEMENT AGENCY

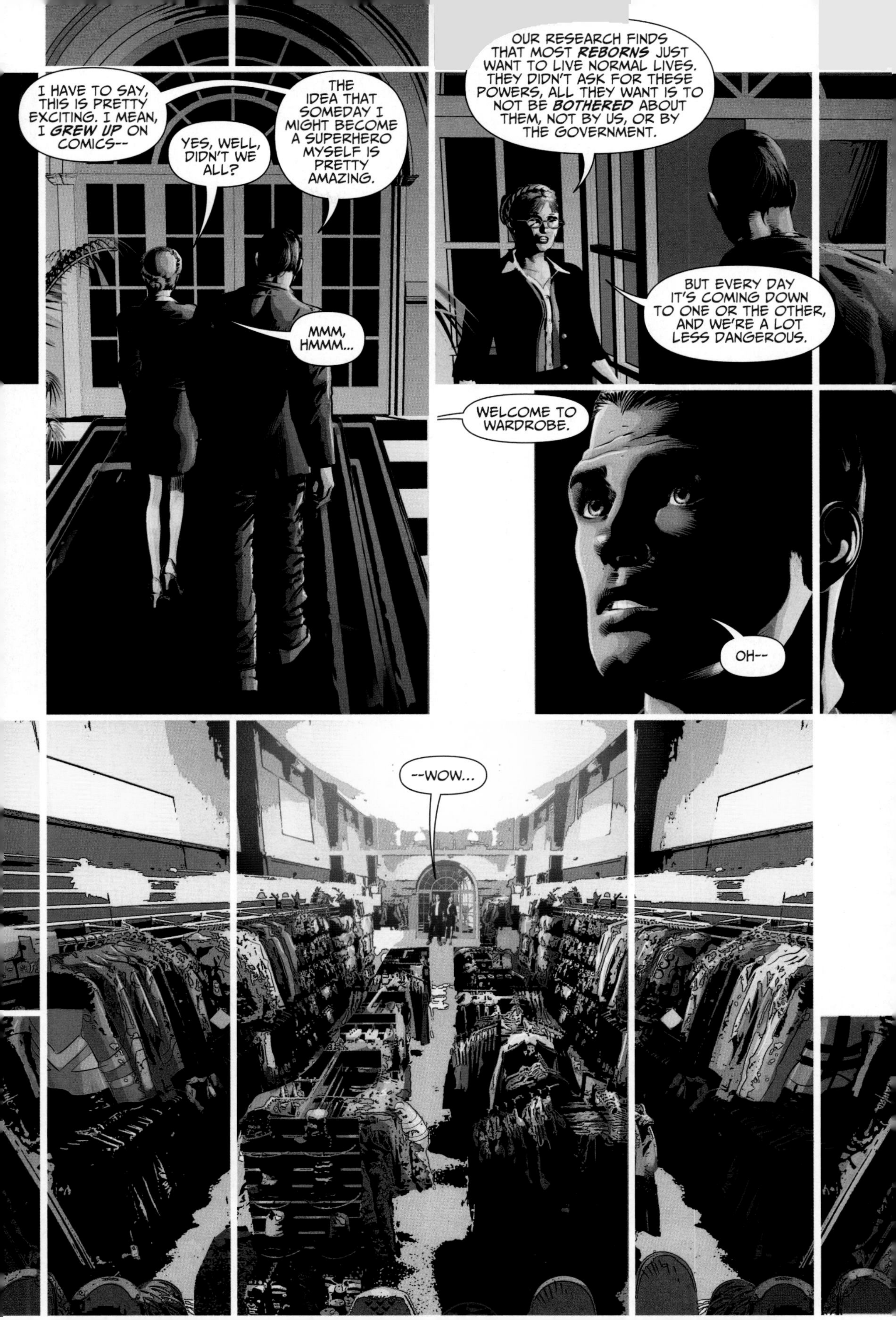
I HAVE TO SAY, THIS IS PRETTY EXCITING. I MEAN, I GREW UP ON COMICS--
YES, WELL, DIDN'T WE ALL?
THE IDEA THAT SOMEDAY I MIGHT BECOME A SUPERHERO MYSELF IS PRETTY AMAZING.
MMM, HMMM...
OUR RESEARCH FINDS THAT MOST REBORNS JUST WANT TO LIVE NORMAL LIVES. THEY DIDN'T ASK FOR THESE POWERS, ALL THEY WANT IS TO NOT BE BOTHERED ABOUT THEM, NOT BY US, OR BY THE GOVERNMENT.
BUT EVERY DAY IT'S COMING DOWN TO ONE OR THE OTHER, AND WE'RE A LOT LESS DANGEROUS.
WELCOME TO WARDROBE.
OH--
--WOW...

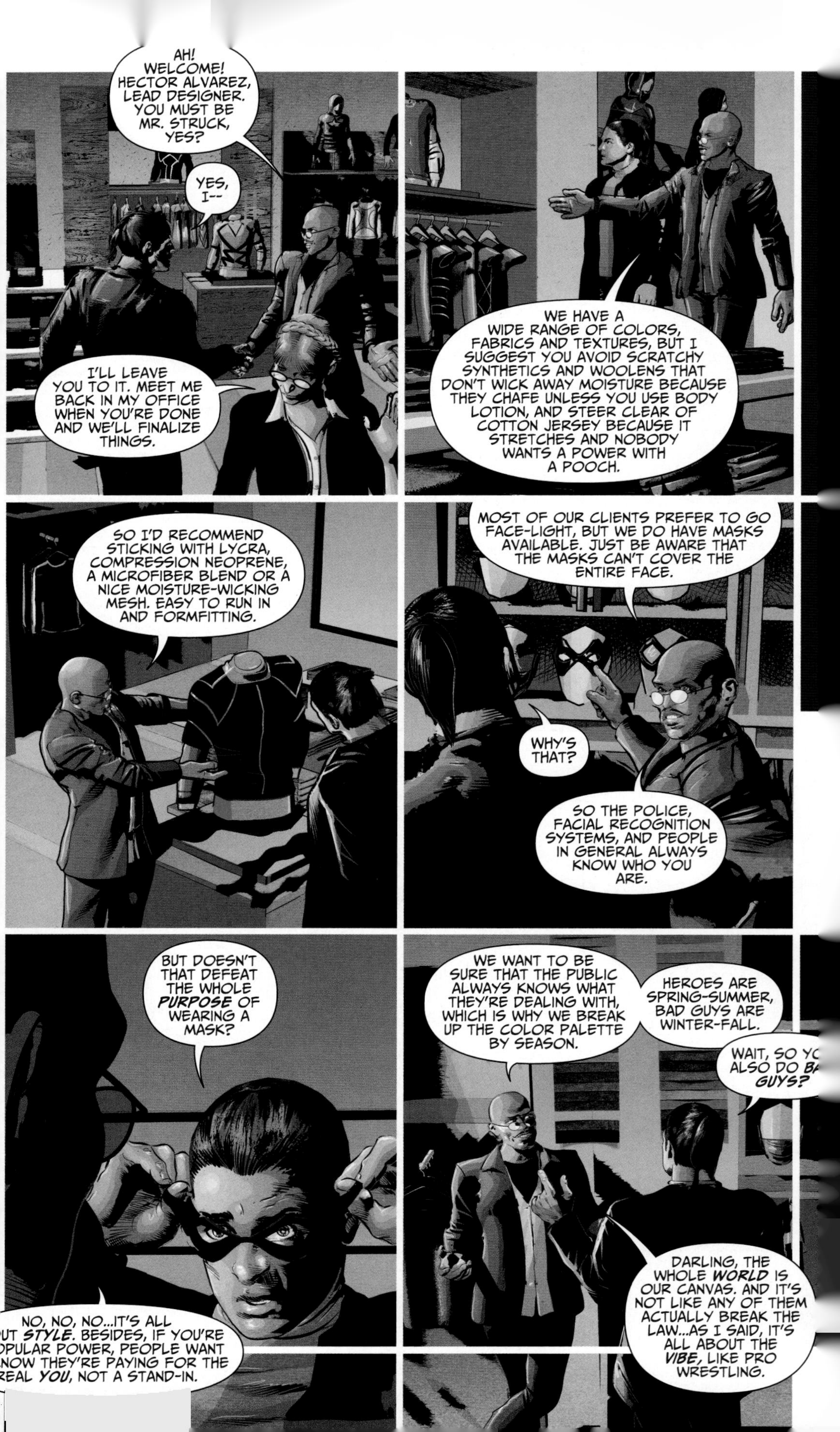
AH! WELCOME! HECTOR ALVAREZ, LEAD DESIGNER. YOU MUST BE MR. STRUCK, YES?
YES, I--
I'LL LEAVE YOU TO IT. MEET ME BACK IN MY OFFICE WHEN YOU'RE DONE AND WE'LL FINALIZE THINGS.
WE HAVE A WIDE RANGE OF COLORS, FABRICS AND TEXTURES, BUT I SUGGEST YOU AVOID SCRATCHY SYNTHETICS AND WOOLENS THAT DON'T WICK AWAY MOISTURE BECAUSE THEY CHAFE UNLESS YOU USE BODY LOTION, AND STEER CLEAR OF COTTON JERSEY BECAUSE IT STRETCHES AND NOBODY WANTS A POWER WITH A POOCH.
SO I'D RECOMMEND STICKING WITH LYCRA, COMPRESSION NEOPRENE, A MICROFIBER BLEND OR A NICE MOISTURE-WICKING MESH. EASY TO RUN IN AND FORMFITTING.
MOST OF OUR CLIENTS PREFER TO GO FACE-LIGHT, BUT WE DO HAVE MASKS AVAILABLE. JUST BE AWARE THAT THE MASKS CAN'T COVER THE ENTIRE FACE.
WHY'S THAT?
SO THE POLICE, FACIAL RECOGNITION SYSTEMS, AND PEOPLE IN GENERAL ALWAYS KNOW WHO YOU ARE.
BUT DOESN'T THAT DEFEAT THE WHOLE *PURPOSE* OF WEARING A MASK?
NO, NO, NO...IT'S ALL UT *STYLE*. BESIDES, IF YOU'RE OPULAR POWER, PEOPLE WANT NOW THEY'RE PAYING FOR THE REAL *YOU*, NOT A STAND-IN.
WE WANT TO BE SURE THAT THE PUBLIC ALWAYS KNOWS WHAT THEY'RE DEALING WITH, WHICH IS WHY WE BREAK UP THE COLOR PALETTE BY SEASON.
HEROES ARE SPRING-SUMMER, BAD GUYS ARE WINTER-FALL.
WAIT, SO YO ALSO DO *BA* *GUYS?*
DARLING, THE WHOLE *WORLD* IS OUR CANVAS. AND IT'S NOT LIKE ANY OF THEM ACTUALLY BREAK THE LAW...AS I SAID, IT'S ALL ABOUT THE *VIBE*, LIKE PRO WRESTLING.

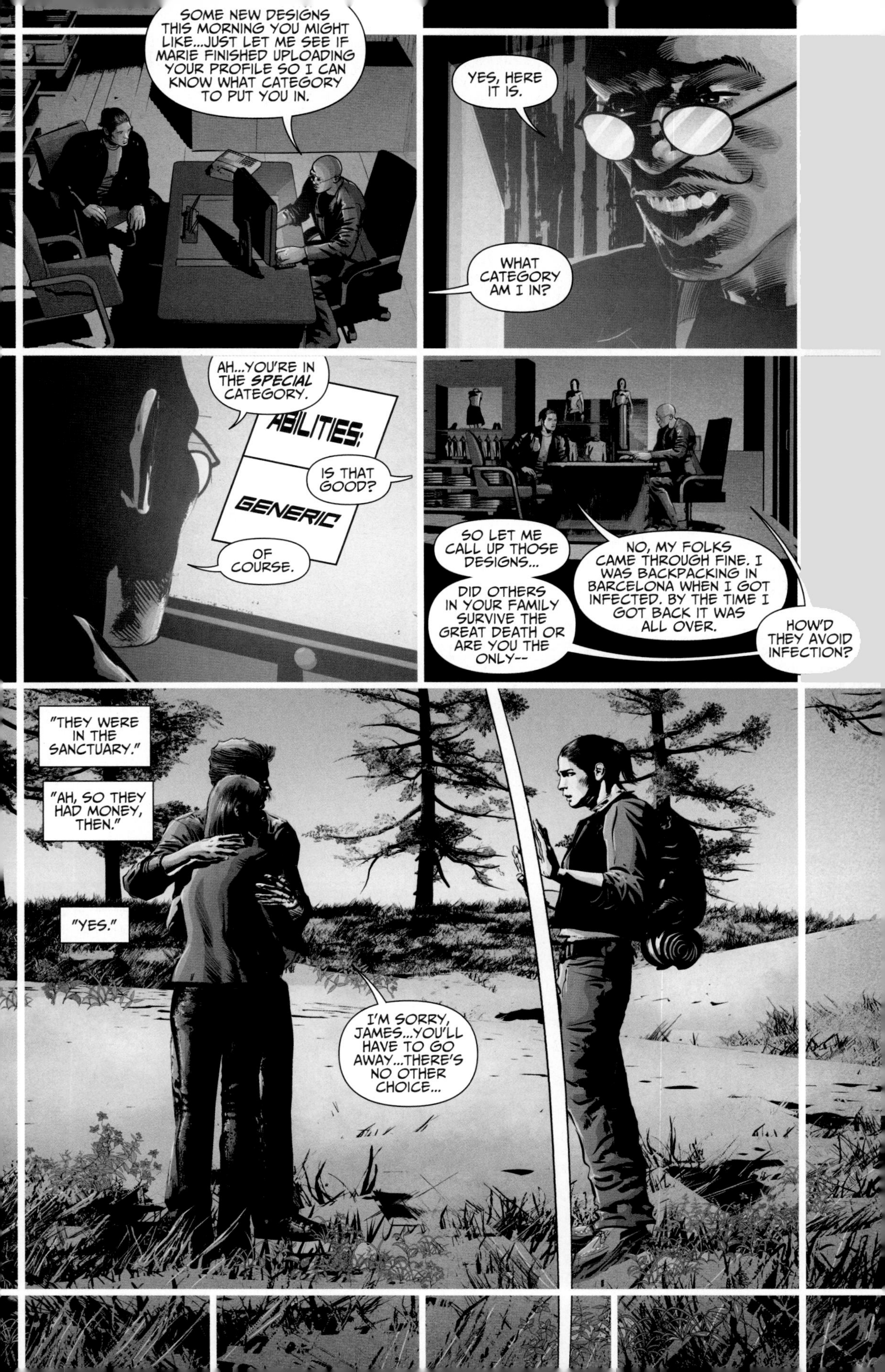
SOME NEW DESIGNS THIS MORNING YOU MIGHT LIKE...JUST LET ME SEE IF MARIE FINISHED UPLOADING YOUR PROFILE SO I CAN KNOW WHAT CATEGORY TO PUT YOU IN.
YES, HERE IT IS.
WHAT CATEGORY AM I IN?
AH...YOU'RE IN THE *SPECIAL* CATEGORY.
ABILITIES:
GENERIC
IS THAT GOOD?
OF COURSE.
SO LET ME CALL UP THOSE DESIGNS...
DID OTHERS IN YOUR FAMILY SURVIVE THE GREAT DEATH OR ARE YOU THE ONLY--
NO, MY FOLKS CAME THROUGH FINE. I WAS BACKPACKING IN BARCELONA WHEN I GOT INFECTED. BY THE TIME I GOT BACK IT WAS ALL OVER.
HOW'D THEY AVOID INFECTION?
"THEY WERE IN THE SANCTUARY."
"AH, SO THEY HAD MONEY, THEN."
"YES."
I'M SORRY, JAMES...YOU'LL HAVE TO GO AWAY...THERE'S NO OTHER CHOICE...

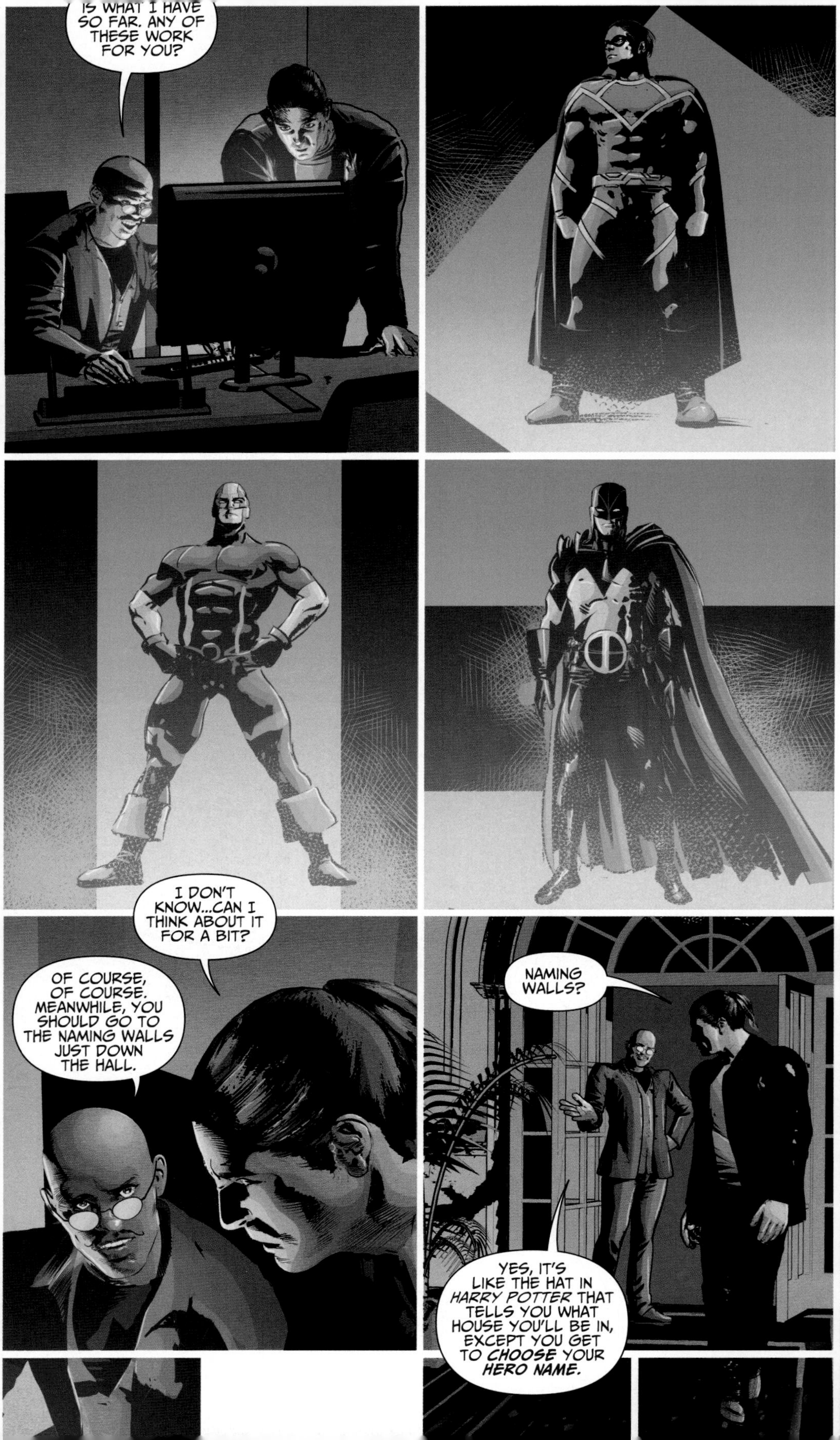
IS WHAT I HAVE SO FAR. ANY OF THESE WORK FOR YOU?
I DON'T KNOW...CAN I THINK ABOUT IT FOR A BIT?
OF COURSE, OF COURSE. MEANWHILE, YOU SHOULD GO TO THE NAMING WALLS JUST DOWN THE HALL.
NAMING WALLS?
YES, IT'S LIKE THE HAT IN *HARRY POTTER* THAT TELLS YOU WHAT HOUSE YOU'LL BE IN, EXCEPT YOU GET TO ***CHOOSE*** YOUR ***HERO NAME.***

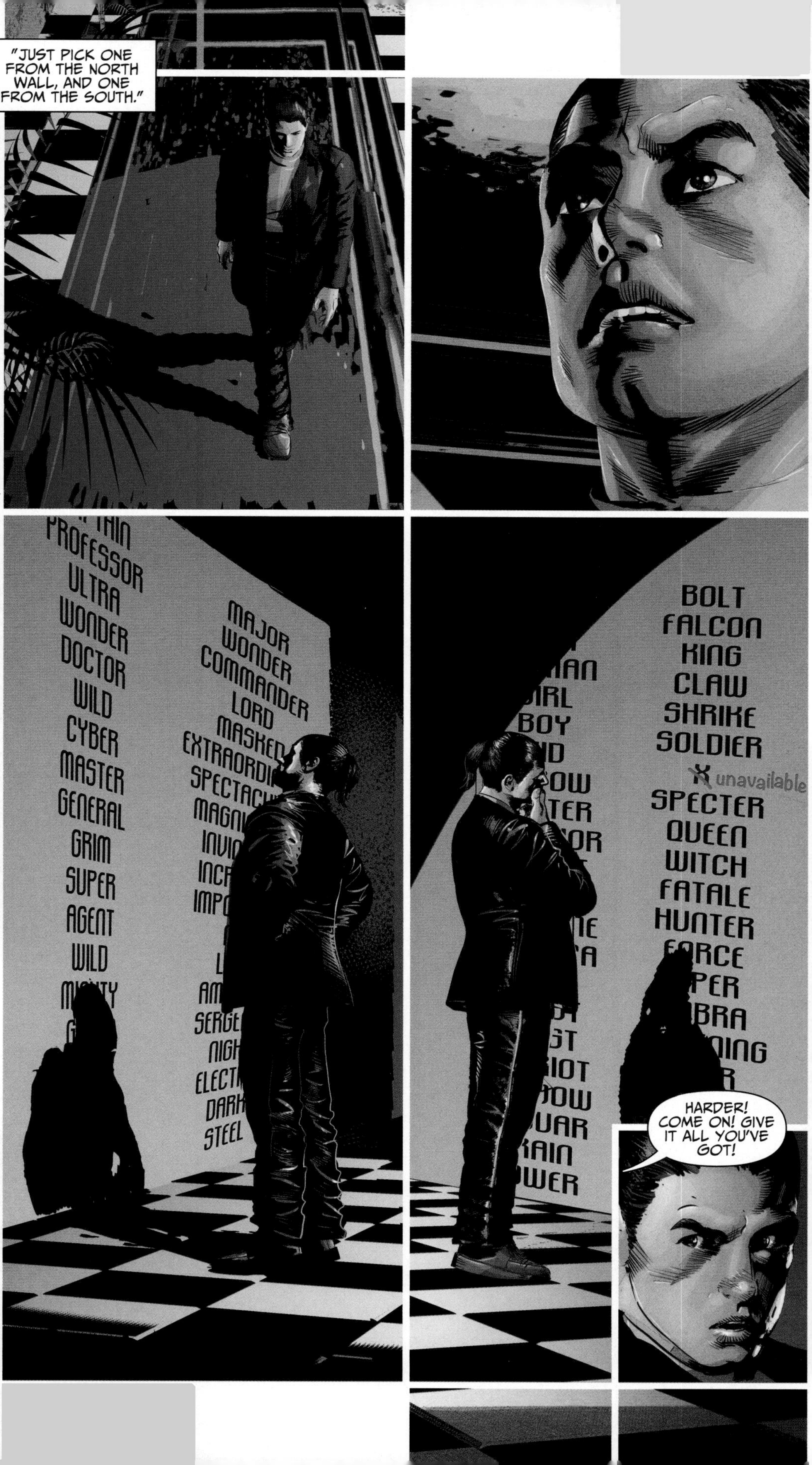
"JUST PICK ONE FROM THE NORTH WALL, AND ONE FROM THE SOUTH."
PROFESSOR
ULTRA
WONDER
DOCTOR
WILD
CYBER
MASTER
GENERAL
GRIM
SUPER
AGENT
WILD
MAJOR
WONDER
COMMANDER
LORD
STEEL
BOLT
FALCON
KING
CLAW
SHRIKE
SOLDIER
unavailable
SPECTER
QUEEN
WITCH
FATALE
HUNTER
HARDER! COME ON! GIVE IT ALL YOU'VE GOT!

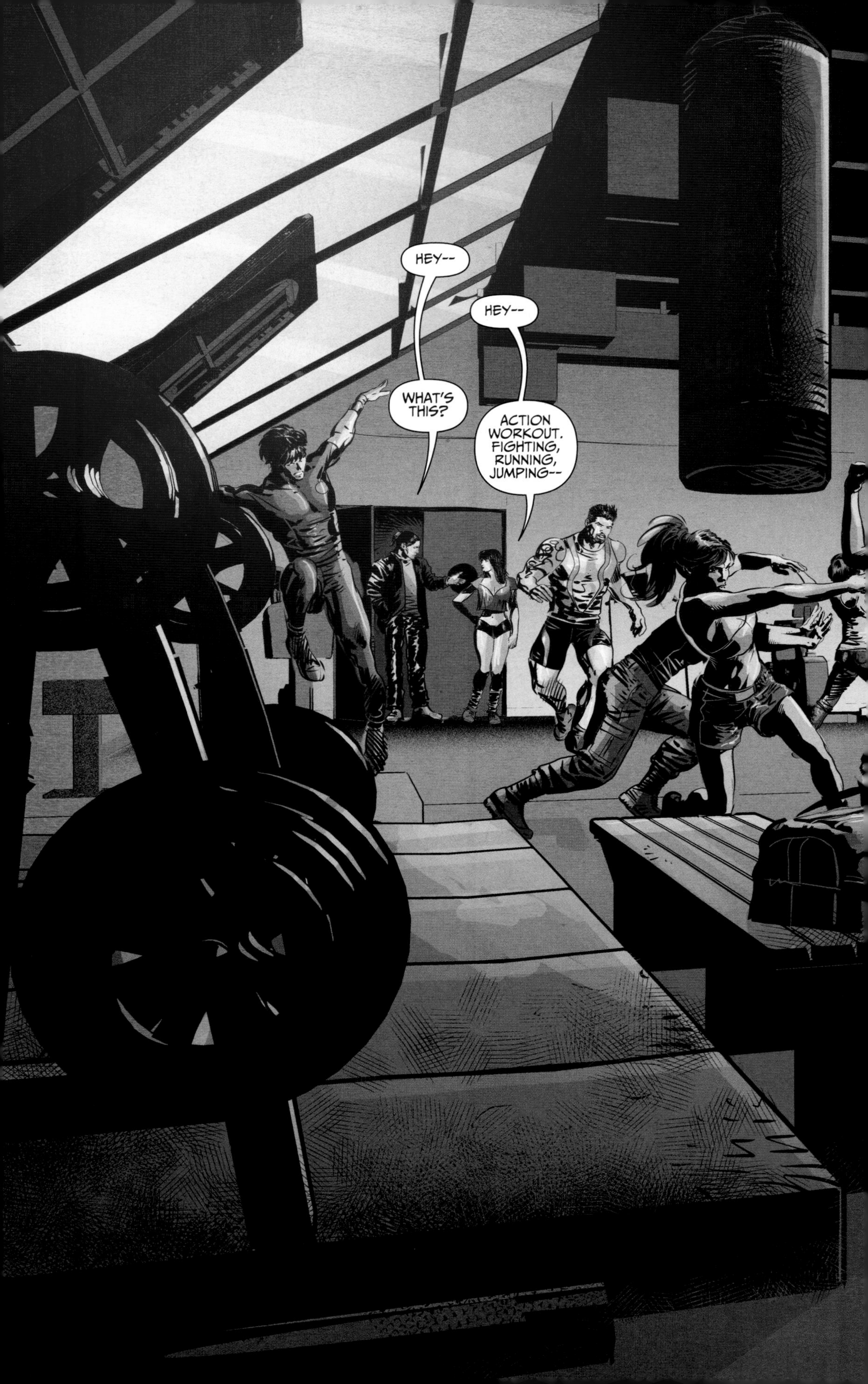
HEY--
HEY--
WHAT'S THIS?
ACTION WORKOUT. FIGHTING, RUNNING, JUMPING--

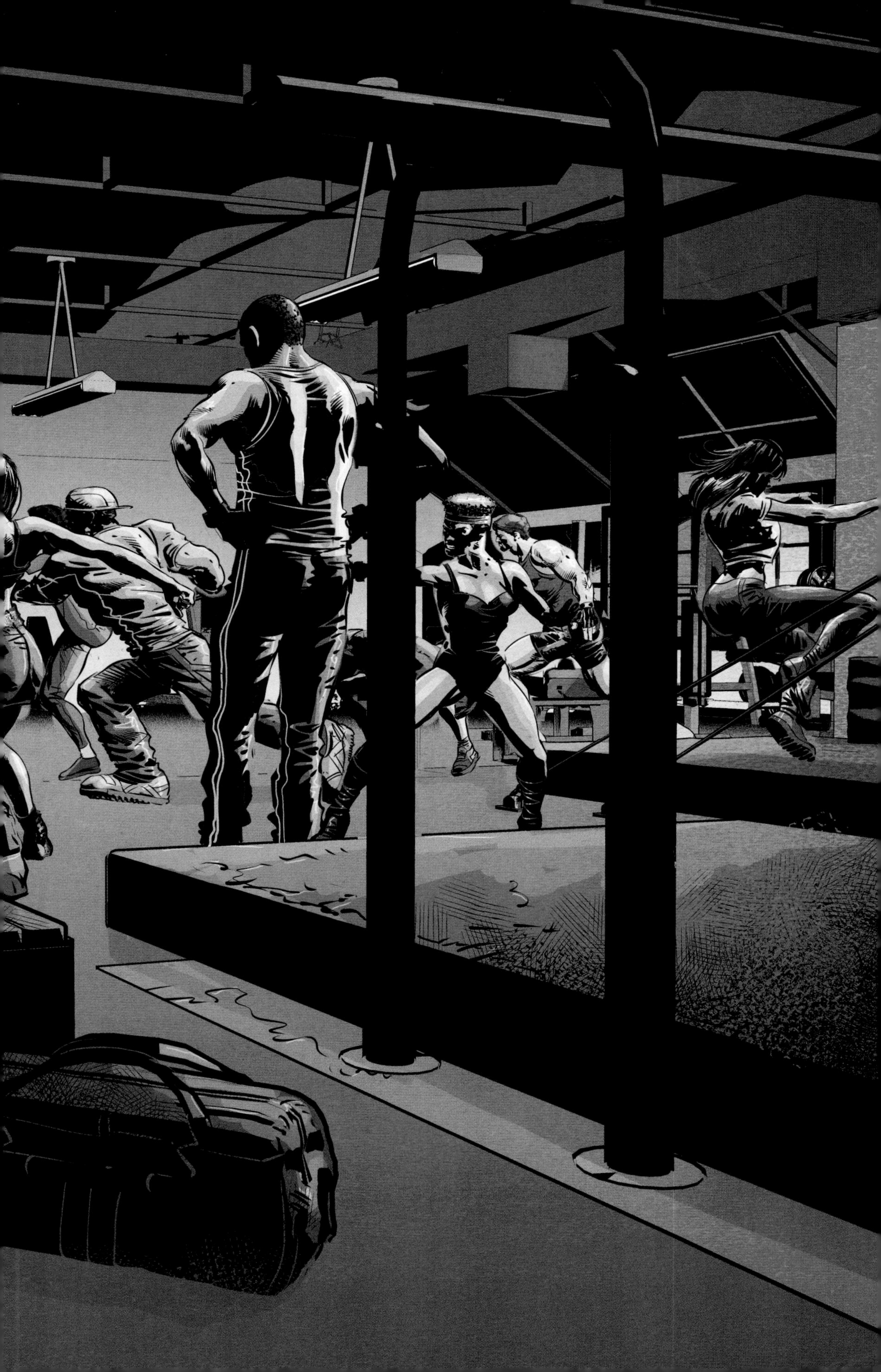

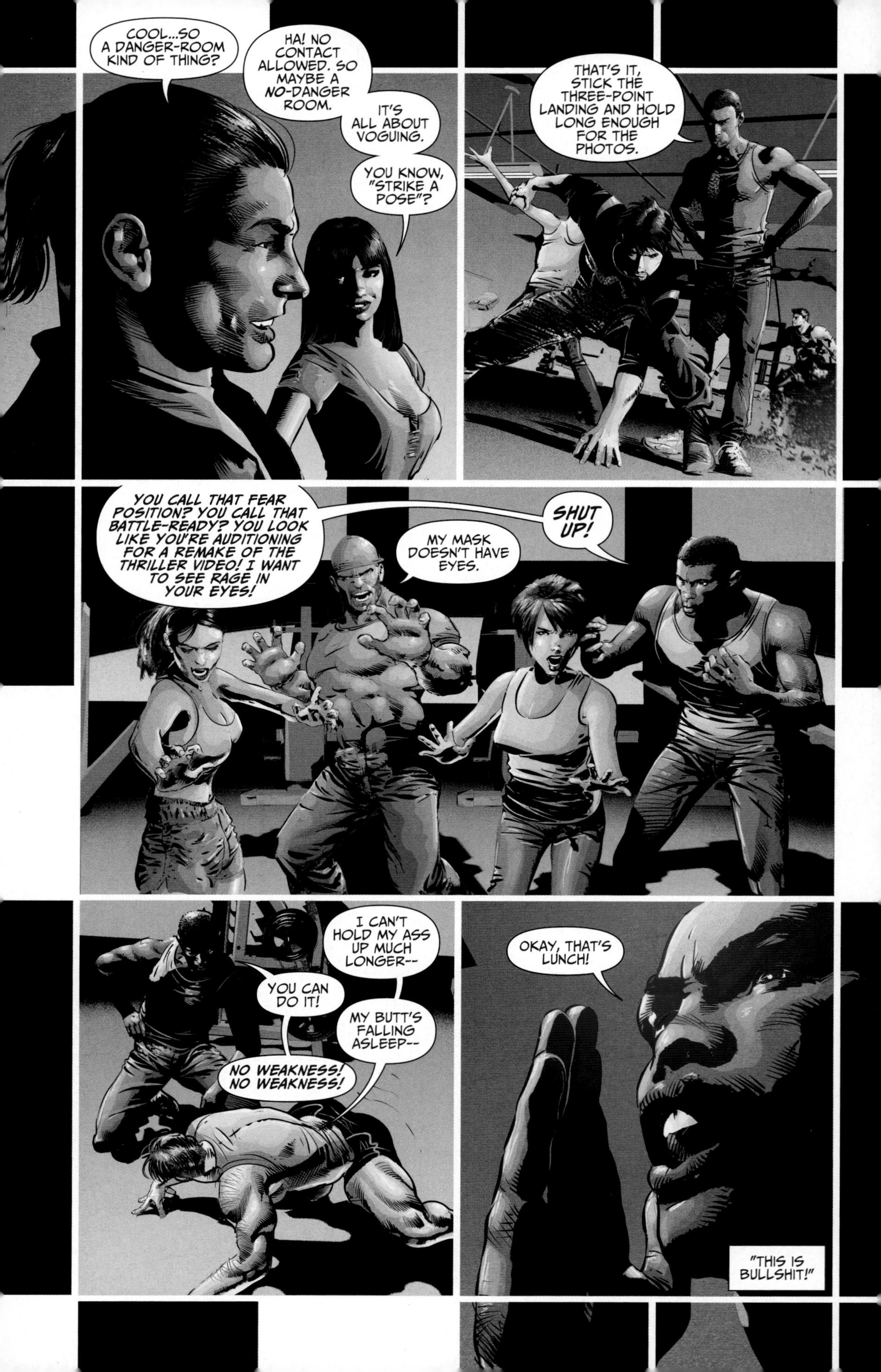

COOL...SO A DANGER-ROOM KIND OF THING?
HA! NO CONTACT ALLOWED. SO MAYBE A NO-DANGER ROOM.
IT'S ALL ABOUT VOGUING.
YOU KNOW, "STRIKE A POSE"?
THAT'S IT, STICK THE THREE-POINT LANDING AND HOLD LONG ENOUGH FOR THE PHOTOS.
YOU CALL THAT FEAR POSITION? YOU CALL THAT BATTLE-READY? YOU LOOK LIKE YOU'RE AUDITIONING FOR A REMAKE OF THE THRILLER VIDEO! I WANT TO SEE RAGE IN YOUR EYES!
MY MASK DOESN'T HAVE EYES.
SHUT UP!
I CAN'T HOLD MY ASS UP MUCH LONGER--
YOU CAN DO IT!
MY BUTT'S FALLING ASLEEP--
NO WEAKNESS! NO WEAKNESS!
OKAY, THAT'S LUNCH!
"THIS IS BULLSHIT!"

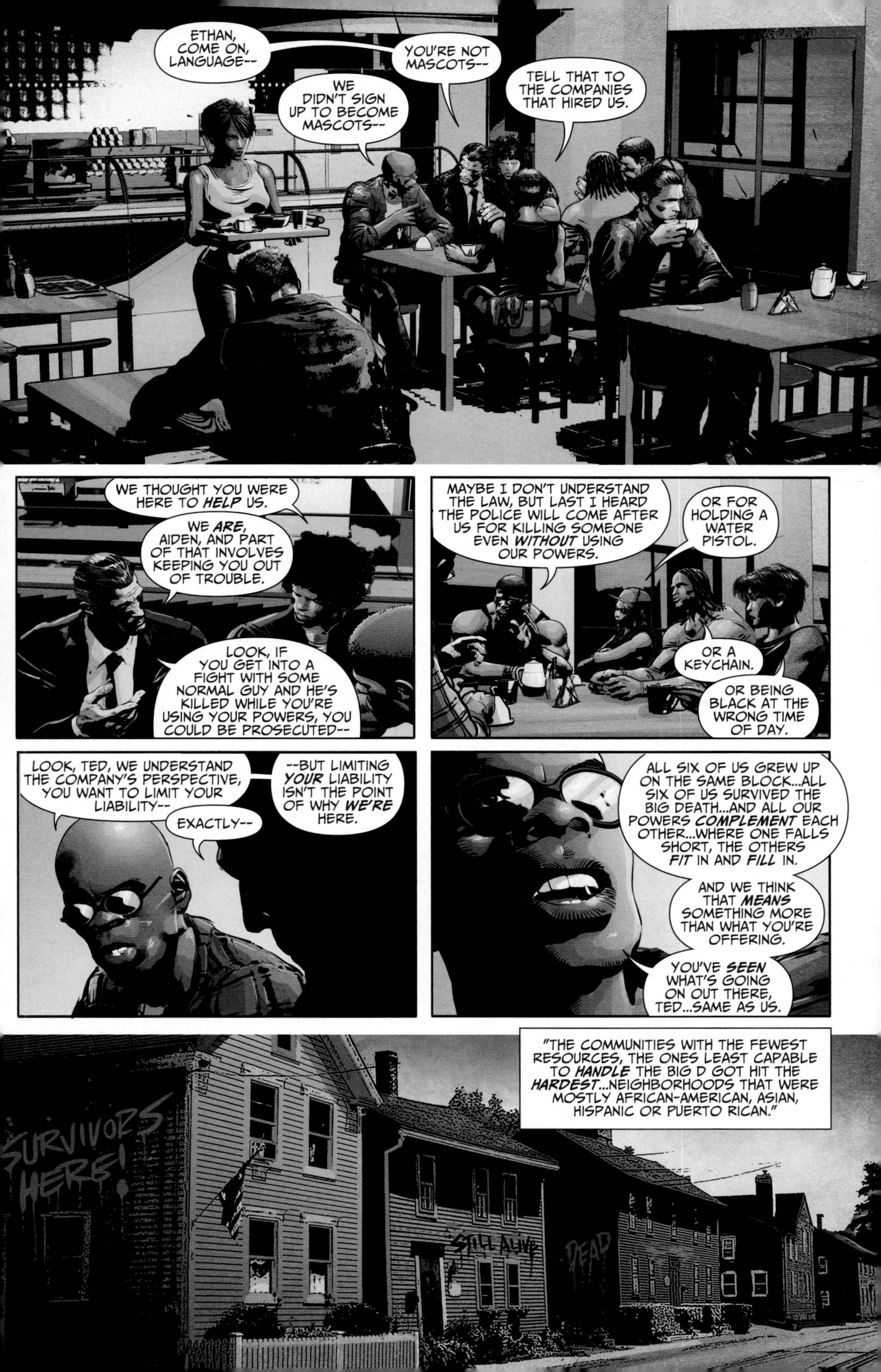
ETHAN, COME ON, LANGUAGE--
WE DIDN'T SIGN UP TO BECOME MASCOTS--
YOU'RE NOT MASCOTS--
TELL THAT TO THE COMPANIES THAT HIRED US.
WE THOUGHT YOU WERE HERE TO HELP US.
WE ARE, AIDEN, AND PART OF THAT INVOLVES KEEPING YOU OUT OF TROUBLE.
LOOK, IF YOU GET INTO A FIGHT WITH SOME NORMAL GUY AND HE'S KILLED WHILE YOU'RE USING YOUR POWERS, YOU COULD BE PROSECUTED--
MAYBE I DON'T UNDERSTAND THE LAW, BUT LAST I HEARD THE POLICE WILL COME AFTER US FOR KILLING SOMEONE EVEN WITHOUT USING OUR POWERS.
OR FOR HOLDING A WATER PISTOL.
OR A KEYCHAIN.
OR BEING BLACK AT THE WRONG TIME OF DAY.
LOOK, TED, WE UNDERSTAND THE COMPANY'S PERSPECTIVE, YOU WANT TO LIMIT YOUR LIABILITY--
EXACTLY--
--BUT LIMITING YOUR LIABILITY ISN'T THE POINT OF WHY WE'RE HERE.
ALL SIX OF US GREW UP ON THE SAME BLOCK...ALL SIX OF US SURVIVED THE BIG DEATH...AND ALL OUR POWERS COMPLEMENT EACH OTHER...WHERE ONE FALLS SHORT, THE OTHERS FIT IN AND FILL IN.
AND WE THINK THAT MEANS SOMETHING MORE THAN WHAT YOU'RE OFFERING.
YOU'VE SEEN WHAT'S GOING ON OUT THERE, TED...SAME AS US.
"THE COMMUNITIES WITH THE FEWEST RESOURCES, THE ONES LEAST CAPABLE TO HANDLE THE BIG D GOT HIT THE HARDEST...NEIGHBORHOODS THAT WERE MOSTLY AFRICAN-AMERICAN, ASIAN, HISPANIC OR PUERTO RICAN."
SURVIVORS HERE!
STILL ALIVE
DEAD

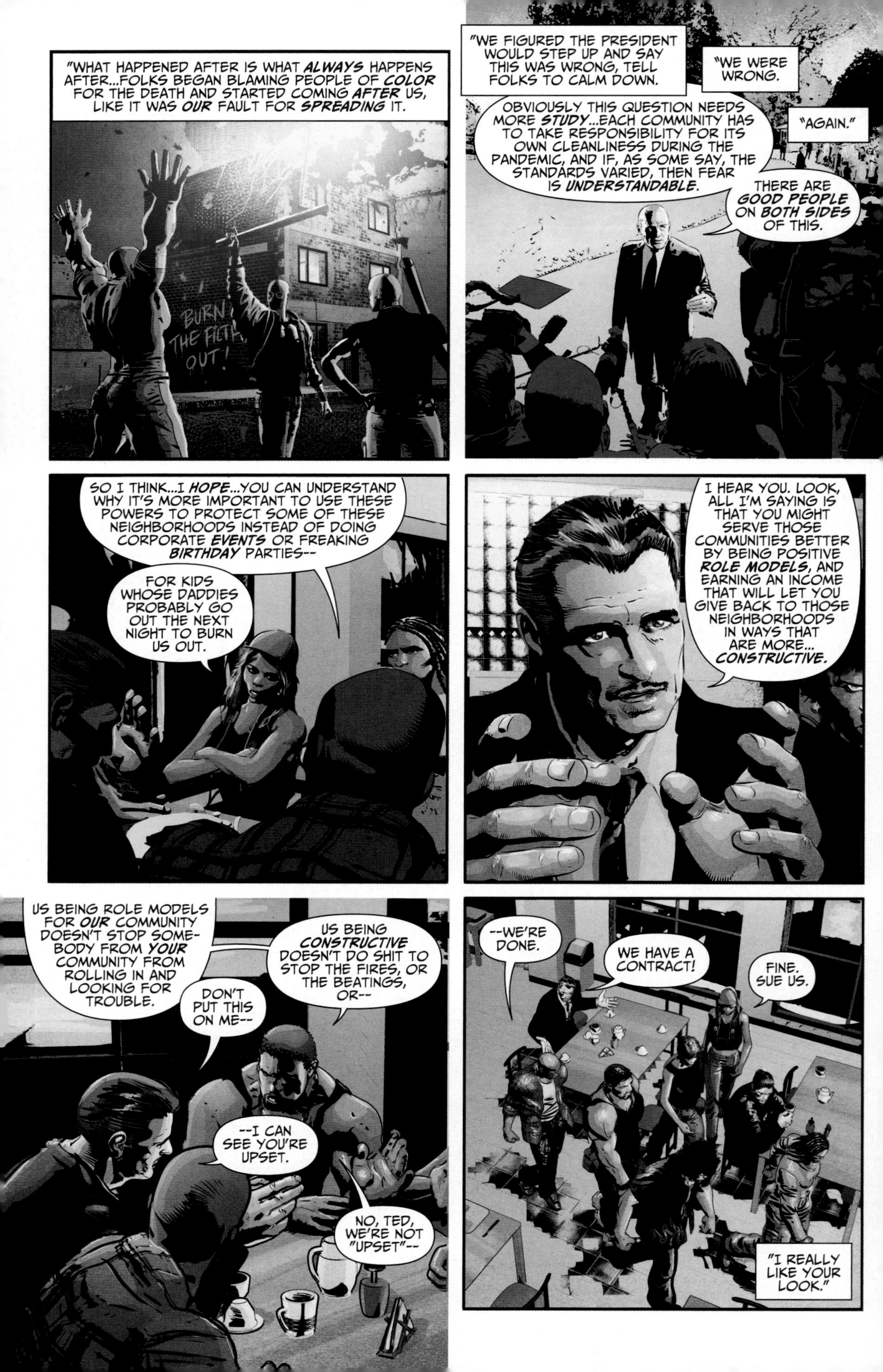

"WHAT HAPPENED AFTER IS WHAT ALWAYS HAPPENS AFTER...FOLKS BEGAN BLAMING PEOPLE OF COLOR FOR THE DEATH AND STARTED COMING AFTER US, LIKE IT WAS OUR FAULT FOR SPREADING IT.
BURN THE FILTH OUT!
"WE FIGURED THE PRESIDENT WOULD STEP UP AND SAY THIS WAS WRONG, TELL FOLKS TO CALM DOWN.
"WE WERE WRONG.
"AGAIN."
OBVIOUSLY THIS QUESTION NEEDS MORE STUDY...EACH COMMUNITY HAS TO TAKE RESPONSIBILITY FOR ITS OWN CLEANLINESS DURING THE PANDEMIC, AND IF, AS SOME SAY, THE STANDARDS VARIED, THEN FEAR IS UNDERSTANDABLE.
THERE ARE GOOD PEOPLE ON BOTH SIDES OF THIS.
SO I THINK...I HOPE...YOU CAN UNDERSTAND WHY IT'S MORE IMPORTANT TO USE THESE POWERS TO PROTECT SOME OF THESE NEIGHBORHOODS INSTEAD OF DOING CORPORATE EVENTS OR FREAKING BIRTHDAY PARTIES--
FOR KIDS WHOSE DADDIES PROBABLY GO OUT THE NEXT NIGHT TO BURN US OUT.
I HEAR YOU. LOOK, ALL I'M SAYING IS THAT YOU MIGHT SERVE THOSE COMMUNITIES BETTER BY BEING POSITIVE ROLE MODELS, AND EARNING AN INCOME THAT WILL LET YOU GIVE BACK TO THOSE NEIGHBORHOODS IN WAYS THAT ARE MORE... CONSTRUCTIVE.
US BEING ROLE MODELS FOR OUR COMMUNITY DOESN'T STOP SOME-BODY FROM YOUR COMMUNITY FROM ROLLING IN AND LOOKING FOR TROUBLE.
US BEING CONSTRUCTIVE DOESN'T DO SHIT TO STOP THE FIRES, OR THE BEATINGS, OR--
DON'T PUT THIS ON ME--
--I CAN SEE YOU'RE UPSET.
NO, TED, WE'RE NOT "UPSET"--
--WE'RE DONE.
WE HAVE A CONTRACT!
FINE. SUE US.
"I REALLY LIKE YOUR LOOK."

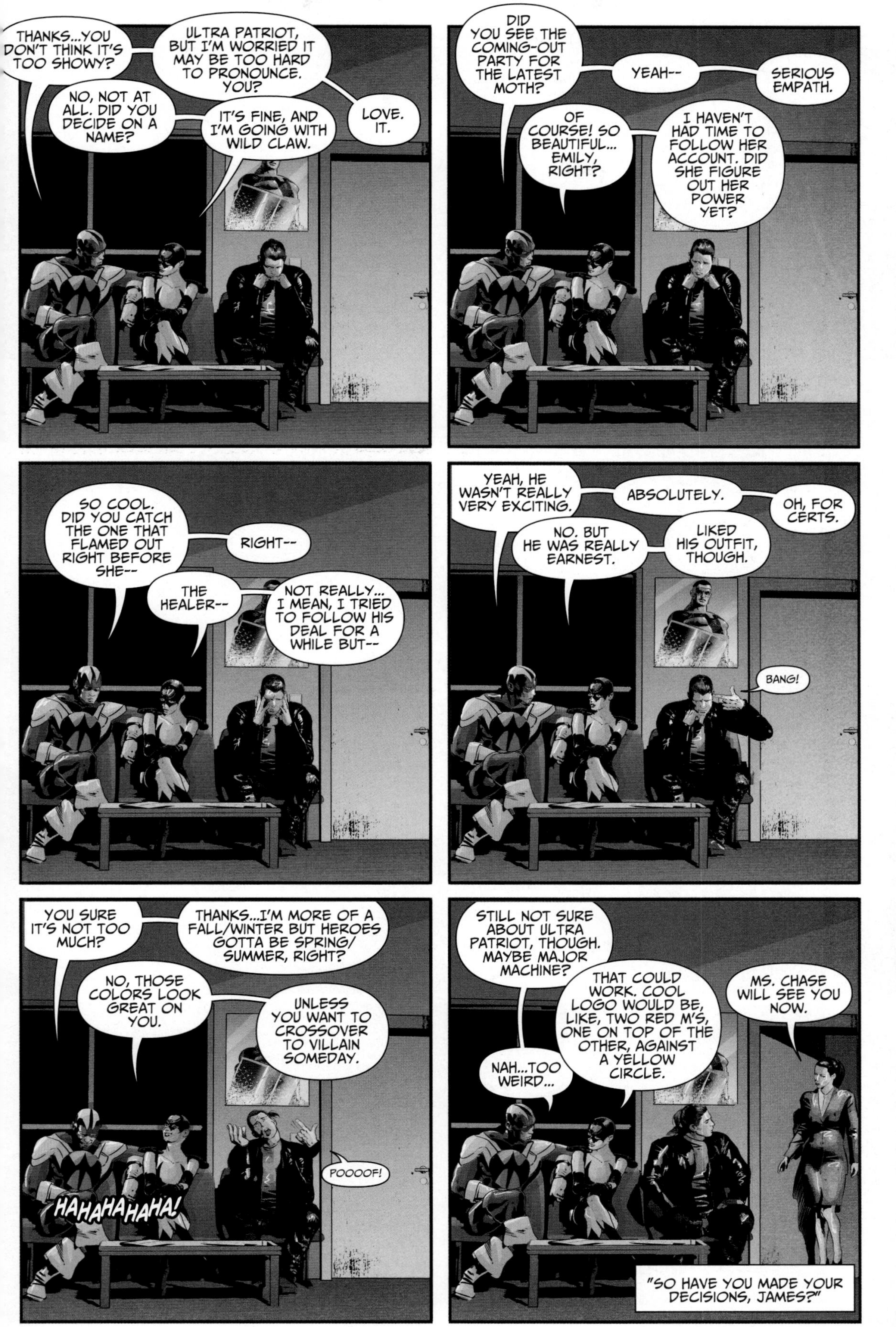
THANKS...YOU DON'T THINK IT'S TOO SHOWY?
ULTRA PATRIOT, BUT I'M WORRIED IT MAY BE TOO HARD TO PRONOUNCE. YOU?
NO, NOT AT ALL. DID YOU DECIDE ON A NAME?
IT'S FINE, AND I'M GOING WITH WILD CLAW.
LOVE. IT.
DID YOU SEE THE COMING-OUT PARTY FOR THE LATEST MOTH?
YEAH--
SERIOUS EMPATH.
OF COURSE! SO BEAUTIFUL... EMILY, RIGHT?
I HAVEN'T HAD TIME TO FOLLOW HER ACCOUNT. DID SHE FIGURE OUT HER POWER YET?
SO COOL. DID YOU CATCH THE ONE THAT FLAMED OUT RIGHT BEFORE SHE--
RIGHT--
THE HEALER--
NOT REALLY... I MEAN, I TRIED TO FOLLOW HIS DEAL FOR A WHILE BUT--
YEAH, HE WASN'T REALLY VERY EXCITING.
ABSOLUTELY.
OH, FOR CERTS.
NO. BUT HE WAS REALLY EARNEST.
LIKED HIS OUTFIT, THOUGH.
BANG!
YOU SURE IT'S NOT TOO MUCH?
THANKS...I'M MORE OF A FALL/WINTER BUT HEROES GOTTA BE SPRING/ SUMMER, RIGHT?
NO, THOSE COLORS LOOK GREAT ON YOU.
UNLESS YOU WANT TO CROSSOVER TO VILLAIN SOMEDAY.
POOOOF!
HAHAHAHAHA!
STILL NOT SURE ABOUT ULTRA PATRIOT, THOUGH. MAYBE MAJOR MACHINE?
THAT COULD WORK. COOL LOGO WOULD BE, LIKE, TWO RED M'S, ONE ON TOP OF THE OTHER, AGAINST A YELLOW CIRCLE.
NAH...TOO WEIRD...
MS. CHASE WILL SEE YOU NOW.
"SO HAVE YOU MADE YOUR DECISIONS, JAMES?"

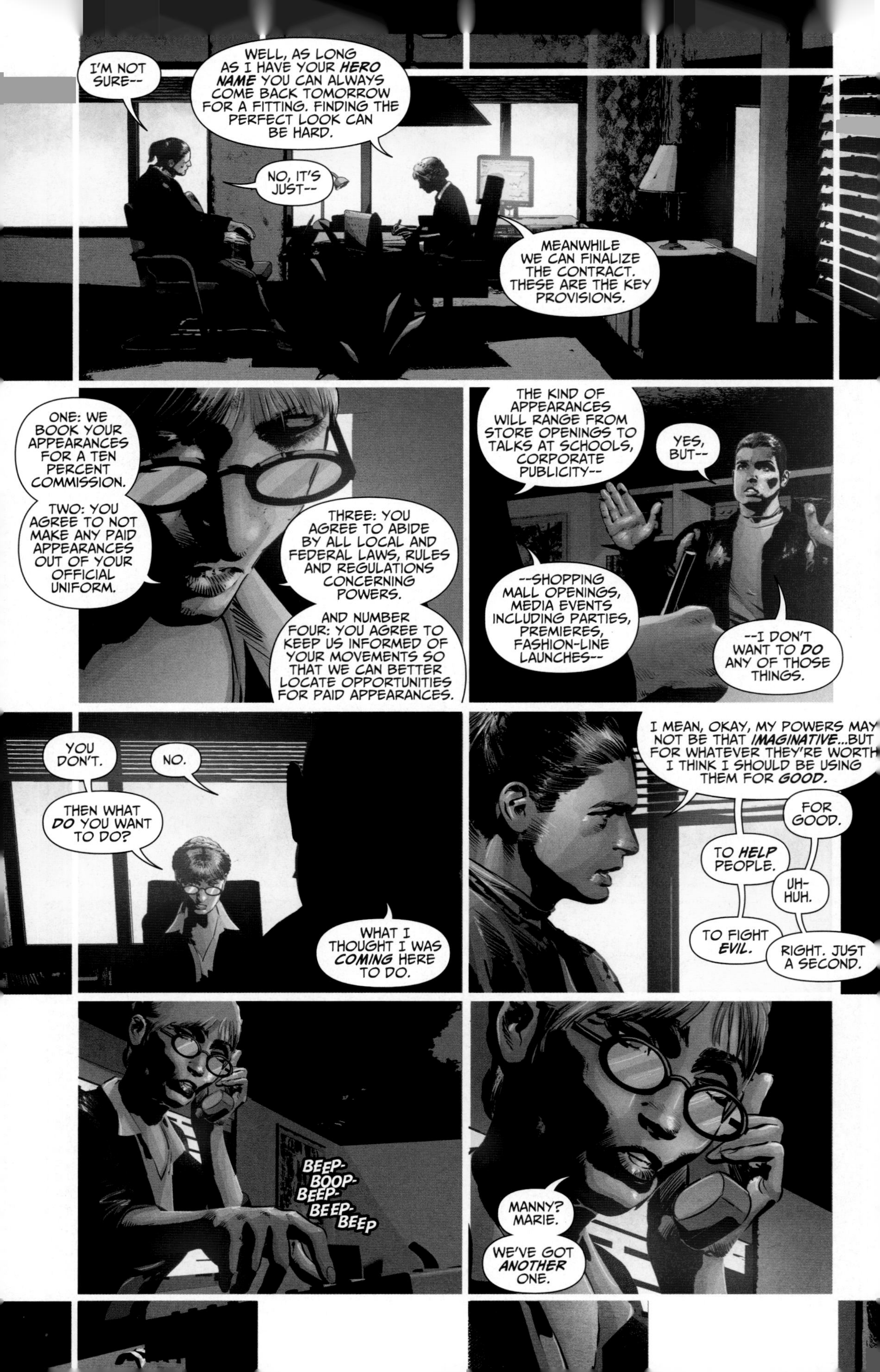

I'M NOT SURE--
WELL, AS LONG AS I HAVE YOUR *HERO NAME* YOU CAN ALWAYS COME BACK TOMORROW FOR A FITTING. FINDING THE PERFECT LOOK CAN BE HARD.
NO, IT'S JUST--
MEANWHILE WE CAN FINALIZE THE CONTRACT. THESE ARE THE KEY PROVISIONS.
ONE: WE BOOK YOUR APPEARANCES FOR A TEN PERCENT COMMISSION.
TWO: YOU AGREE TO NOT MAKE ANY PAID APPEARANCES OUT OF YOUR OFFICIAL UNIFORM.
THREE: YOU AGREE TO ABIDE BY ALL LOCAL AND FEDERAL LAWS, RULES AND REGULATIONS CONCERNING POWERS.
AND NUMBER FOUR: YOU AGREE TO KEEP US INFORMED OF YOUR MOVEMENTS SO THAT WE CAN BETTER LOCATE OPPORTUNITIES FOR PAID APPEARANCES.
THE KIND OF APPEARANCES WILL RANGE FROM STORE OPENINGS TO TALKS AT SCHOOLS, CORPORATE PUBLICITY--
YES, BUT--
--SHOPPING MALL OPENINGS, MEDIA EVENTS INCLUDING PARTIES, PREMIERES, FASHION-LINE LAUNCHES--
--I DON'T WANT TO *DO* ANY OF THOSE THINGS.
YOU DON'T.
NO.
THEN WHAT *DO* YOU WANT TO DO?
WHAT I THOUGHT I WAS *COMING* HERE TO DO.
I MEAN, OKAY, MY POWERS MAY NOT BE THAT *IMAGINATIVE*...BUT FOR WHATEVER THEY'RE WORTH I THINK I SHOULD BE USING THEM FOR *GOOD.*
FOR GOOD.
TO *HELP* PEOPLE.
UH-HUH.
TO FIGHT *EVIL.*
RIGHT. JUST A SECOND.
BEEP-BOOP-BEEP-BEEP-BEEP
MANNY? MARIE.
WE'VE GOT *ANOTHER* ONE.

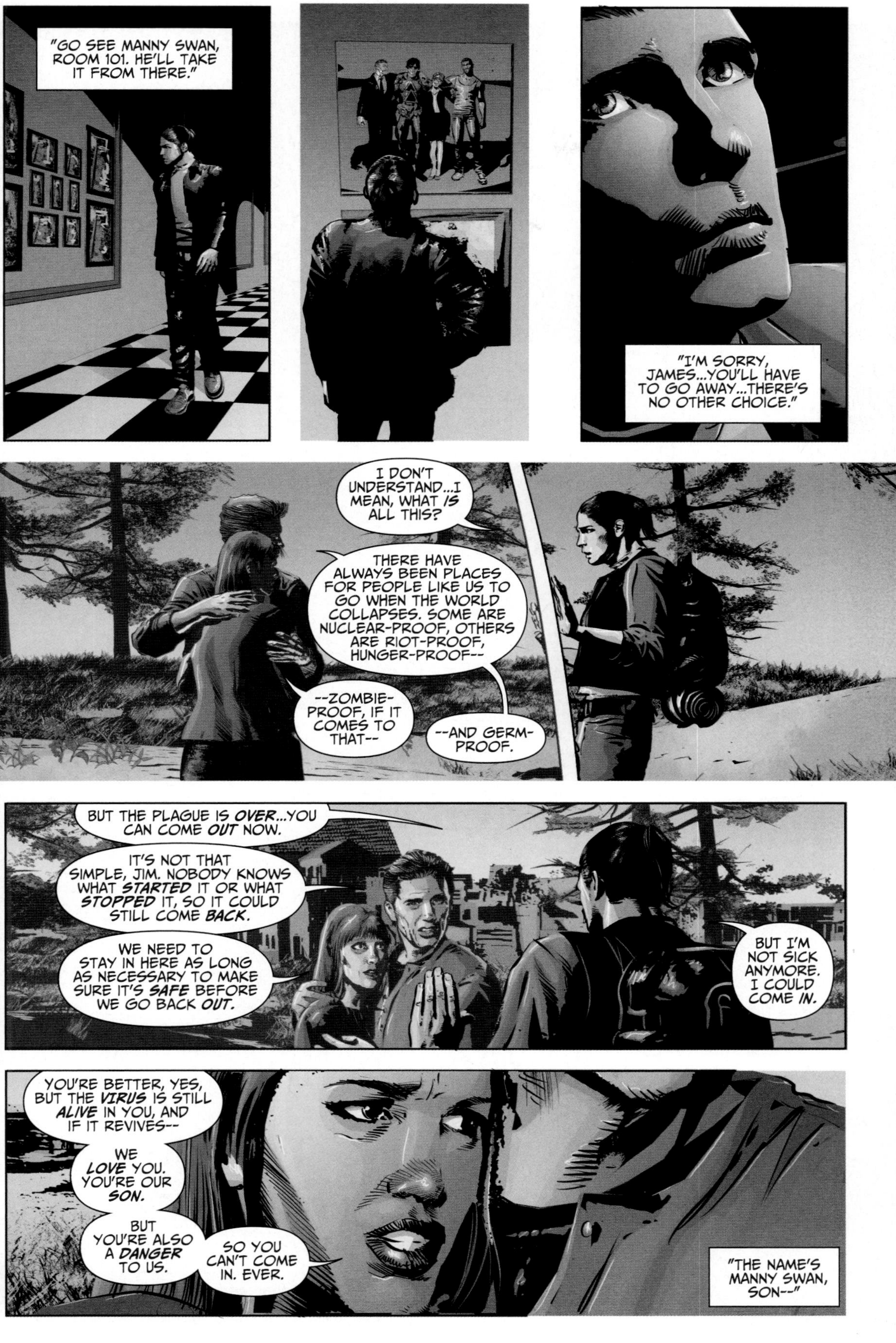
"GO SEE MANNY SWAN, ROOM 101. HE'LL TAKE IT FROM THERE."
"I'M SORRY, JAMES...YOU'LL HAVE TO GO AWAY...THERE'S NO OTHER CHOICE."
I DON'T UNDERSTAND...I MEAN, WHAT *IS* ALL THIS?
THERE HAVE ALWAYS BEEN PLACES FOR PEOPLE LIKE US TO GO WHEN THE WORLD COLLAPSES. SOME ARE NUCLEAR-PROOF, OTHERS ARE RIOT-PROOF, HUNGER-PROOF--
--ZOMBIE-PROOF, IF IT COMES TO THAT--
--AND GERM-PROOF.
BUT THE PLAGUE IS *OVER*...YOU CAN COME *OUT* NOW.
IT'S NOT THAT SIMPLE, JIM. NOBODY KNOWS WHAT *STARTED* IT OR WHAT *STOPPED* IT, SO IT COULD STILL COME *BACK*.
WE NEED TO STAY IN HERE AS LONG AS NECESSARY TO MAKE SURE IT'S *SAFE* BEFORE WE GO BACK *OUT*.
BUT I'M NOT SICK ANYMORE. I COULD COME *IN*.
YOU'RE BETTER, YES, BUT THE *VIRUS* IS STILL *ALIVE* IN YOU, AND IF IT REVIVES--
WE *LOVE* YOU. YOU'RE OUR *SON*.
BUT YOU'RE ALSO A *DANGER* TO US.
SO YOU CAN'T COME IN. EVER.
"THE NAME'S MANNY SWAN, SON--"

--AND THERE'S A LOT YOU DON'T *UNDERSTAND* ABOUT YOUR SITUATION, AND ALL THE WAYS THAT WE CAN *HELP* YOU.

SEE, YOU HAVE ALL THESE AMAZING *ABILITIES*...A LITTLE GENERIC, SURE, BUT POWERS NONETHELESS...BUT THE GOVERNMENT DOESN'T WANT PEOPLE *USING* THESE POWERS IN UNLICENSED WAYS.

IF SOMEBODY CAN TURN A TREE TO ICE WITH A LOOK, THEY DON'T WANT THAT PERSON FREEZING UP YOSEMITE. THEY NEED TO KNOW THE POWERS WILL BE USED *PROPERLY* AND *REASONABLY*.

[WH]EN YOU BUY A CAR, THERE'S A [LIC]ENSE AND *REGISTRATION*. THE [REGI]STRATION JUST SAYS YOU OWN IT, [AN]D SINCE YOU OBVIOUSLY OWN [YO]UR OWN POWERS, THERE'S NO NEED TO REGISTER IT.

SO THERE'S NO, LIKE, *REGISTRATION ACT?*

NO. NONE. THIS IS NOTHING LIKE THAT AT ALL.

SO THERE'S, LIKE, NO REASON FOR ANYBODY TO SUE ANYBODY.

YEAH, I GET THAT.

A [LICENSE] IS WHAT *ALLOWS* YOU TO [B]E ON THE ROADS THE GOVERNMENT [P]AID FOR. IT AUTHORIZES YOU TO *OPERATE* THE VEHICLE.

[AND] THAT'S [WHE]RE WE COME [IN.] PROVIDE YOU [A] LICENSE TO [OPE]RATE YOUR [P]OWERS.

WITHOUT THAT LICENSE, YOU MAY *HAVE* POWERS BUT YOU CAN'T *USE* THEM WITHOUT GETTING INTO TROUBLE.

SO WHEN YOU COME RIGHT DOWN TO IT, WE'RE THE ONLY GAME IN TOWN, JAMES.

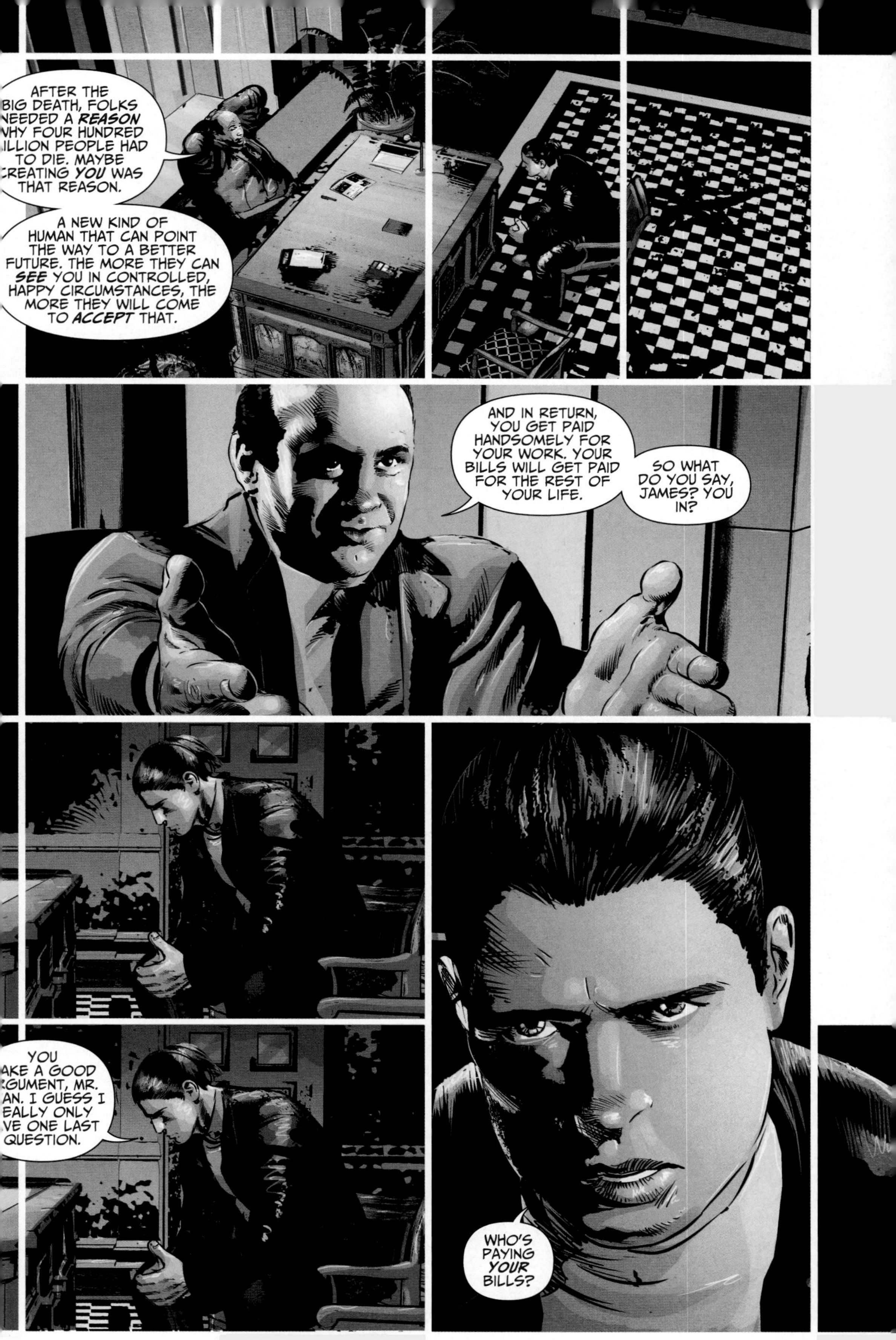

AFTER THE BIG DEATH, FOLKS NEEDED A *REASON* WHY FOUR HUNDRED ILLION PEOPLE HAD TO DIE. MAYBE CREATING *YOU* WAS THAT REASON.
A NEW KIND OF HUMAN THAT CAN POINT THE WAY TO A BETTER FUTURE. THE MORE THEY CAN *SEE* YOU IN CONTROLLED, HAPPY CIRCUMSTANCES, THE MORE THEY WILL COME TO *ACCEPT* THAT.
AND IN RETURN, YOU GET PAID HANDSOMELY FOR YOUR WORK. YOUR BILLS WILL GET PAID FOR THE REST OF YOUR LIFE.
SO WHAT DO YOU SAY, JAMES? YOU IN?
YOU AKE A GOOD RGUMENT, MR. AN. I GUESS I EALLY ONLY VE ONE LAST QUESTION.
WHO'S PAYING *YOUR* BILLS?

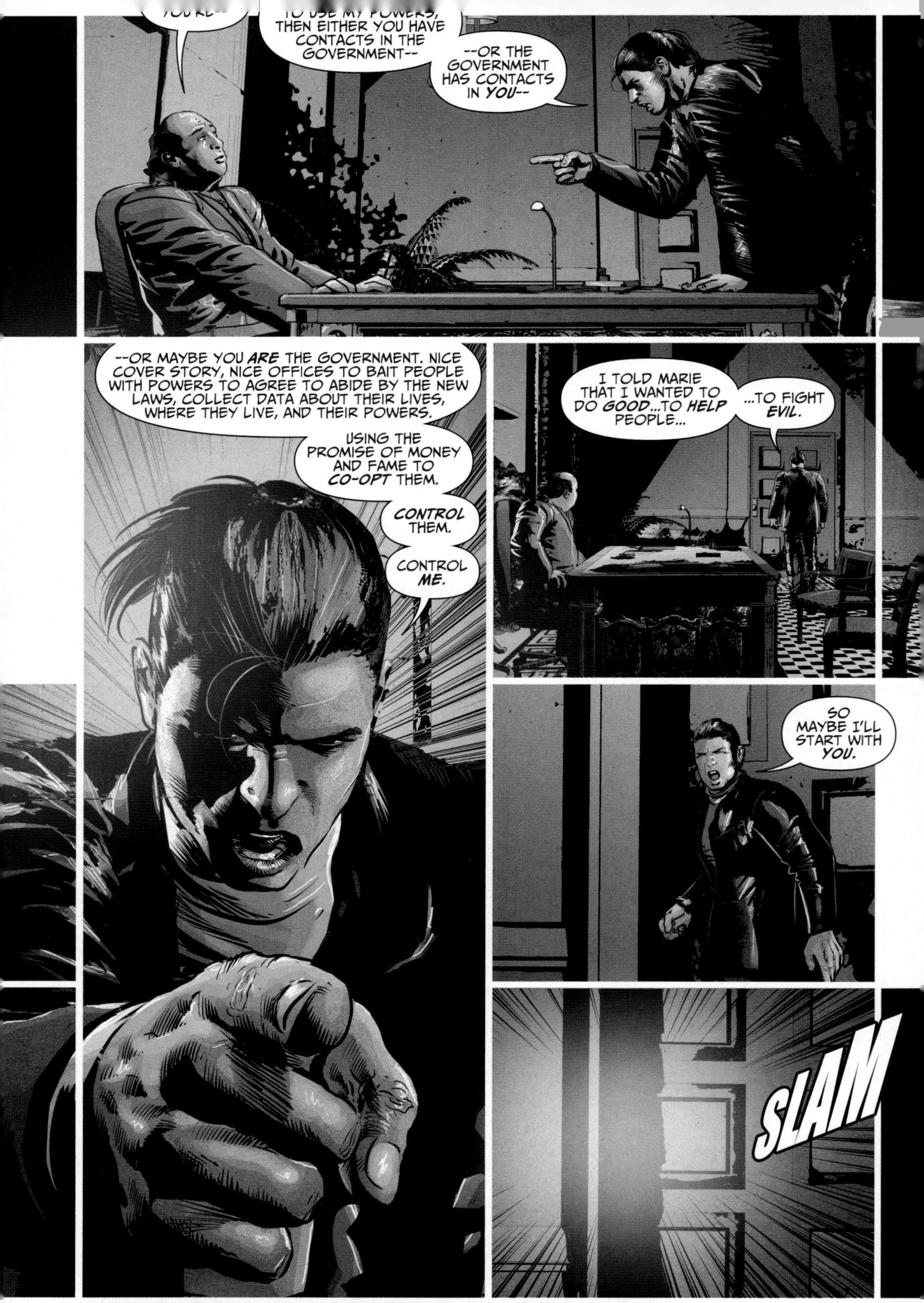
THEN EITHER YOU HAVE CONTACTS IN THE GOVERNMENT--
--OR THE GOVERNMENT HAS CONTACTS IN YOU--
--OR MAYBE YOU ARE THE GOVERNMENT. NICE COVER STORY, NICE OFFICES TO BAIT PEOPLE WITH POWERS TO AGREE TO ABIDE BY THE NEW LAWS, COLLECT DATA ABOUT THEIR LIVES, WHERE THEY LIVE, AND THEIR POWERS.
USING THE PROMISE OF MONEY AND FAME TO CO-OPT THEM.
CONTROL THEM.
CONTROL ME.
I TOLD MARIE THAT I WANTED TO DO GOOD...TO HELP PEOPLE...
...TO FIGHT EVIL.
SO MAYBE I'LL START WITH YOU.
SLAM

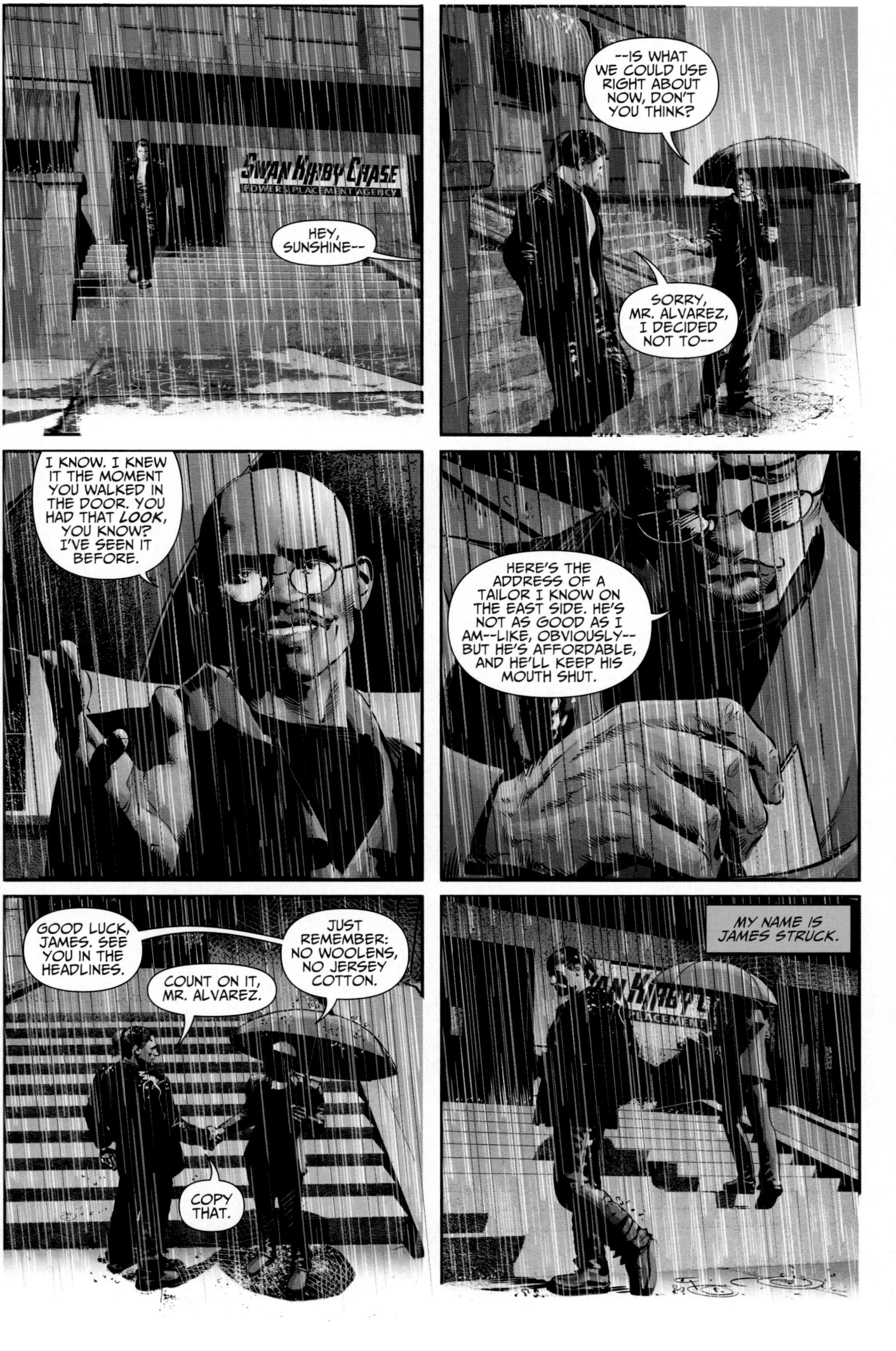
SWAN KIRBY CHASE
POWERS PLACEMENT AGENCY
HEY, SUNSHINE--
--IS WHAT WE COULD USE RIGHT ABOUT NOW, DON'T YOU THINK?
SORRY, MR. ALVAREZ, I DECIDED NOT TO--
I KNOW. I KNEW IT THE MOMENT YOU WALKED IN THE DOOR. YOU HAD THAT LOOK, YOU KNOW? I'VE SEEN IT BEFORE.
HERE'S THE ADDRESS OF A TAILOR I KNOW ON THE EAST SIDE. HE'S NOT AS GOOD AS I AM--LIKE, OBVIOUSLY--BUT HE'S AFFORDABLE, AND HE'LL KEEP HIS MOUTH SHUT.
GOOD LUCK, JAMES. SEE YOU IN THE HEADLINES.
JUST REMEMBER: NO WOOLENS, NO JERSEY COTTON.
COUNT ON IT, MR. ALVAREZ.
COPY THAT.
MY NAME IS JAMES STRUCK.

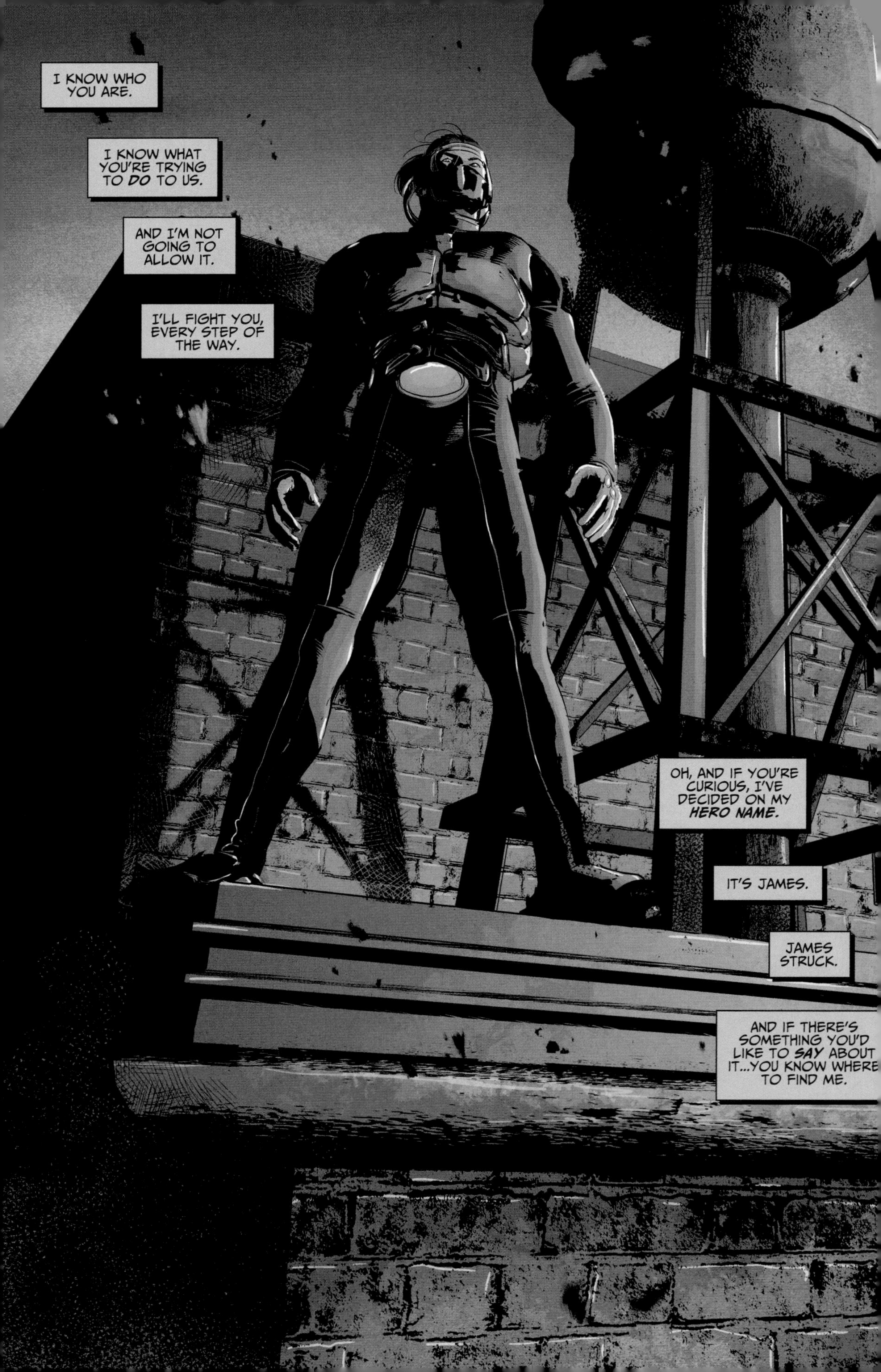
I KNOW WHO YOU ARE.
I KNOW WHAT YOU'RE TRYING TO *DO* TO US.
AND I'M NOT GOING TO ALLOW IT.
I'LL FIGHT YOU, EVERY STEP OF THE WAY.
OH, AND IF YOU'RE CURIOUS, I'VE DECIDED ON MY *HERO NAME.*
IT'S JAMES.
JAMES STRUCK.
AND IF THERE'S SOMETHING YOU'D LIKE TO *SAY* ABOUT IT...YOU KNOW WHERE TO FIND ME.

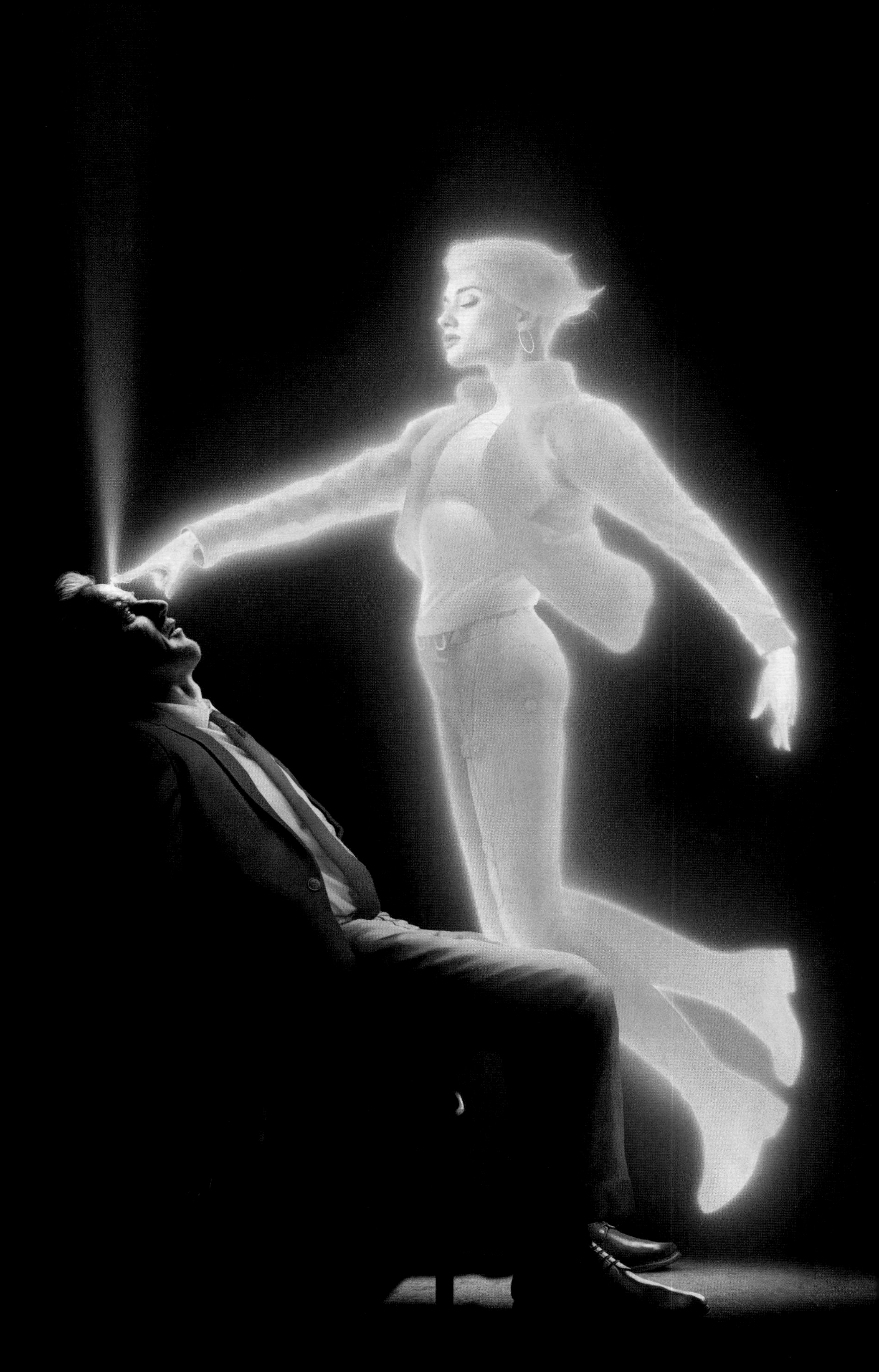

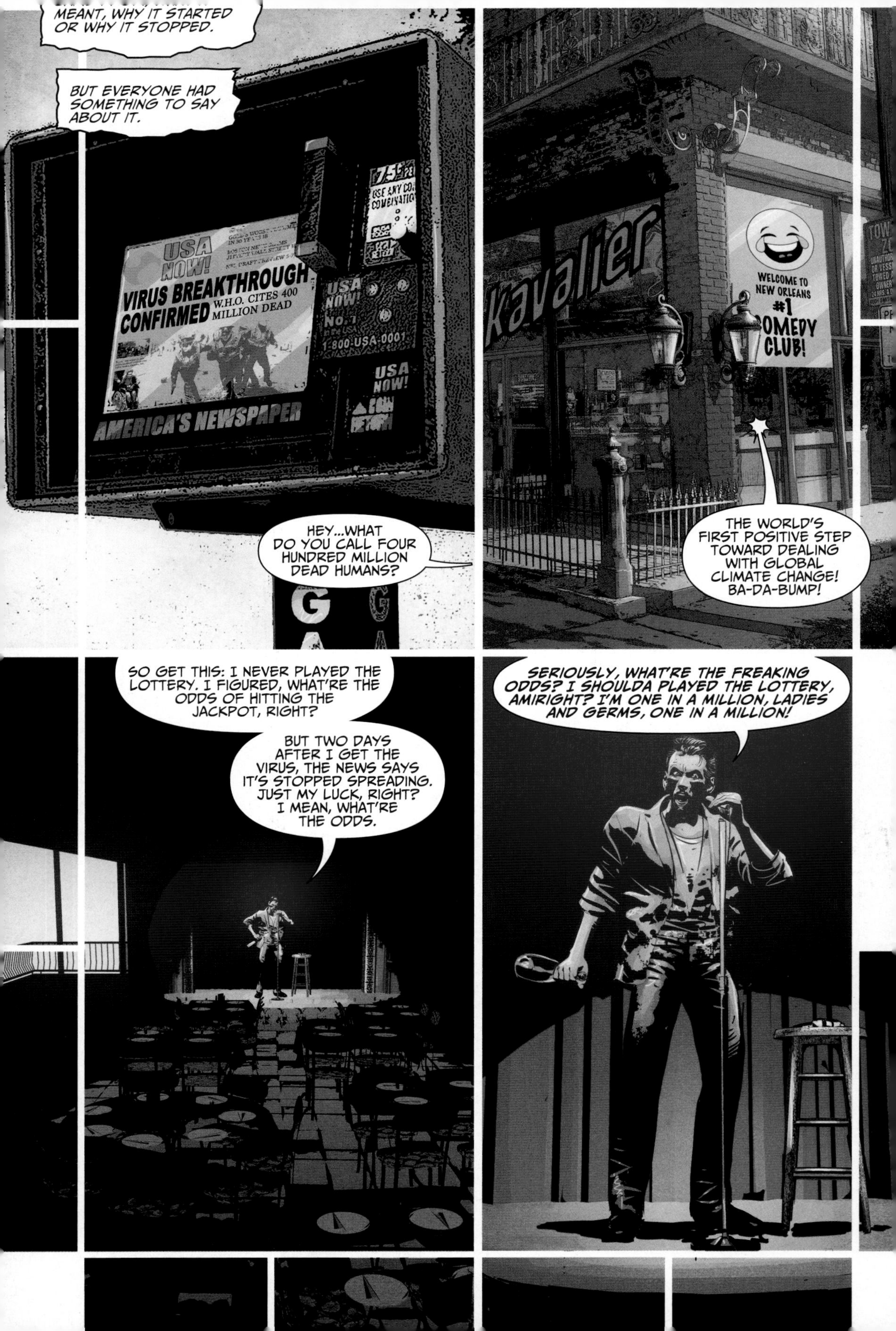
MEANT, WHY IT STARTED OR WHY IT STOPPED.
BUT EVERYONE HAD SOMETHING TO SAY ABOUT IT.
USA NOW!
VIRUS BREAKTHROUGH CONFIRMED
W.H.O. CITES 400 MILLION DEAD
AMERICA'S NEWSPAPER
1-800-USA-0001
HEY...WHAT DO YOU CALL FOUR HUNDRED MILLION DEAD HUMANS?
kavalier
WELCOME TO NEW ORLEANS #1 COMEDY CLUB!
THE WORLD'S FIRST POSITIVE STEP TOWARD DEALING WITH GLOBAL CLIMATE CHANGE! BA-DA-BUMP!
SO GET THIS: I NEVER PLAYED THE LOTTERY. I FIGURED, WHAT'RE THE ODDS OF HITTING THE JACKPOT, RIGHT?
BUT TWO DAYS AFTER I GET THE VIRUS, THE NEWS SAYS IT'S STOPPED SPREADING. JUST MY LUCK, RIGHT? I MEAN, WHAT'RE THE ODDS.
SERIOUSLY, WHAT'RE THE FREAKING ODDS? I SHOULDA PLAYED THE LOTTERY, AMIRIGHT? I'M ONE IN A MILLION, LADIES AND GERMS, ONE IN A MILLION!

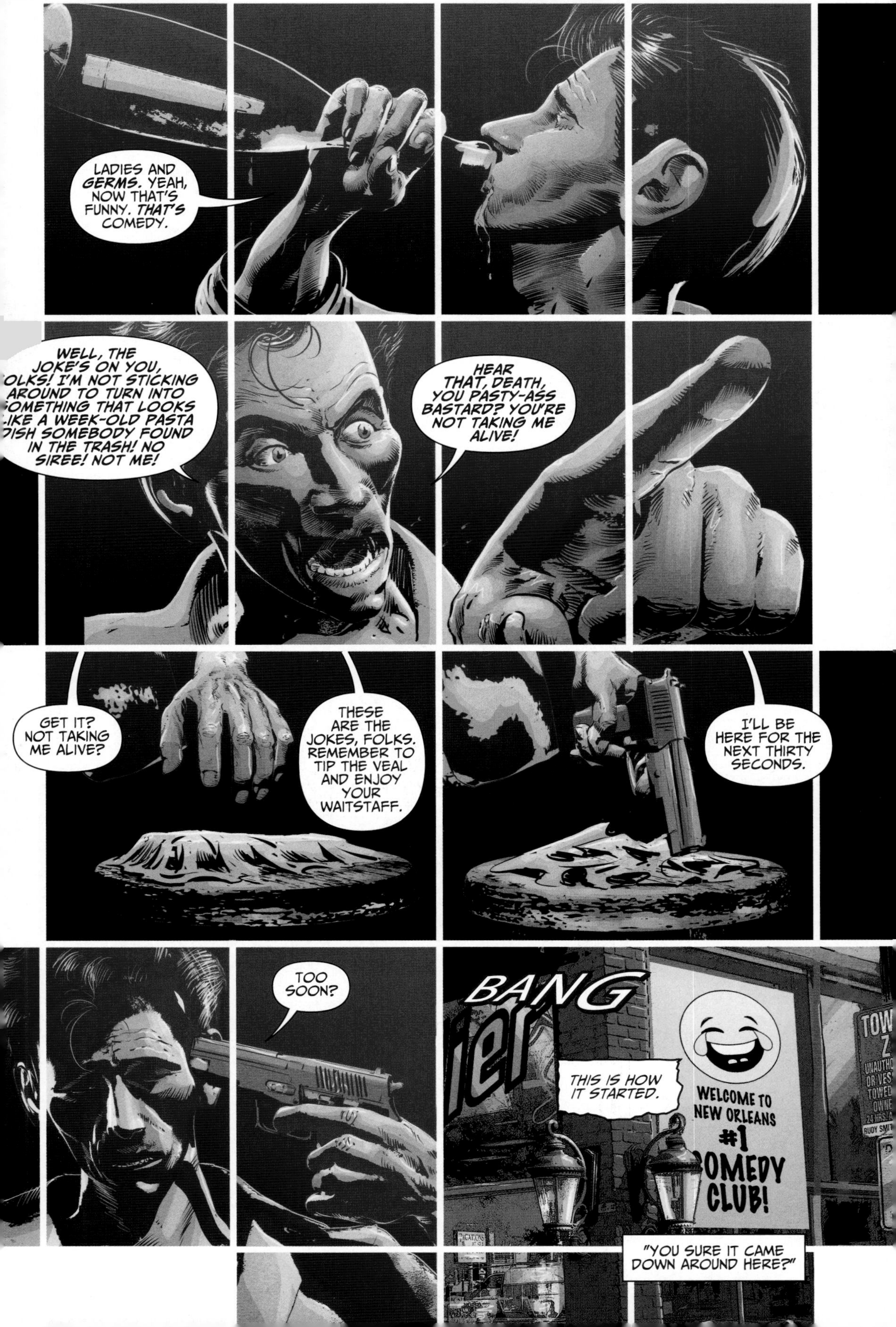
LADIES AND GERMS. YEAH, NOW THAT'S FUNNY. THAT'S COMEDY.
WELL, THE JOKE'S ON YOU, FOLKS! I'M NOT STICKING AROUND TO TURN INTO SOMETHING THAT LOOKS LIKE A WEEK-OLD PASTA DISH SOMEBODY FOUND IN THE TRASH! NO SIREE! NOT ME!
HEAR THAT, DEATH, YOU PASTY-ASS BASTARD? YOU'RE NOT TAKING ME ALIVE!
GET IT? NOT TAKING ME ALIVE?
THESE ARE THE JOKES, FOLKS. REMEMBER TO TIP THE VEAL AND ENJOY YOUR WAITSTAFF.
I'LL BE HERE FOR THE NEXT THIRTY SECONDS.
TOO SOON?
BANG
THIS IS HOW IT STARTED.
WELCOME TO NEW ORLEANS #1 OMEDY CLUB!
"YOU SURE IT CAME DOWN AROUND HERE?"

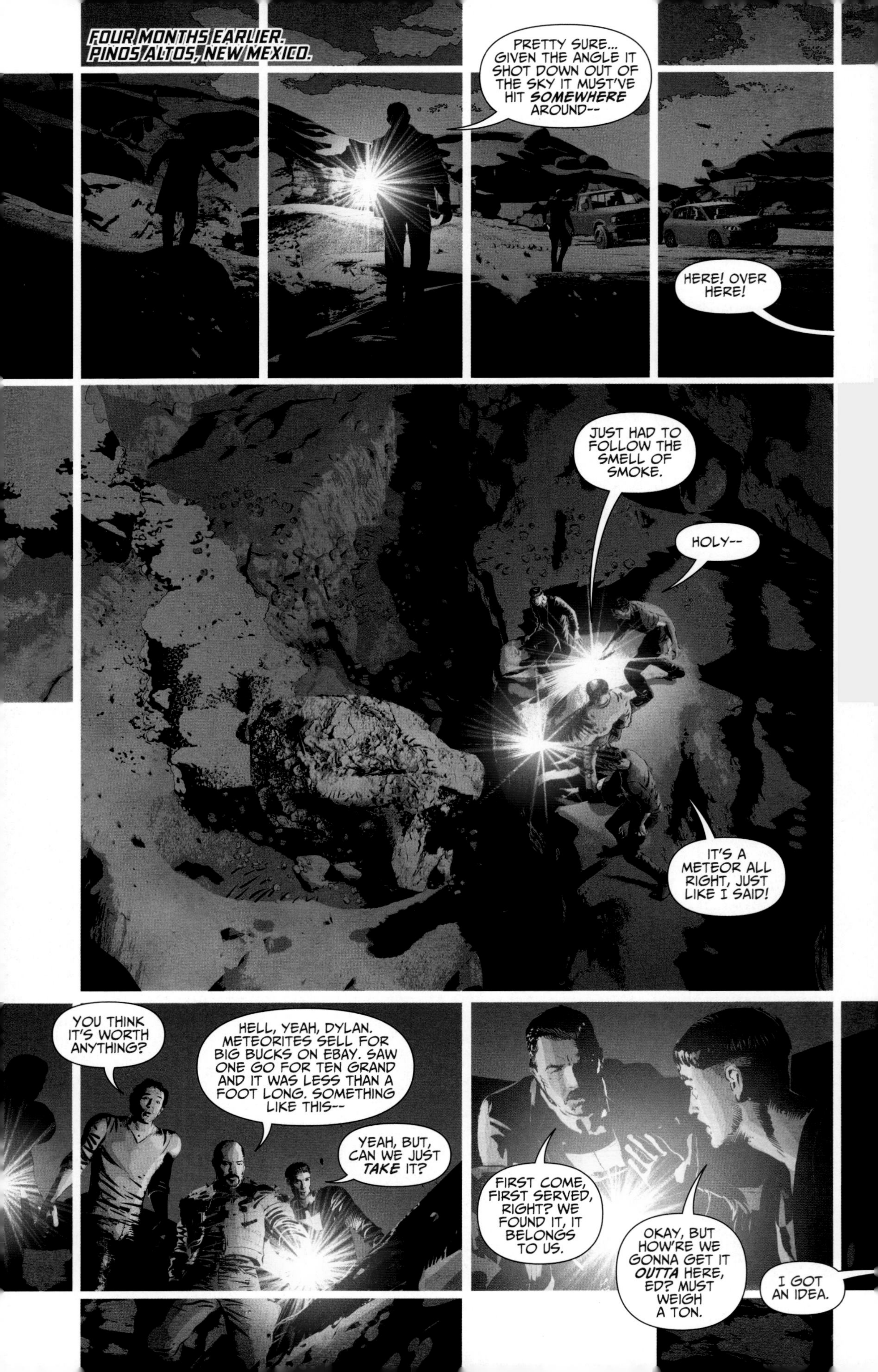
FOUR MONTHS EARLIER.
PINOS ALTOS, NEW MEXICO.
PRETTY SURE... GIVEN THE ANGLE IT SHOT DOWN OUT OF THE SKY IT MUST'VE HIT SOMEWHERE AROUND--
HERE! OVER HERE!
JUST HAD TO FOLLOW THE SMELL OF SMOKE.
HOLY--
IT'S A METEOR ALL RIGHT, JUST LIKE I SAID!
YOU THINK IT'S WORTH ANYTHING?
HELL, YEAH, DYLAN. METEORITES SELL FOR BIG BUCKS ON EBAY. SAW ONE GO FOR TEN GRAND AND IT WAS LESS THAN A FOOT LONG. SOMETHING LIKE THIS--
YEAH, BUT, CAN WE JUST TAKE IT?
FIRST COME, FIRST SERVED, RIGHT? WE FOUND IT, IT BELONGS TO US.
OKAY, BUT HOW'RE WE GONNA GET IT OUTTA HERE, ED? MUST WEIGH A TON.
I GOT AN IDEA.

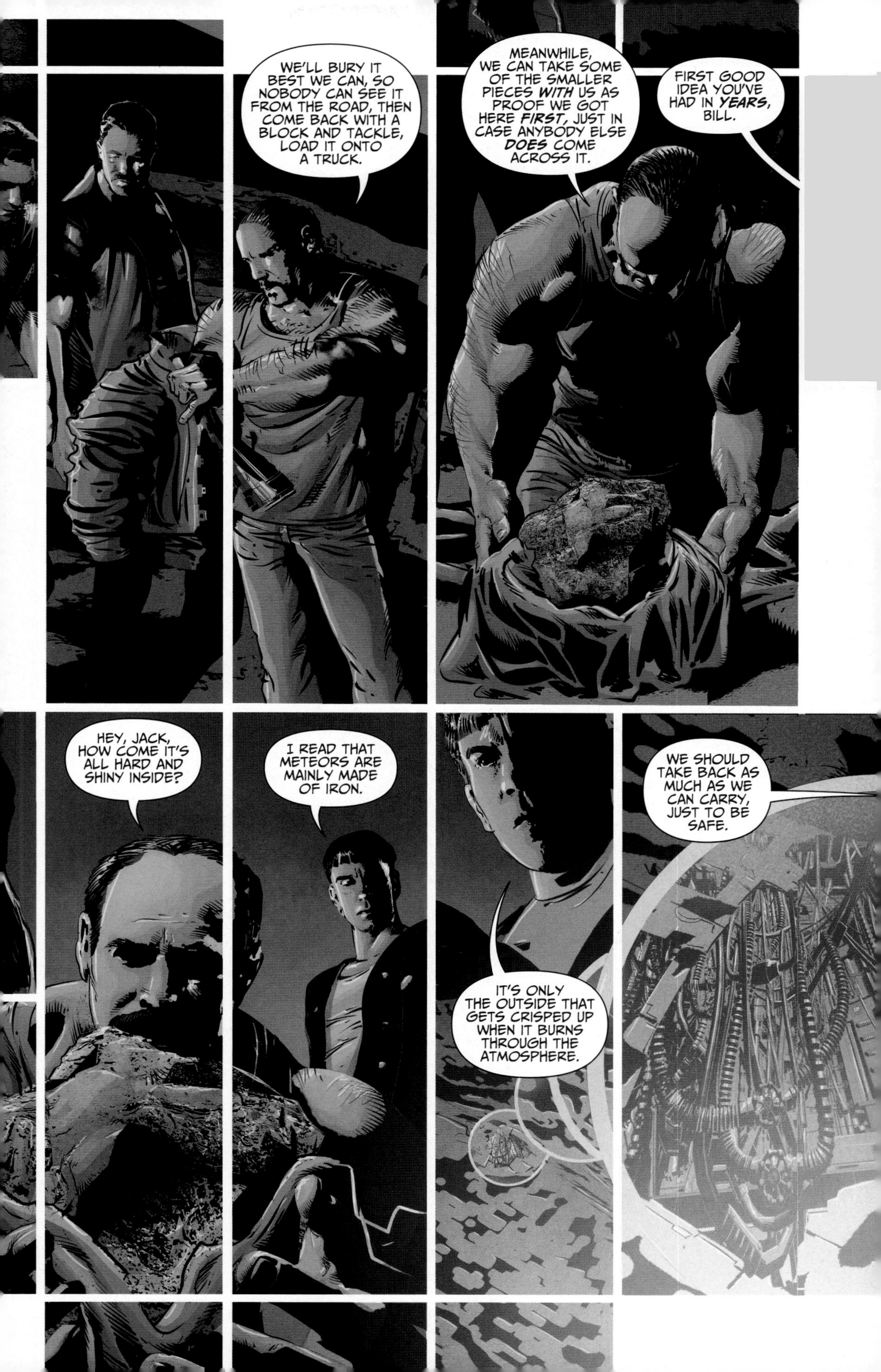
WE'LL BURY IT BEST WE CAN, SO NOBODY CAN SEE IT FROM THE ROAD, THEN COME BACK WITH A BLOCK AND TACKLE, LOAD IT ONTO A TRUCK.
MEANWHILE, WE CAN TAKE SOME OF THE SMALLER PIECES WITH US AS PROOF WE GOT HERE FIRST, JUST IN CASE ANYBODY ELSE DOES COME ACROSS IT.
FIRST GOOD IDEA YOU'VE HAD IN YEARS, BILL.
HEY, JACK, HOW COME IT'S ALL HARD AND SHINY INSIDE?
I READ THAT METEORS ARE MAINLY MADE OF IRON.
IT'S ONLY THE OUTSIDE THAT GETS CRISPED UP WHEN IT BURNS THROUGH THE ATMOSPHERE.
WE SHOULD TAKE BACK AS MUCH AS WE CAN CARRY, JUST TO BE SAFE.

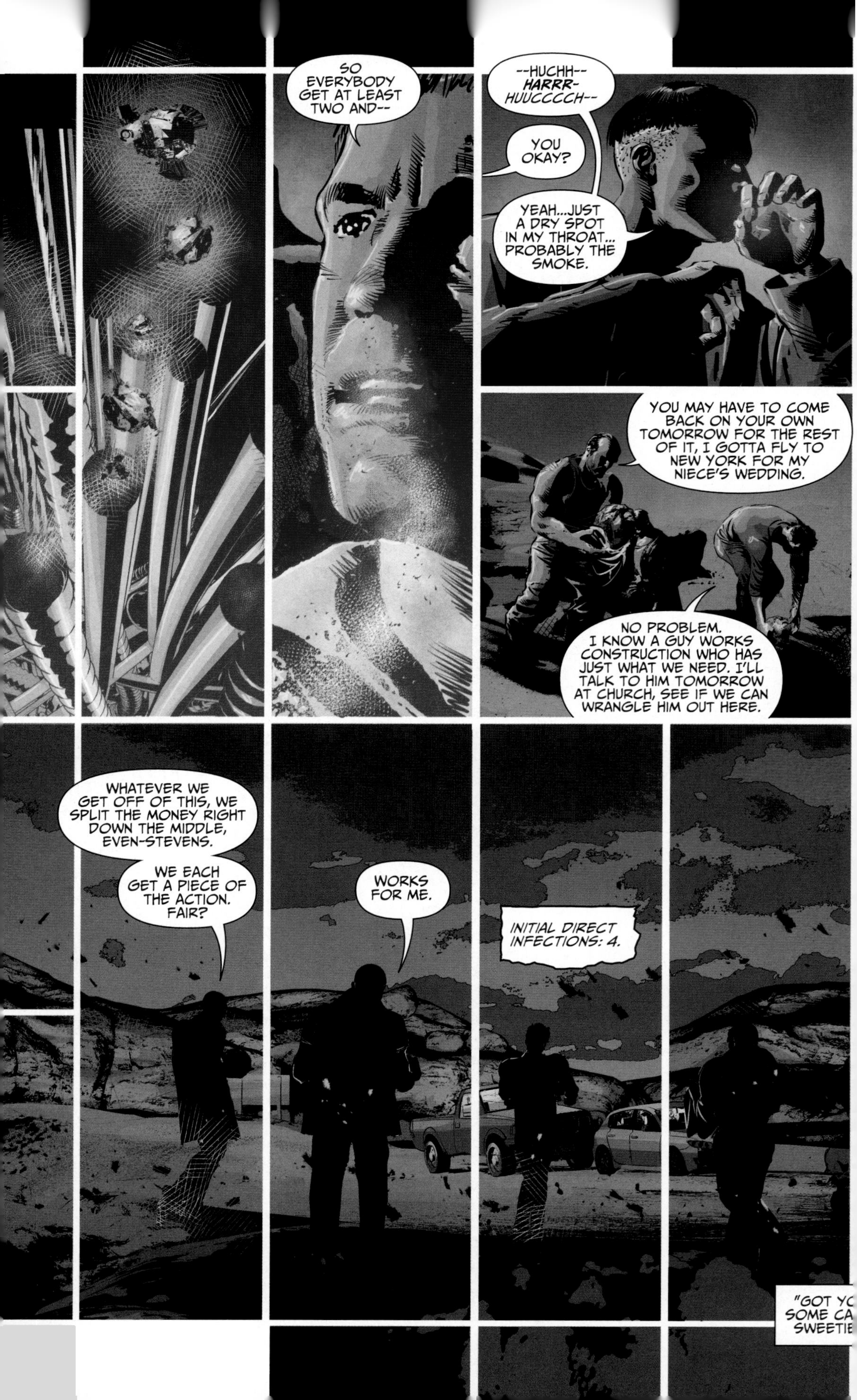
SO EVERYBODY GET AT LEAST TWO AND--
--HUCHH-- HARRR- HUUCCCCH--
YOU OKAY?
YEAH...JUST A DRY SPOT IN MY THROAT... PROBABLY THE SMOKE.
YOU MAY HAVE TO COME BACK ON YOUR OWN TOMORROW FOR THE REST OF IT, I GOTTA FLY TO NEW YORK FOR MY NIECE'S WEDDING.
NO PROBLEM. I KNOW A GUY WORKS CONSTRUCTION WHO HAS JUST WHAT WE NEED. I'LL TALK TO HIM TOMORROW AT CHURCH, SEE IF WE CAN WRANGLE HIM OUT HERE.
WHATEVER WE GET OFF OF THIS, WE SPLIT THE MONEY RIGHT DOWN THE MIDDLE, EVEN-STEVENS.
WE EACH GET A PIECE OF THE ACTION. FAIR?
WORKS FOR ME.
INITIAL DIRECT INFECTIONS: 4.
"GOT YO
SOME CA
SWEETIE

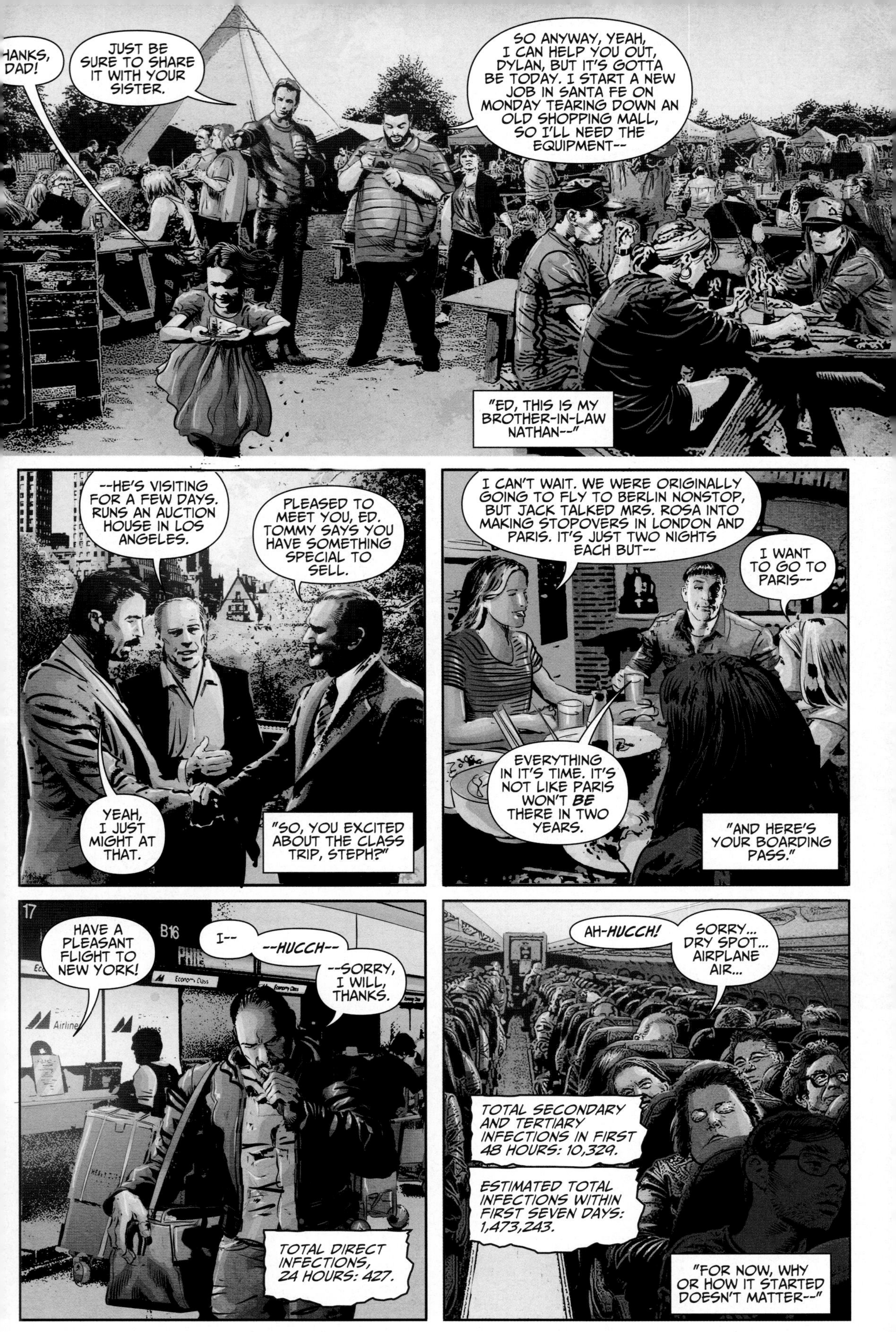

HANKS, DAD!
JUST BE SURE TO SHARE IT WITH YOUR SISTER.
SO ANYWAY, YEAH, I CAN HELP YOU OUT, DYLAN, BUT IT'S GOTTA BE TODAY. I START A NEW JOB IN SANTA FE ON MONDAY TEARING DOWN AN OLD SHOPPING MALL, SO I'LL NEED THE EQUIPMENT--
"ED, THIS IS MY BROTHER-IN-LAW NATHAN--"
--HE'S VISITING FOR A FEW DAYS. RUNS AN AUCTION HOUSE IN LOS ANGELES.
PLEASED TO MEET YOU, ED. TOMMY SAYS YOU HAVE SOMETHING SPECIAL TO SELL.
YEAH, I JUST MIGHT AT THAT.
"SO, YOU EXCITED ABOUT THE CLASS TRIP, STEPH?"
I CAN'T WAIT. WE WERE ORIGINALLY GOING TO FLY TO BERLIN NONSTOP, BUT JACK TALKED MRS. ROSA INTO MAKING STOPOVERS IN LONDON AND PARIS. IT'S JUST TWO NIGHTS EACH BUT--
I WANT TO GO TO PARIS--
EVERYTHING IN IT'S TIME. IT'S NOT LIKE PARIS WON'T BE THERE IN TWO YEARS.
"AND HERE'S YOUR BOARDING PASS."
17
B16
HAVE A PLEASANT FLIGHT TO NEW YORK!
I--
--HUCCH--
--SORRY, I WILL, THANKS.
TOTAL DIRECT INFECTIONS, 24 HOURS: 427.
AH-HUCCH!
SORRY... DRY SPOT... AIRPLANE AIR...
TOTAL SECONDARY AND TERTIARY INFECTIONS IN FIRST 48 HOURS: 10,329.
ESTIMATED TOTAL INFECTIONS WITHIN FIRST SEVEN DAYS: 1,473,243.
"FOR NOW, WHY OR HOW IT STARTED DOESN'T MATTER--"

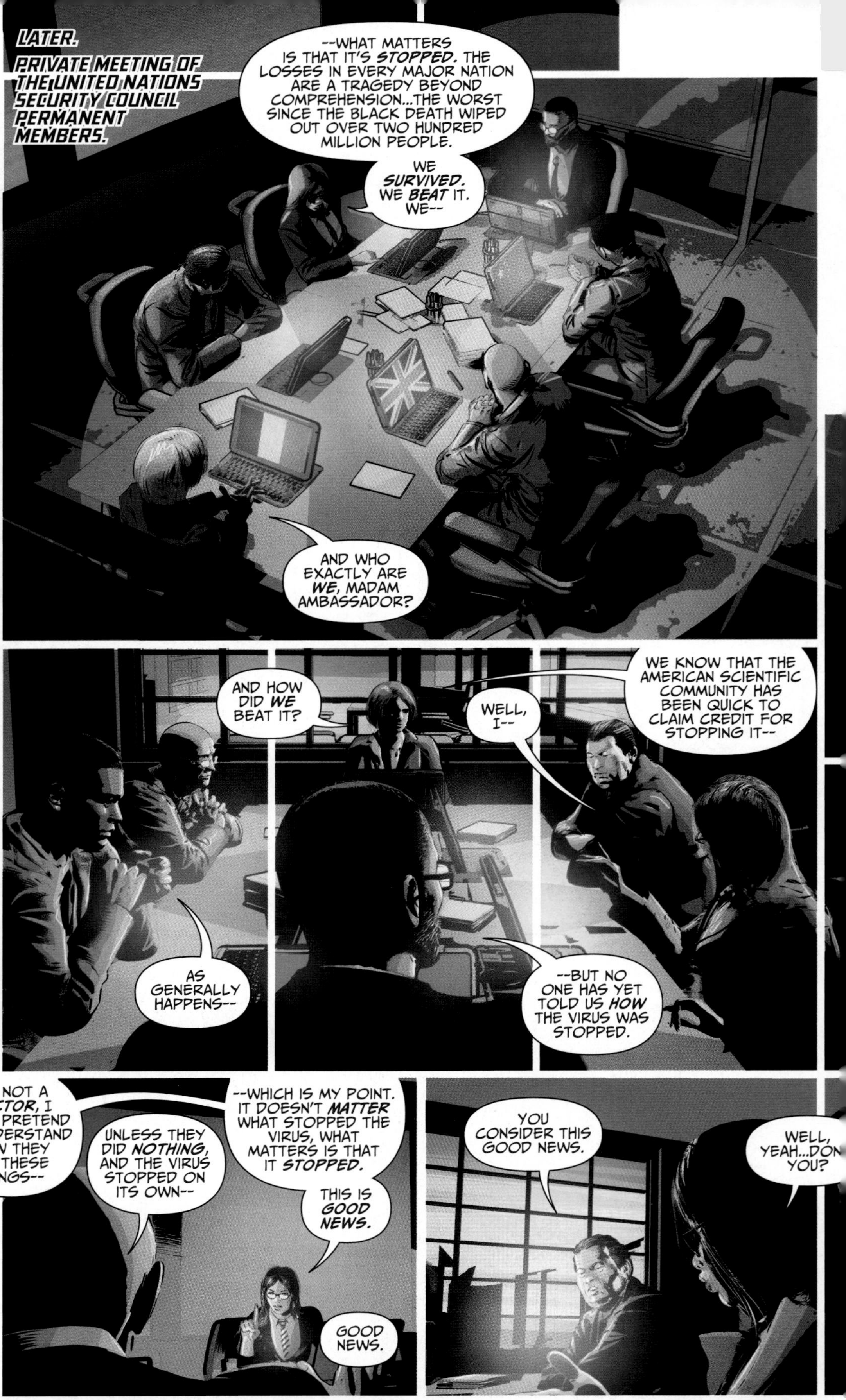
LATER.
PRIVATE MEETING OF THE UNITED NATIONS SECURITY COUNCIL PERMANENT MEMBERS.
--WHAT MATTERS IS THAT IT'S STOPPED. THE LOSSES IN EVERY MAJOR NATION ARE A TRAGEDY BEYOND COMPREHENSION...THE WORST SINCE THE BLACK DEATH WIPED OUT OVER TWO HUNDRED MILLION PEOPLE.
WE SURVIVED. WE BEAT IT. WE--
AND WHO EXACTLY ARE WE, MADAM AMBASSADOR?
AND HOW DID WE BEAT IT?
WELL, I--
WE KNOW THAT THE AMERICAN SCIENTIFIC COMMUNITY HAS BEEN QUICK TO CLAIM CREDIT FOR STOPPING IT--
AS GENERALLY HAPPENS--
--BUT NO ONE HAS YET TOLD US HOW THE VIRUS WAS STOPPED.
UNLESS THEY DID NOTHING, AND THE VIRUS STOPPED ON ITS OWN--
--WHICH IS MY POINT. IT DOESN'T MATTER WHAT STOPPED THE VIRUS, WHAT MATTERS IS THAT IT STOPPED.
THIS IS GOOD NEWS.
GOOD NEWS.
YOU CONSIDER THIS GOOD NEWS.
WELL, YEAH...DON YOU?

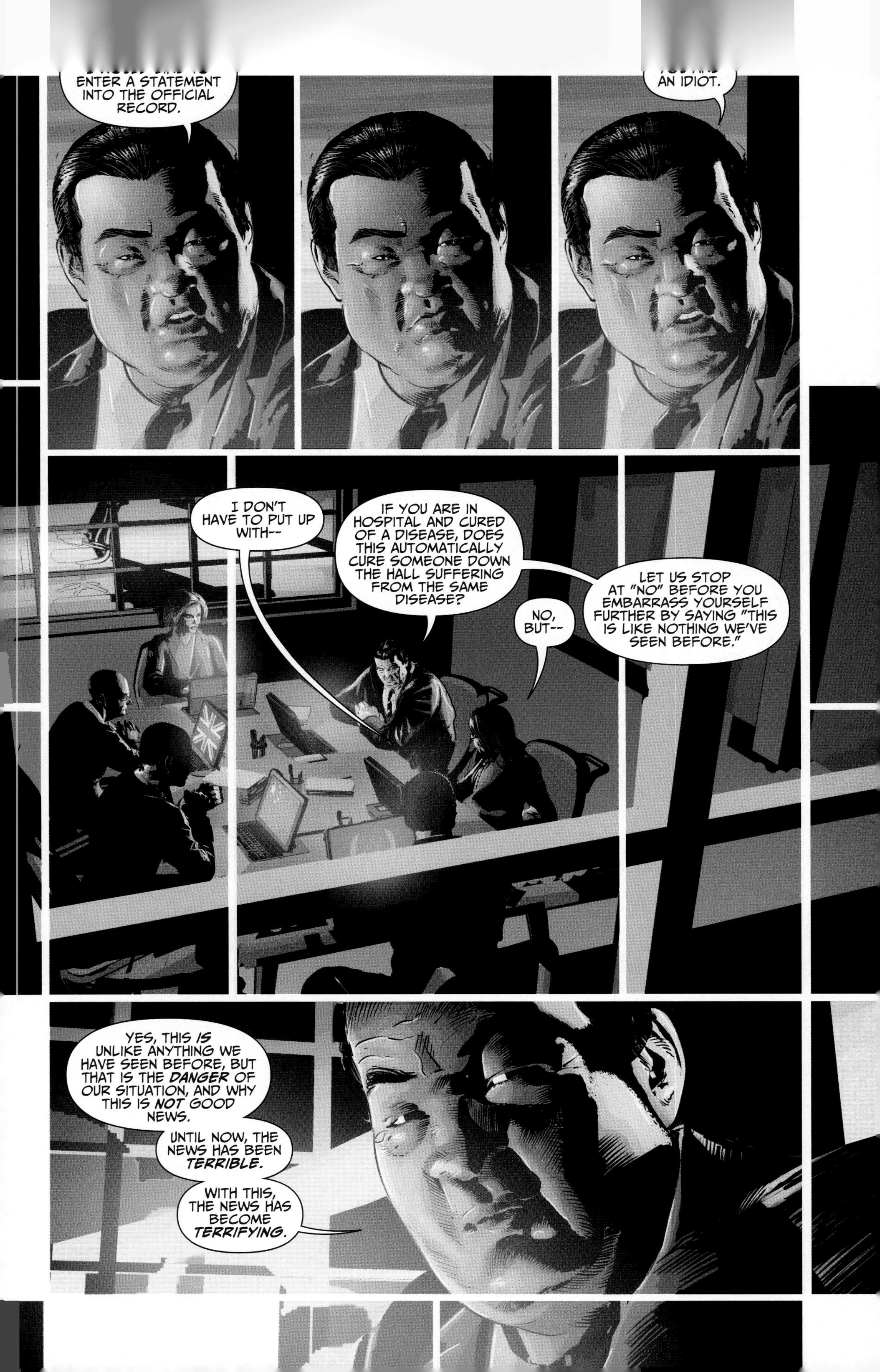
ENTER A STATEMENT INTO THE OFFICIAL RECORD.
AN IDIOT.
I DON'T HAVE TO PUT UP WITH--
IF YOU ARE IN HOSPITAL AND CURED OF A DISEASE, DOES THIS AUTOMATICALLY CURE SOMEONE DOWN THE HALL SUFFERING FROM THE SAME DISEASE?
NO, BUT--
LET US STOP AT "NO" BEFORE YOU EMBARRASS YOURSELF FURTHER BY SAYING "THIS IS LIKE NOTHING WE'VE SEEN BEFORE."
YES, THIS *IS* UNLIKE ANYTHING WE HAVE SEEN BEFORE, BUT THAT IS THE ***DANGER*** OF OUR SITUATION, AND WHY THIS IS ***NOT*** GOOD NEWS.
UNTIL NOW, THE NEWS HAS BEEN ***TERRIBLE.***
WITH THIS, THE NEWS HAS BECOME ***TERRIFYING.***

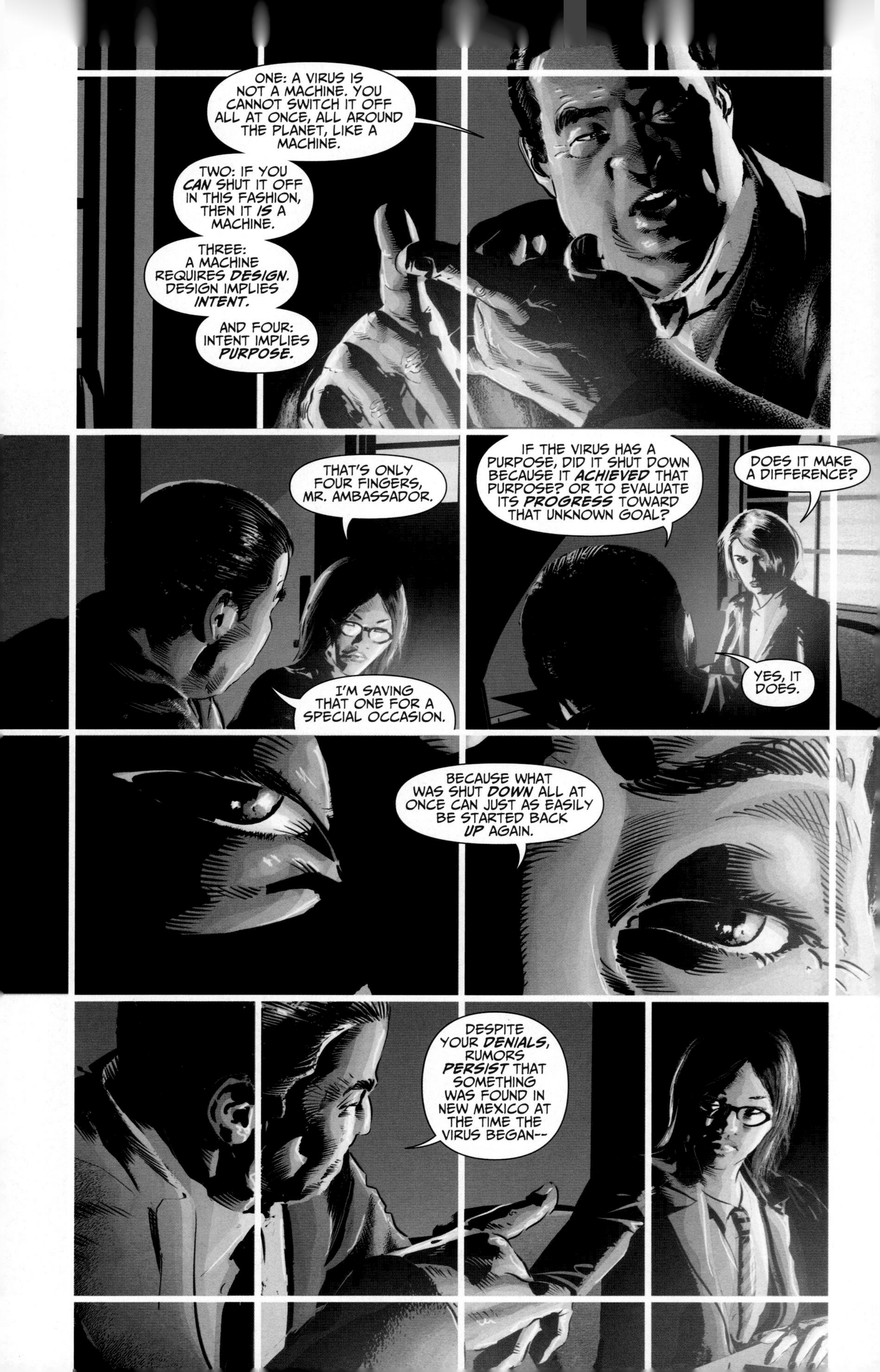
ONE: A VIRUS IS NOT A MACHINE. YOU CANNOT SWITCH IT OFF ALL AT ONCE, ALL AROUND THE PLANET, LIKE A MACHINE.
TWO: IF YOU *CAN* SHUT IT OFF IN THIS FASHION, THEN IT *IS* A MACHINE.
THREE: A MACHINE REQUIRES ***DESIGN.*** DESIGN IMPLIES ***INTENT.***
AND FOUR: INTENT IMPLIES ***PURPOSE.***
THAT'S ONLY FOUR FINGERS, MR. AMBASSADOR.
I'M SAVING THAT ONE FOR A SPECIAL OCCASION.
IF THE VIRUS HAS A PURPOSE, DID IT SHUT DOWN BECAUSE IT ***ACHIEVED*** THAT PURPOSE? OR TO EVALUATE ITS ***PROGRESS*** TOWARD THAT UNKNOWN GOAL?
DOES IT MAKE A DIFFERENCE?
YES, IT DOES.
BECAUSE WHAT WAS SHUT ***DOWN*** ALL AT ONCE CAN JUST AS EASILY BE STARTED BACK ***UP*** AGAIN.
DESPITE YOUR ***DENIALS,*** RUMORS ***PERSIST*** THAT SOMETHING WAS FOUND IN NEW MEXICO AT THE TIME THE VIRUS BEGAN--

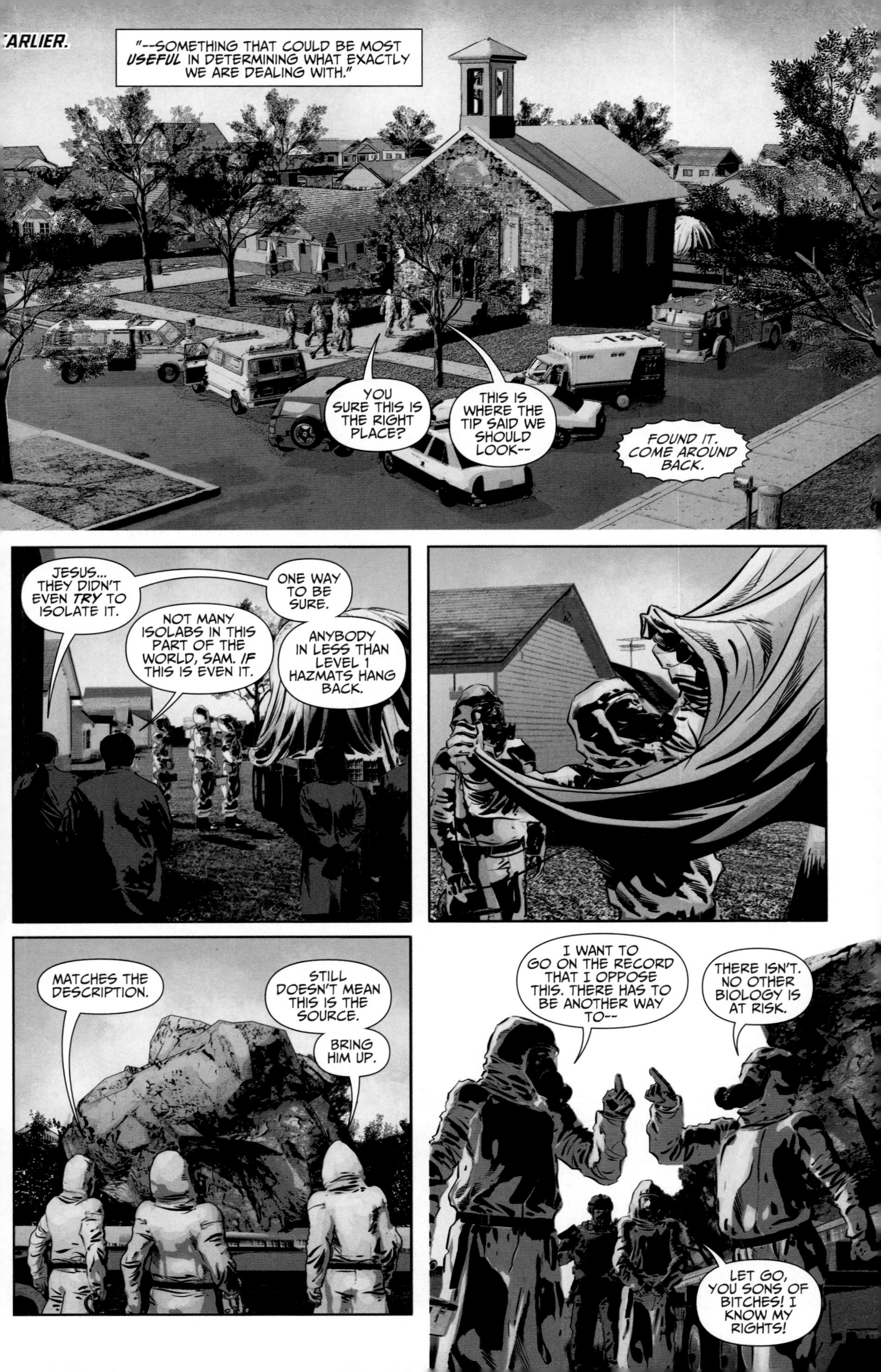

ARLIER.
"--SOMETHING THAT COULD BE MOST USEFUL IN DETERMINING WHAT EXACTLY WE ARE DEALING WITH."
YOU SURE THIS IS THE RIGHT PLACE?
THIS IS WHERE THE TIP SAID WE SHOULD LOOK--
FOUND IT. COME AROUND BACK.
JESUS... THEY DIDN'T EVEN TRY TO ISOLATE IT.
NOT MANY ISOLABS IN THIS PART OF THE WORLD, SAM. IF THIS IS EVEN IT.
ONE WAY TO BE SURE.
ANYBODY IN LESS THAN LEVEL 1 HAZMATS HANG BACK.
MATCHES THE DESCRIPTION.
STILL DOESN'T MEAN THIS IS THE SOURCE.
BRING HIM UP.
I WANT TO GO ON THE RECORD THAT I OPPOSE THIS. THERE HAS TO BE ANOTHER WAY TO--
THERE ISN'T. NO OTHER BIOLOGY IS AT RISK.
LET GO, YOU SONS OF BITCHES! I KNOW MY RIGHTS!

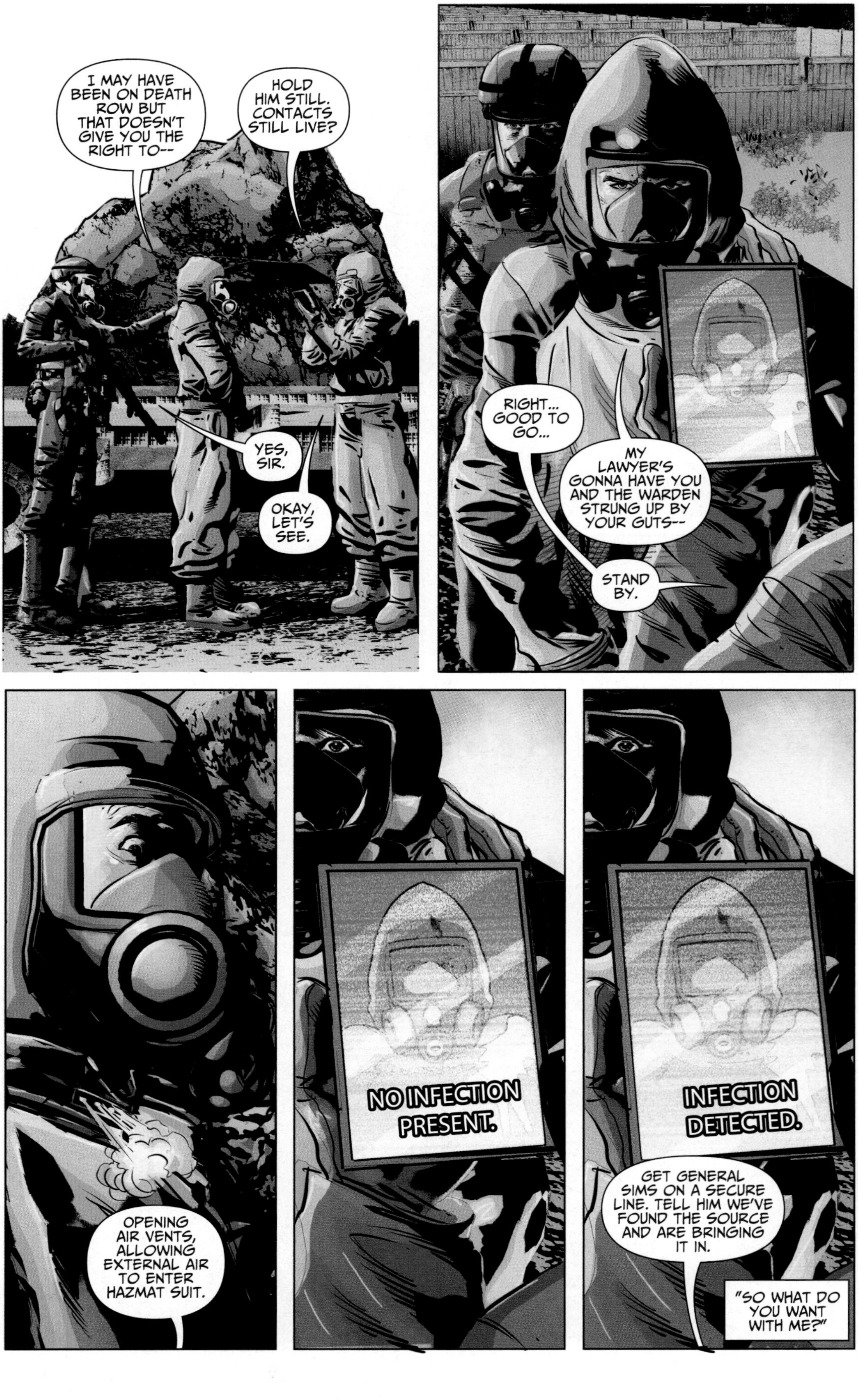
I MAY HAVE BEEN ON DEATH ROW BUT THAT DOESN'T GIVE YOU THE RIGHT TO--
HOLD HIM STILL. CONTACTS STILL LIVE?
YES, SIR.
OKAY, LET'S SEE.
RIGHT... GOOD TO GO...
MY LAWYER'S GONNA HAVE YOU AND THE WARDEN STRUNG UP BY YOUR GUTS--
STAND BY.
OPENING AIR VENTS, ALLOWING EXTERNAL AIR TO ENTER HAZMAT SUIT.
NO INFECTION PRESENT.
INFECTION DETECTED.
GET GENERAL SIMS ON A SECURE LINE. TELL HIM WE'VE FOUND THE SOURCE AND ARE BRINGING IT IN.
"SO WHAT DO YOU WANT WITH ME?"

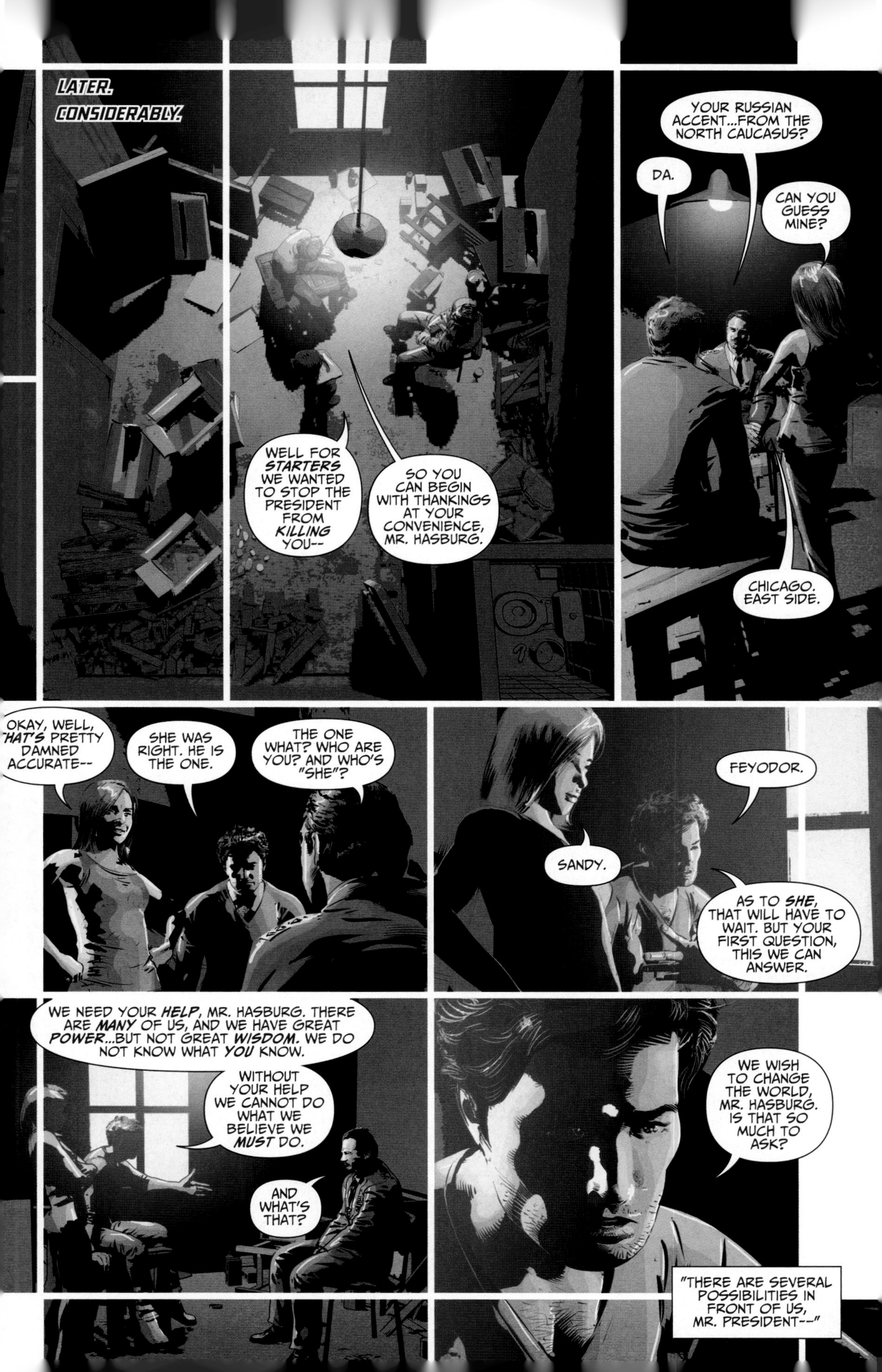
LATER. CONSIDERABLY.
WELL FOR STARTERS WE WANTED TO STOP THE PRESIDENT FROM KILLING YOU--
SO YOU CAN BEGIN WITH THANKINGS AT YOUR CONVENIENCE, MR. HASBURG.
YOUR RUSSIAN ACCENT...FROM THE NORTH CAUCASUS?
DA.
CAN YOU GUESS MINE?
CHICAGO. EAST SIDE.
OKAY, WELL, THAT'S PRETTY DAMNED ACCURATE--
SHE WAS RIGHT. HE IS THE ONE.
THE ONE WHAT? WHO ARE YOU? AND WHO'S "SHE"?
FEYODOR.
SANDY.
AS TO SHE, THAT WILL HAVE TO WAIT. BUT YOUR FIRST QUESTION, THIS WE CAN ANSWER.
WE NEED YOUR HELP, MR. HASBURG. THERE ARE MANY OF US, AND WE HAVE GREAT POWER...BUT NOT GREAT WISDOM. WE DO NOT KNOW WHAT YOU KNOW.
WITHOUT YOUR HELP WE CANNOT DO WHAT WE BELIEVE WE MUST DO.
AND WHAT'S THAT?
WE WISH TO CHANGE THE WORLD, MR. HASBURG. IS THAT SO MUCH TO ASK?
"THERE ARE SEVERAL POSSIBILITIES IN FRONT OF US, MR. PRESIDENT--"

EARLIER. BUT NOT BY MUCH.

--OUR VARIABLES ARE THE NON-TERRESTRIAL ORIGIN OF XV1N1, ITS CLEARLY ARTIFICIAL DESIGN, AND THE SUDDEN MANNER IN WHICH IT STOPPED.

POSSIBILITY ONE: THE VIRAL HOST WAS SENT BY AN OUTSIDE CIVILIZATION AS A MEANS OF SIMPLY WIPING OUT POTENTIAL COMPETITORS, OR EXTERMINATING ALL HUMAN LIFE AS A PRELUDE TO COLONIZATION, MOVING INTO A TECH-READY PLANET LIKE HERMIT CRABS.

IN EITHER SCENARIO, THOSE RESPONSIBLE WOULD NOT SEND THE STOP SIGNAL UNTIL THE JOB WAS DONE, UNLESS THE VIRUS WAS ATTACKED BY SOMETHING WE STILL HAVEN'T IDENTIFIED.

LIKE THE WAR OF THE WORLDS... YOU KNOW, WHERE THE MARTIANS GOT SICK BECAUSE THEY WEREN'T READY FOR OUR WORLD.

YES, MR. PRESIDENT... JUST LIKE WAR OF THE WORLDS.

POSSIBILITY NUMBER TWO--

--IS THAT XV1N1 WAS DESIGNED TO KILL EVERYONE WHOSE GENETICS WERE NOT CONDUCIVE TO THE CREATION OF POWERED INDIVIDUALS WHO COULD BE USED FOR SOME UNKNOWN PURPOSE.

SOLDIERS IN A WAR, PERHAPS. OR WORKERS ON A CONSTRUCTION PROJECT OF AN UNIMAGINABLE SCALE.

SO IN THIS SCENARIO, THE HUMAN BEINGS WHO DIED TO CREATE THIS ARMY ARE SIMPLY--

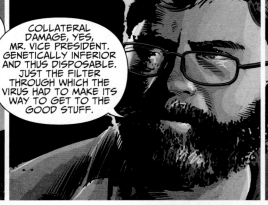

COLLATERAL DAMAGE, YES, MR. VICE PRESIDENT. GENETICALLY INFERIOR AND THUS DISPOSABLE. JUST THE FILTER THROUGH WHICH THE VIRUS HAD TO MAKE ITS WAY TO GET TO THE GOOD STUFF.

MY COLLEAGUES AND I BELIEVE THAT THIS MAY HAVE BEEN DONE IN ORDER TO CREATE AN ARMY OF *FIFTH COLUMNISTS* WHOSE GENETICS HAVE BEEN ALTERED TO MAKE THEM MORE CONDUCIVE TO DOING--

THE LAST POSSIBILITY IS, IN ITS WAY, THE MOST DISTURBING OF ALL.

AFTER KILLING 400 MILLION PEOPLE AND GIVING POWERS TO AS MANY AS TEN MILLION OTHERS, IF THE VIRUS WAS *INTENTIONALLY* TURNED OFF BY THOSE WHO SENT IT, THEN WE HAVE TO ASK *WHY?*

DOING WHAT?

...HATEVER THEY'VE BEEN *PROGRAMMED* TO DO. ...EY COULD BE WORKING ...F DATA SENT DIRECTLY TO THEIR BRAINS THAT THEY DON'T EVEN KNOW IS *THERE.*

BECAUSE OF THIS PROGRAMMING, THEY ...OULD BELIEVE THEY'RE DOING SOMETHING *POSITIVE* WITHOUT EVEN ...EALIZING THAT THEY'RE DOING SOMETHING DESTRUCTIVE.

FOR ALL WE KNOW, THEY COULD'VE BEEN CREATED TO START A *WAR* BETWEEN *US* AND THE *SURVIVORS* BECAUSE THE RACE WHO SENT THE VIRUS HERE WANTS TO SEE WHAT HAPPENS.

THE WORST PART IS, THESE PEOPLE WOULDN'T KNOW THAT THEIR POWERS HAVE *STRINGS* ATTACHED--

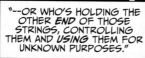

"--OR WHO'S HOLDING THE OTHER *END* OF THOSE STRINGS, CONTROLLING THEM AND *USING* THEM FOR UNKNOWN PURPOSES."

"I CAN *DO* THIS, LISA."

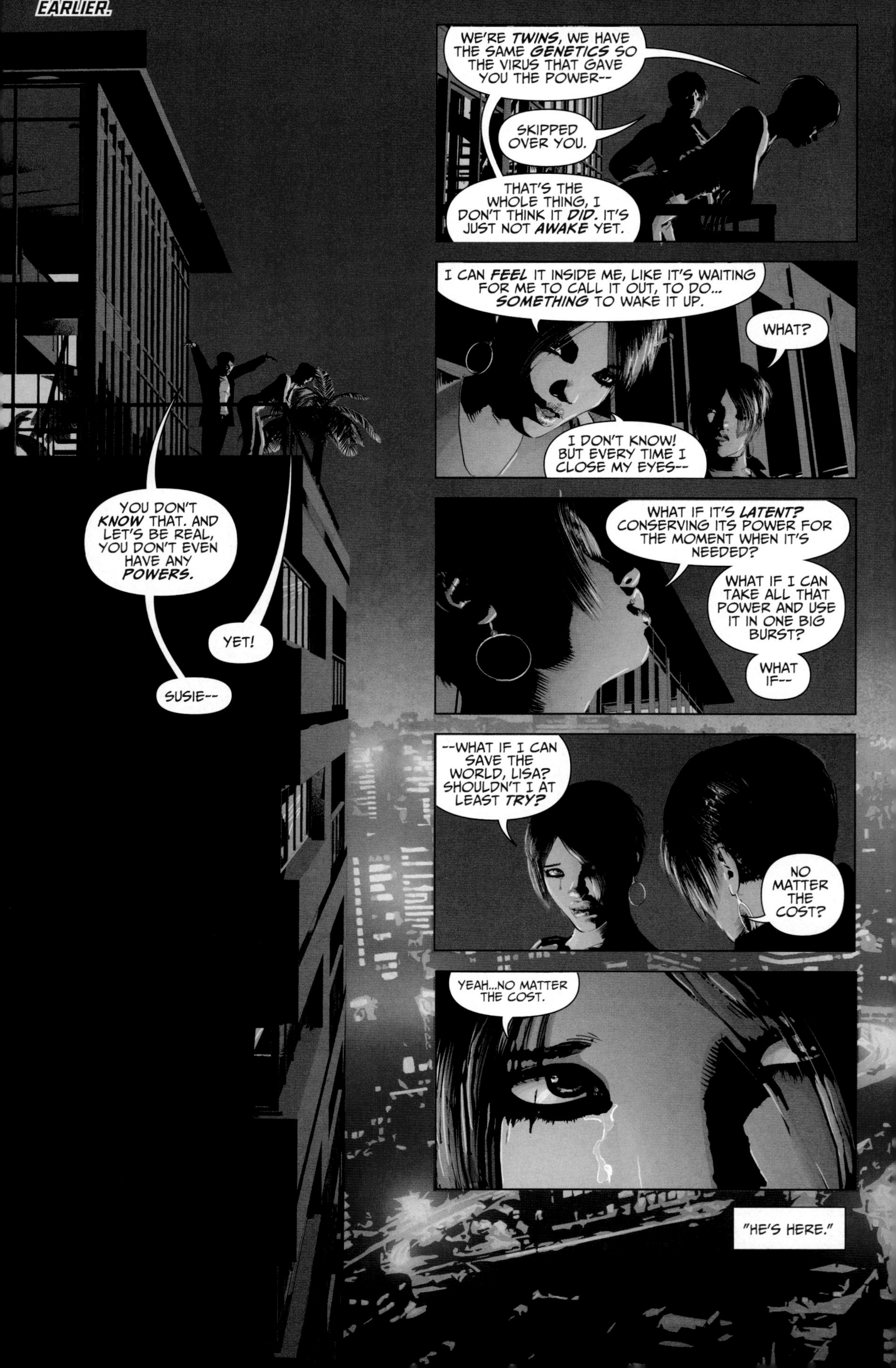
EARLIER.
WE'RE TWINS, WE HAVE THE SAME GENETICS SO THE VIRUS THAT GAVE YOU THE POWER--
SKIPPED OVER YOU.
THAT'S THE WHOLE THING, I DON'T THINK IT DID. IT'S JUST NOT AWAKE YET.
I CAN FEEL IT INSIDE ME, LIKE IT'S WAITING FOR ME TO CALL IT OUT, TO DO... SOMETHING TO WAKE IT UP.
WHAT?
I DON'T KNOW! BUT EVERY TIME I CLOSE MY EYES--
WHAT IF IT'S LATENT? CONSERVING ITS POWER FOR THE MOMENT WHEN IT'S NEEDED?
WHAT IF I CAN TAKE ALL THAT POWER AND USE IT IN ONE BIG BURST?
WHAT IF--
--WHAT IF I CAN SAVE THE WORLD, LISA? SHOULDN'T I AT LEAST TRY?
NO MATTER THE COST?
YEAH...NO MATTER THE COST.
YOU DON'T KNOW THAT. AND LET'S BE REAL, YOU DON'T EVEN HAVE ANY POWERS.
YET!
SUSIE--
"HE'S HERE."

HEY, FEYODOR--

HELLO, JAMES.

--SANDY?

PRESENT AND ACCOUNTED FOR.

SO WEIRD TO MEET IN PERSON AFTER WE'VE ALREADY MET THROUGH *HER*.

I KNOW, RIGHT? IT'S LIKE I KNOW YOU AND I DON'T KNOW YOU.

SO BASICALLY LIKE MOST OF MY PRIOR RELATIONSHIPS.

TMI, FEYODOR.

THE EMPLOYMENT AGENCY, DID IT TURN OUT TO BE--

RECRUITMENT, CONTROL AND ISOLATION, JUST LIKE SHE SAID.

GOOD, THEN WE ARE *SO* TAKING THEM DOWN, I--

EXCUSE ME--

--WHAT DOES *ANY* OF THIS HAVE TO DO TO ME?

YOU'LL SEE.

CUT HIM LOOSE, FEYODOR. SHE DOESN'T WANT HIM UNCOMFORTABLE.

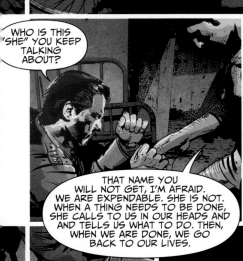

WHO IS THIS "SHE" YOU KEEP TALKING ABOUT?

THAT NAME YOU WILL NOT GET, I'M AFRAID. WE ARE EXPENDABLE. SHE IS NOT. WHEN A THING NEEDS TO BE DONE, SHE CALLS TO US IN OUR HEADS AND AND TELLS US WHAT TO DO. THEN, WHEN WE ARE DONE, WE GO BACK TO OUR LIVES.

WE DO NOT HAVE A NAME OTHER THAN THE *RESISTANCE.* WE ARE WHO AND WHAT WE NEED TO BE WHEN WE ARE NEEDED...AND THEN WE ARE NOT.

THROUGH HER, WE ARE *INVISIBLE.* WE ARE *LEGION.* WE ARE *EVERYWHERE.*

BUT THAT IS THE *LEAST* OF WHO AND *WHAT* SHE IS...AND WHAT SHE CAN DO.

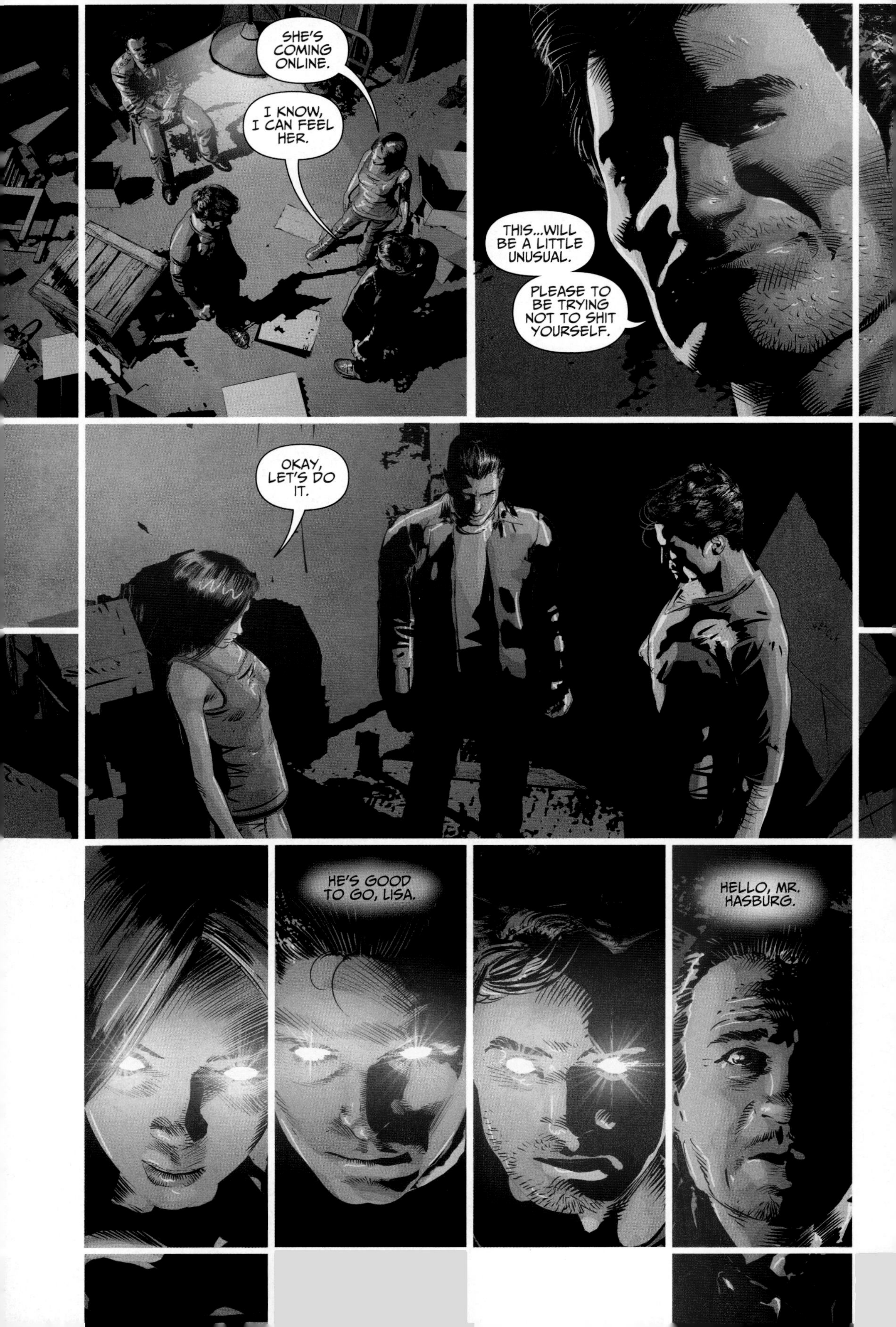
SHE'S COMING ONLINE.
I KNOW, I CAN FEEL HER.
THIS...WILL BE A LITTLE UNUSUAL.
PLEASE TO BE TRYING NOT TO SHIT YOURSELF.
OKAY, LET'S DO IT.
HE'S GOOD TO GO, LISA.
HELLO, MR. HASBURG.

I APOLOGIZE FOR MEETING UNDER SUCH CIRCUMSTANCES, BUT IF WE HAD NOT INTERVENED WHEN WE DID, WE WOULD NOT EVEN BE *HAVING* THIS CONVERSATION.

FEYODOR ALREADY TOLD YOU THAT WE INTEND TO *CHANGE* THINGS, AND THAT WE NEED YOUR *HELP*.

I AM HERE TO HELP YOU *UNDERSTAND*.

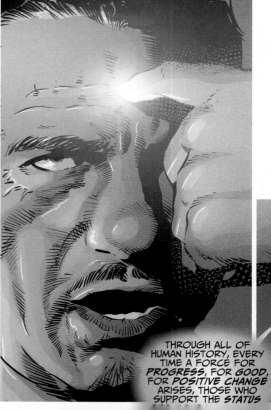

THROUGH ALL OF HUMAN HISTORY, EVERY TIME A FORCE FOR *PROGRESS*, FOR *GOOD*, FOR *POSITIVE CHANGE* ARISES, THOSE WHO SUPPORT THE *STATUS*

I AM HERE TO HELP YOU *SEE*.

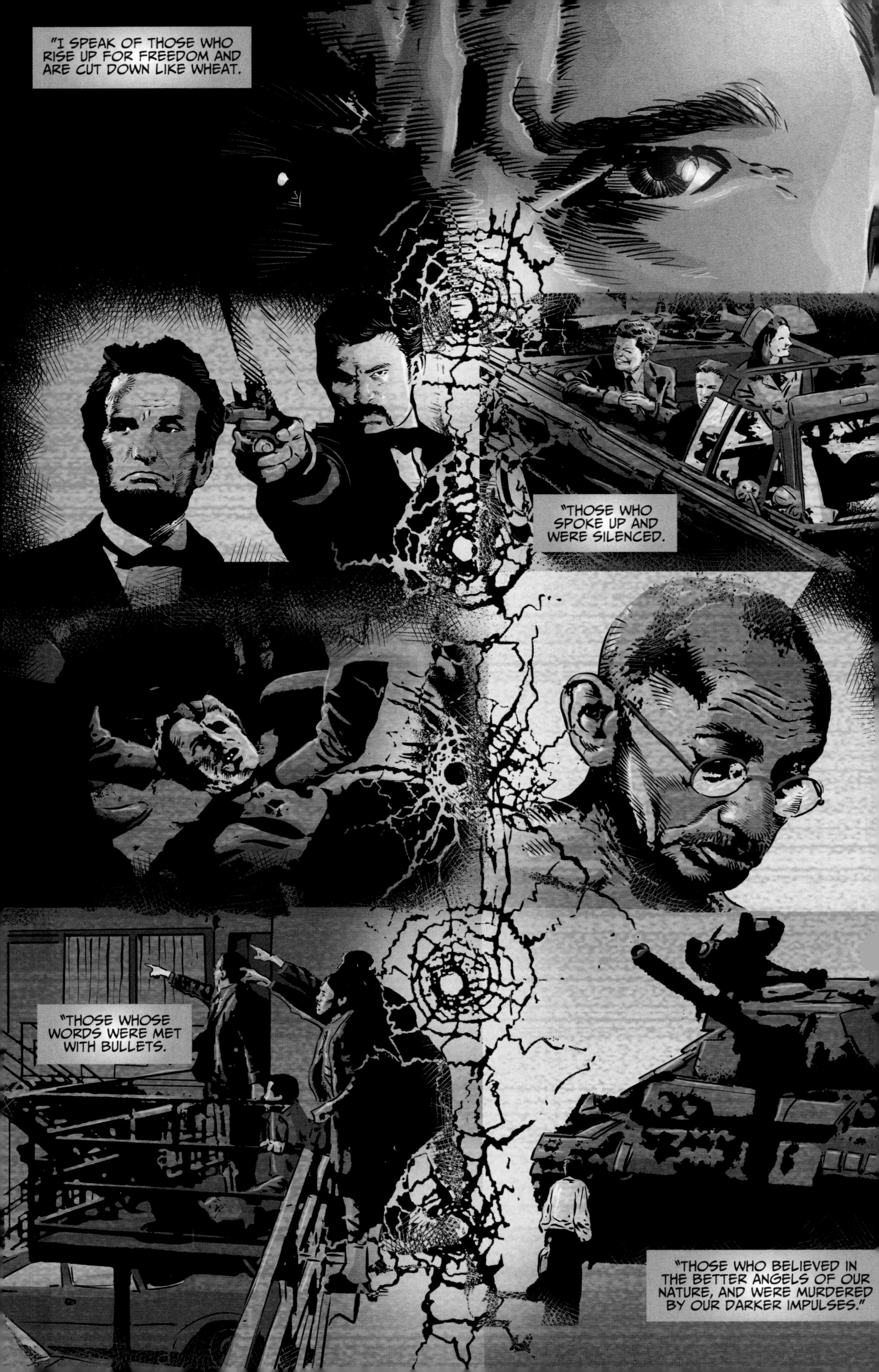
"I SPEAK OF THOSE WHO RISE UP FOR FREEDOM AND ARE CUT DOWN LIKE WHEAT.
"THOSE WHO SPOKE UP AND WERE SILENCED.
"THOSE WHOSE WORDS WERE MET WITH BULLETS.
"THOSE WHO BELIEVED IN THE BETTER ANGELS OF OUR NATURE, AND WERE MURDERED BY OUR DARKER IMPULSES."

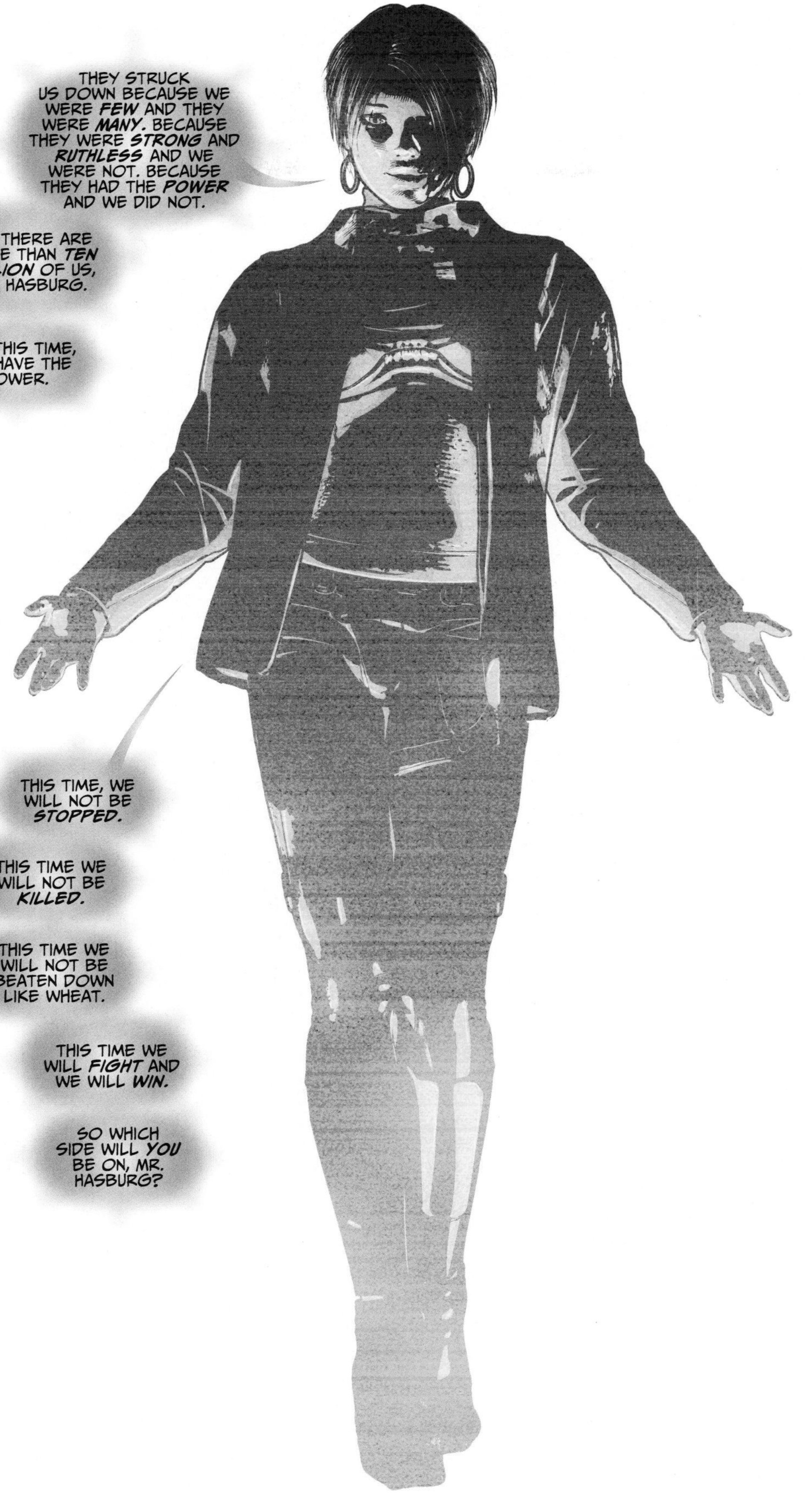
THEY STRUCK US DOWN BECAUSE WE WERE FEW AND THEY WERE MANY. BECAUSE THEY WERE STRONG AND RUTHLESS AND WE WERE NOT. BECAUSE THEY HAD THE POWER AND WE DID NOT.
BUT THERE ARE MORE THAN TEN MILLION OF US, MR. HASBURG.
AND THIS TIME, WE HAVE THE POWER.
THIS TIME, WE WILL NOT BE STOPPED.
THIS TIME WE WILL NOT BE KILLED.
THIS TIME WE WILL NOT BE BEATEN DOWN LIKE WHEAT.
THIS TIME WE WILL FIGHT AND WE WILL WIN.
SO WHICH SIDE WILL YOU BE ON, MR. HASBURG?

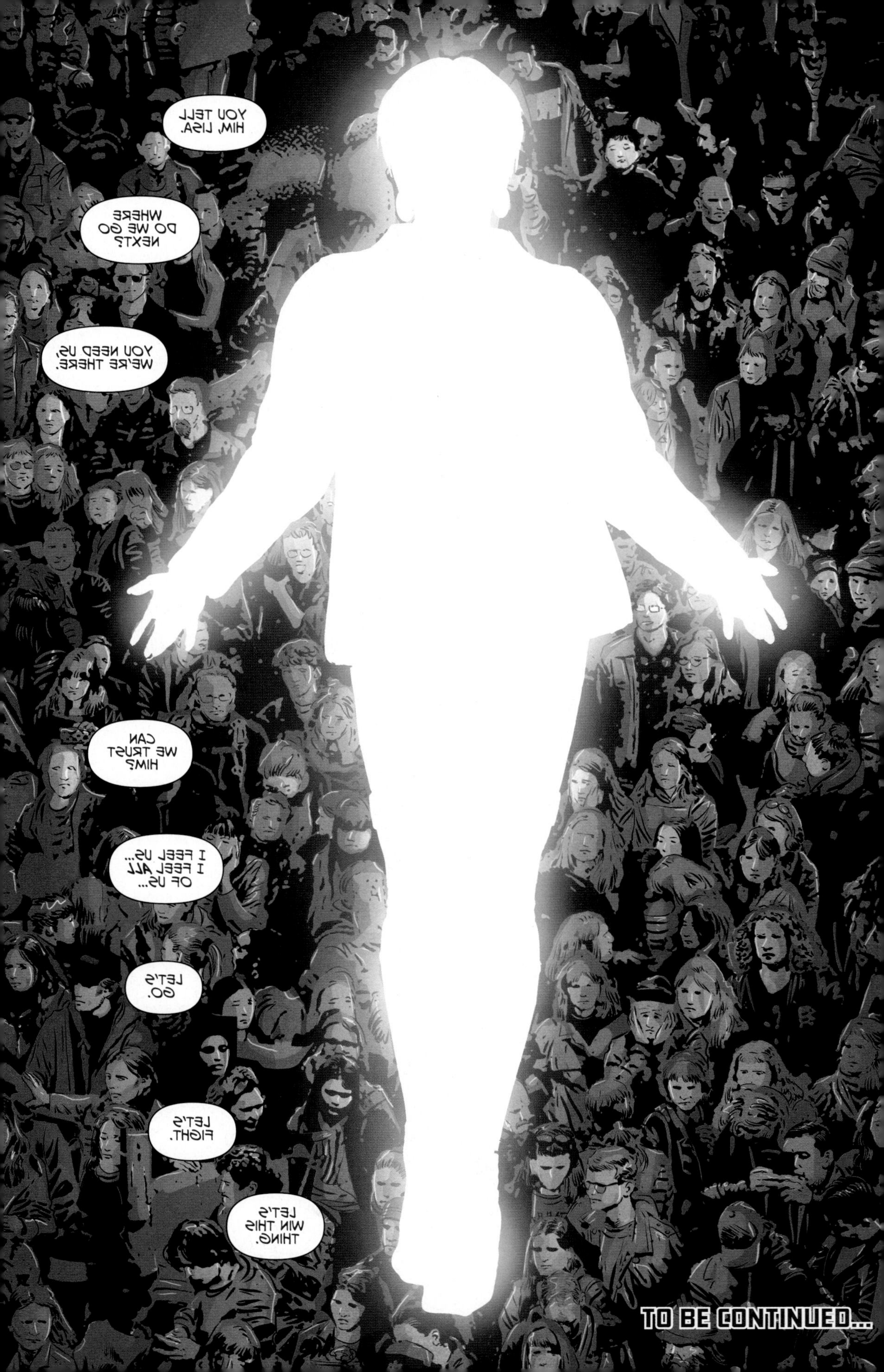
YOU TELL HIM, LISA.
WHERE DO WE GO NEXT?
YOU NEED US, WE'RE THERE.
CAN WE TRUST HIM?
I FEEL US... I FEEL ALL OF US...
LET'S GO.
LET'S FIGHT.
LET'S WIN THIS THING.
TO BE CONTINUED...

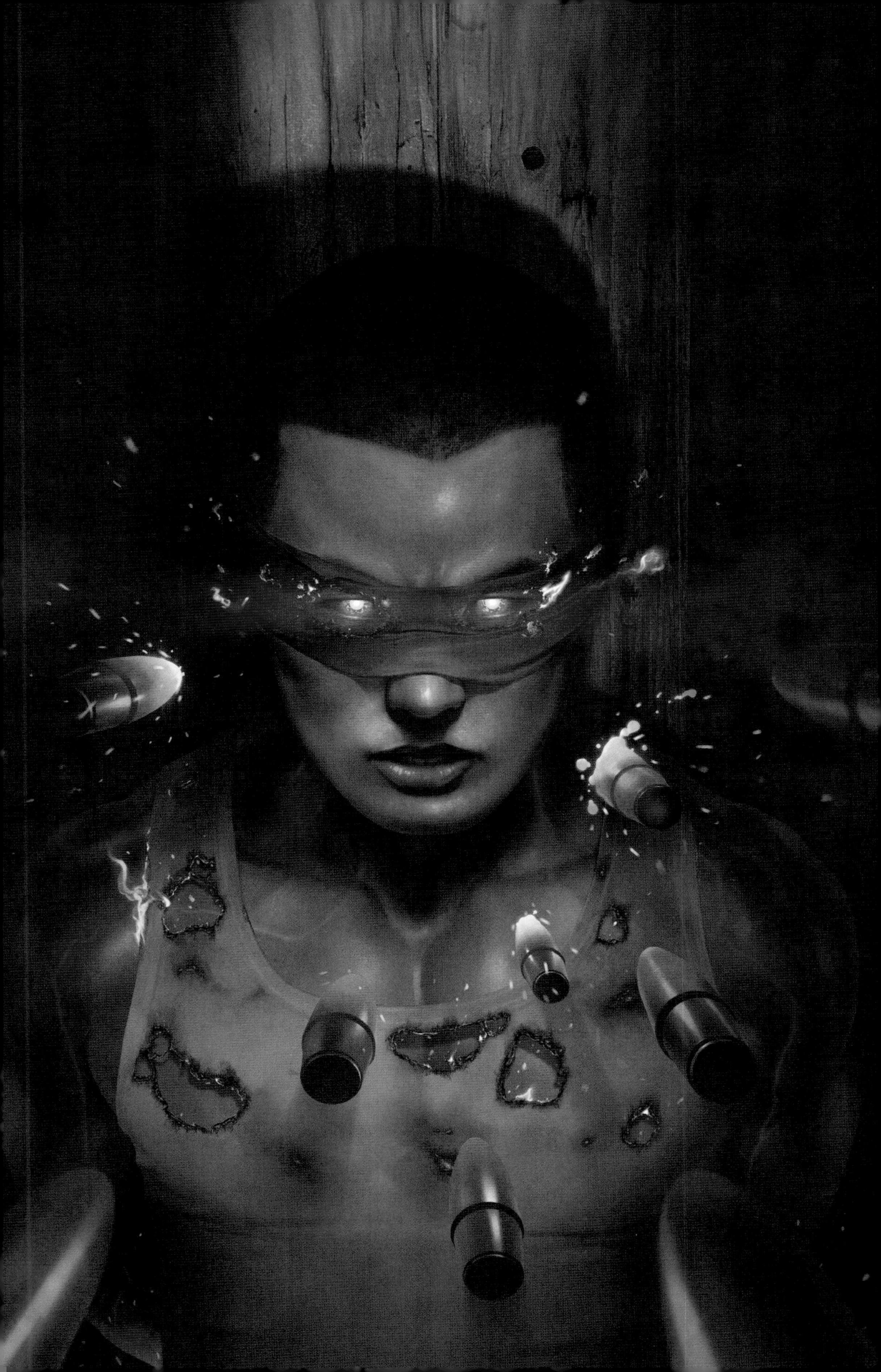

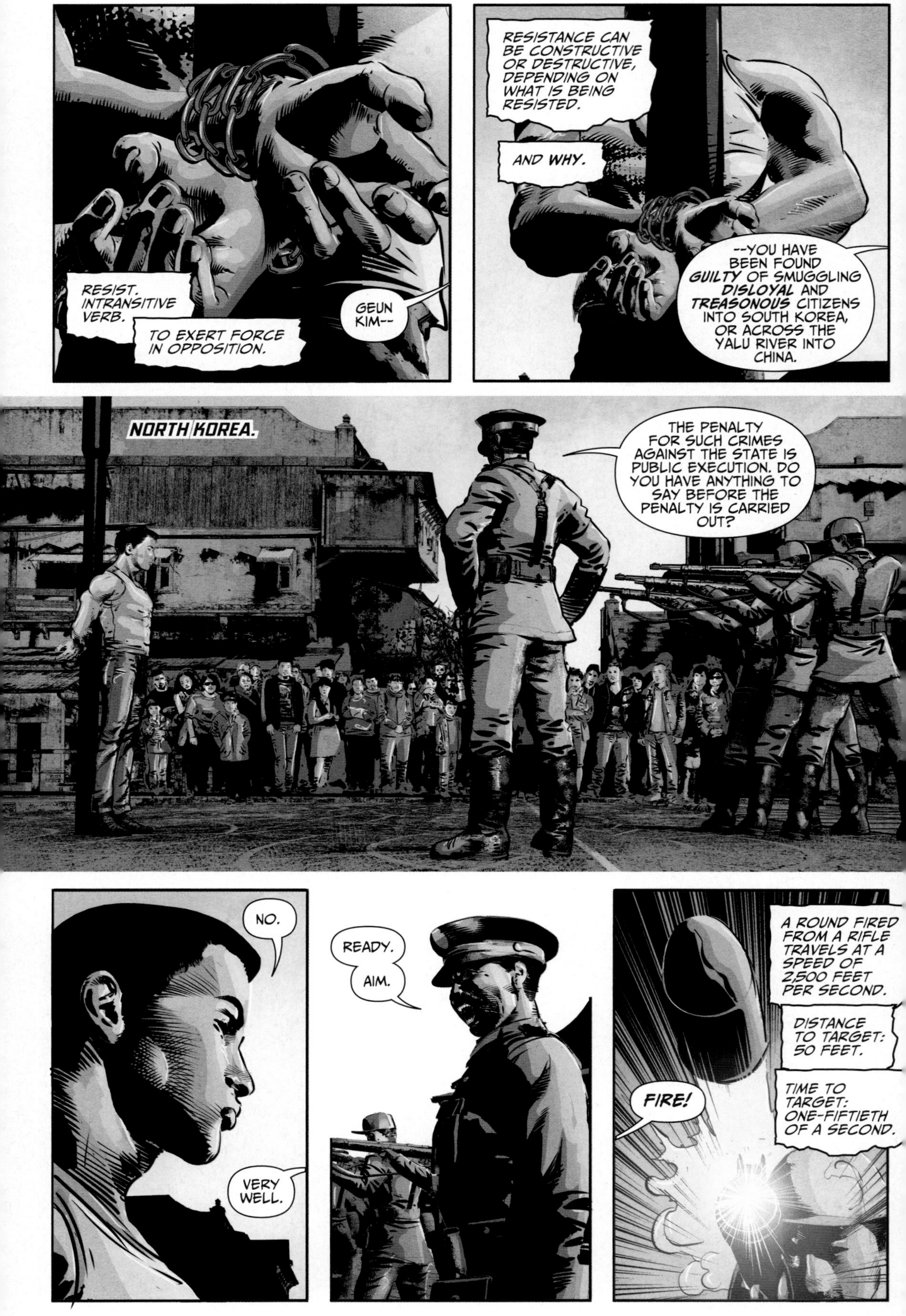
RESIST. INTRANSITIVE VERB.
TO EXERT FORCE IN OPPOSITION.
GEUN KIM--
RESISTANCE CAN BE CONSTRUCTIVE OR DESTRUCTIVE, DEPENDING ON WHAT IS BEING RESISTED.
AND WHY.
--YOU HAVE BEEN FOUND GUILTY OF SMUGGLING DISLOYAL AND TREASONOUS CITIZENS INTO SOUTH KOREA, OR ACROSS THE YALU RIVER INTO CHINA.
NORTH KOREA.
THE PENALTY FOR SUCH CRIMES AGAINST THE STATE IS PUBLIC EXECUTION. DO YOU HAVE ANYTHING TO SAY BEFORE THE PENALTY IS CARRIED OUT?
NO.
VERY WELL.
READY.
AIM.
FIRE!
A ROUND FIRED FROM A RIFLE TRAVELS AT A SPEED OF 2,500 FEET PER SECOND.
DISTANCE TO TARGET: 50 FEET.
TIME TO TARGET: ONE-FIFTIETH OF A SECOND.

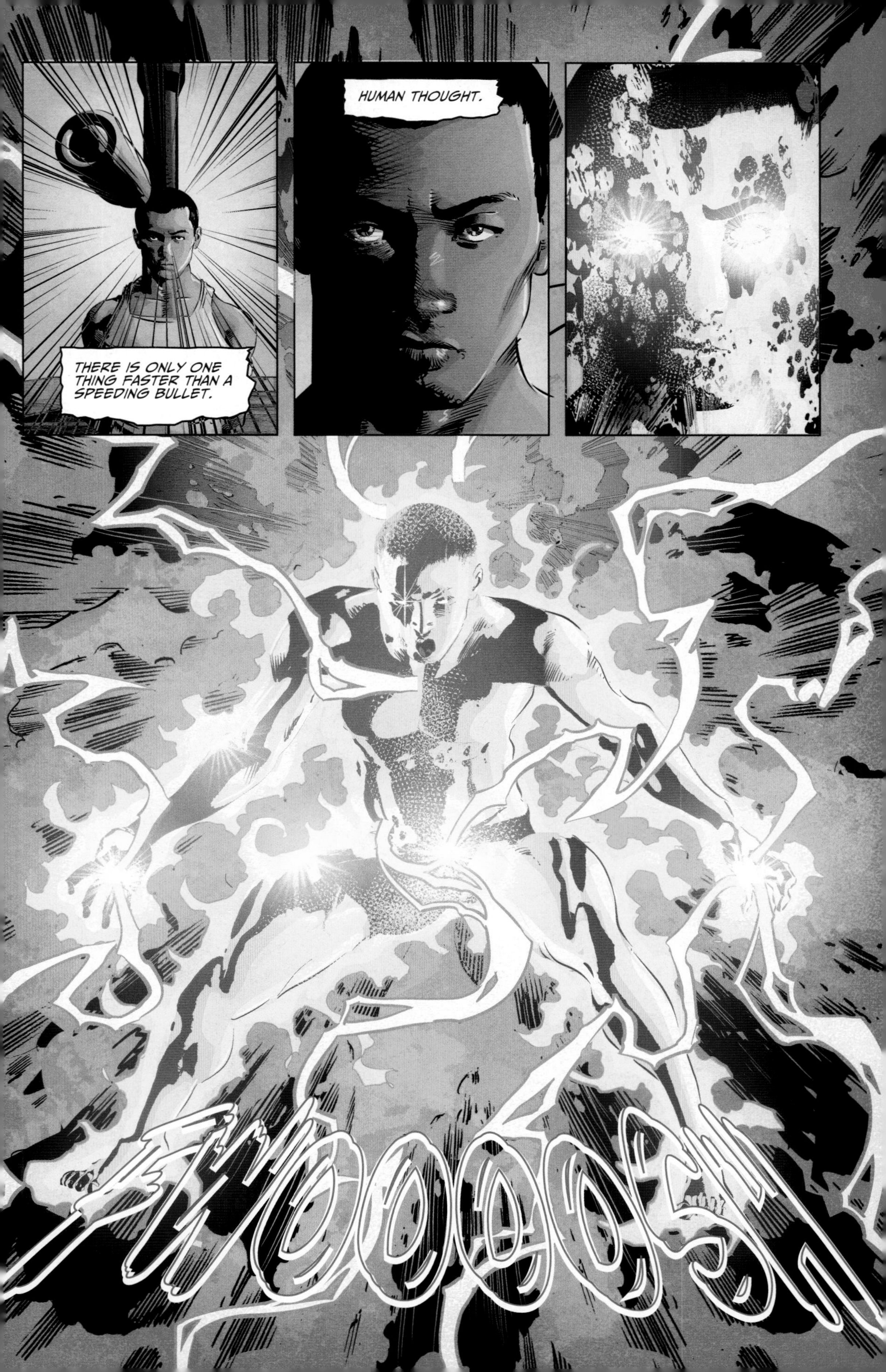
THERE IS ONLY ONE THING FASTER THAN A SPEEDING BULLET.
HUMAN THOUGHT.
FWOOOOOSH!

I ALLOWED YOU TO CAPTURE ME SO I COULD GIVE YOU A *MESSAGE.* SO THAT YOU WOULD *UNDERSTAND.*

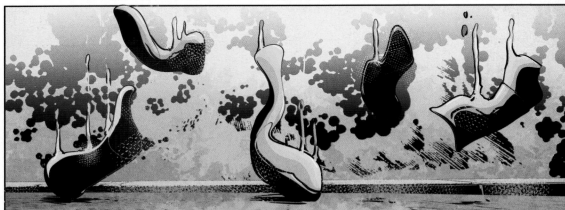

I WILL NOT BE STOPPED. I *CANNOT* BE STOPPED.

NOT BY YOU.

NOT BY *ANYONE.*

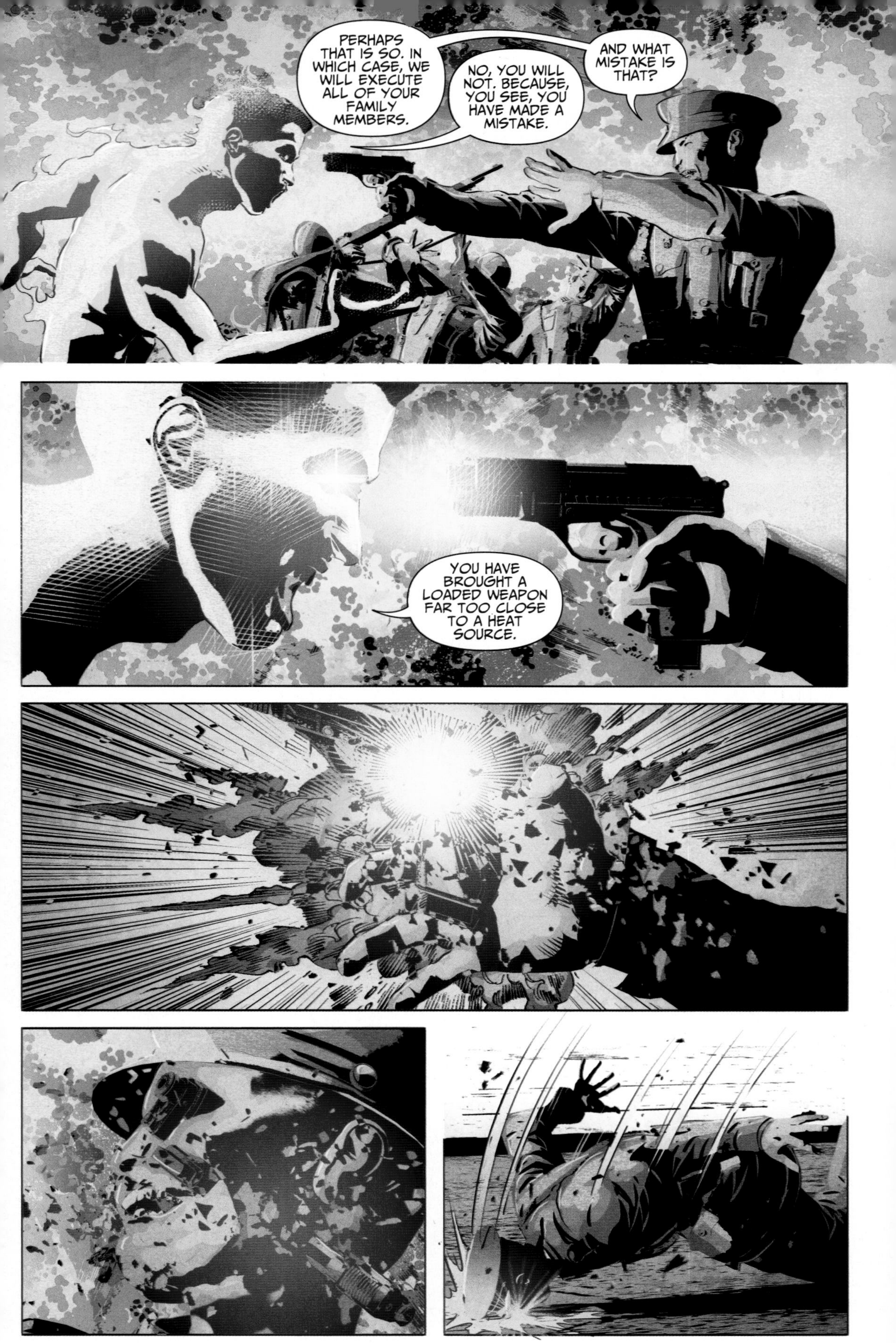
PERHAPS THAT IS SO. IN WHICH CASE, WE WILL EXECUTE ALL OF YOUR FAMILY MEMBERS.
NO, YOU WILL NOT. BECAUSE, YOU SEE, YOU HAVE MADE A MISTAKE.
AND WHAT MISTAKE IS THAT?
YOU HAVE BROUGHT A LOADED WEAPON FAR TOO CLOSE TO A HEAT SOURCE.

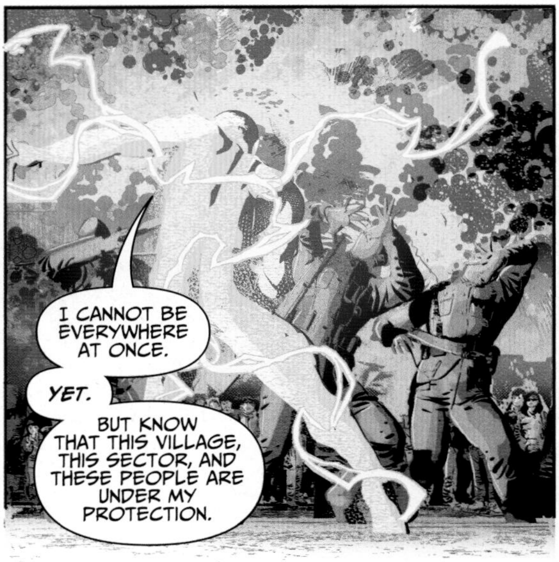
I CANNOT BE EVERYWHERE AT ONCE.
YET.
BUT KNOW THAT THIS VILLAGE, THIS SECTOR, AND THESE PEOPLE ARE UNDER MY PROTECTION.

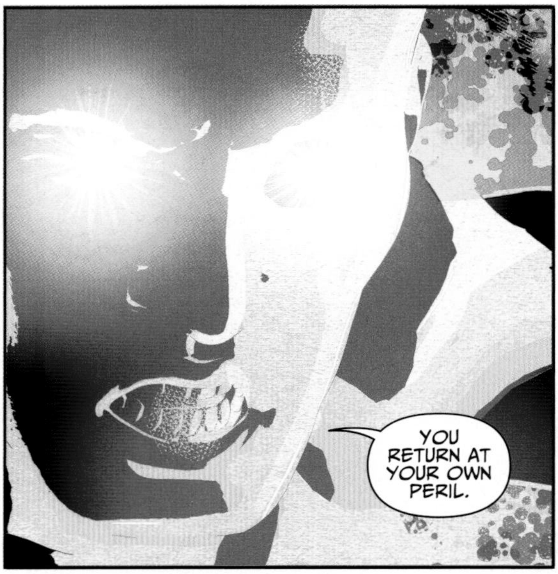
YOU RETURN AT YOUR OWN PERIL.

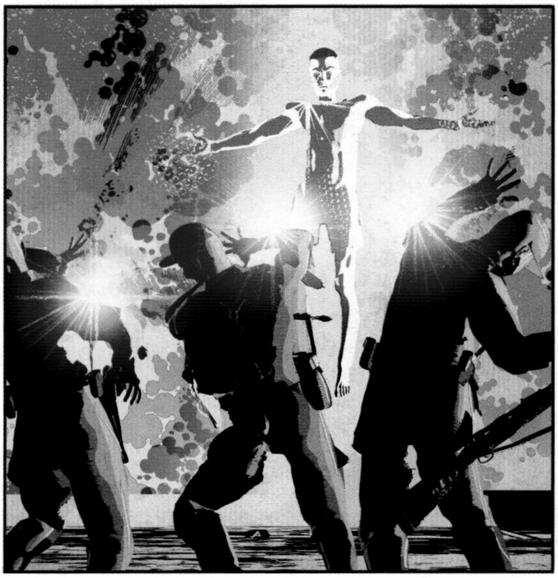

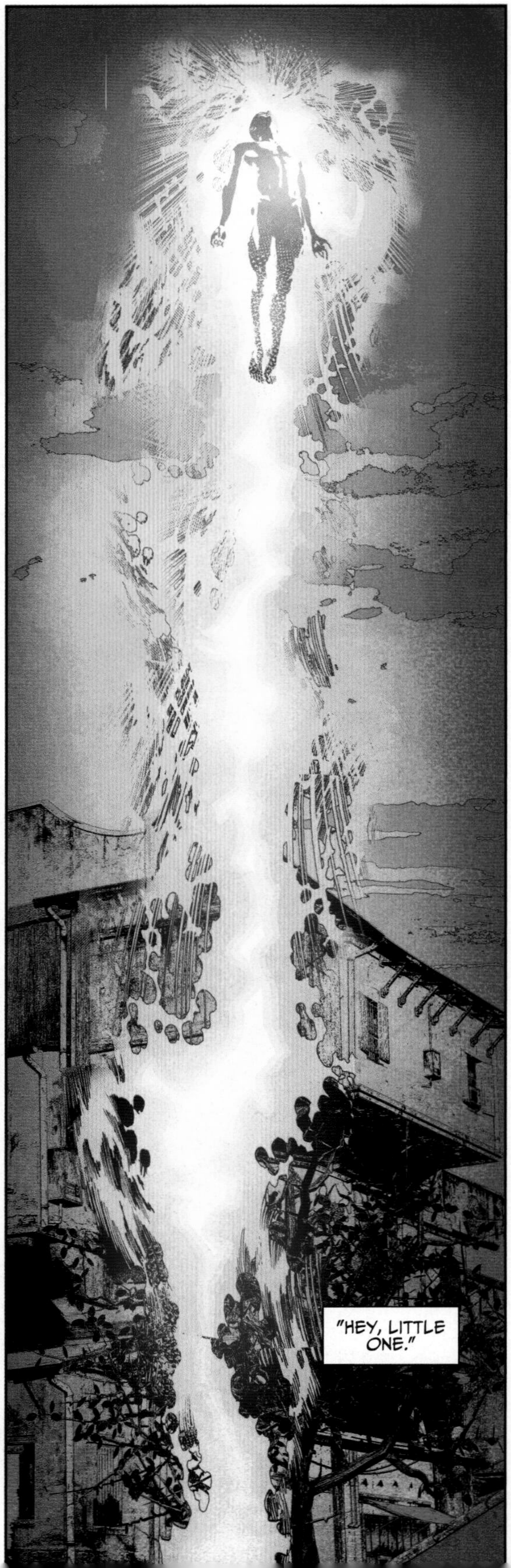
"HEY, LITTLE ONE."

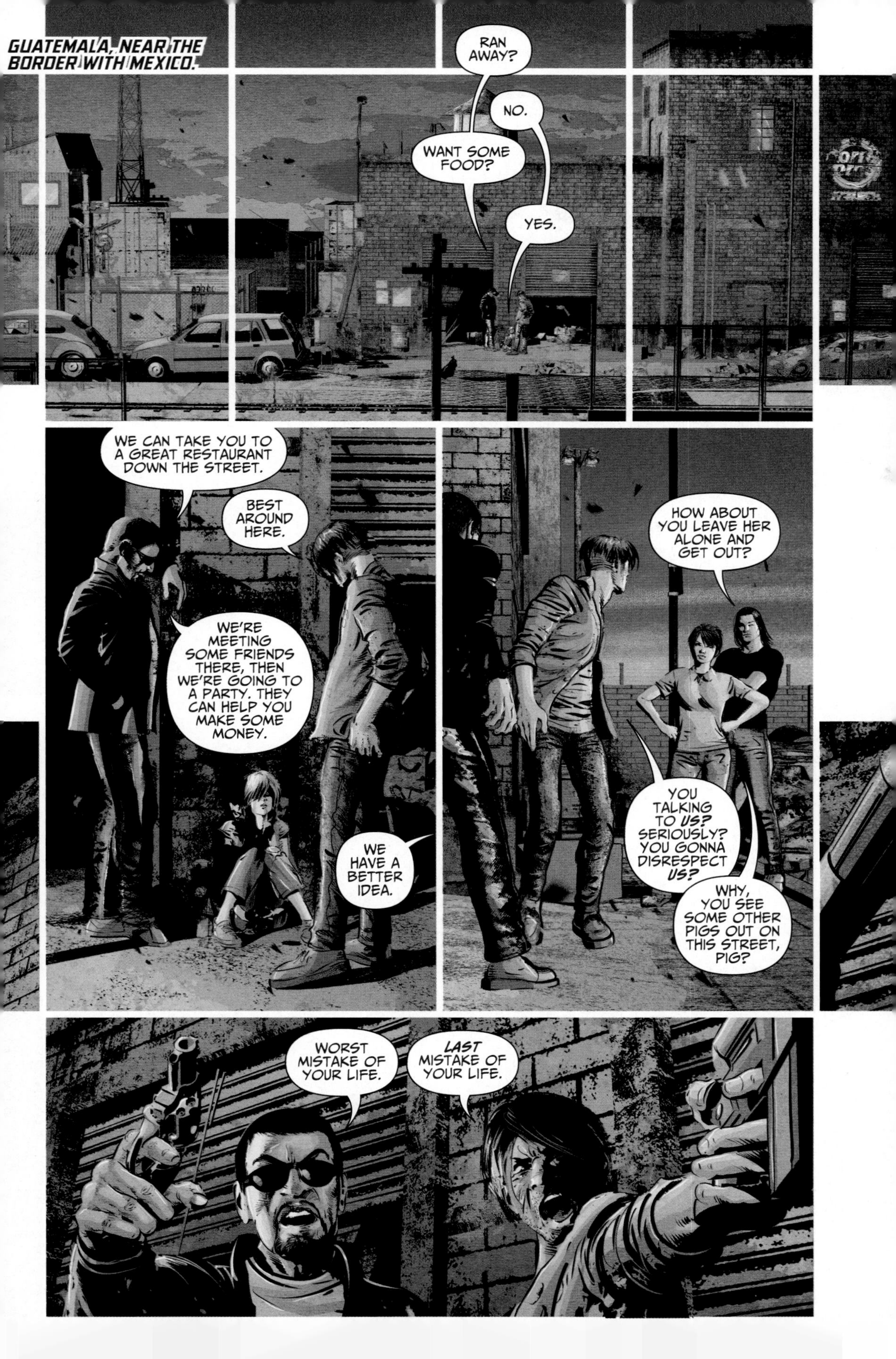
GUATEMALA, NEAR THE BORDER WITH MEXICO.
RAN AWAY?
NO.
WANT SOME FOOD?
YES.
WE CAN TAKE YOU TO A GREAT RESTAURANT DOWN THE STREET.
BEST AROUND HERE.
WE'RE MEETING SOME FRIENDS THERE, THEN WE'RE GOING TO A PARTY. THEY CAN HELP YOU MAKE SOME MONEY.
WE HAVE A BETTER IDEA.
HOW ABOUT YOU LEAVE HER ALONE AND GET OUT?
YOU TALKING TO *US?* SERIOUSLY? YOU GONNA DISRESPECT *US?*
WHY, YOU SEE SOME OTHER PIGS OUT ON THIS STREET, PIG?
WORST MISTAKE OF YOUR LIFE.
LAST MISTAKE OF YOUR LIFE.

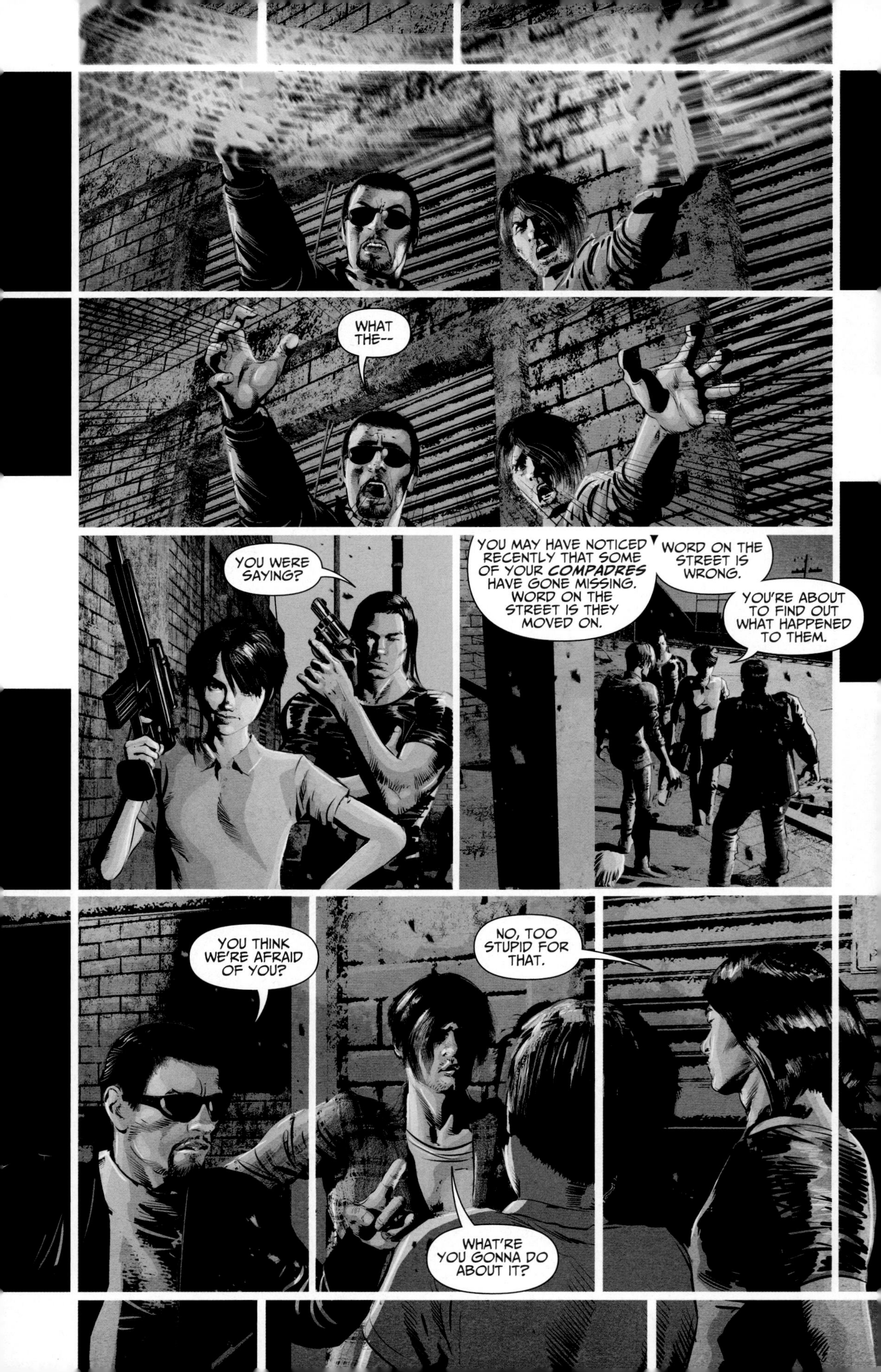
WHAT THE--
YOU WERE SAYING?
YOU MAY HAVE NOTICED RECENTLY THAT SOME OF YOUR *COMPADRES* HAVE GONE MISSING. WORD ON THE STREET IS THEY MOVED ON.
WORD ON THE STREET IS WRONG.
YOU'RE ABOUT TO FIND OUT WHAT HAPPENED TO THEM.
YOU THINK WE'RE AFRAID OF YOU?
NO, TOO STUPID FOR THAT.
WHAT'RE YOU GONNA DO ABOUT IT?

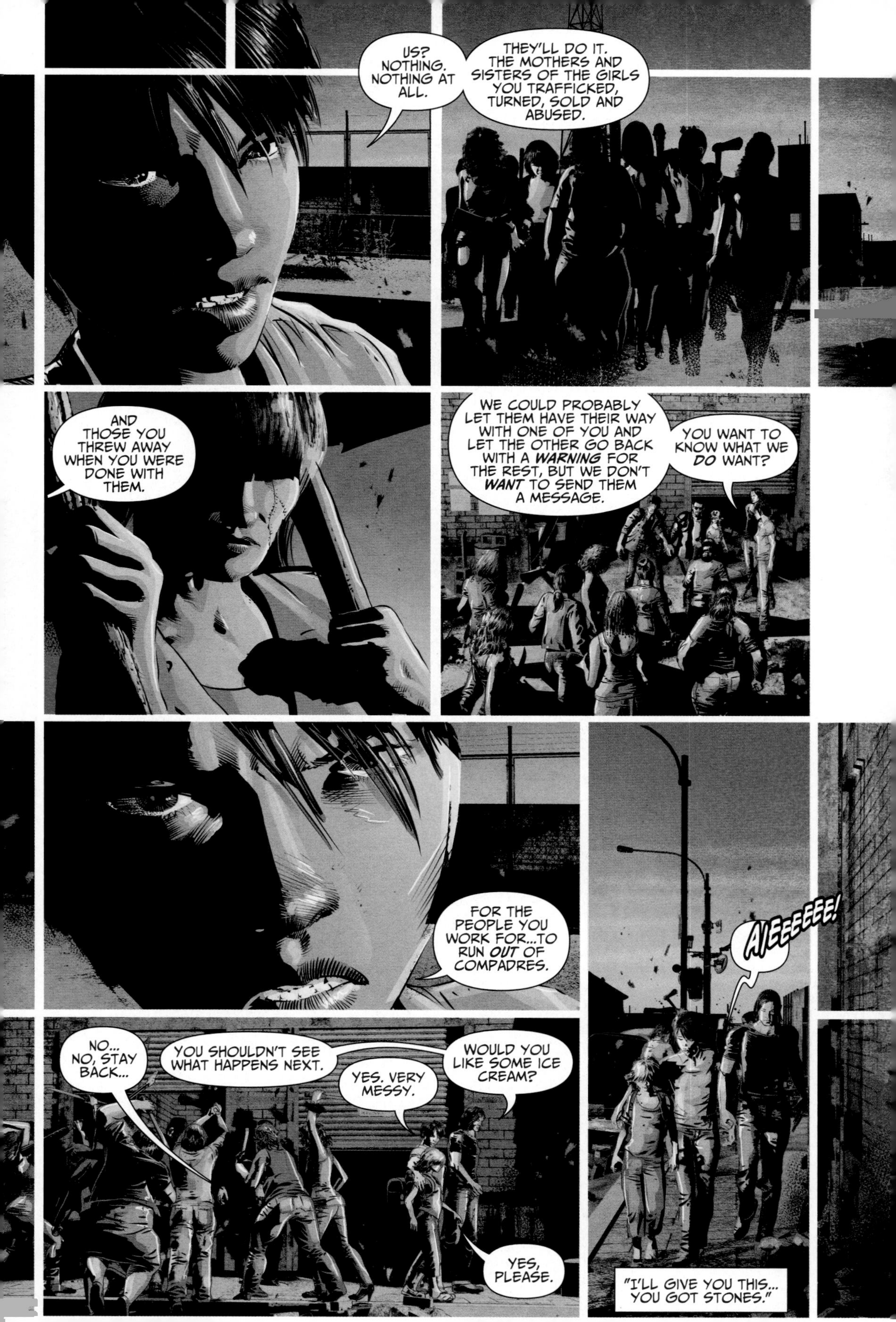
US? NOTHING. NOTHING AT ALL.
THEY'LL DO IT. THE MOTHERS AND SISTERS OF THE GIRLS YOU TRAFFICKED, TURNED, SOLD AND ABUSED.
AND THOSE YOU THREW AWAY WHEN YOU WERE DONE WITH THEM.
WE COULD PROBABLY LET THEM HAVE THEIR WAY WITH ONE OF YOU AND LET THE OTHER GO BACK WITH A WARNING FOR THE REST, BUT WE DON'T WANT TO SEND THEM A MESSAGE.
YOU WANT TO KNOW WHAT WE DO WANT?
FOR THE PEOPLE YOU WORK FOR...TO RUN OUT OF COMPADRES.
AIEEEEEE!
NO... NO, STAY BACK...
YOU SHOULDN'T SEE WHAT HAPPENS NEXT.
YES. VERY MESSY.
WOULD YOU LIKE SOME ICE CREAM?
YES, PLEASE.
"I'LL GIVE YOU THIS... YOU GOT STONES."

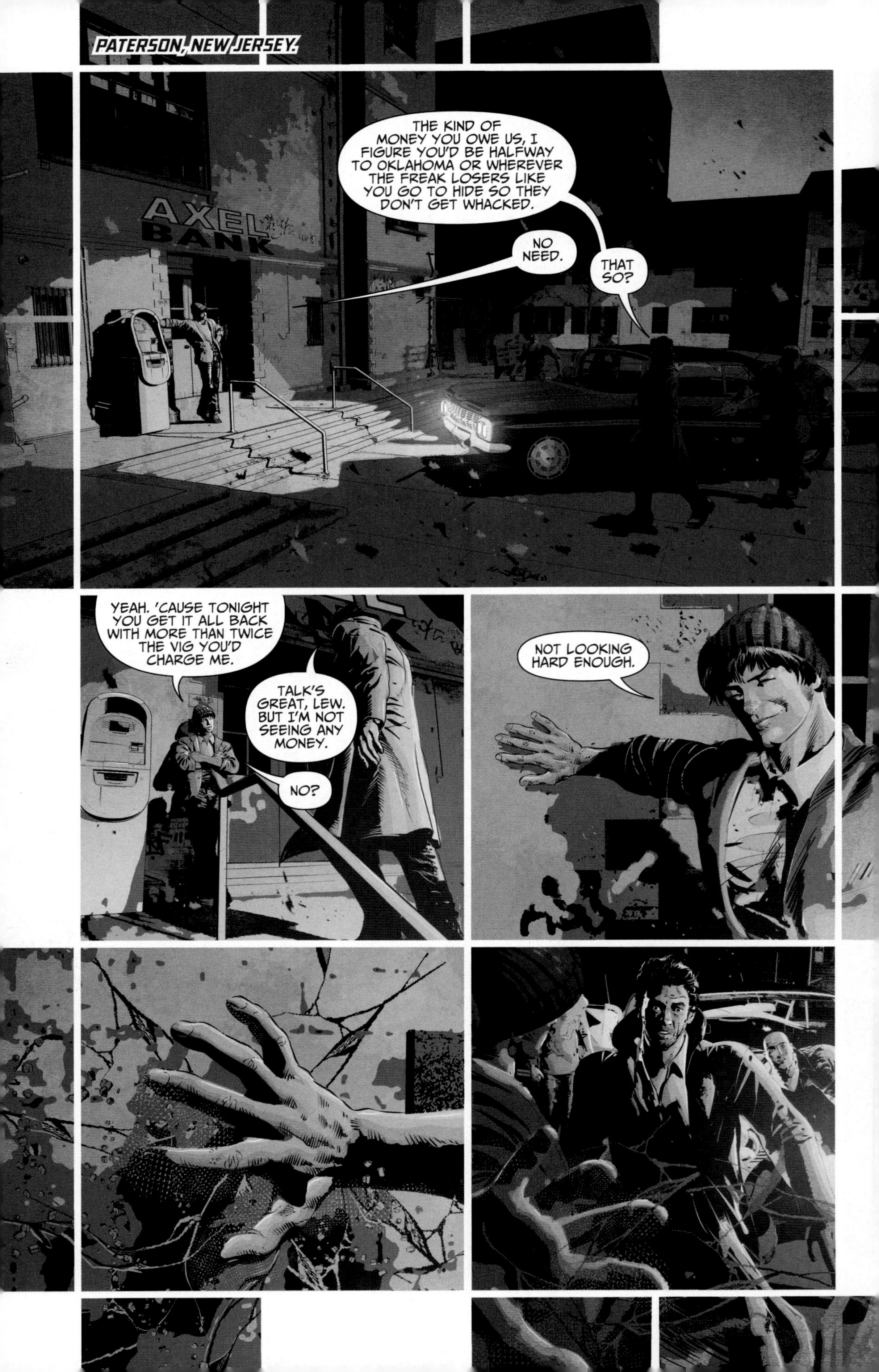
PATERSON, NEW JERSEY.
THE KIND OF MONEY YOU OWE US, I FIGURE YOU'D BE HALFWAY TO OKLAHOMA OR WHEREVER THE FREAK LOSERS LIKE YOU GO TO HIDE SO THEY DON'T GET WHACKED.
NO NEED.
THAT SO?
YEAH. 'CAUSE TONIGHT YOU GET IT ALL BACK WITH MORE THAN TWICE THE VIG YOU'D CHARGE ME.
TALK'S GREAT, LEW. BUT I'M NOT SEEING ANY MONEY.
NO?
NOT LOOKING HARD ENOUGH.
AXEL BANK

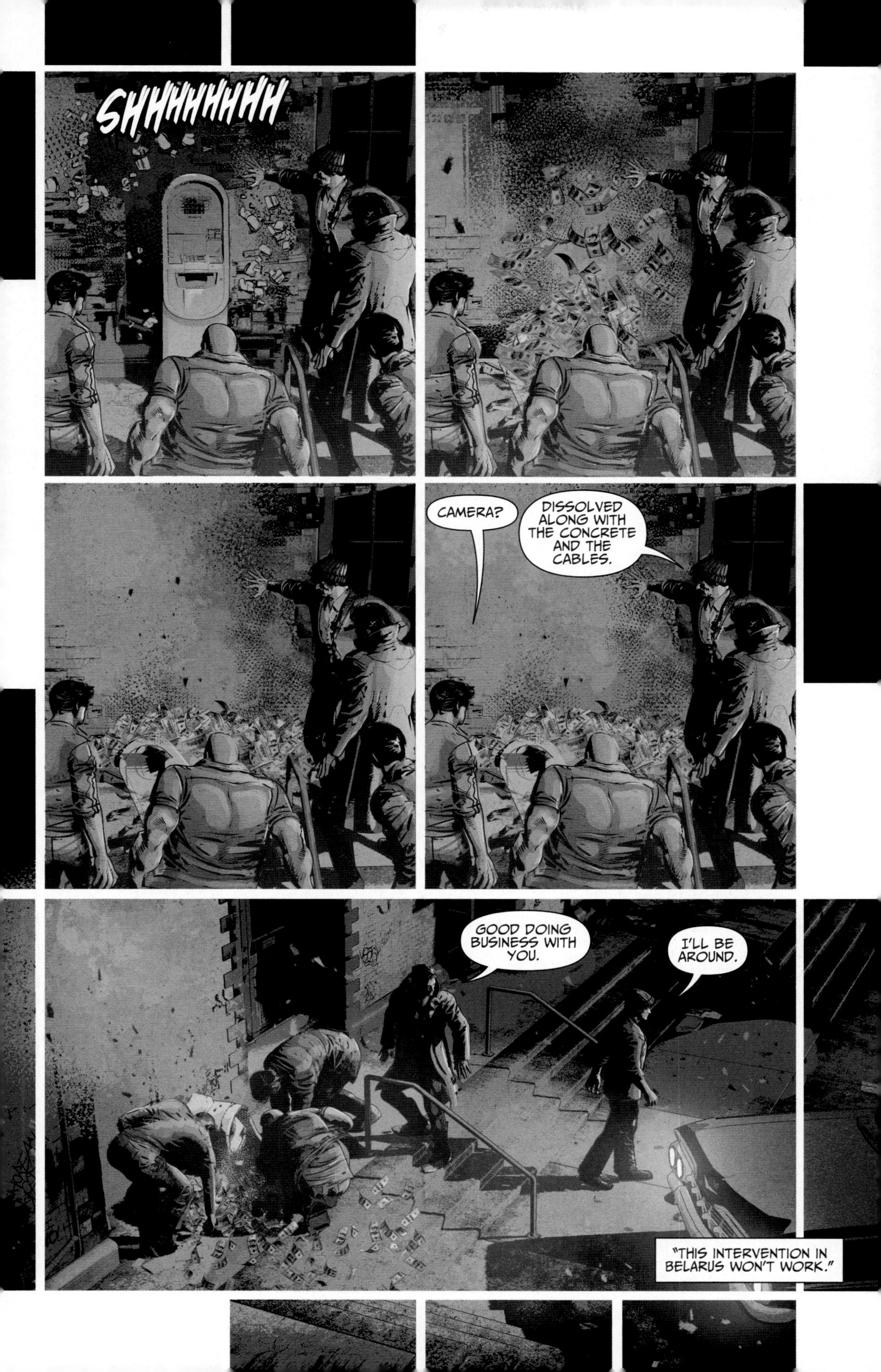
SHHHHHHHH
CAMERA?
DISSOLVED ALONG WITH THE CONCRETE AND THE CABLES.
GOOD DOING BUSINESS WITH YOU.
I'LL BE AROUND.
"THIS INTERVENTION IN BELARUS WON'T WORK."

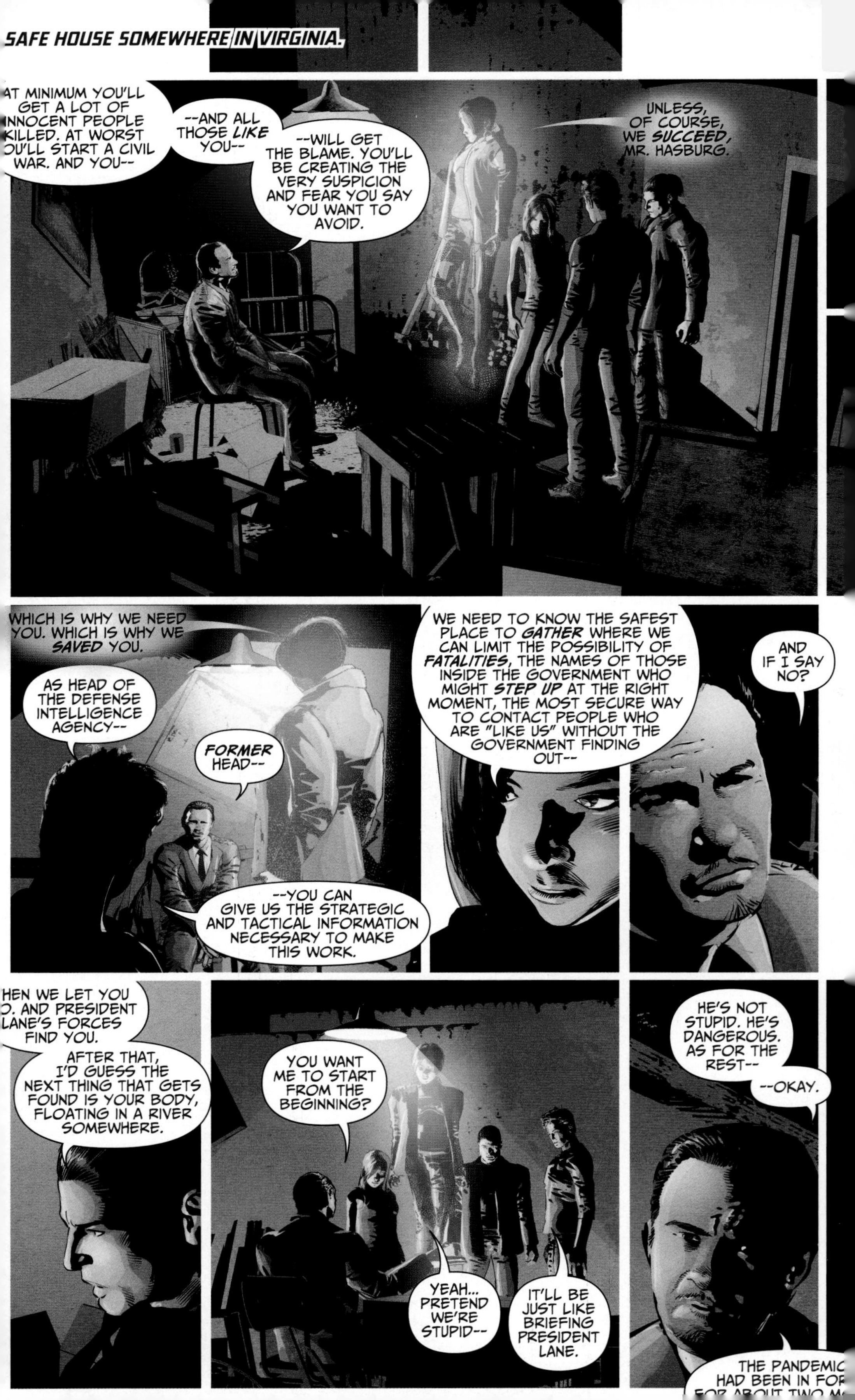
SAFE HOUSE SOMEWHERE IN VIRGINIA.
AT MINIMUM YOU'LL GET A LOT OF INNOCENT PEOPLE KILLED. AT WORST OU'LL START A CIVIL WAR. AND YOU--
--AND ALL THOSE LIKE YOU--
--WILL GET THE BLAME. YOU'LL BE CREATING THE VERY SUSPICION AND FEAR YOU SAY YOU WANT TO AVOID.
UNLESS, OF COURSE, WE SUCCEED, MR. HASBURG.
WHICH IS WHY WE NEED YOU. WHICH IS WHY WE SAVED YOU.
AS HEAD OF THE DEFENSE INTELLIGENCE AGENCY--
FORMER HEAD--
--YOU CAN GIVE US THE STRATEGIC AND TACTICAL INFORMATION NECESSARY TO MAKE THIS WORK.
WE NEED TO KNOW THE SAFEST PLACE TO GATHER WHERE WE CAN LIMIT THE POSSIBILITY OF FATALITIES, THE NAMES OF THOSE INSIDE THE GOVERNMENT WHO MIGHT STEP UP AT THE RIGHT MOMENT, THE MOST SECURE WAY TO CONTACT PEOPLE WHO ARE "LIKE US" WITHOUT THE GOVERNMENT FINDING OUT--
AND IF I SAY NO?
HEN WE LET YOU O. AND PRESIDENT LANE'S FORCES FIND YOU.
AFTER THAT, I'D GUESS THE NEXT THING THAT GETS FOUND IS YOUR BODY, FLOATING IN A RIVER SOMEWHERE.
YOU WANT ME TO START FROM THE BEGINNING?
YEAH... PRETEND WE'RE STUPID--
IT'LL BE JUST LIKE BRIEFING PRESIDENT LANE.
HE'S NOT STUPID. HE'S DANGEROUS. AS FOR THE REST--
--OKAY.
THE PANDEMIC HAD BEEN IN

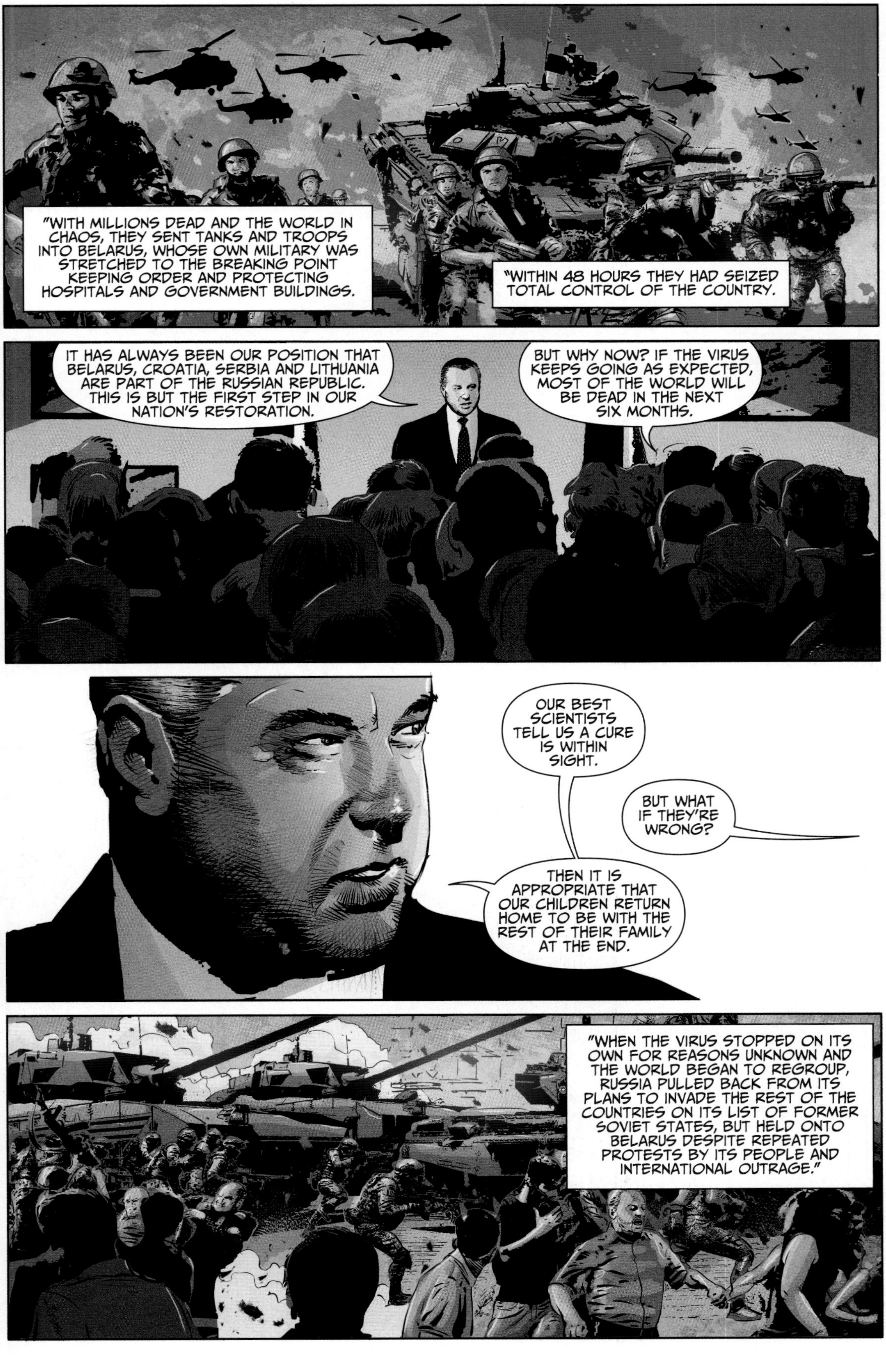
"WITH MILLIONS DEAD AND THE WORLD IN CHAOS, THEY SENT TANKS AND TROOPS INTO BELARUS, WHOSE OWN MILITARY WAS STRETCHED TO THE BREAKING POINT KEEPING ORDER AND PROTECTING HOSPITALS AND GOVERNMENT BUILDINGS.
"WITHIN 48 HOURS THEY HAD SEIZED TOTAL CONTROL OF THE COUNTRY.
IT HAS ALWAYS BEEN OUR POSITION THAT BELARUS, CROATIA, SERBIA AND LITHUANIA ARE PART OF THE RUSSIAN REPUBLIC. THIS IS BUT THE FIRST STEP IN OUR NATION'S RESTORATION.
BUT WHY NOW? IF THE VIRUS KEEPS GOING AS EXPECTED, MOST OF THE WORLD WILL BE DEAD IN THE NEXT SIX MONTHS.
OUR BEST SCIENTISTS TELL US A CURE IS WITHIN SIGHT.
BUT WHAT IF THEY'RE WRONG?
THEN IT IS APPROPRIATE THAT OUR CHILDREN RETURN HOME TO BE WITH THE REST OF THEIR FAMILY AT THE END.
"WHEN THE VIRUS STOPPED ON ITS OWN FOR REASONS UNKNOWN AND THE WORLD BEGAN TO REGROUP, RUSSIA PULLED BACK FROM ITS PLANS TO INVADE THE REST OF THE COUNTRIES ON ITS LIST OF FORMER SOVIET STATES, BUT HELD ONTO BELARUS DESPITE REPEATED PROTESTS BY ITS PEOPLE AND INTERNATIONAL OUTRAGE."

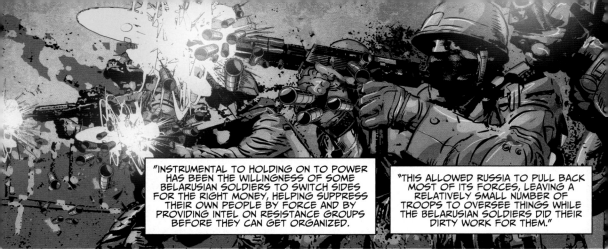

"INSTRUMENTAL TO HOLDING ON TO POWER HAS BEEN THE WILLINGNESS OF SOME BELARUSIAN SOLDIERS TO SWITCH SIDES FOR THE RIGHT MONEY, HELPING SUPPRESS THEIR OWN PEOPLE BY FORCE AND BY PROVIDING INTEL ON RESISTANCE GROUPS BEFORE THEY CAN GET ORGANIZED.

"THIS ALLOWED RUSSIA TO PULL BACK MOST OF ITS FORCES, LEAVING A RELATIVELY SMALL NUMBER OF TROOPS TO OVERSEE THINGS WHILE THE BELARUSIAN SOLDIERS DID THEIR DIRTY WORK FOR THEM."

MOST OF THE RUSSIAN COMMAND AND CONTROL OPERATION IS BASED IN THE BELARUS CAPITAL OF MINSK.

IF YOUR PEOPLE GO IN ON THEIR OWN TO TRY AND OVERTHROW THE OCCUPATION YOU'LL BE SEEN AS WESTERN STOOGES.

IF YOU GET THE PEOPLE TO TAKE PART IN A POPULAR UPRISING, *YOUR* FOLKS MAY SURVIVE BUT EVERYONE *ELSE*, THOSE WITHOUT *POWERS*, WILL BE SLAUGHTERED, TRIGGERING A CIVIL WAR THAT WILL COMPLETELY DESTABILIZE THE REGION.

THERE'S NO VERSION OF THIS IN WHICH YOU COME OUT A WINNER.

NAMES. CONTACTS. HUMAN INTELLIGENCE RESOURCES. COMMUNICATIONS PASSCODES.

LEAVE THE REST TO US.

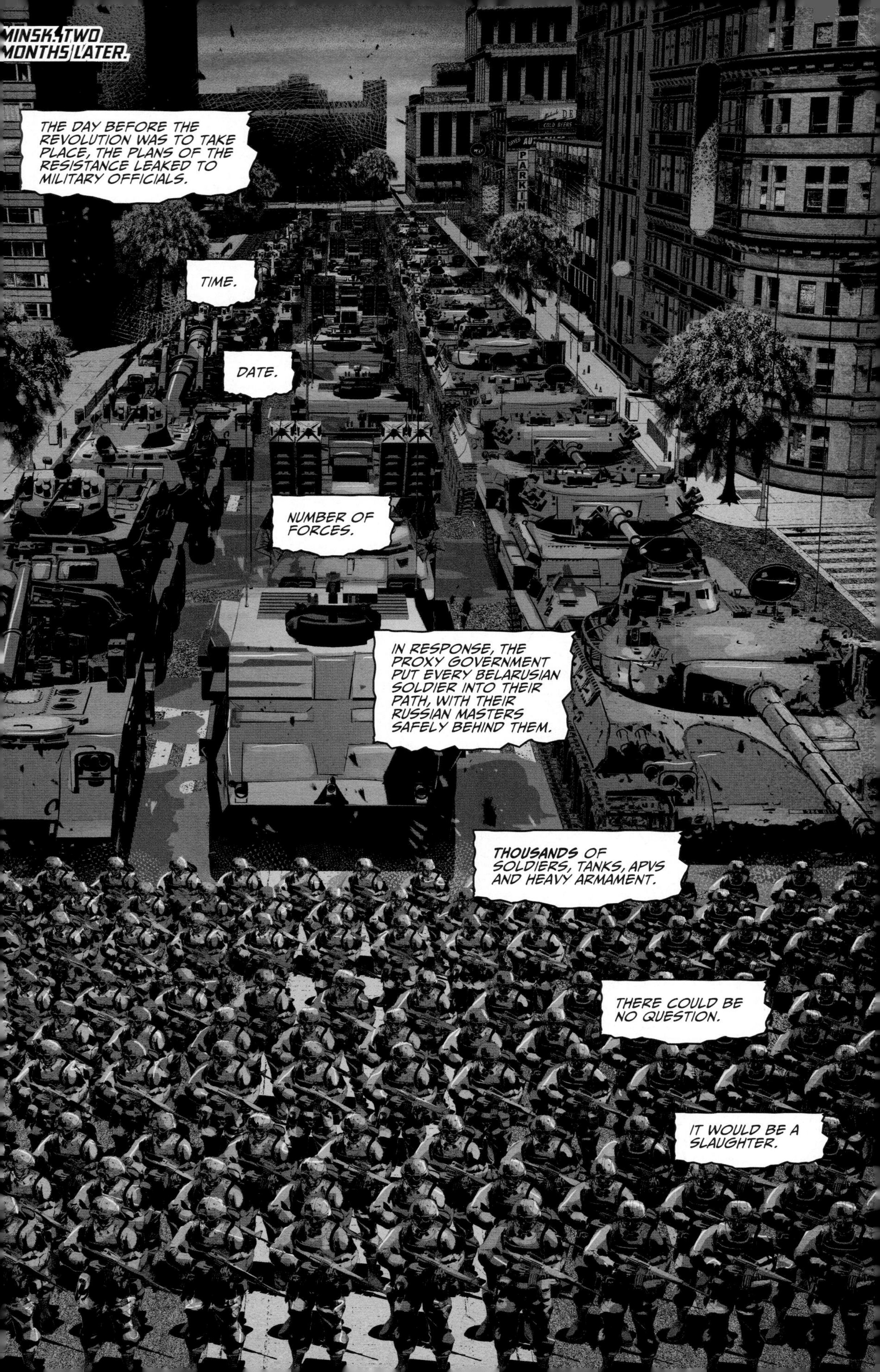
MINSK. TWO MONTHS LATER.
THE DAY BEFORE THE REVOLUTION WAS TO TAKE PLACE, THE PLANS OF THE RESISTANCE LEAKED TO MILITARY OFFICIALS.
TIME.
DATE.
NUMBER OF FORCES.
IN RESPONSE, THE PROXY GOVERNMENT PUT EVERY BELARUSIAN SOLDIER INTO THEIR PATH, WITH THEIR RUSSIAN MASTERS SAFELY BEHIND THEM.
THOUSANDS OF SOLDIERS, TANKS, APVS AND HEAVY ARMAMENT.
THERE COULD BE NO QUESTION.
IT WOULD BE A SLAUGHTER.

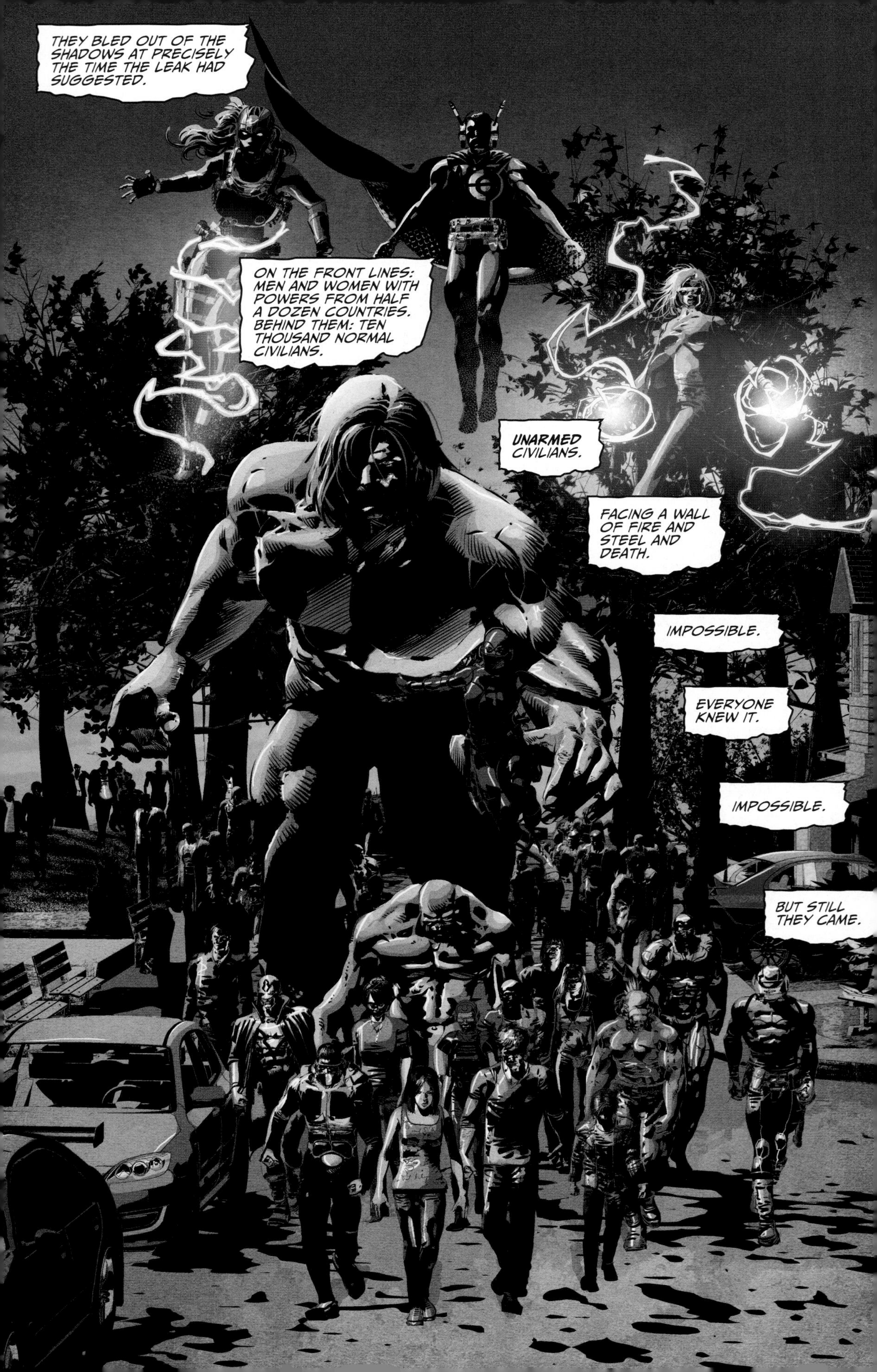
THEY BLED OUT OF THE SHADOWS AT PRECISELY THE TIME THE LEAK HAD SUGGESTED.
ON THE FRONT LINES: MEN AND WOMEN WITH POWERS FROM HALF A DOZEN COUNTRIES. BEHIND THEM: TEN THOUSAND NORMAL CIVILIANS.
UNARMED CIVILIANS.
FACING A WALL OF FIRE AND STEEL AND DEATH.
IMPOSSIBLE.
EVERYONE KNEW IT.
IMPOSSIBLE.
BUT STILL THEY CAME.

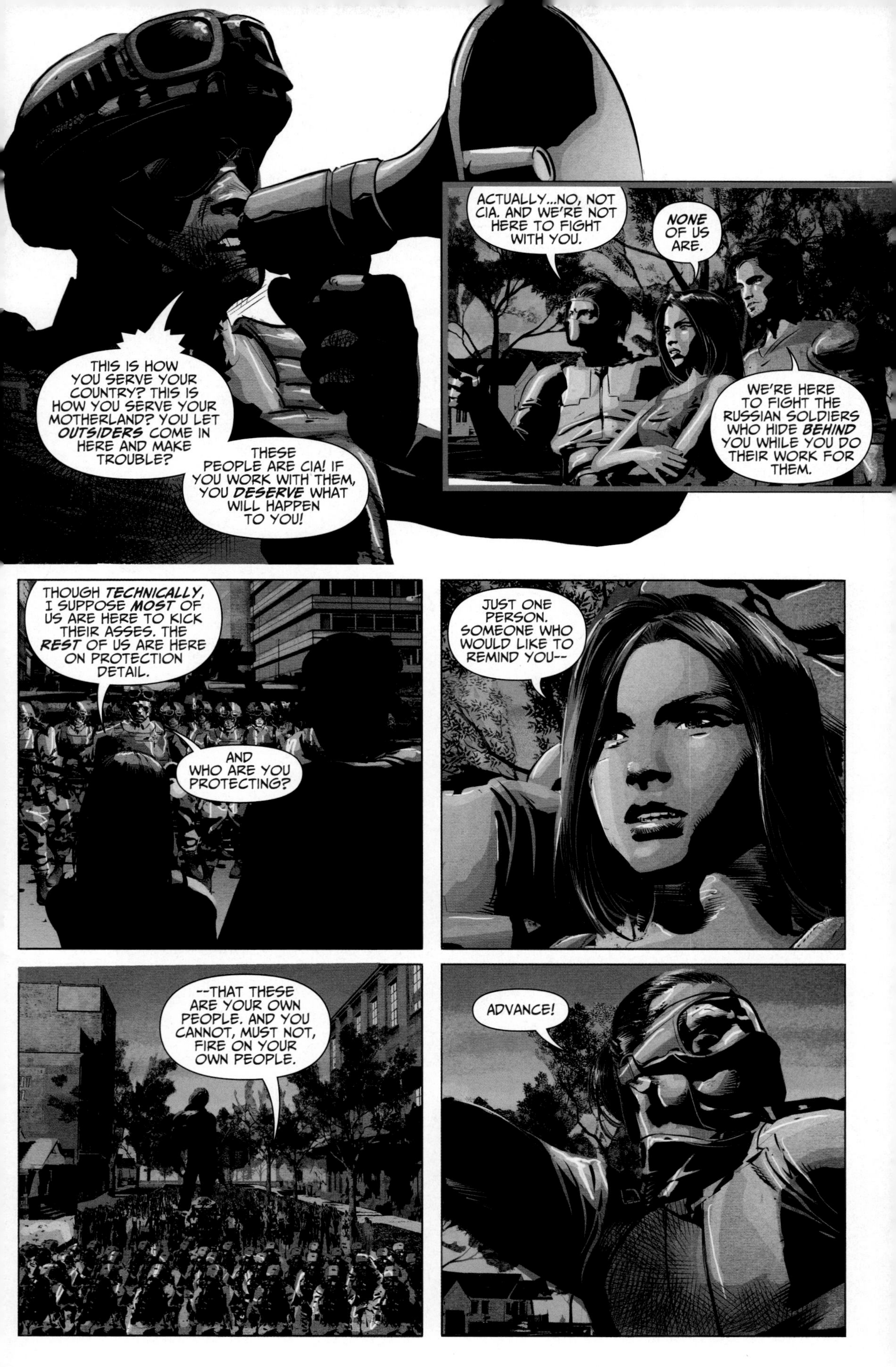
THIS IS HOW YOU SERVE YOUR COUNTRY? THIS IS HOW YOU SERVE YOUR MOTHERLAND? YOU LET OUTSIDERS COME IN HERE AND MAKE TROUBLE?
THESE PEOPLE ARE CIA! IF YOU WORK WITH THEM, YOU DESERVE WHAT WILL HAPPEN TO YOU!
ACTUALLY...NO, NOT CIA. AND WE'RE NOT HERE TO FIGHT WITH YOU.
NONE OF US ARE.
WE'RE HERE TO FIGHT THE RUSSIAN SOLDIERS WHO HIDE BEHIND YOU WHILE YOU DO THEIR WORK FOR THEM.
THOUGH TECHNICALLY, I SUPPOSE MOST OF US ARE HERE TO KICK THEIR ASSES. THE REST OF US ARE HERE ON PROTECTION DETAIL.
AND WHO ARE YOU PROTECTING?
JUST ONE PERSON. SOMEONE WHO WOULD LIKE TO REMIND YOU--
--THAT THESE ARE YOUR OWN PEOPLE. AND YOU CANNOT, MUST NOT, FIRE ON YOUR OWN PEOPLE.
ADVANCE!

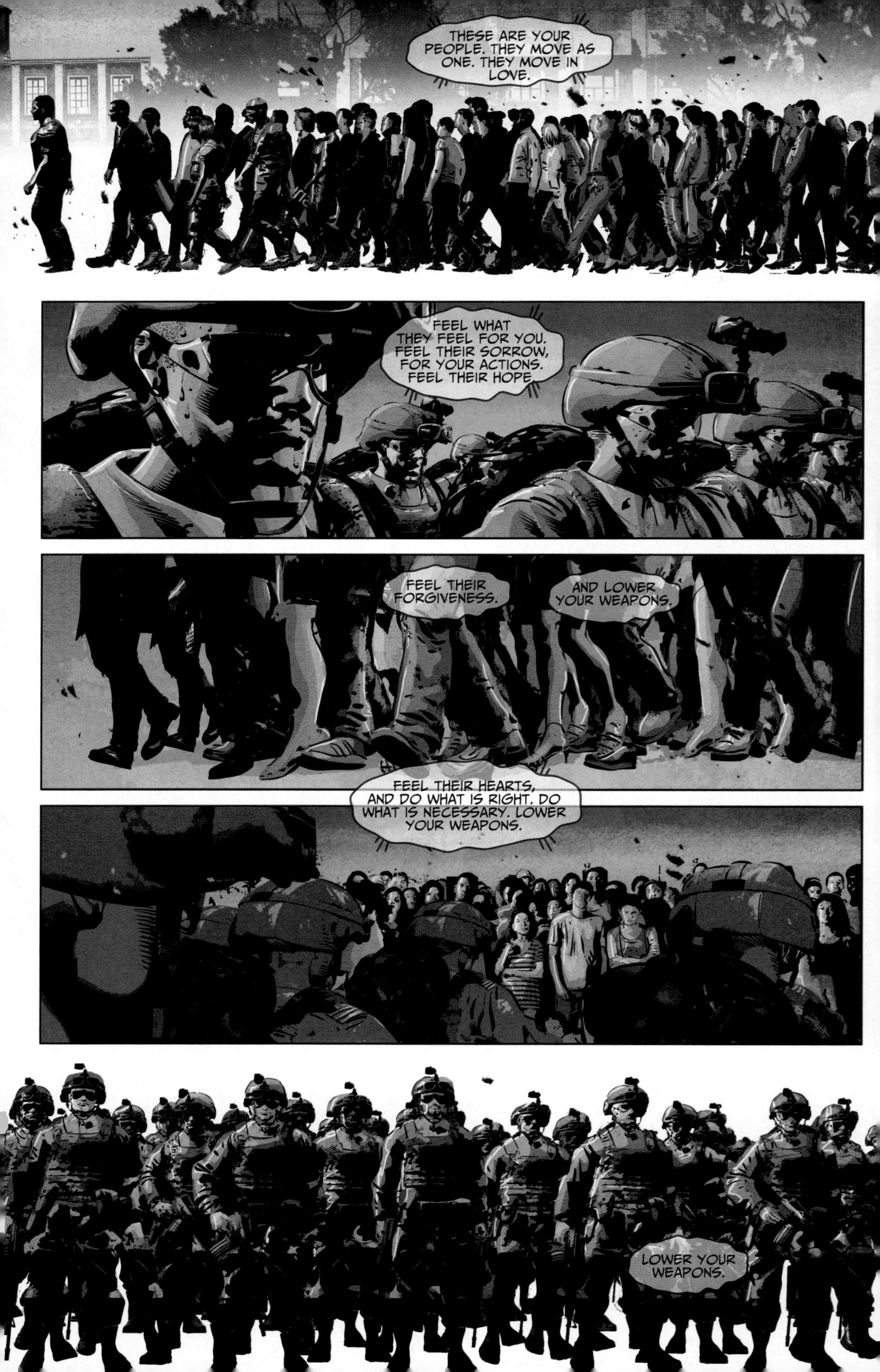
THESE ARE YOUR PEOPLE. THEY MOVE AS ONE. THEY MOVE IN LOVE.
FEEL WHAT THEY FEEL FOR YOU. FEEL THEIR SORROW, FOR YOUR ACTIONS. FEEL THEIR HOPE.
FEEL THEIR FORGIVENESS.
AND LOWER YOUR WEAPONS.
FEEL THEIR HEARTS, AND DO WHAT IS RIGHT. DO WHAT IS NECESSARY. LOWER YOUR WEAPONS.
LOWER YOUR WEAPONS.

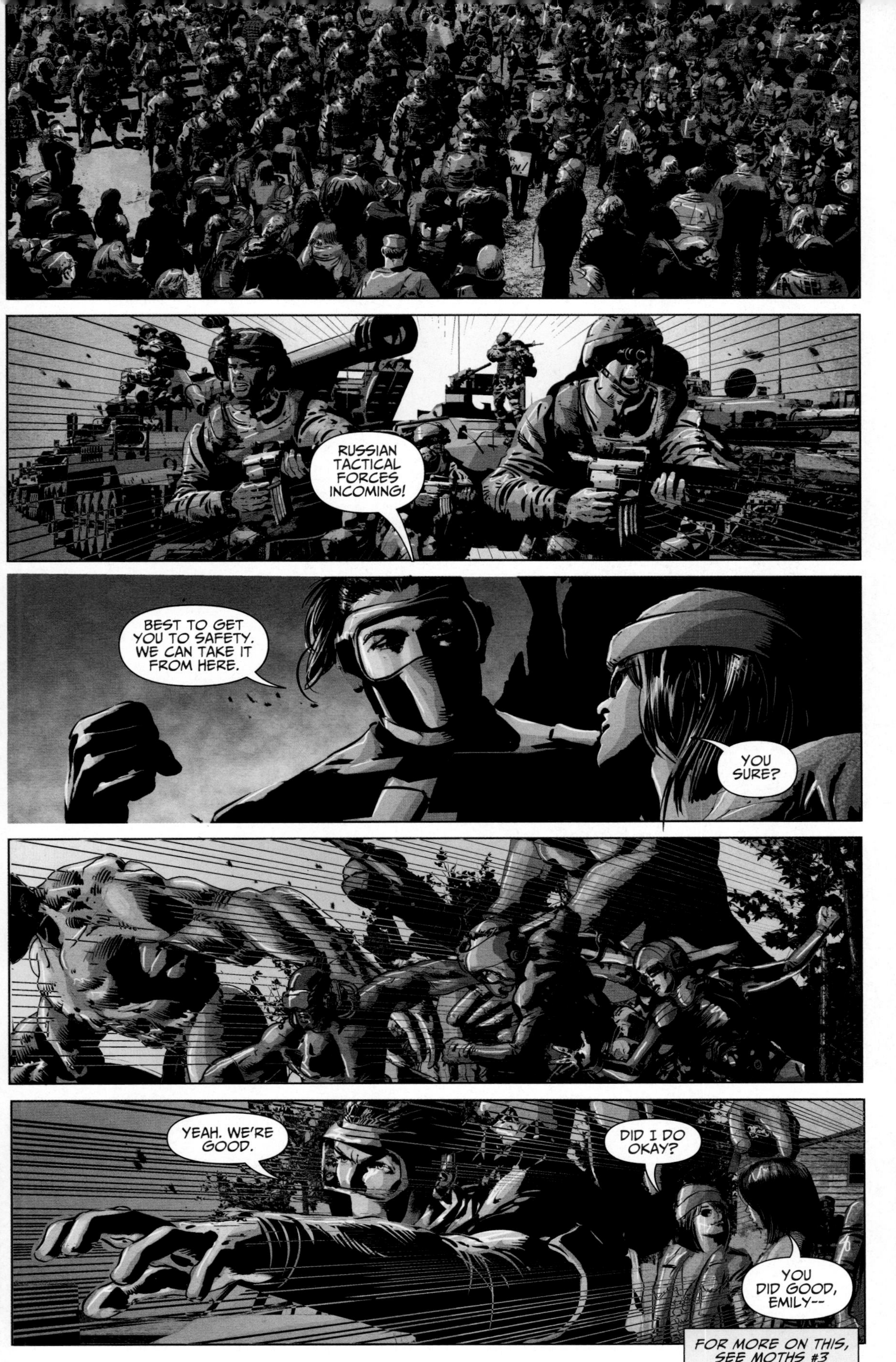
RUSSIAN TACTICAL FORCES INCOMING!
BEST TO GET YOU TO SAFETY. WE CAN TAKE IT FROM HERE.
YOU SURE?
YEAH. WE'RE GOOD.
DID I DO OKAY?
YOU DID GOOD, EMILY--
FOR MORE ON THIS, SEE MOTHS #3

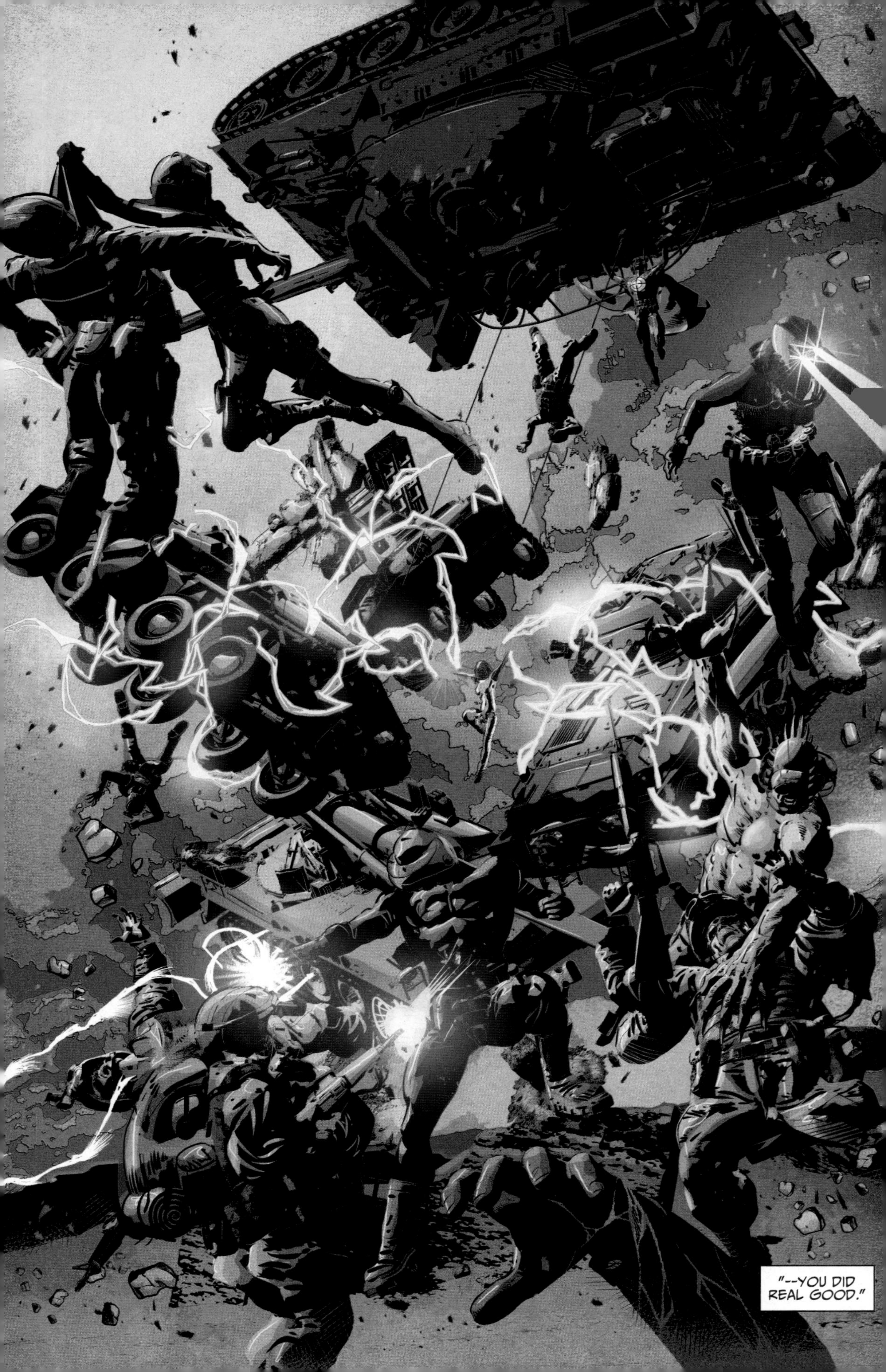
"--YOU DID REAL GOOD."

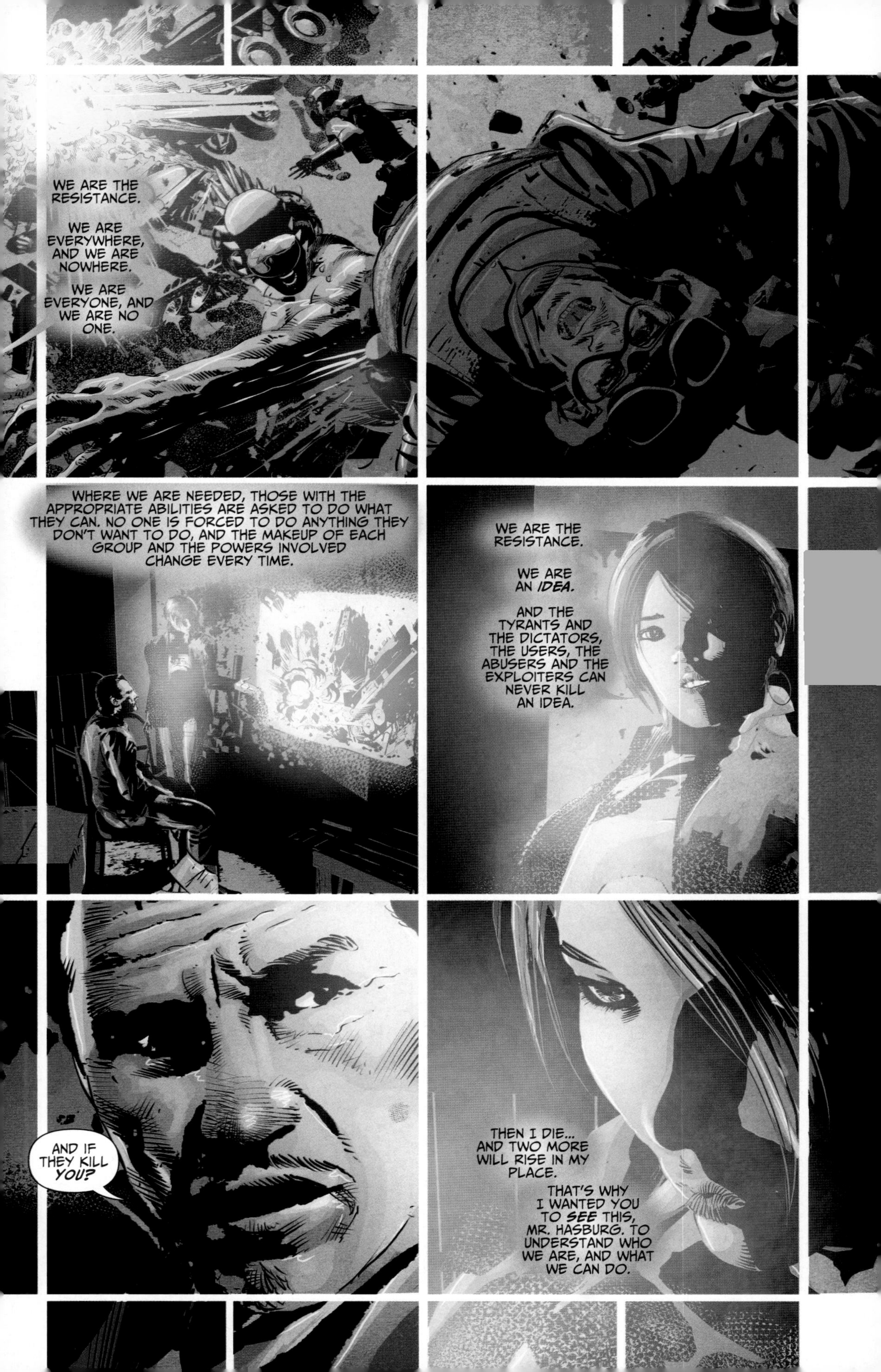
WE ARE THE RESISTANCE.
WE ARE EVERYWHERE, AND WE ARE NOWHERE.
WE ARE EVERYONE, AND WE ARE NO ONE.
WHERE WE ARE NEEDED, THOSE WITH THE APPROPRIATE ABILITIES ARE ASKED TO DO WHAT THEY CAN. NO ONE IS FORCED TO DO ANYTHING THEY DON'T WANT TO DO, AND THE MAKEUP OF EACH GROUP AND THE POWERS INVOLVED CHANGE EVERY TIME.
WE ARE THE RESISTANCE.
WE ARE AN *IDEA.*
AND THE TYRANTS AND THE DICTATORS, THE USERS, THE ABUSERS AND THE EXPLOITERS CAN NEVER KILL AN IDEA.
AND IF THEY KILL *YOU?*
THEN I DIE... AND TWO MORE WILL RISE IN MY PLACE.
THAT'S WHY I WANTED YOU TO ***SEE*** THIS, MR. HASBURG. TO UNDERSTAND WHO WE ARE, AND WHAT WE CAN DO.

BUT WE CAN'T DO WHAT'S *NECESSARY* THROUGH POWER ALONE. THAT WOULD MAKE US NO BETTER THAN THOSE WE OPPOSE.

WE NEED *WISDOM.* WE NEED *PLANNING.* WE NEED *CONNECTIONS.* WE NEED PEOPLE LIKE *YOU.*

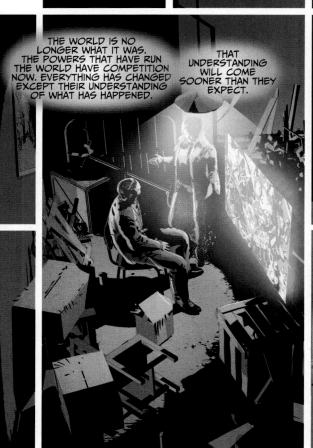

THE WORLD IS NO LONGER WHAT IT WAS. THE POWERS THAT HAVE RUN THE WORLD HAVE COMPETITION NOW. EVERYTHING HAS CHANGED EXCEPT THEIR UNDERSTANDING OF WHAT HAS HAPPENED.

THAT UNDERSTANDING WILL COME SOONER THAN THEY EXPECT.

BECAUSE WHAT WE HAVE DONE IN OTHER PLACES, AND WHAT WE ARE *DOING* IN OTHER PLACES... WE MAY NEED TO DO HERE AS WELL, IF PRESIDENT LANE CONTINUES DOWN THE PATH HE HAS BEGUN.

IN THAT EVENT, WE WILL BE ASKING A GREAT DEAL OF YOU.

I LEFT THE ADMINISTRATION BECAUSE I SAW LANE TRYING TO MOVE THE COUNTRY TOWARD FASCISM. TOTAL CONTROL AND TOTAL POWER. NOBODY ON THE INSIDE HAS THE STOMACH TO CONFRONT HIM. THIS RESISTANCE OF YOURS MAY BE OUR ONLY SHOT AT HOLDING ON TO ANYTHING RESEMBLING DEMOCRACY.

BESIDES, IT'S NOT LIKE I CAN GO BACK TO MY OFFICE OR MY HOUSE OR ANYTHING ELSE UNDER THE CIRCUMSTANCES. I'M A MAN WITHOUT A COUNTRY WITH NO OTHER PLANS, AT LEAST FOR NOW.

SO HOW DO I SIGN UP?

YOU JUST DID, MR. HASBURG. YOU JUST DID.

TO BE CONCLUDED.

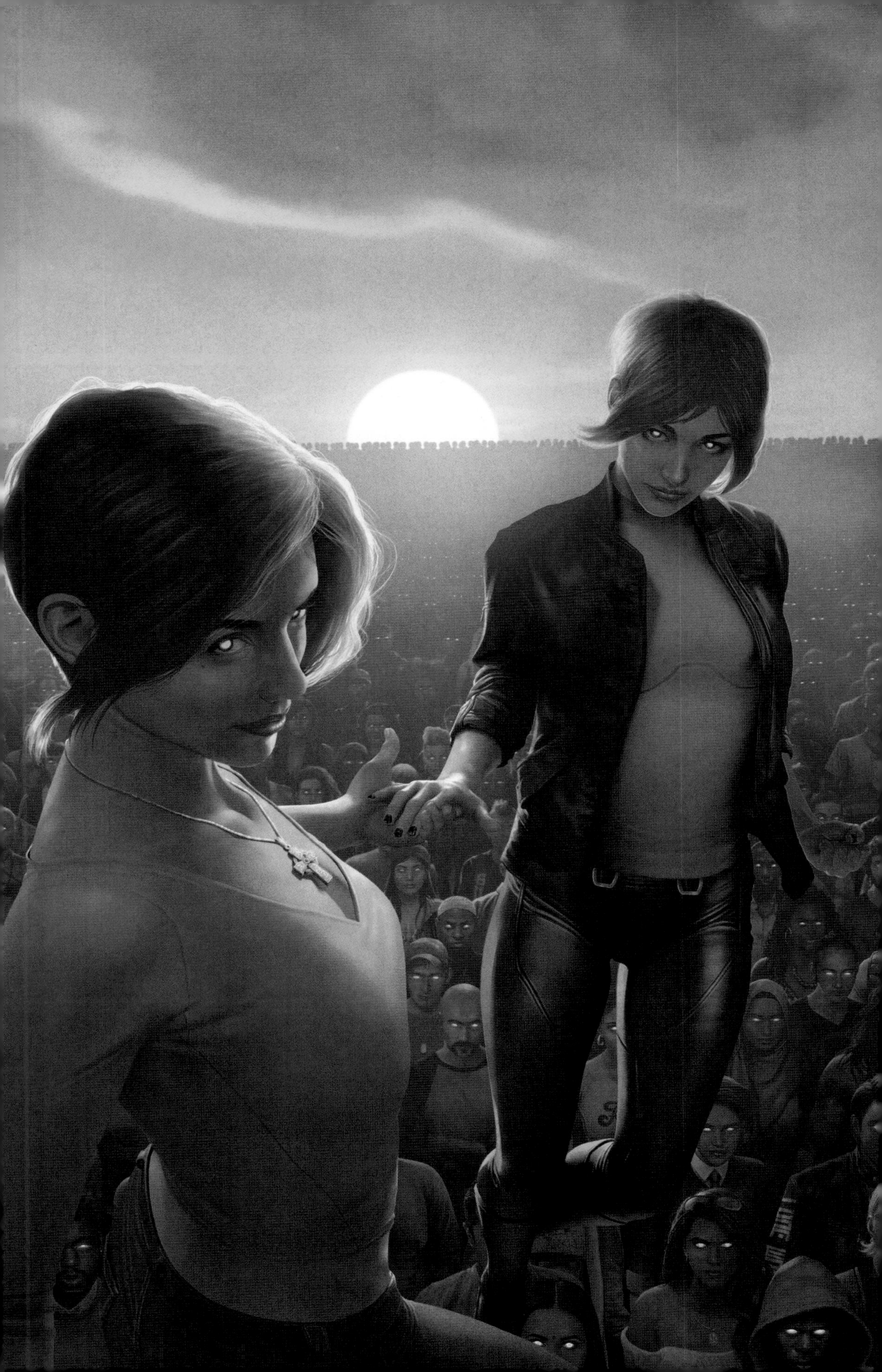

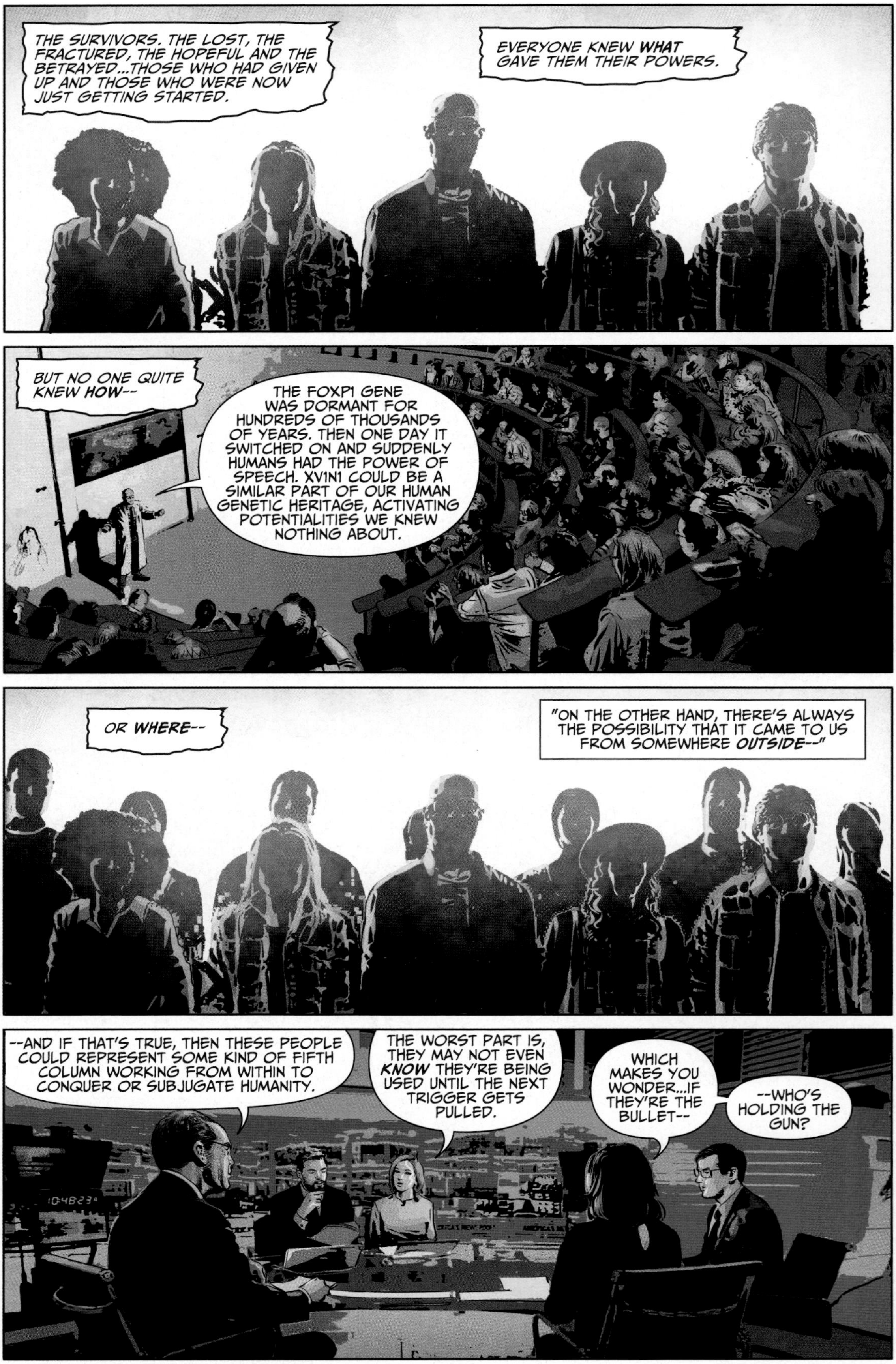
THE SURVIVORS. THE LOST, THE FRACTURED, THE HOPEFUL AND THE BETRAYED...THOSE WHO HAD GIVEN UP AND THOSE WHO WERE NOW JUST GETTING STARTED.
EVERYONE KNEW WHAT GAVE THEM THEIR POWERS.
BUT NO ONE QUITE KNEW HOW--
THE FOXP1 GENE WAS DORMANT FOR HUNDREDS OF THOUSANDS OF YEARS. THEN ONE DAY IT SWITCHED ON AND SUDDENLY HUMANS HAD THE POWER OF SPEECH. XV1N1 COULD BE A SIMILAR PART OF OUR HUMAN GENETIC HERITAGE, ACTIVATING POTENTIALITIES WE KNEW NOTHING ABOUT.
OR WHERE--
"ON THE OTHER HAND, THERE'S ALWAYS THE POSSIBILITY THAT IT CAME TO US FROM SOMEWHERE OUTSIDE--"
--AND IF THAT'S TRUE, THEN THESE PEOPLE COULD REPRESENT SOME KIND OF FIFTH COLUMN WORKING FROM WITHIN TO CONQUER OR SUBJUGATE HUMANITY.
THE WORST PART IS, THEY MAY NOT EVEN KNOW THEY'RE BEING USED UNTIL THE NEXT TRIGGER GETS PULLED.
WHICH MAKES YOU WONDER...IF THEY'RE THE BULLET--
--WHO'S HOLDING THE GUN?

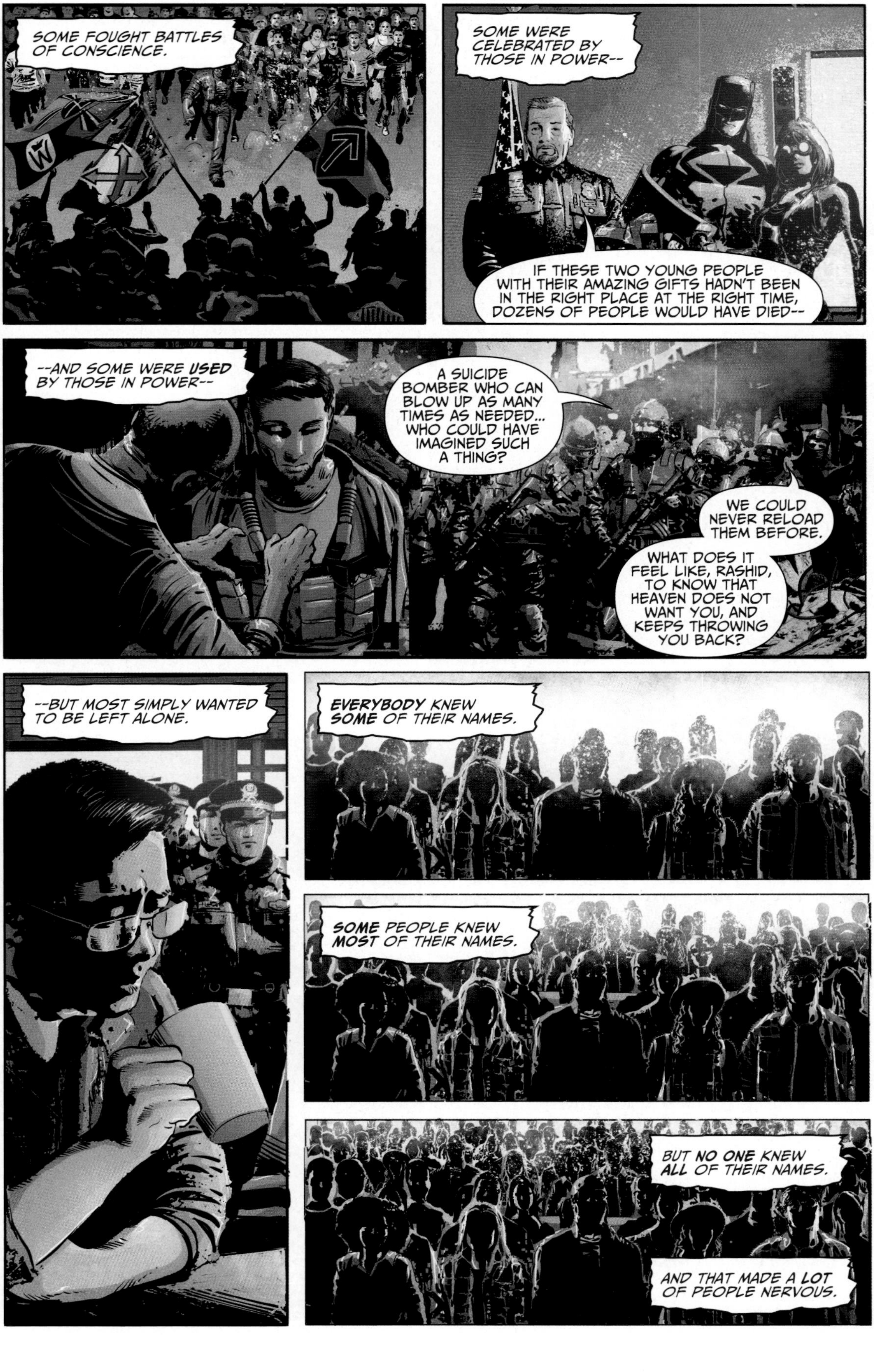
SOME FOUGHT BATTLES OF CONSCIENCE.
SOME WERE CELEBRATED BY THOSE IN POWER--
IF THESE TWO YOUNG PEOPLE WITH THEIR AMAZING GIFTS HADN'T BEEN IN THE RIGHT PLACE AT THE RIGHT TIME, DOZENS OF PEOPLE WOULD HAVE DIED--
--AND SOME WERE USED BY THOSE IN POWER--
A SUICIDE BOMBER WHO CAN BLOW UP AS MANY TIMES AS NEEDED... WHO COULD HAVE IMAGINED SUCH A THING?
WE COULD NEVER RELOAD THEM BEFORE.
WHAT DOES IT FEEL LIKE, RASHID, TO KNOW THAT HEAVEN DOES NOT WANT YOU, AND KEEPS THROWING YOU BACK?
--BUT MOST SIMPLY WANTED TO BE LEFT ALONE.
EVERYBODY KNEW SOME OF THEIR NAMES.
SOME PEOPLE KNEW MOST OF THEIR NAMES.
BUT NO ONE KNEW ALL OF THEIR NAMES.
AND THAT MADE A LOT OF PEOPLE NERVOUS.

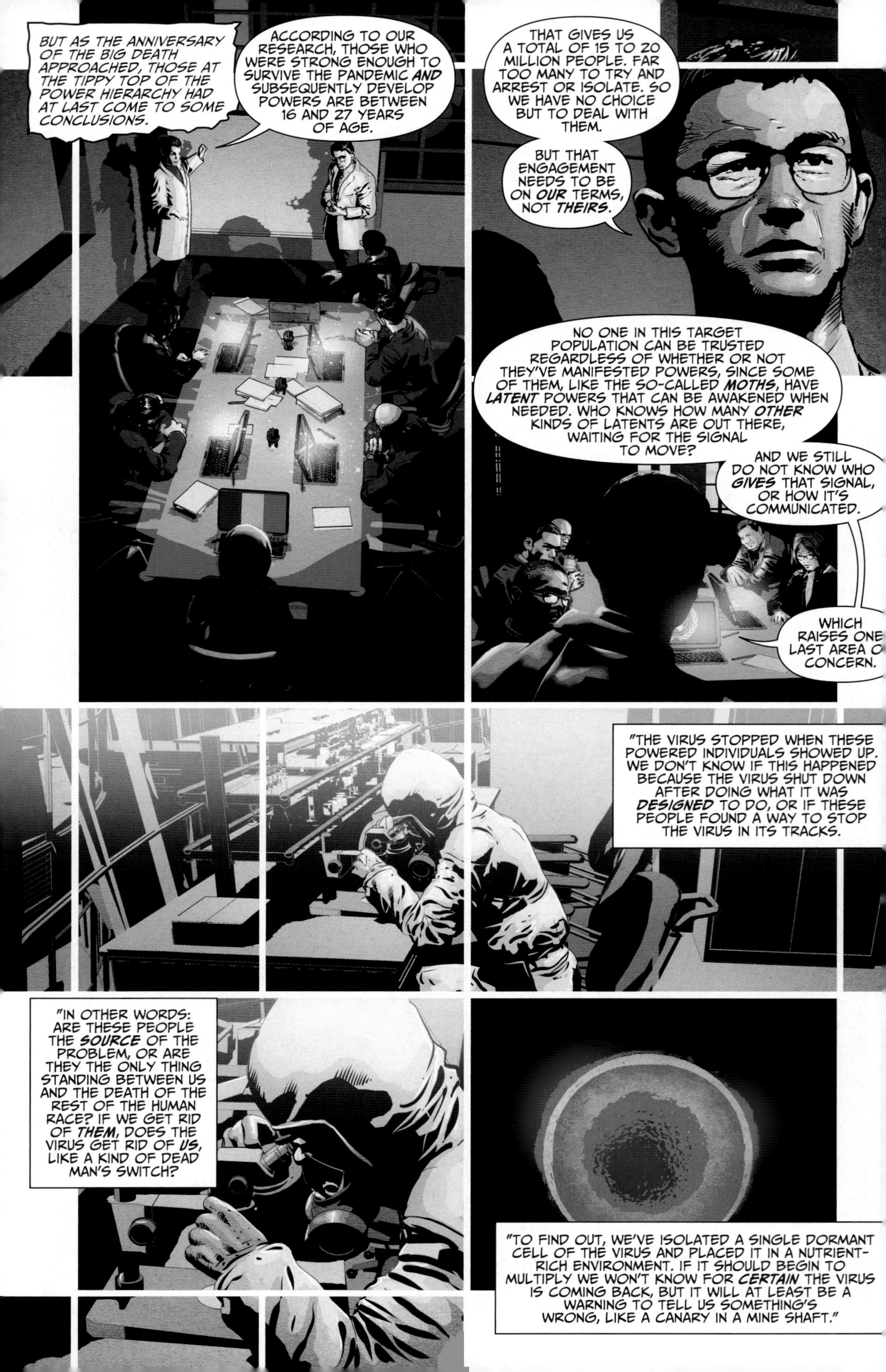
BUT AS THE ANNIVERSARY OF THE BIG DEATH APPROACHED, THOSE AT THE TIPPY TOP OF THE POWER HIERARCHY HAD AT LAST COME TO SOME CONCLUSIONS.
ACCORDING TO OUR RESEARCH, THOSE WHO WERE STRONG ENOUGH TO SURVIVE THE PANDEMIC AND SUBSEQUENTLY DEVELOP POWERS ARE BETWEEN 16 AND 27 YEARS OF AGE.
THAT GIVES US A TOTAL OF 15 TO 20 MILLION PEOPLE. FAR TOO MANY TO TRY AND ARREST OR ISOLATE. SO WE HAVE NO CHOICE BUT TO DEAL WITH THEM.
BUT THAT ENGAGEMENT NEEDS TO BE ON OUR TERMS, NOT THEIRS.
NO ONE IN THIS TARGET POPULATION CAN BE TRUSTED REGARDLESS OF WHETHER OR NOT THEY'VE MANIFESTED POWERS, SINCE SOME OF THEM, LIKE THE SO-CALLED MOTHS, HAVE LATENT POWERS THAT CAN BE AWAKENED WHEN NEEDED. WHO KNOWS HOW MANY OTHER KINDS OF LATENTS ARE OUT THERE, WAITING FOR THE SIGNAL TO MOVE?
AND WE STILL DO NOT KNOW WHO GIVES THAT SIGNAL, OR HOW IT'S COMMUNICATED.
WHICH RAISES ONE LAST AREA O CONCERN.
"THE VIRUS STOPPED WHEN THESE POWERED INDIVIDUALS SHOWED UP. WE DON'T KNOW IF THIS HAPPENED BECAUSE THE VIRUS SHUT DOWN AFTER DOING WHAT IT WAS DESIGNED TO DO, OR IF THESE PEOPLE FOUND A WAY TO STOP THE VIRUS IN ITS TRACKS.
"IN OTHER WORDS: ARE THESE PEOPLE THE SOURCE OF THE PROBLEM, OR ARE THEY THE ONLY THING STANDING BETWEEN US AND THE DEATH OF THE REST OF THE HUMAN RACE? IF WE GET RID OF THEM, DOES THE VIRUS GET RID OF US, LIKE A KIND OF DEAD MAN'S SWITCH?
"TO FIND OUT, WE'VE ISOLATED A SINGLE DORMANT CELL OF THE VIRUS AND PLACED IT IN A NUTRIENT-RICH ENVIRONMENT. IF IT SHOULD BEGIN TO MULTIPLY WE WON'T KNOW FOR CERTAIN THE VIRUS IS COMING BACK, BUT IT WILL AT LEAST BE A WARNING TO TELL US SOMETHING'S WRONG, LIKE A CANARY IN A MINE SHAFT."

THANK YOU FOR YOUR DILIGENCE AND THE DEPTH OF YOUR ANALYSIS. THIS GIVES US MUCH TO CONSIDER.

YOU'RE WELCOME, AMBASSADOR.

ABSOLUTELY. WE COMPARTMENTALIZED THE RESEARCH SO NO ONE HAD A FULL PICTURE EXCEPT FOR US.

NOW THAT OUR DATA HAS BEEN COMPILED, WE'VE WIPED THE DRIVES. YOU HAVE THE ONLY COPIES.

YOU'RE SURE THE ONLY COPIES OF THE REPORT ARE IN OUR HANDS? WE DON'T WANT ANY LEAKS.

VERY GOOD. THANK YOU.

YOU'LL STILL HAVE TO BE DEBRIEFED, OF COURSE--

OF COURSE--

--SO ONCE THAT'S DONE, YOU CAN COLLECT ON THE REST OF YOUR FEES.

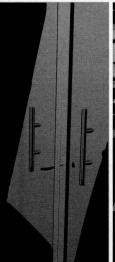

THANK YOU AGAIN FOR YOUR HELP.

HONORED, MADAM AMBASSADOR.

CLICK   PFFT

PFFT

"WE ALL SAW WHAT HAPPENED IN BELARUS."

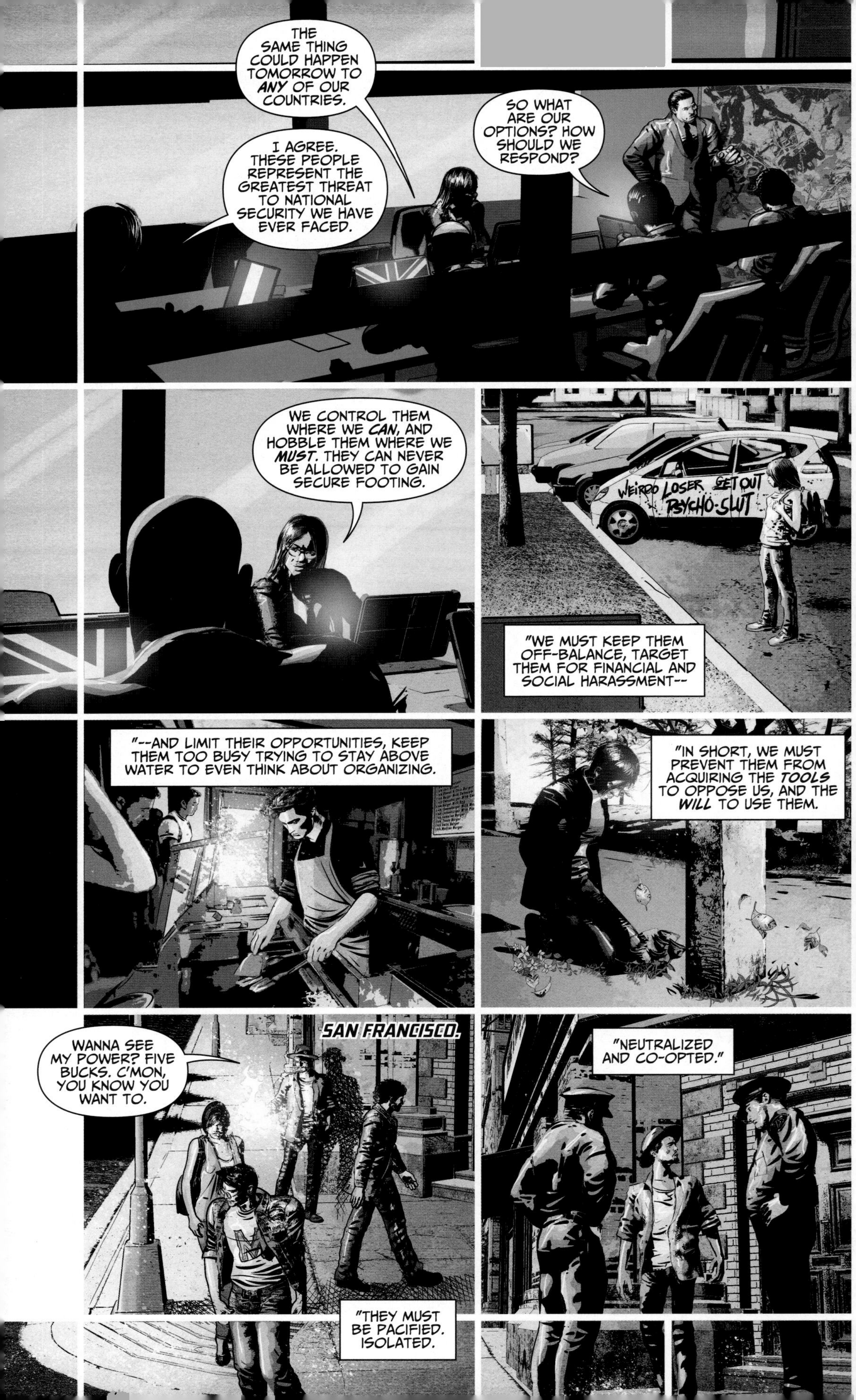
THE SAME THING COULD HAPPEN TOMORROW TO ANY OF OUR COUNTRIES.
I AGREE. THESE PEOPLE REPRESENT THE GREATEST THREAT TO NATIONAL SECURITY WE HAVE EVER FACED.
SO WHAT ARE OUR OPTIONS? HOW SHOULD WE RESPOND?
WE CONTROL THEM WHERE WE CAN, AND HOBBLE THEM WHERE WE MUST. THEY CAN NEVER BE ALLOWED TO GAIN SECURE FOOTING.
WEIRDO LOSER GET OUT
PSYCHO-SLUT
"WE MUST KEEP THEM OFF-BALANCE, TARGET THEM FOR FINANCIAL AND SOCIAL HARASSMENT--
"--AND LIMIT THEIR OPPORTUNITIES, KEEP THEM TOO BUSY TRYING TO STAY ABOVE WATER TO EVEN THINK ABOUT ORGANIZING.
"IN SHORT, WE MUST PREVENT THEM FROM ACQUIRING THE TOOLS TO OPPOSE US, AND THE WILL TO USE THEM.
SAN FRANCISCO.
WANNA SEE MY POWER? FIVE BUCKS. C'MON, YOU KNOW YOU WANT TO.
"THEY MUST BE PACIFIED. ISOLATED.
"NEUTRALIZED AND CO-OPTED."

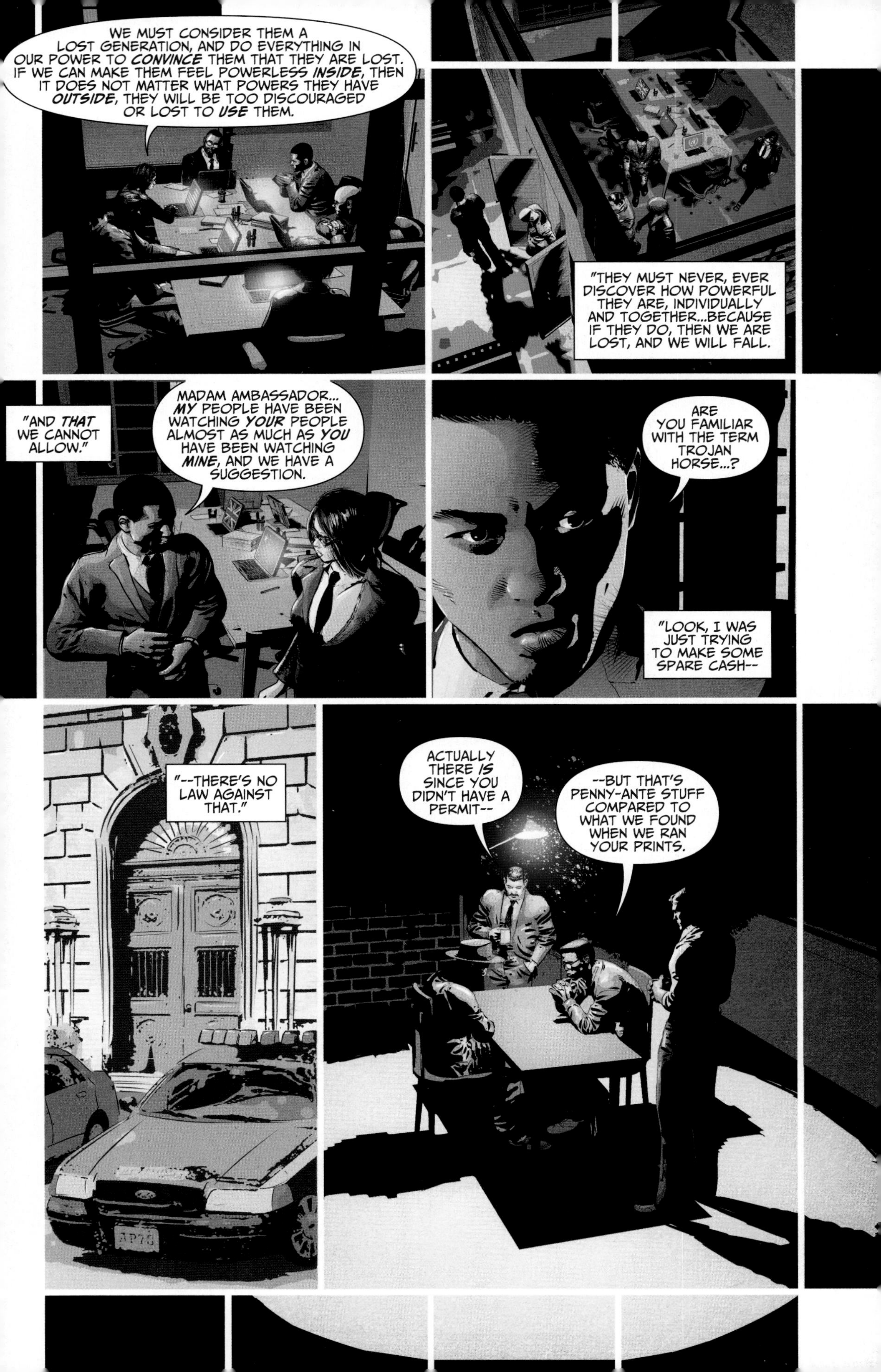
WE MUST CONSIDER THEM A LOST GENERATION, AND DO EVERYTHING IN OUR POWER TO CONVINCE THEM THAT THEY ARE LOST. IF WE CAN MAKE THEM FEEL POWERLESS INSIDE, THEN IT DOES NOT MATTER WHAT POWERS THEY HAVE OUTSIDE, THEY WILL BE TOO DISCOURAGED OR LOST TO USE THEM.
"THEY MUST NEVER, EVER DISCOVER HOW POWERFUL THEY ARE, INDIVIDUALLY AND TOGETHER...BECAUSE IF THEY DO, THEN WE ARE LOST, AND WE WILL FALL.
"AND THAT WE CANNOT ALLOW."
MADAM AMBASSADOR... MY PEOPLE HAVE BEEN WATCHING YOUR PEOPLE ALMOST AS MUCH AS YOU HAVE BEEN WATCHING MINE, AND WE HAVE A SUGGESTION.
ARE YOU FAMILIAR WITH THE TERM TROJAN HORSE...?
"LOOK, I WAS JUST TRYING TO MAKE SOME SPARE CASH--
"--THERE'S NO LAW AGAINST THAT."
ACTUALLY THERE IS SINCE YOU DIDN'T HAVE A PERMIT--
--BUT THAT'S PENNY-ANTE STUFF COMPARED TO WHAT WE FOUND WHEN WE RAN YOUR PRINTS.

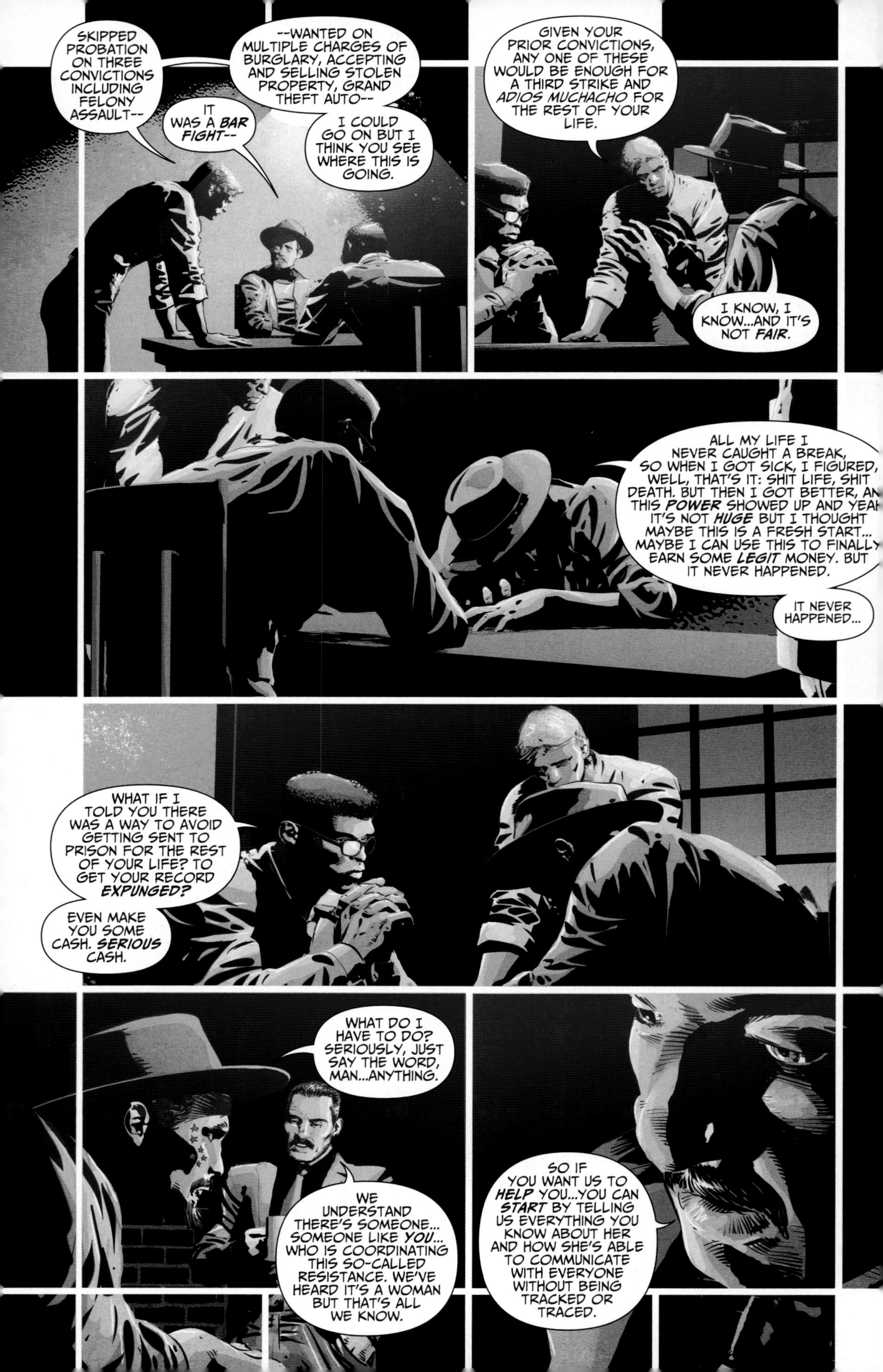
SKIPPED PROBATION ON THREE CONVICTIONS INCLUDING FELONY ASSAULT--
--WANTED ON MULTIPLE CHARGES OF BURGLARY, ACCEPTING AND SELLING STOLEN PROPERTY, GRAND THEFT AUTO--
IT WAS A BAR FIGHT--
I COULD GO ON BUT I THINK YOU SEE WHERE THIS IS GOING.
GIVEN YOUR PRIOR CONVICTIONS, ANY ONE OF THESE WOULD BE ENOUGH FOR A THIRD STRIKE AND ADIOS MUCHACHO FOR THE REST OF YOUR LIFE.
I KNOW, I KNOW...AND IT'S NOT FAIR.
ALL MY LIFE I NEVER CAUGHT A BREAK, SO WHEN I GOT SICK, I FIGURED, WELL, THAT'S IT: SHIT LIFE, SHIT DEATH. BUT THEN I GOT BETTER, AN THIS POWER SHOWED UP AND YEAH IT'S NOT HUGE BUT I THOUGHT MAYBE THIS IS A FRESH START... MAYBE I CAN USE THIS TO FINALLY EARN SOME LEGIT MONEY. BUT IT NEVER HAPPENED.
IT NEVER HAPPENED...
WHAT IF I TOLD YOU THERE WAS A WAY TO AVOID GETTING SENT TO PRISON FOR THE REST OF YOUR LIFE? TO GET YOUR RECORD EXPUNGED?
EVEN MAKE YOU SOME CASH. SERIOUS CASH.
WHAT DO I HAVE TO DO? SERIOUSLY, JUST SAY THE WORD, MAN...ANYTHING.
WE UNDERSTAND THERE'S SOMEONE... SOMEONE LIKE YOU... WHO IS COORDINATING THIS SO-CALLED RESISTANCE. WE'VE HEARD IT'S A WOMAN BUT THAT'S ALL WE KNOW.
SO IF YOU WANT US TO HELP YOU...YOU CAN START BY TELLING US EVERYTHING YOU KNOW ABOUT HER AND HOW SHE'S ABLE TO COMMUNICATE WITH EVERYONE WITHOUT BEING TRACKED OR TRACED.

SAFE HOUSE, SOMEWHERE IN VIRGINIA.
The New York
White House vows more resources in search for Intelligence Director Hasburg
CREEAAAKK
FREEZE!

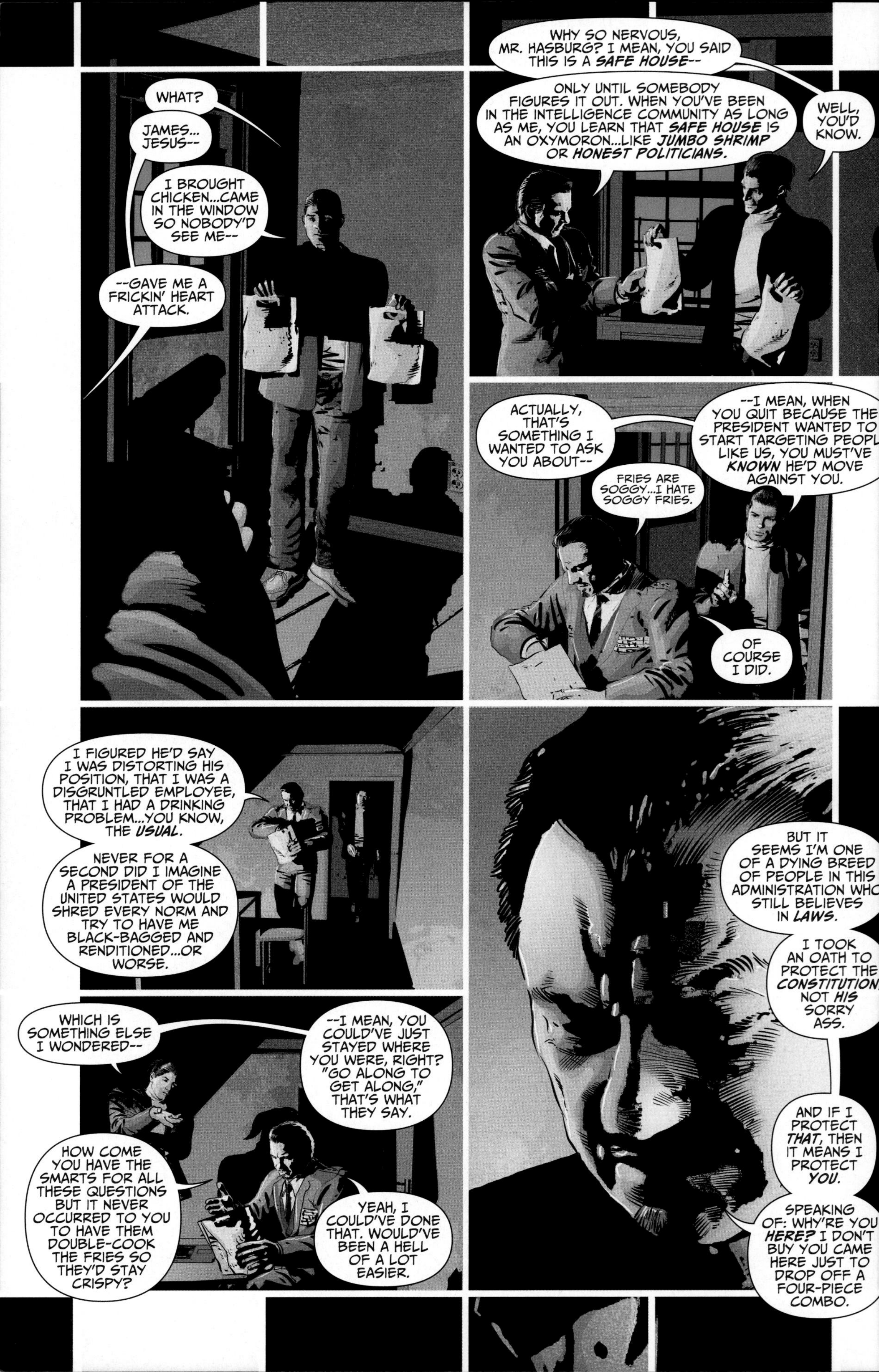
WHAT?
JAMES... JESUS--
I BROUGHT CHICKEN...CAME IN THE WINDOW SO NOBODY'D SEE ME--
--GAVE ME A FRICKIN' HEART ATTACK.
WHY SO NERVOUS, MR. HASBURG? I MEAN, YOU SAID THIS IS A SAFE HOUSE--
ONLY UNTIL SOMEBODY FIGURES IT OUT. WHEN YOU'VE BEEN IN THE INTELLIGENCE COMMUNITY AS LONG AS ME, YOU LEARN THAT SAFE HOUSE IS AN OXYMORON...LIKE JUMBO SHRIMP OR HONEST POLITICIANS.
WELL, YOU'D KNOW.
ACTUALLY, THAT'S SOMETHING I WANTED TO ASK YOU ABOUT--
--I MEAN, WHEN YOU QUIT BECAUSE THE PRESIDENT WANTED TO START TARGETING PEOPL LIKE US, YOU MUST'VE KNOWN HE'D MOVE AGAINST YOU.
FRIES ARE SOGGY...I HATE SOGGY FRIES.
OF COURSE I DID.
I FIGURED HE'D SAY I WAS DISTORTING HIS POSITION, THAT I WAS A DISGRUNTLED EMPLOYEE, THAT I HAD A DRINKING PROBLEM...YOU KNOW, THE USUAL.
NEVER FOR A SECOND DID I IMAGINE A PRESIDENT OF THE UNITED STATES WOULD SHRED EVERY NORM AND TRY TO HAVE ME BLACK-BAGGED AND RENDITIONED...OR WORSE.
WHICH IS SOMETHING ELSE I WONDERED--
--I MEAN, YOU COULD'VE JUST STAYED WHERE YOU WERE, RIGHT? "GO ALONG TO GET ALONG," THAT'S WHAT THEY SAY.
HOW COME YOU HAVE THE SMARTS FOR ALL THESE QUESTIONS BUT IT NEVER OCCURRED TO YOU TO HAVE THEM DOUBLE-COOK THE FRIES SO THEY'D STAY CRISPY?
YEAH, I COULD'VE DONE THAT. WOULD'VE BEEN A HELL OF A LOT EASIER.
BUT IT SEEMS I'M ONE OF A DYING BREED OF PEOPLE IN THIS ADMINISTRATION WHO STILL BELIEVES IN LAWS.
I TOOK AN OATH TO PROTECT THE CONSTITUTION NOT HIS SORRY ASS.
AND IF I PROTECT THAT, THEN IT MEANS I PROTECT YOU.
SPEAKING OF: WHY'RE YOU HERE? I DON'T BUY YOU CAME HERE JUST TO DROP OFF A FOUR-PIECE COMBO.

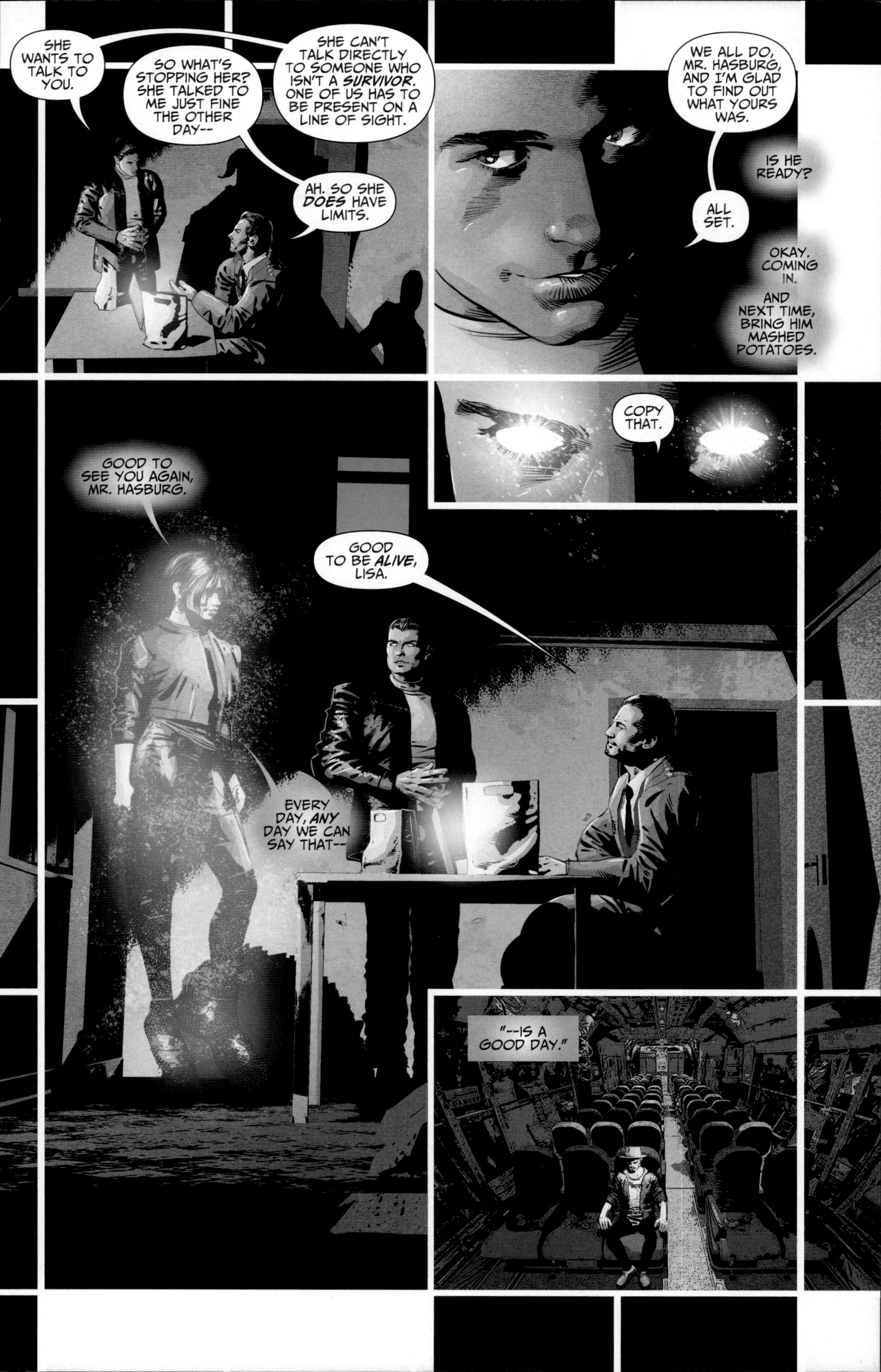
SHE WANTS TO TALK TO YOU.
SO WHAT'S STOPPING HER? SHE TALKED TO ME JUST FINE THE OTHER DAY--
SHE CAN'T TALK DIRECTLY TO SOMEONE WHO ISN'T A SURVIVOR. ONE OF US HAS TO BE PRESENT ON A LINE OF SIGHT.
AH. SO SHE DOES HAVE LIMITS.
WE ALL DO, MR. HASBURG, AND I'M GLAD TO FIND OUT WHAT YOURS WAS.
IS HE READY?
ALL SET.
OKAY. COMING IN.
AND NEXT TIME, BRING HIM MASHED POTATOES.
COPY THAT.
GOOD TO SEE YOU AGAIN, MR. HASBURG.
GOOD TO BE ALIVE, LISA.
EVERY DAY, ANY DAY WE CAN SAY THAT--
"--IS A GOOD DAY."

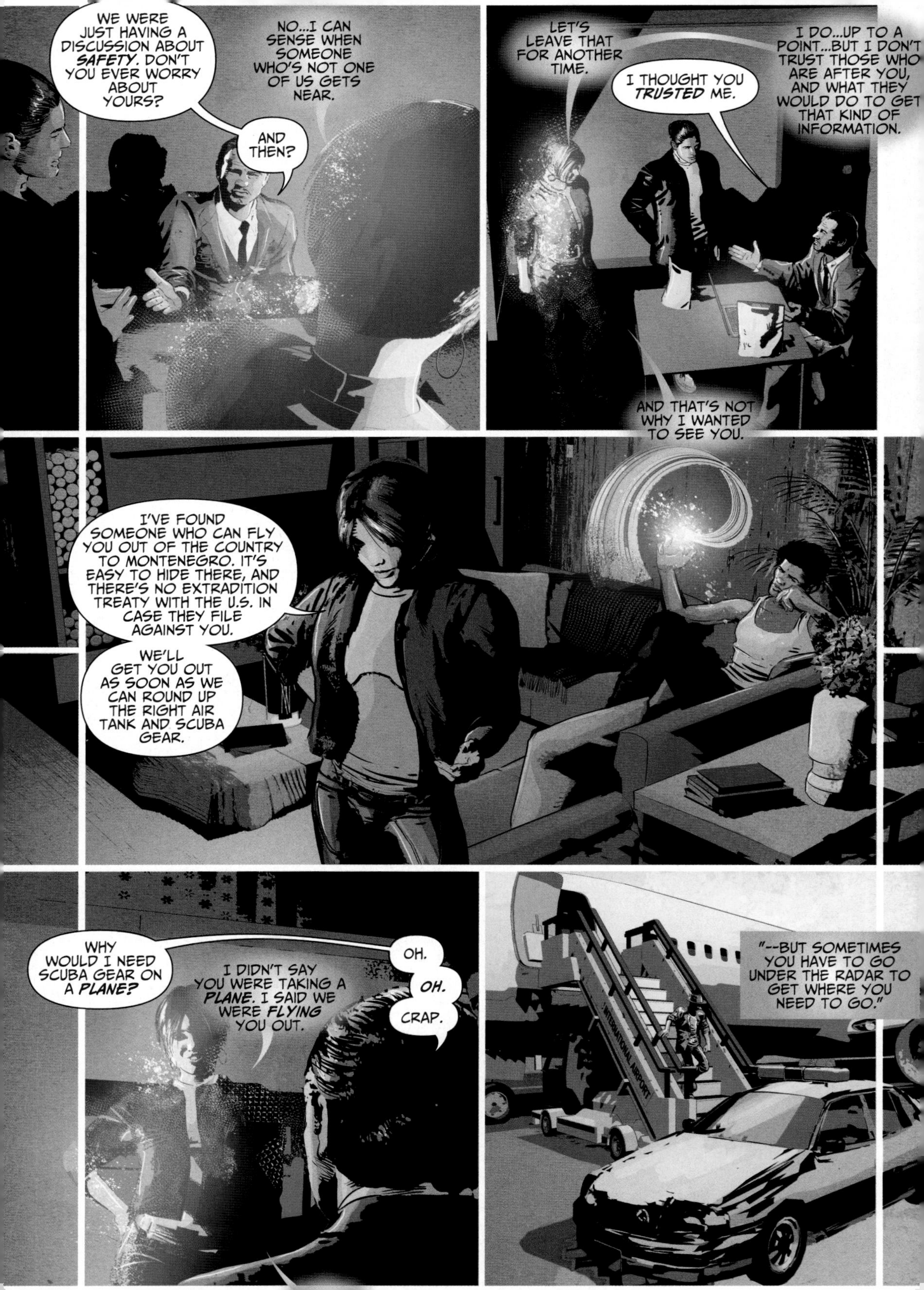
WE WERE JUST HAVING A DISCUSSION ABOUT *SAFETY*. DON'T YOU EVER WORRY ABOUT YOURS?
NO...I CAN SENSE WHEN SOMEONE WHO'S NOT ONE OF US GETS NEAR.
AND THEN?
LET'S LEAVE THAT FOR ANOTHER TIME.
I THOUGHT YOU *TRUSTED* ME.
I DO...UP TO A POINT...BUT I DON'T TRUST THOSE WHO ARE AFTER YOU, AND WHAT THEY WOULD DO TO GET THAT KIND OF INFORMATION.
AND THAT'S NOT WHY I WANTED TO SEE YOU.
I'VE FOUND SOMEONE WHO CAN FLY YOU OUT OF THE COUNTRY TO MONTENEGRO. IT'S EASY TO HIDE THERE, AND THERE'S NO EXTRADITION TREATY WITH THE U.S. IN CASE THEY FILE AGAINST YOU.
WE'LL GET YOU OUT AS SOON AS WE CAN ROUND UP THE RIGHT AIR TANK AND SCUBA GEAR.
WHY WOULD I NEED SCUBA GEAR ON A *PLANE?*
I DIDN'T SAY YOU WERE TAKING A *PLANE*. I SAID WE WERE *FLYING* YOU OUT.
OH.
OH.
CRAP.
INTERNATIONAL AIRPORT
"--BUT SOMETIMES YOU HAVE TO GO UNDER THE RADAR TO GET WHERE YOU NEED TO GO."

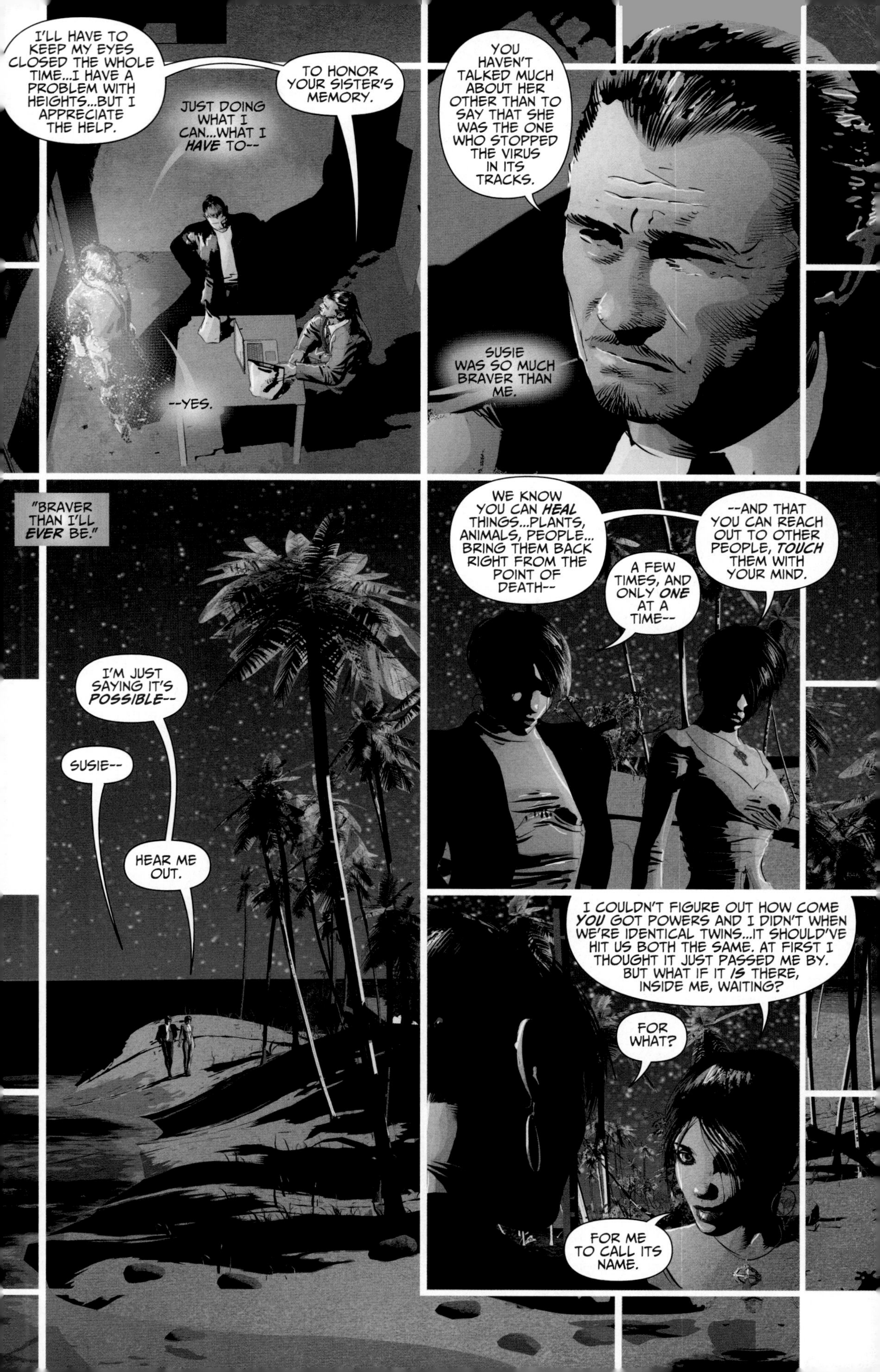
I'LL HAVE TO KEEP MY EYES CLOSED THE WHOLE TIME...I HAVE A PROBLEM WITH HEIGHTS...BUT I APPRECIATE THE HELP.
TO HONOR YOUR SISTER'S MEMORY.
JUST DOING WHAT I CAN...WHAT I *HAVE* TO--
--YES.
YOU HAVEN'T TALKED MUCH ABOUT HER OTHER THAN TO SAY THAT SHE WAS THE ONE WHO STOPPED THE VIRUS IN ITS TRACKS.
SUSIE WAS SO MUCH BRAVER THAN ME.
"BRAVER THAN I'LL *EVER* BE."
I'M JUST SAYING IT'S *POSSIBLE*--
SUSIE--
HEAR ME OUT.
WE KNOW YOU CAN *HEAL* THINGS...PLANTS, ANIMALS, PEOPLE... BRING THEM BACK RIGHT FROM THE POINT OF DEATH--
--AND THAT YOU CAN REACH OUT TO OTHER PEOPLE, *TOUCH* THEM WITH YOUR MIND.
A FEW TIMES, AND ONLY *ONE* AT A TIME--
I COULDN'T FIGURE OUT HOW COME *YOU* GOT POWERS AND I DIDN'T WHEN WE'RE IDENTICAL TWINS...IT SHOULD'VE HIT US BOTH THE SAME. AT FIRST I THOUGHT IT JUST PASSED ME BY. BUT WHAT IF IT *IS* THERE, INSIDE ME, WAITING?
FOR WHAT?
FOR ME TO CALL ITS NAME.

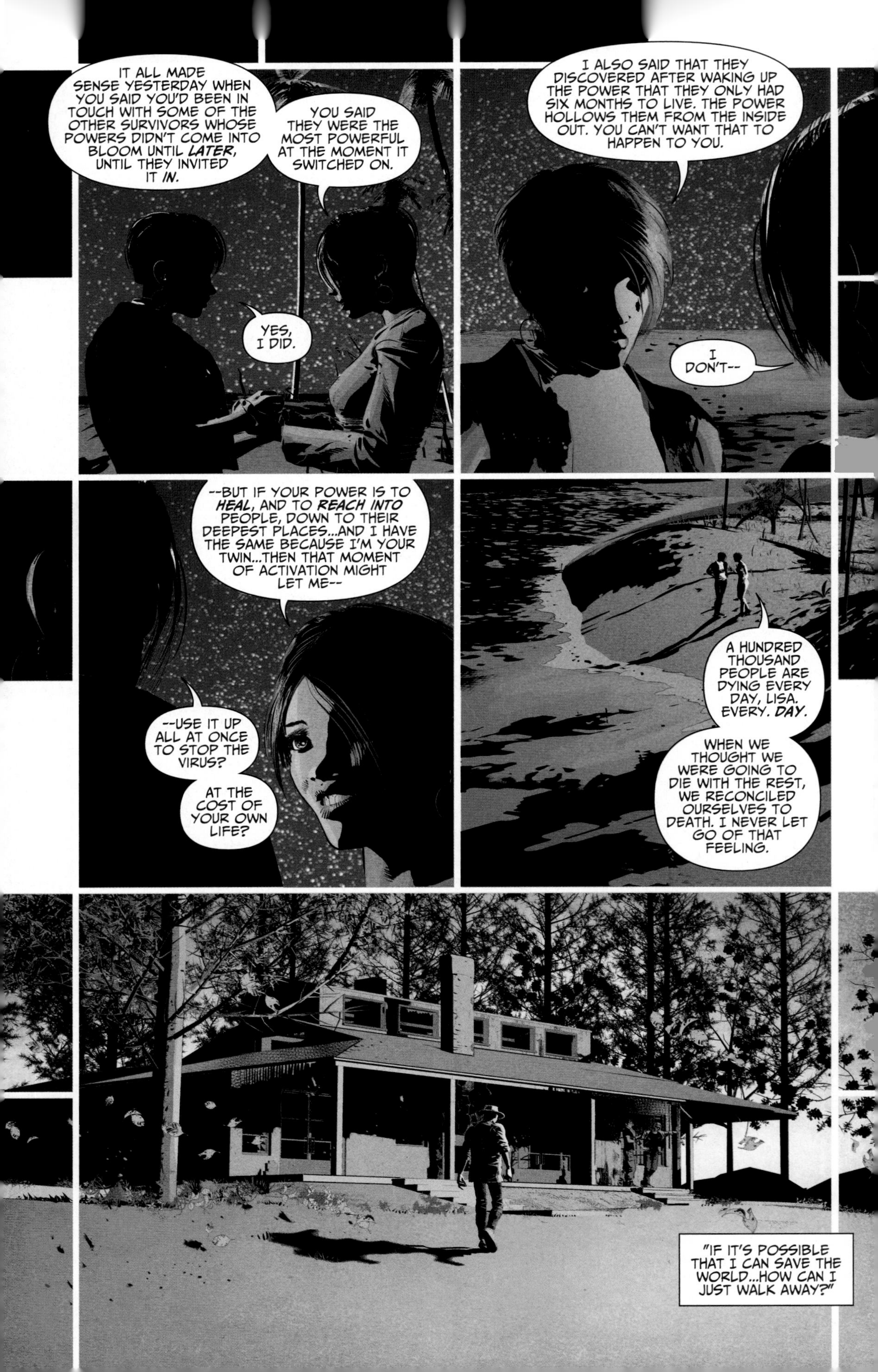
IT ALL MADE SENSE YESTERDAY WHEN YOU SAID YOU'D BEEN IN TOUCH WITH SOME OF THE OTHER SURVIVORS WHOSE POWERS DIDN'T COME INTO BLOOM UNTIL *LATER*, UNTIL THEY INVITED IT *IN*.
YOU SAID THEY WERE THE MOST POWERFUL AT THE MOMENT IT SWITCHED ON.
YES, I DID.
I ALSO SAID THAT THEY DISCOVERED AFTER WAKING UP THE POWER THAT THEY ONLY HAD SIX MONTHS TO LIVE. THE POWER HOLLOWS THEM FROM THE INSIDE OUT. YOU CAN'T WANT THAT TO HAPPEN TO YOU.
I DON'T--
--BUT IF YOUR POWER IS TO *HEAL*, AND TO *REACH INTO* PEOPLE, DOWN TO THEIR DEEPEST PLACES...AND I HAVE THE SAME BECAUSE I'M YOUR TWIN...THEN THAT MOMENT OF ACTIVATION MIGHT LET ME--
--USE IT UP ALL AT ONCE TO STOP THE VIRUS?
AT THE COST OF YOUR OWN LIFE?
A HUNDRED THOUSAND PEOPLE ARE DYING EVERY DAY, LISA. EVERY. *DAY*.
WHEN WE THOUGHT WE WERE GOING TO DIE WITH THE REST, WE RECONCILED OURSELVES TO DEATH. I NEVER LET GO OF THAT FEELING.
"IF IT'S POSSIBLE THAT I CAN SAVE THE WORLD...HOW CAN I JUST WALK AWAY?"

SO WHO'S THAT AND WHAT'S HE DOING HERE?

DUNNO...BUT HE'S ONE OF US, OR SHE'D BE RINGING THE ALARM.

HEY... WHAT'S UP?

JUST LOOKING FOR A PLACE TO CRASH FOR A WHILE...SHE SAID SHE NEEDED FOLKS TO HELP OUT, JUST SCUT WORK--

YEAH, JUST TO BE SURE.

SHOW US WHAT YOU CAN DO.

NO PROB.

PRETTY, HUH? NOW IF YOU *REALLY* WANT TO SEE SOMETHING, WATCH *THIS*.

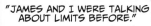

"JAMES AND I WERE TALKING ABOUT LIMITS BEFORE."

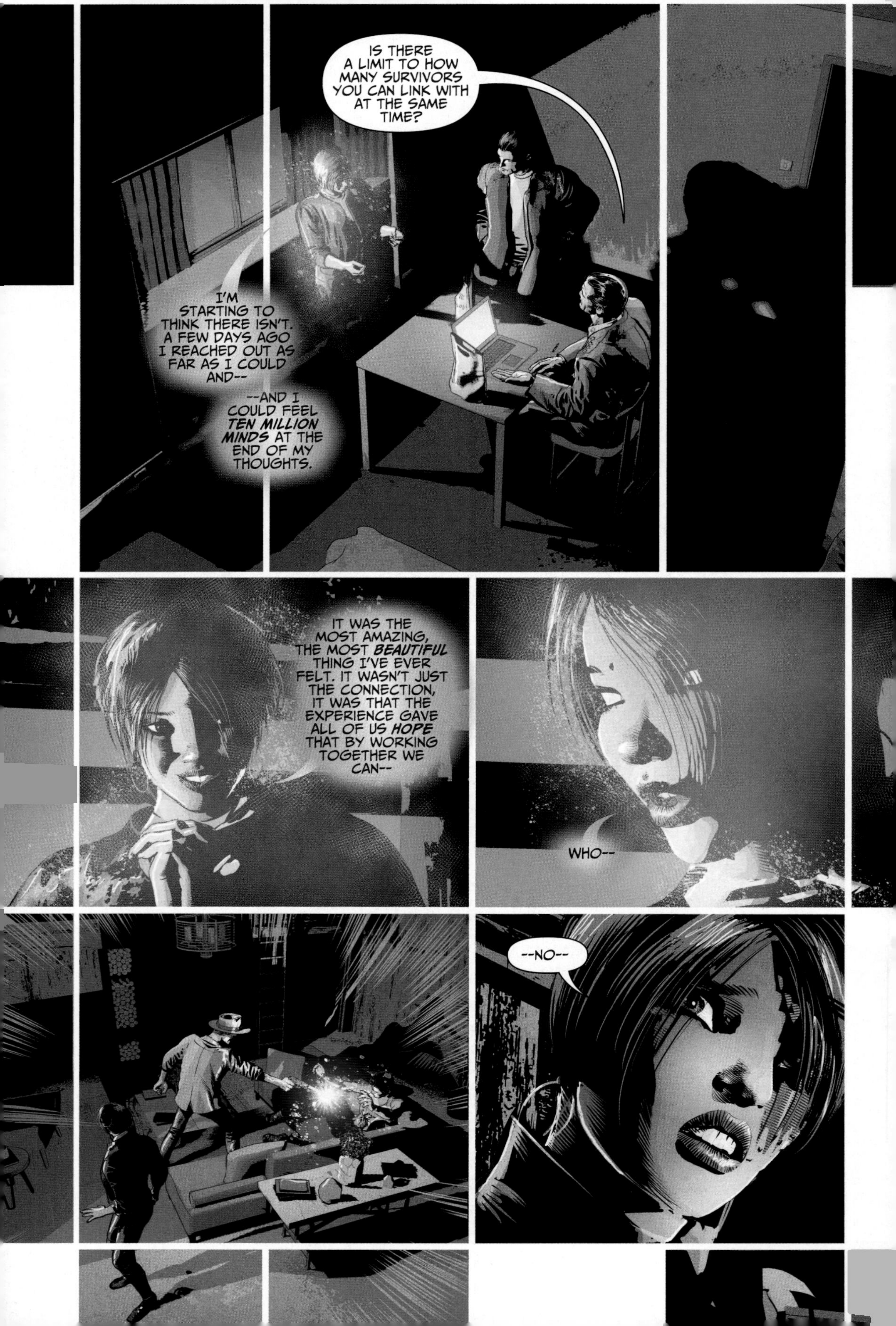
IS THERE A LIMIT TO HOW MANY SURVIVORS YOU CAN LINK WITH AT THE SAME TIME?
I'M STARTING TO THINK THERE ISN'T. A FEW DAYS AGO I REACHED OUT AS FAR AS I COULD AND--
--AND I COULD FEEL TEN MILLION MINDS AT THE END OF MY THOUGHTS.
IT WAS THE MOST AMAZING, THE MOST BEAUTIFUL THING I'VE EVER FELT. IT WASN'T JUST THE CONNECTION, IT WAS THAT THE EXPERIENCE GAVE ALL OF US HOPE THAT BY WORKING TOGETHER WE CAN--
WHO--
--NO--

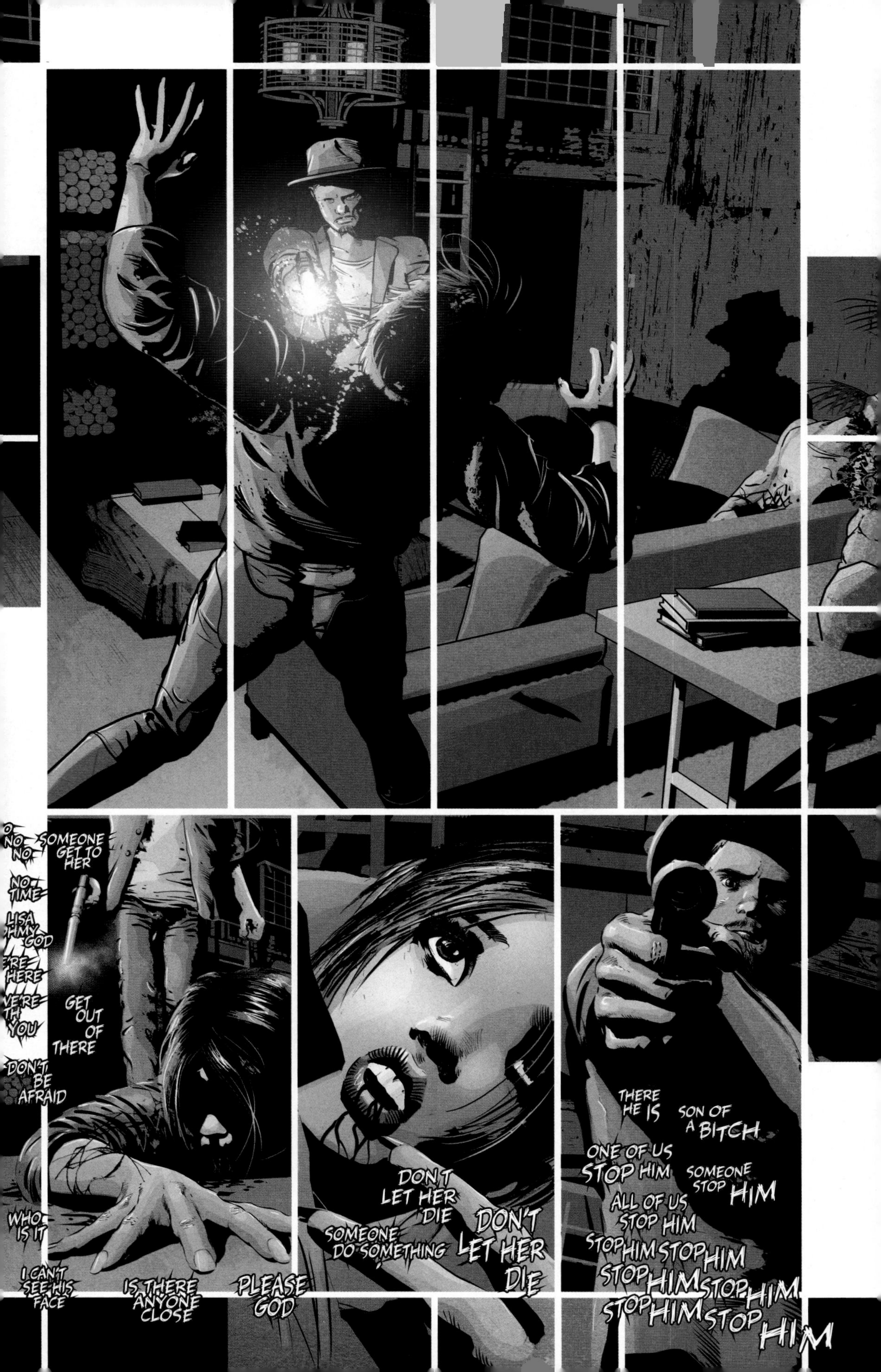
NO NO
SOMEONE GET TO HER
NO TIME
LISA OHMY GOD
'RE HERE
VE'RE TH YOU
GET OUT OF THERE
DON'T BE AFRAID
WHO IS IT
I CAN'T SEE HIS FACE
IS THERE ANYONE CLOSE
PLEASE GOD
DON'T LET HER DIE
SOMEONE DO SOMETHING
DON'T LET HER DIE
THERE HE IS
SON OF A BITCH
ONE OF US STOP HIM
SOMEONE STOP HIM
ALL OF US STOP HIM
STOP HIM STOP HIM
STOP HIM STOP HIM
STOP HIM STOP HIM

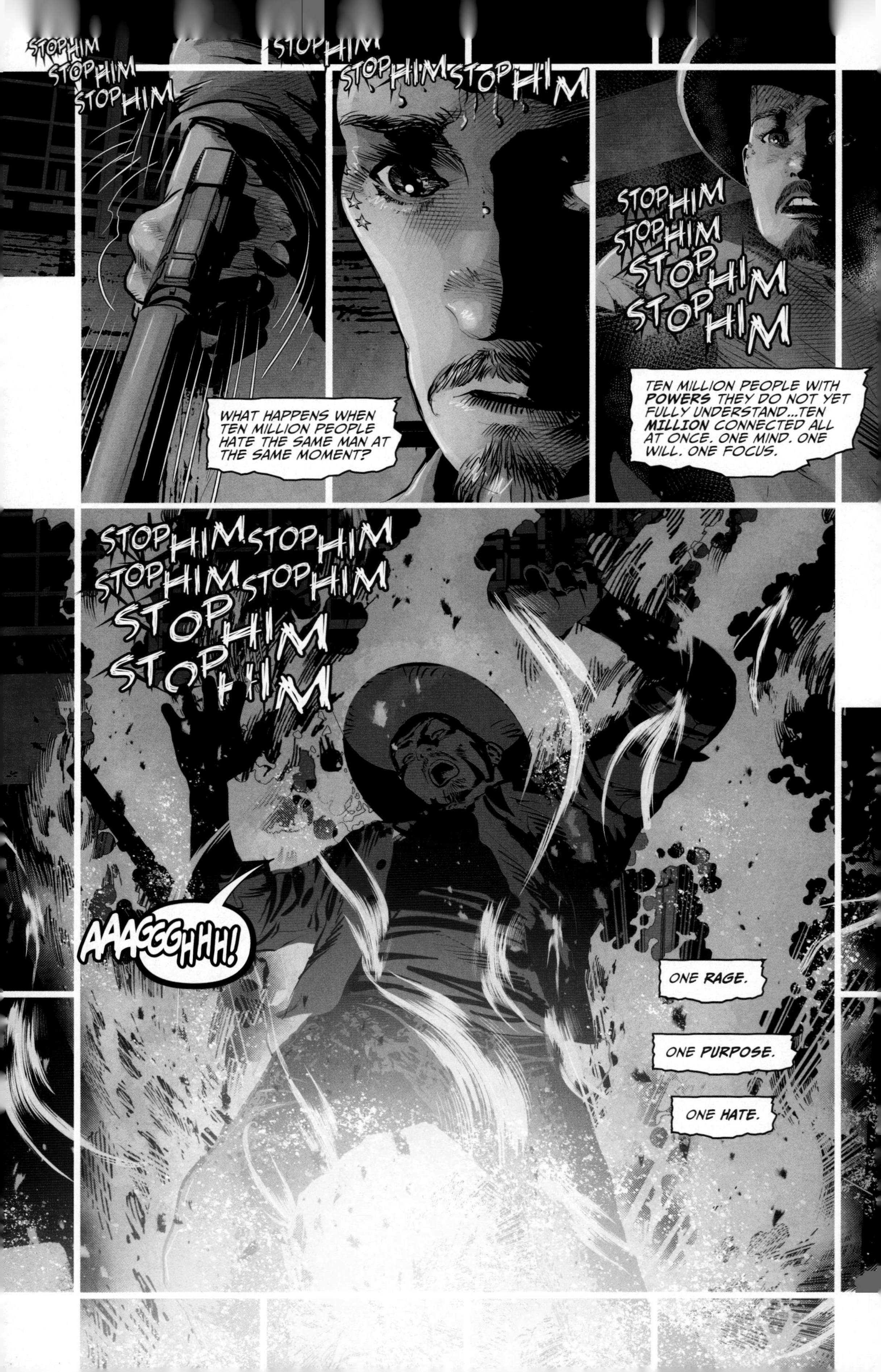
STOP HIM STOP HIM STOP HIM
STOP HIM
STOP HIM STOP HIM
WHAT HAPPENS WHEN TEN MILLION PEOPLE HATE THE SAME MAN AT THE SAME MOMENT?
STOP HIM STOP HIM STOP HIM STOP HIM
TEN MILLION PEOPLE WITH POWERS THEY DO NOT YET FULLY UNDERSTAND...TEN MILLION CONNECTED ALL AT ONCE. ONE MIND. ONE WILL. ONE FOCUS.
STOP HIM STOP HIM STOP HIM STOP HIM STOP HIM STOP HIM
AAAGGGHHH!
ONE RAGE.
ONE PURPOSE.
ONE HATE.

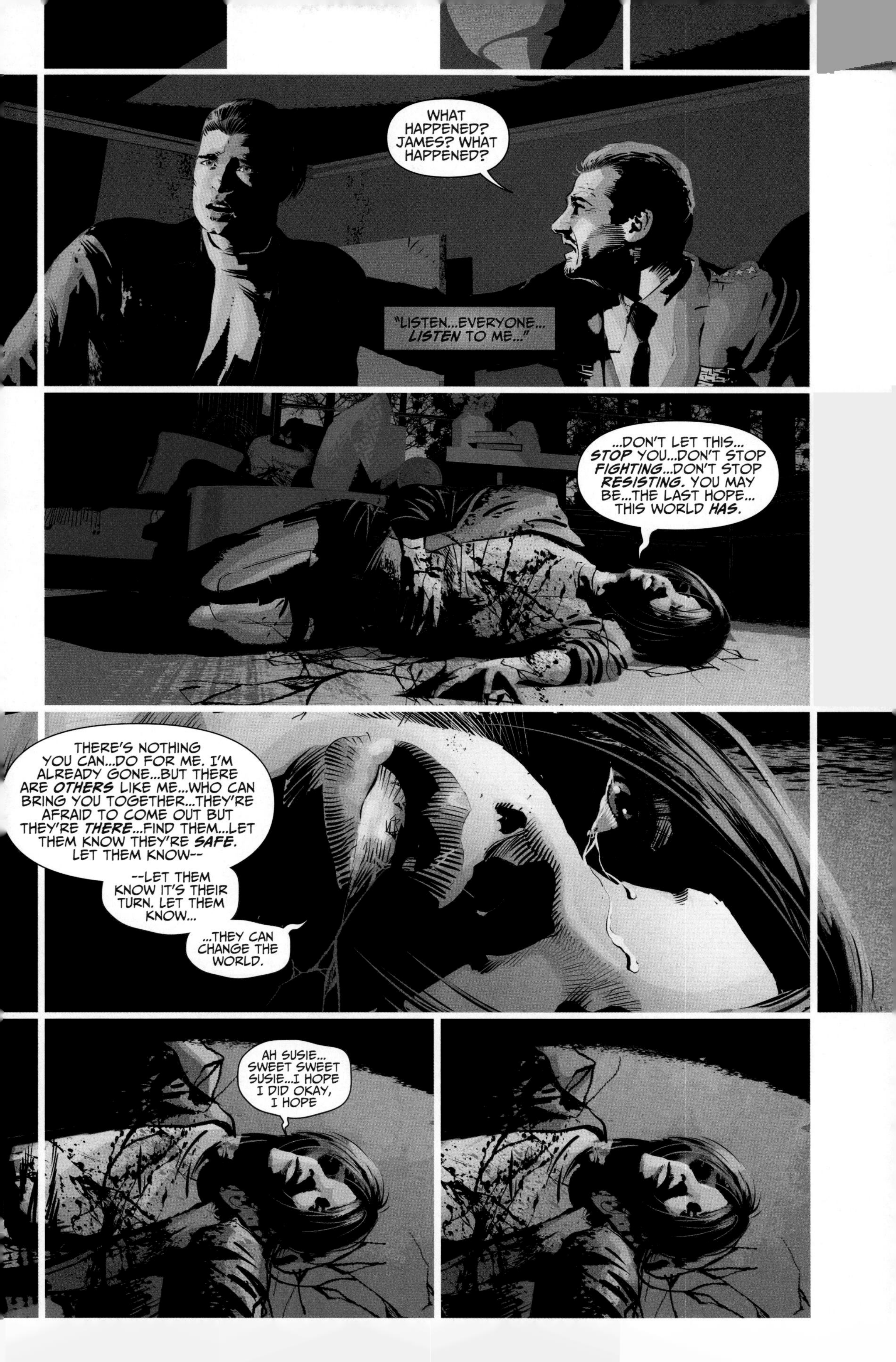
WHAT HAPPENED? JAMES? WHAT HAPPENED?
"LISTEN...EVERYONE... LISTEN TO ME..."
...DON'T LET THIS... STOP YOU...DON'T STOP FIGHTING...DON'T STOP RESISTING. YOU MAY BE...THE LAST HOPE... THIS WORLD HAS.
THERE'S NOTHING YOU CAN...DO FOR ME. I'M ALREADY GONE...BUT THERE ARE OTHERS LIKE ME...WHO CAN BRING YOU TOGETHER...THEY'RE AFRAID TO COME OUT BUT THEY'RE THERE...FIND THEM...LET THEM KNOW THEY'RE SAFE. LET THEM KNOW--
--LET THEM KNOW IT'S THEIR TURN. LET THEM KNOW...
...THEY CAN CHANGE THE WORLD.
AH SUSIE... SWEET SWEET SUSIE...I HOPE I DID OKAY, I HOPE

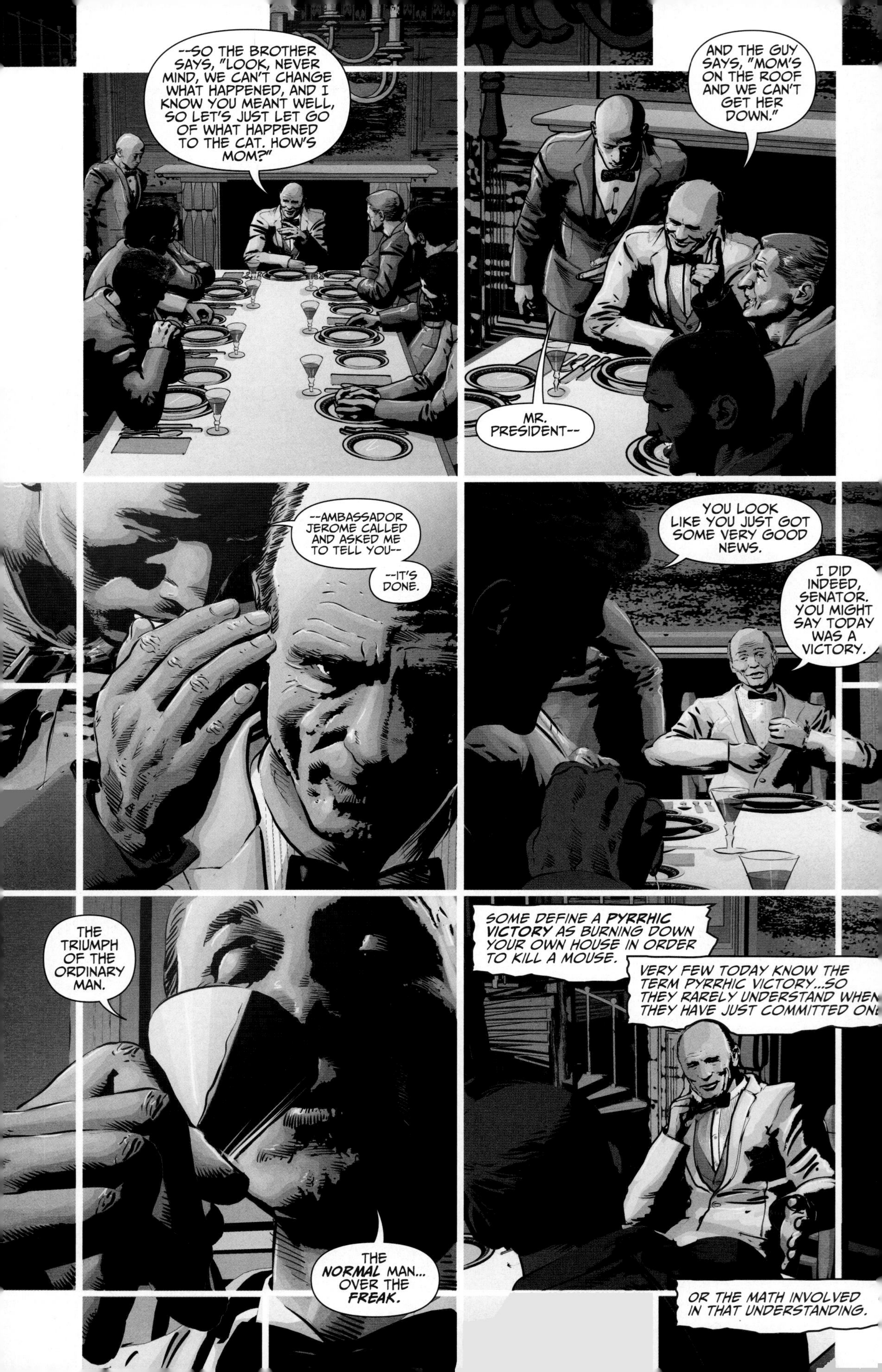
--SO THE BROTHER SAYS, "LOOK, NEVER MIND, WE CAN'T CHANGE WHAT HAPPENED, AND I KNOW YOU MEANT WELL, SO LET'S JUST LET GO OF WHAT HAPPENED TO THE CAT. HOW'S MOM?"
AND THE GUY SAYS, "MOM'S ON THE ROOF AND WE CAN'T GET HER DOWN."
MR. PRESIDENT--
--AMBASSADOR JEROME CALLED AND ASKED ME TO TELL YOU--
--IT'S DONE.
YOU LOOK LIKE YOU JUST GOT SOME VERY GOOD NEWS.
I DID INDEED, SENATOR. YOU MIGHT SAY TODAY WAS A VICTORY.
THE TRIUMPH OF THE ORDINARY MAN.
THE NORMAL MAN... OVER THE FREAK.
SOME DEFINE A PYRRHIC VICTORY AS BURNING DOWN YOUR OWN HOUSE IN ORDER TO KILL A MOUSE.
VERY FEW TODAY KNOW THE TERM PYRRHIC VICTORY...SO THEY RARELY UNDERSTAND WHEN THEY HAVE JUST COMMITTED ONE
OR THE MATH INVOLVED IN THAT UNDERSTANDING.

ONE CONNECTION. ONE *HEALER* NO LONGER ABLE TO *HEAL*...TO HOLD BACK THE *TIDE*.

ONE DORMANT CELL. ONE CANARY IN THE MINE SHAFT.

TWO MOURNERS, ENRAGED AT THE WORLD.

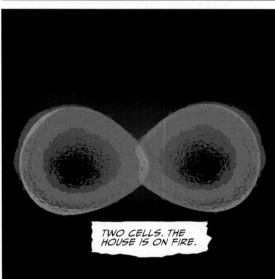

TWO CELLS. THE HOUSE IS ON FIRE.

FOUR MOURNERS. THE MOUSE HAS THE ONLY KEY.

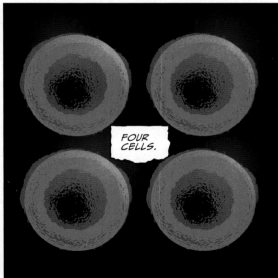

FOUR CELLS.

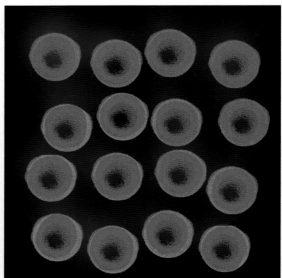

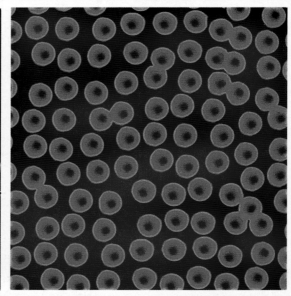

THE CLOCK IS TICKING,
THE FUTURE POISED ON
THE EDGE OF A KNIFE.

READY--

STEADY--

GO.

LETTER FROM THE CREATOR OF THE RESISTANCE

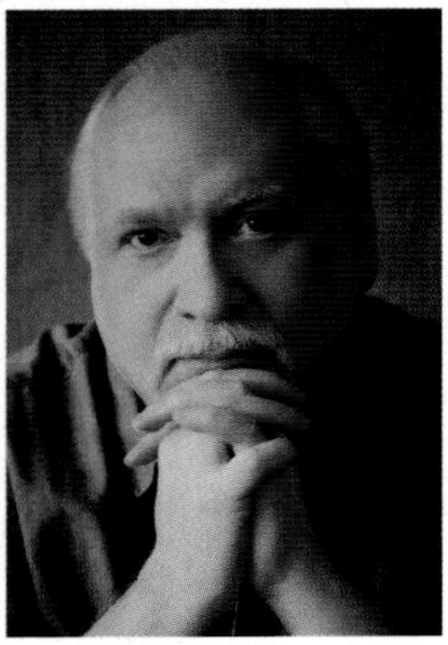

On the morning of June 4, 2018, a mysterious email arrived in my inbox under the subject **Hello from Axel Alonso**. It contained just two sentences: *I'd love to catch up sometime soon and let you know what I'm up to. Would you be available to chat sometime in the next few weeks?*

Now, Axel's a nice guy, a lovely guy, a snappy dresser and (I'm told) a good dancer, but nobody ever just comes by the house to catch up and tell me what they're up to. One does not simply walk into Mordor to talk to Sauron about having just taken up Zorbing. (It's a thing, look it up.) So I knew something was up.

The last time I'd worked directly with Axel was during my 6-year-plus run on *The Amazing Spider-Man*, during which time I came to understand why Axel is one of the best and most highly regarded editors in the comics field when it comes to working with writers, artists and the legion of other folks involved in producing these books. He knows that creative folks are like feral cats: we are cute and fuzzy from a distance, but inside our heads we're running all kinds of tapes that you have no idea even exist until you put your hand out too fast and it comes back a bloody stump. We all have rules of engagement. Mine is simple: don't touch my stuff. It's not that my stuff is better than anybody else's, it's just that it's mine, it has my name on it, it's just the way I want it, so don't touch my frickin' stuff.

Six years of *ASM* plus a clutch of minis, and Axel never touched my frickin' stuff.

So when we met up two weeks later here at Casa Joe, I was eager to learn what he was up to, provided it did not *actually* involve Zorbing. He explained that he and former Marvel Publisher and all around swell guy Bill Jemas had formed a new company called AWA (for Artists, Writers and Artisans, because I guess Artists, Writers and Astronauts was already taken) and together they were quietly lining up some of the best and brightest people in the business to come and play in their yard, a list that included folks like Reggie Hudlin, Margaret Stohl, Gregg Hurwitz, Frank Cho, Peter Milligan, Tommy Lee Edwards and Garth Freaking Ennis, whose Sacred Name has replaced Yog-Sothoth when it comes to opening the gate to strang worlds. *Iä! Iä! Alonso fhtagn!*

Against that catalog of luminaries, I couldn't figur out what the hell Axel could possibly want with *me*

So he told me.

"Along with the creator-owned books, I want t create a shared storytelling universe that othe writers can dial into if they choose to do so, wher all of the books complement and line up with eac other in specific ways that tie together but not i a way that requires readers to buy all of them. It' an added value: the more you read, the more yo begin to experience a much bigger story.

"What that shared universe is, how it works the parts and pieces, how to lay it all out so it' easy for other writers to dial into if they choos to do so, something that will add to their storytel ing process without interfering with their uniqu vision or limiting the scope of their imagination.. have no idea what that is or how it works. I jus know that it has to be unlike anything anybody' ever done before. That's why I'm here. You're world-builder, this is what you *do*, so if anyon can figure it out, you're the guy."

We spent the next several hours (and man days afterward by email) discussing not just sto ry ideas, but the themes and subjects that ma tered to us on a personal basis. Good stories ar about the connective material of emotional con sequence, not just stuff happening, which is wh *The king died then the queen died* is an inciden and *The king died then the queen died of grief* i a story. So our universe couldn't just be a box i which stuff happened in various titles, there ha

What is the paradigm right now?

to be emotionally connective material that woul serve as the foundation for a macro story con taining a multitude of individual, complementar stories.

We talked about the need to write somethin that would speak to our current paradigm as society, just as the early DC books spoke to post-WW2 environment that was about the rol of government and authorities as heroes, and th Marvel books that arose during the turbulent six ties reflected a paradigm that favored anti- autho ity figures. What is the paradigm *right now*? What did we want to say with this story and why should it matter to the readership of an already crowded comics marketplace? Who is it ultimately *about* and who is it ultimately *for*?

Out of these discussions came the Axelverse. Well, *I* call it the Axelverse, partly because Axel was the Prime Mover in reaching out, it's his (and Bill's and the backers') company, but mainly because he hates it when I call it the Axelverse, so nobody reading this should call it that either. Seriously. If you see him at a convention and you ask about the books, don't call it the Axelverse. That would be a terrible thing to do so I would never, ever suggest it.

The story would be told on a planetary scale, and since there are very few things that can af-

It's the democratization of superpowers

fect everyone on the planet without destroying it, we agreed that the logical choice was a genetic-based pandemic of some sort (which by a weird quirk of fate has resonance in the current coronavirus situation). The virus causes the death of over 400 million people worldwide, forcing the human race to confront the very real probability of extinction until, suddenly and without explanation, it goes dormant, after which we discover that many of those who survived have developed extraordinary abilities as a consequence of changes to their DNA caused by the virus.

We're talking millions of people who suddenly find themselves with powers, and are spread through every country, in every social class and caste. Good people, bad people, and people who simply don't want to get involved one way or another. It's the democratization of superpowers, but not in any political sense of that term. It means that you don't need to be an industrialist with billions of dollars to spend on making high-powered armored suits, you don't need to be a scientist or a pilot or be in exactly the right spot as a radioactive spider falls out of the drop-ceiling… t strikes students and store clerks and CEOs and petty criminals and dancers and ravers and reverends and geeks and the Beautiful People and the Unseen People and the Hidden People and the Lost People and the locked-up and the runaway and the thrown-away and the neglected and the powerful…the process is totally random and absolutely, utterly unmindful of borders or personalities or resources.

And that randomness is both beautiful and deeply terrifying.

(My theory on power is that it operates the same as fame and money. If you were a nice person before fame&money, you're a nicer person afterward; if you were a jerk before fame&money, you're a bigger jerk afterward. So the power makes you more of what you were in the first place.)

How would *you* react, or your family and friends, if you were among those affected? What would you do? What wouldn't you do? What *couldn't* you do?

How would governments and churches and corporations and medical institutions and militaries and security forces respond? And in turn, how would you react to the prospect of being exploited, co-opted, jailed, interrogated, blackmailed, sponsored, compromised, exiled, purchased, elevated, worshipped, pursued or denied your basic human rights?

If you've been poor and put down and beat up your whole life, do you give in to revenge or rise above it?

How do you react to being given the gift of extraordinary powers if you live in the Miami club world? Or how about Saudi Arabia? North Korea? Colombia? Afghanistan? China? The Bronx?

If you've lived your whole life on the wrong side of the law not because you had to but because you liked it, with your ambitions constrained only by fear of being locked in a cell the rest of your life, and one day that concern no longer applies to you…how far and how dark would you go?

If you're a dictator presiding over a beaten, repressed population and suddenly there are several thousand people among them powerful enough to destroy your entire army and yank the spine out of your dead body just for kicks, but you have no intention of surrendering power…what do you do?

If you're a President and you want to try and get your hands around the problem even if that means abridging civil rights, how far are you prepared to go? And how far will someone else go to stop you?

Did the virus go dormant because it was beaten or because it's achieved what it was designed to do? Were people given these abilities as a gift, or in order to create Fifth Columnists inside every nation of the world? If so, to what end, and who's responsible? And what does all of that mean to the ten million people who have been affected?

Emotional consequence.

The king died, then the queen died of grief.

That is the universe which some of the brightest lights of the comics industry have been invited to explore, and play in, and create stories about people and ideas and themes that *matter* to them. Stories you won't find in any other comics universe.

That, in short…is the Axelverse.

Just, whatever you do, don't call it that around Axel. I got enough problems.

-J. Michael Straczynski

The Resistance #1 Variant Cover by Mike Deodato Jr., Colored by Snakebite Cortez

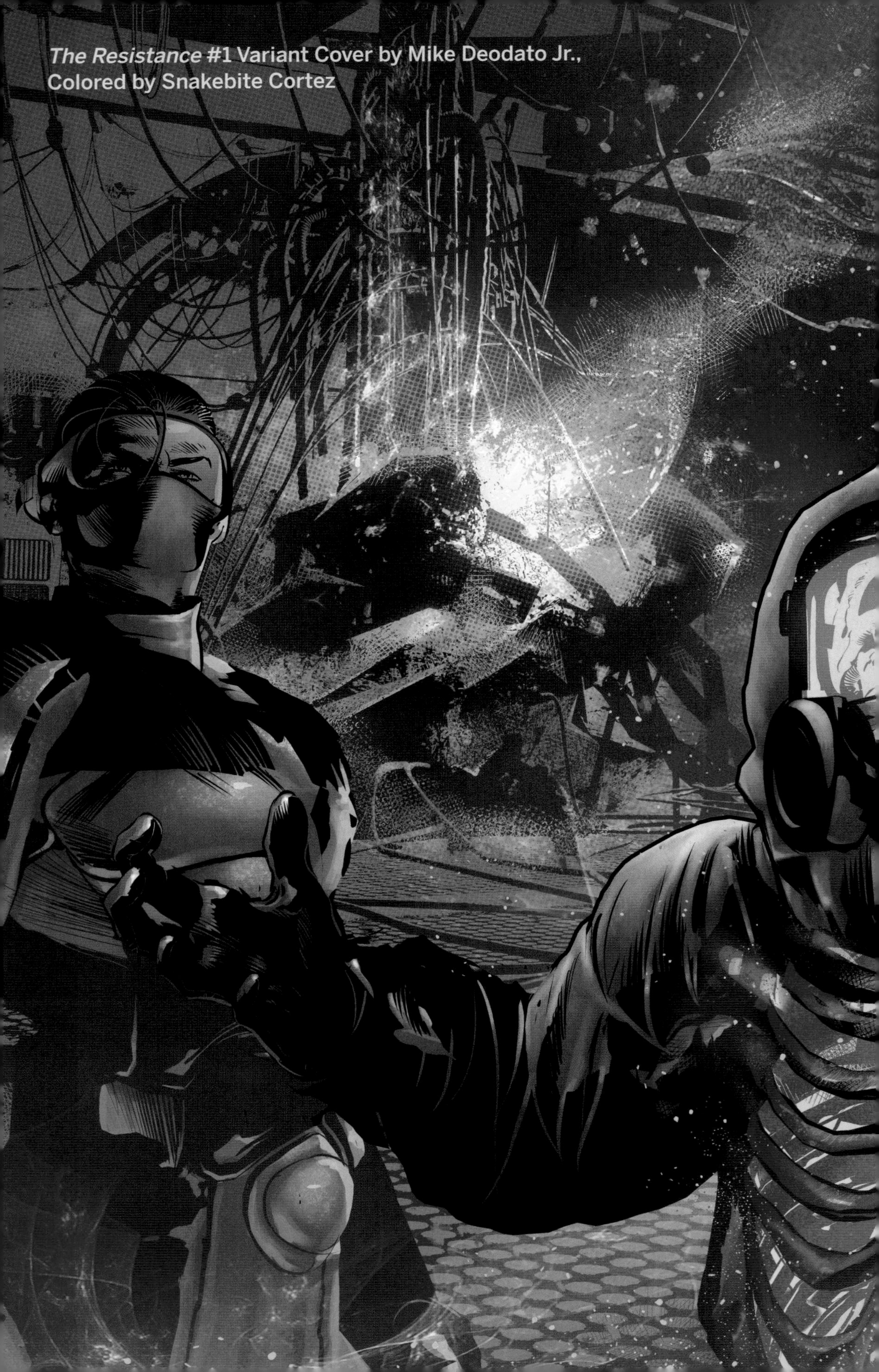

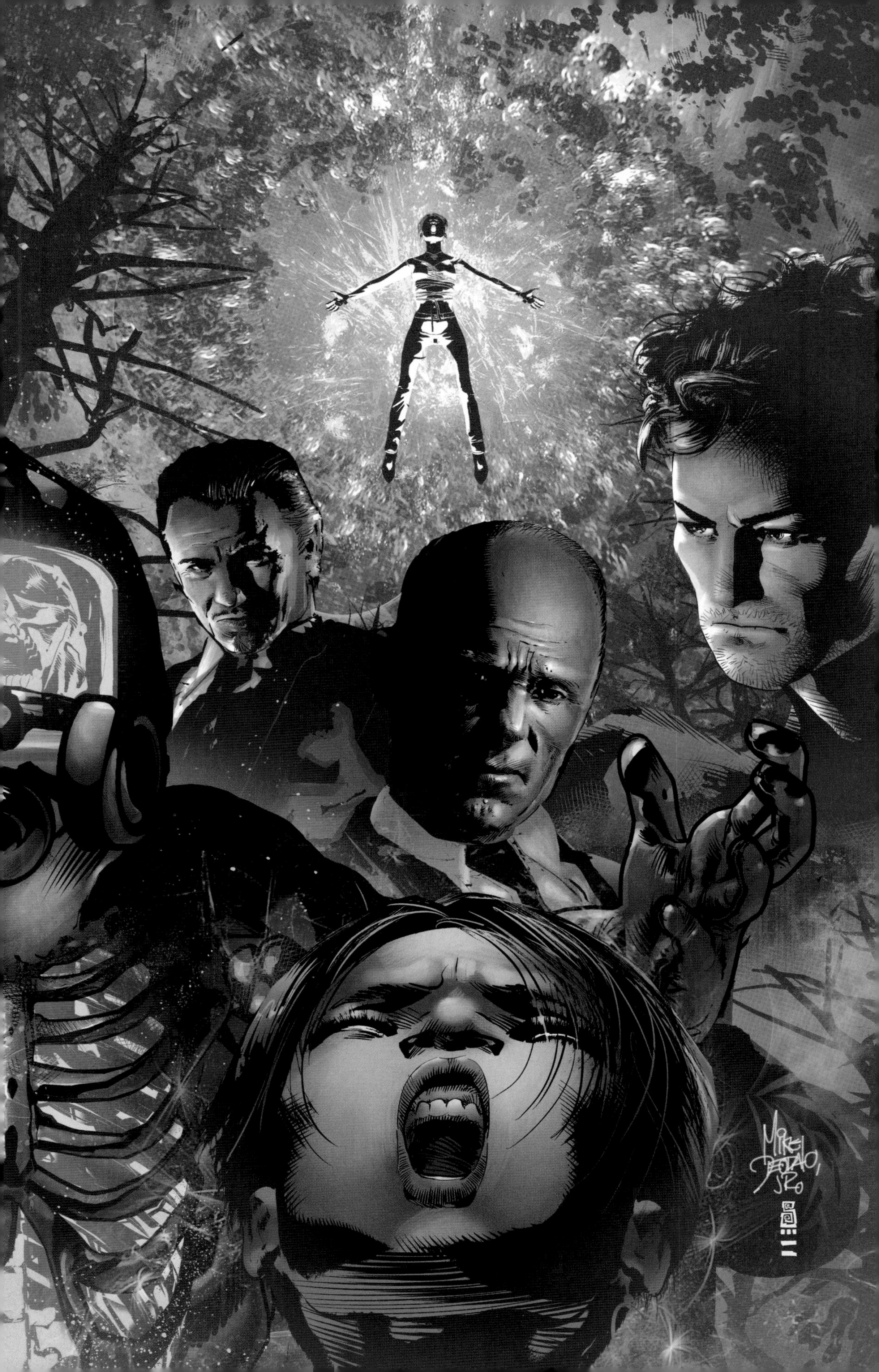

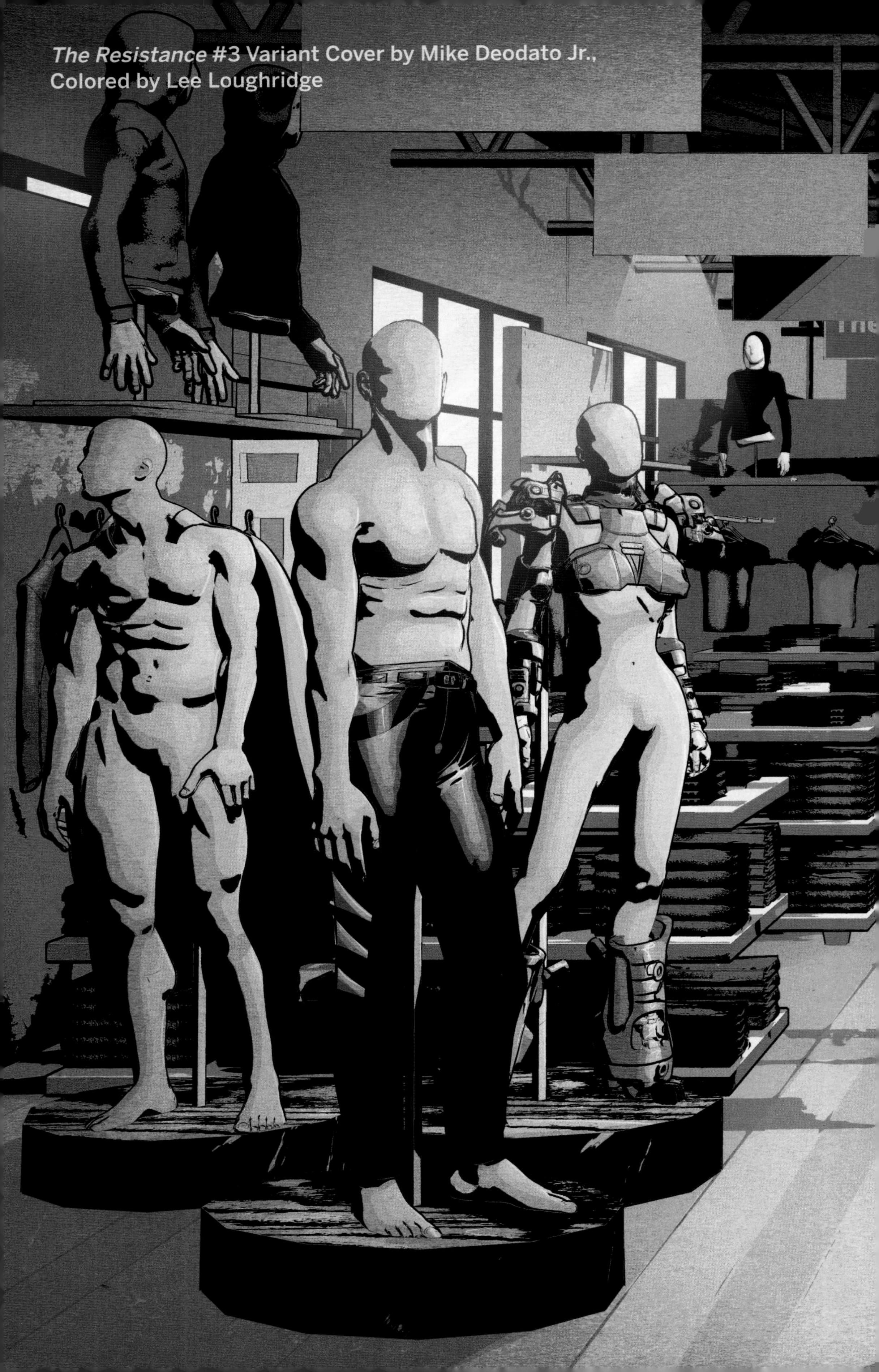

The Resistance #3 Variant Cover by Mike Deodato Jr., Colored by Lee Loughridge

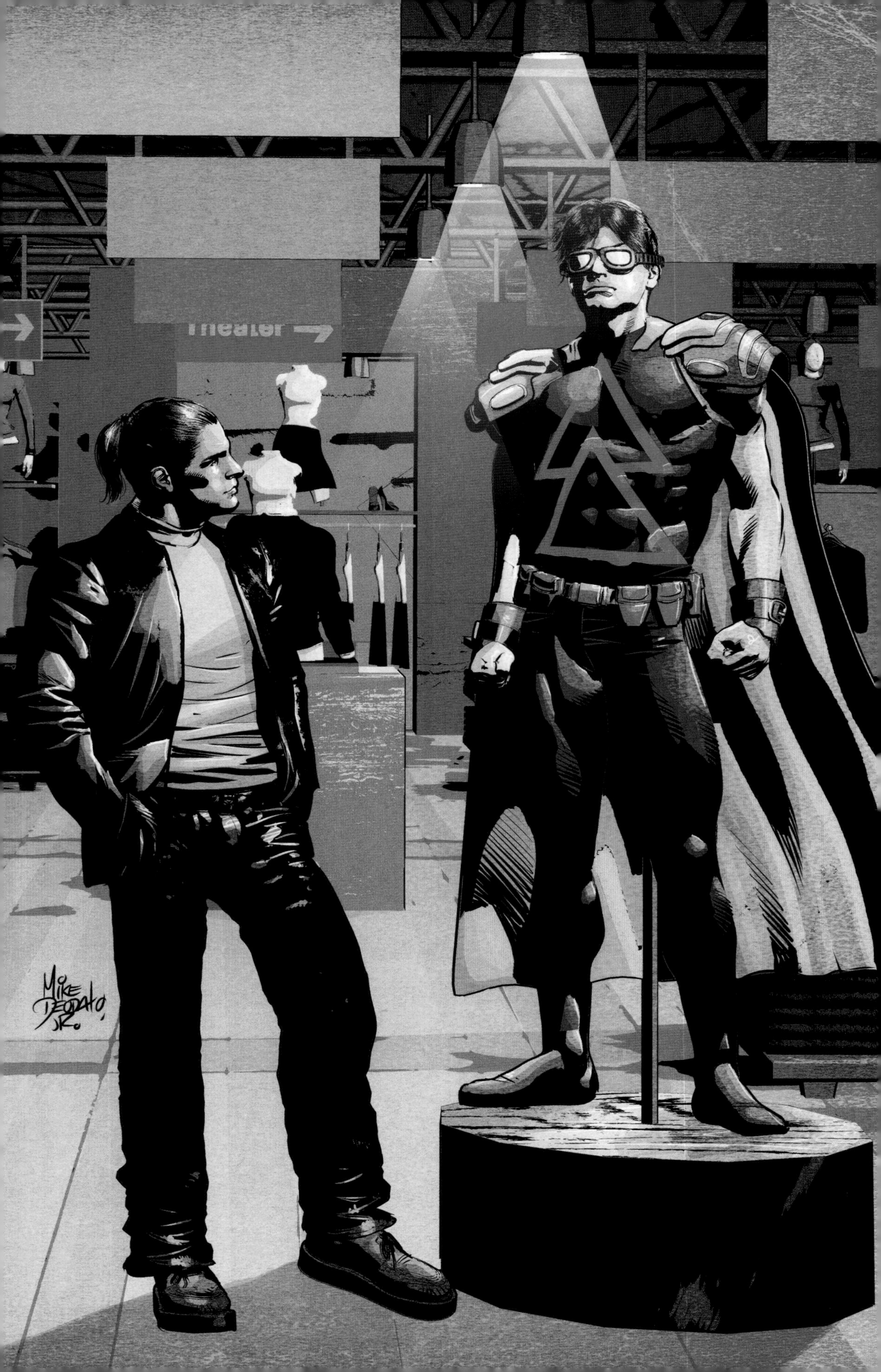
Theater
Mike Deodato, Jr.

PANELS ONE THROUGH SIX

PANEL ONE

A newscaster sits at a desk covered
with printouts and coffee cups.
It's been a long night. The sense
of disorder is still there...but
something's changed.

NEWSCASTER
Starting around ten p.m. Eastern time
we began receiving reports that we
held off covering because there have
been so many rumors...we wanted to be
sure they were true before --

PANEL TWO

Joy comes into his face.

NEWSCASTER
Over the last twelve hours, the xv1n1
virus has gone dormant in patients
around the world...almost as though
a switch had been thrown and it all
just...STOPPED.
(second) Everywhere.
(third) Simultaneously.

PANEL THREE

A downshot into the studio.

NEWSCASTER
The crisis is over...the human race is
safe...it's over....
(second)
...it's over....

PANEL FOUR

Time's Square in daylight. Crowds
celebrate the news, streamers and
confetti like New Year's Eve.

RADIO CAPTION
"We are getting reports of spontaneous
celebrations in Melbourne, Chicago,
St. Petersburg, Seoul, Nairobi --"

PANEL ONE

A montage of holy places around
the world as celebrants cheer and
embrace.

PANEL TWO

CAPTION
And in all the holy places the air
was electric with cries of joy,
a million voices fructifying into
prayers and hosannas, shouts of God
is great and Inshallah and Shalom.

A press conference in a medical
facility, with white-robed scientists
facing the press.

CAPTION
And because success has a million
mothers....

SCIENTIST
-- so we kept our attempts to develop
a counter-virus that would wipe out
xv1n1 secret because we were afraid
of getting people's hopes up while we
introduced it into a trial population
and, from there, the rest of the
world.
(second)
But it seems our efforts have won the
day. The virus has been defeated.

SCIENTIST #2
We've subsequently decided to take
our company public, so any investors
who want to jump on, this would be
the time.

PANEL ONE

PANELS ONE THROUGH SIX

Two rows of three panels each, faces of
people (maybe some we've seen before)
and politicians and parties in Vatican
Square and elsewhere.

CAPTION
It seemed EVERYONE had theories as to
why the virus had simply...stopped.

RADIO CAPTION
"-- a Resistance movement inside the
organization that unleashed this virus
in order to to create a New World Order
were able to turn it off. It's the only
way to explain how it happened all at
once --"

(second)
"The whole thing was just a false flag to
cover genocide --"

(third)
"It was a shot across the bow of the
sinful and the aberrant, and it was the
prayers of the pious that saved them, so
they better get in line --"

(fourth)
"I don't want to rain on anybody's
parade but someone should point out
that the virus is still there, it's just
dormant --"

(fifth)
"The question now is what do we do about
those who survived the virus, and are
dealing with after-effects that range
from the minimal to the horrific to the
unknown --"

(sixth)
"I don't care about any of that!
What matters I that I'm alive, my whole
family is alive and BEING ALIVE IS
AMAZING!"

PANEL ONE

A wide view of a cemetery. We can see
in the distance a young woman kneeling
on the ground by a fresh grave and
tombstone.

PANEL TWO

CAPTION
Everyone had theories. But no one knew
what REALLY happened.

Same angle, but pushing in.

CAPTION
Or why, or how.

PANEL THREE

Another angle, revealing LISA STAMER,
slender, straight brown hair, so pale
she's almost ethereal, early 20s,
kneeling on the soft ground, a white
rose dangling from her hand. Crying.

CAPTION
Or what it cost.

PANEL FOUR

Closer.

LISA
You just wouldn't listen. You NEVER
listened.

CAPTION
"Don't do it, Susie...please...please,
don't do it!"

PANEL FIVE

A forest. Night. Lisa stands facing
her twin sister SUSIE.

SUSIE
I have to --

LISA
No you don't --

SUSIE
Lisa --

LISA
There has to be someone else --

SUSIE
There hasn't been, there isn't going
to be, and we can't wait any longer.

PAGE TWENTY

PANEL ONE

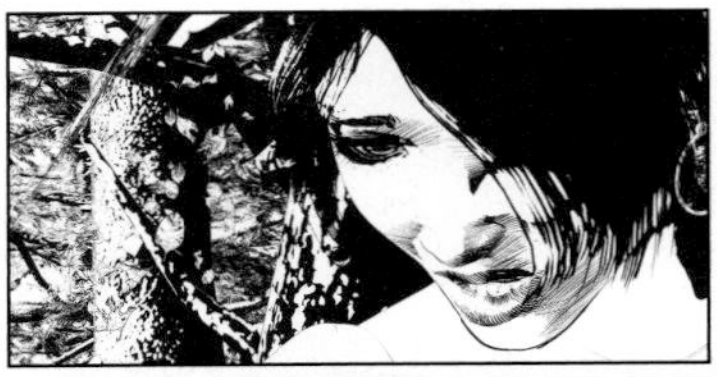

Favoring Susie. Strangely calm.
Her mind is made up. Resigned to what she has to do.A part of her is already gone.

PANEL TWO

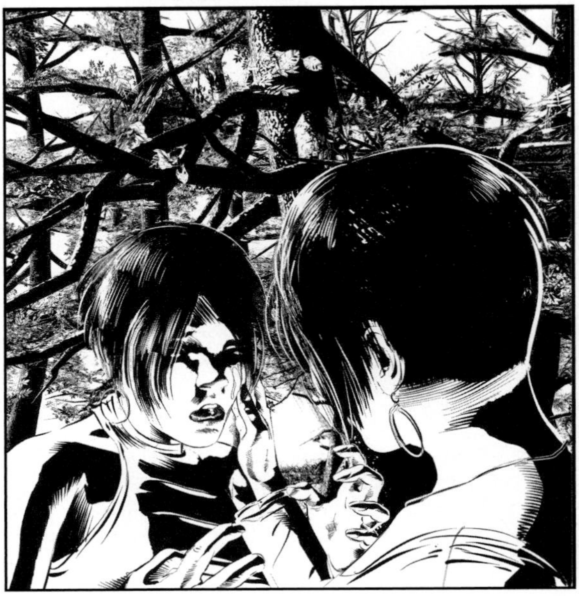

SUSIE
When we survived the virus...when we were part of that impossibly lucky five percent...I thought it was a miracle. We BOTH did.
(second)
Then afterward, when we learned what we could DO...it became even MORE of a miracle.

She touches Lisa's tearful face.

SUSIE
This gift comes with a REASON, Lisa. Something that can only be done by one of us.

LISA
And what if you're wrong? What if we're not as powerful as you THINK we are, together or apart?
(second)
What if it tears you apart? What if you throw it all away for nothing?

PANEL THREE

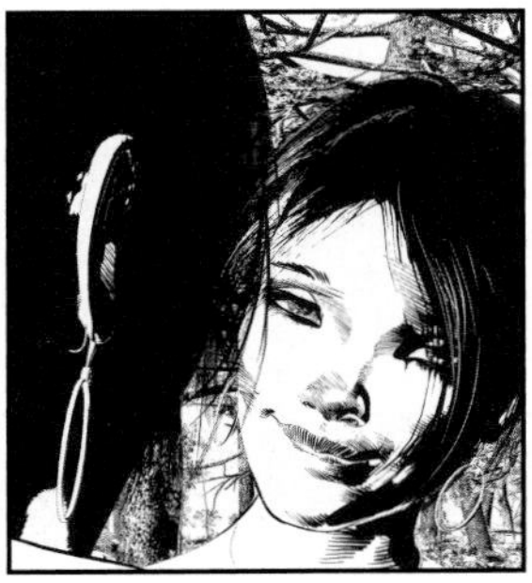

On Susie. Beatific.

SUSIE
Then I'll know I tried. (second) I tried to save the world. (third)
How many can say that?

PANEL FOUR

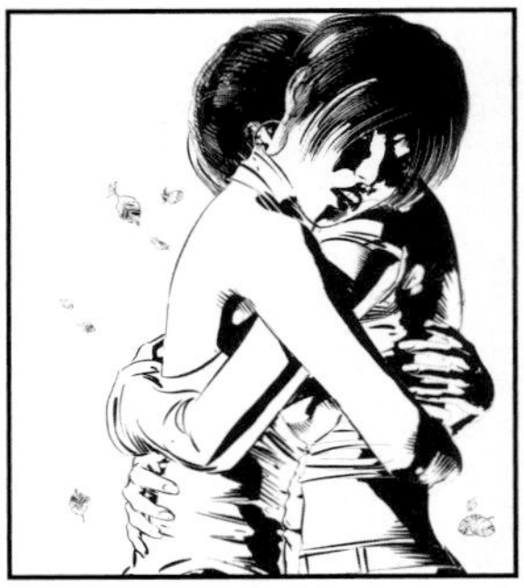

They embrace.

SUSIE
Goodbye, little sister.

LISA
No...don't...please, Susie...don't leave me....

SUSIE
Goodbye...goodbye my better self, my beautiful reflection...

PANEL FIVE

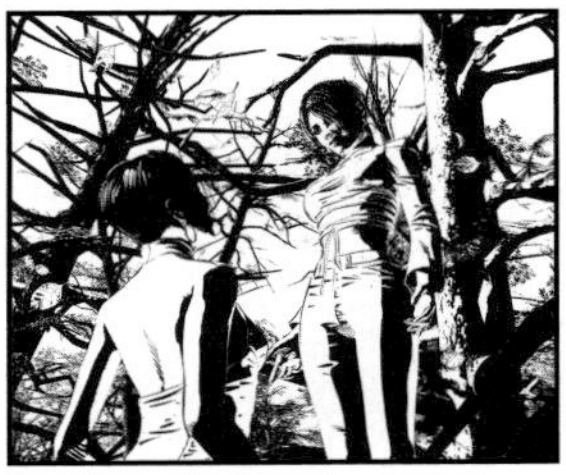

Past Lisa to Susie, who seems somewhat higher up than she did a moment ago.

SUSIE
...goodbye....

PANEL ONE

Susie rises into the night air, the
moon bright in the sky above, her skin
starting to glow.

LISA
Susie, please...

PANEL TWO

Susie stretches her arms out to the
world, her skin brighter by the second.

PANEL THREE

On her face, luminous, eyes closed.

PANEL FOUR

She opens her eyes, and LIGHT pours out
of them.

PAGE TWENTY-TWO

FULL PAGE SPLASH

Susie hovers above the trees, arms thrown back with the force of what she is doing...her form as bright as a supernova, sending her life force out into humanity, mouth open in a silent scream.

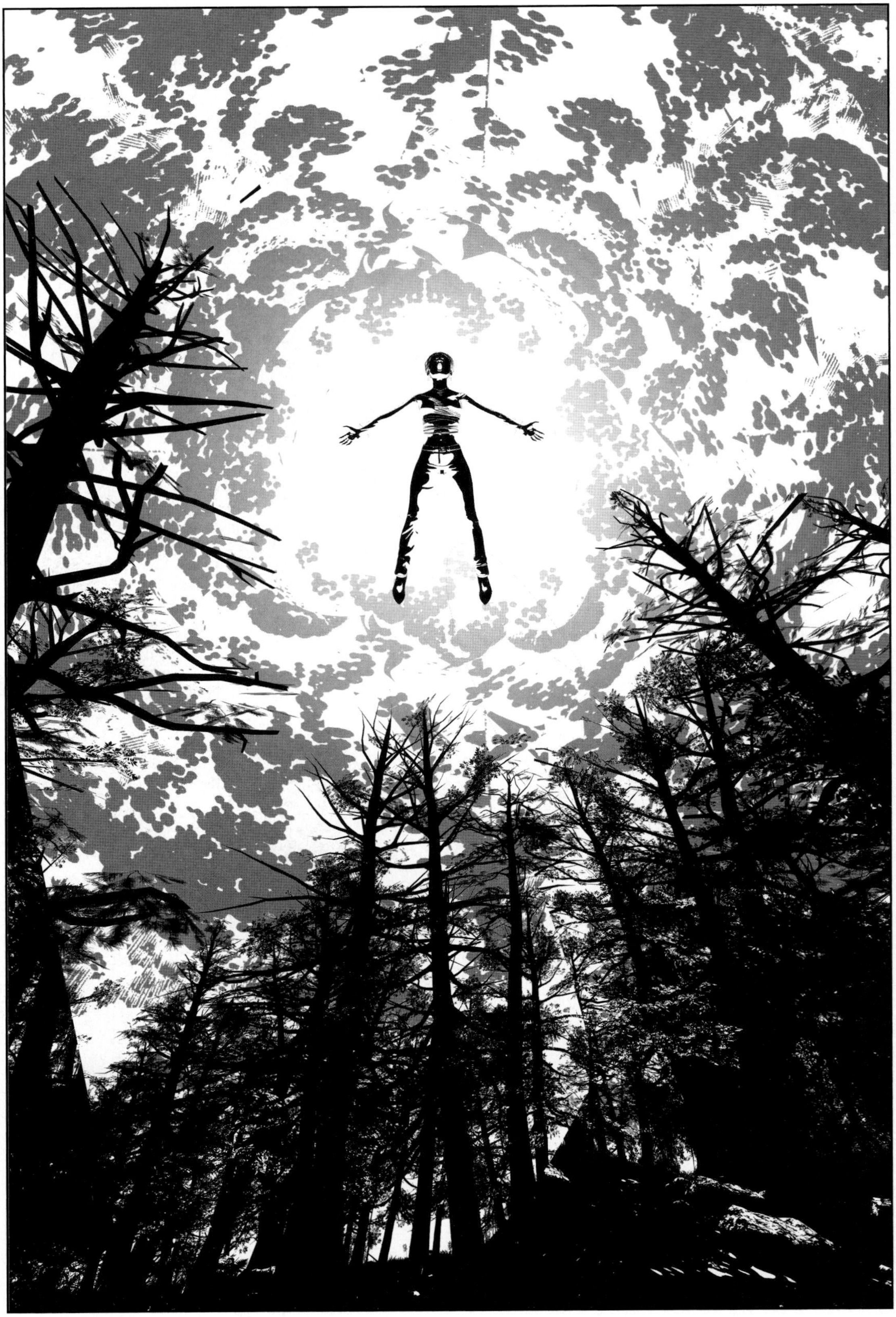

PAGE TWENTY-THREE

PANEL ONE

Tight on the headstone set into the ground.We only see part of it no dates. SUSIE STAMER. LOVING TWIN SISTER. YOU WERE BRAVER IN DEATH THAN I WILL EVER BE IN LIFE. GOODBYE.

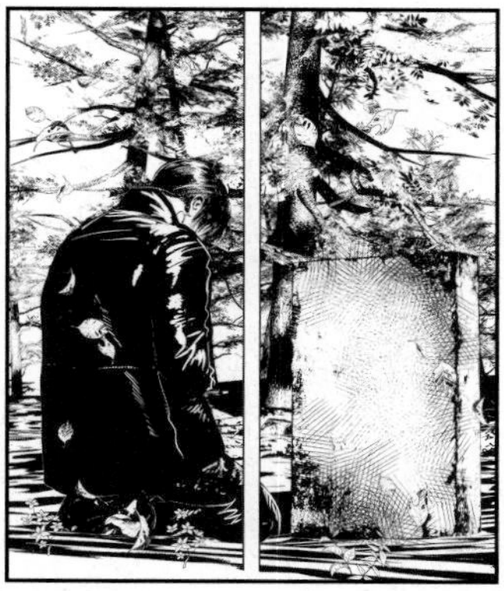

PANEL TWO

Lisa puts the white rose atop the still-fresh mound of earth, the stem gently inserted into the ground so it stands up.

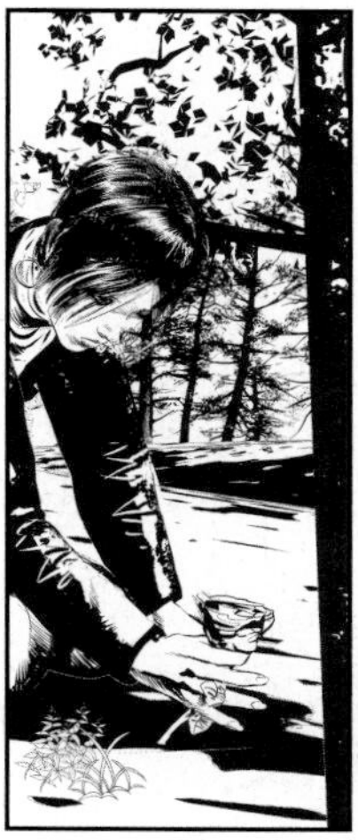

PANEL THREE

She touches it, her finger glowing where it makes contact.

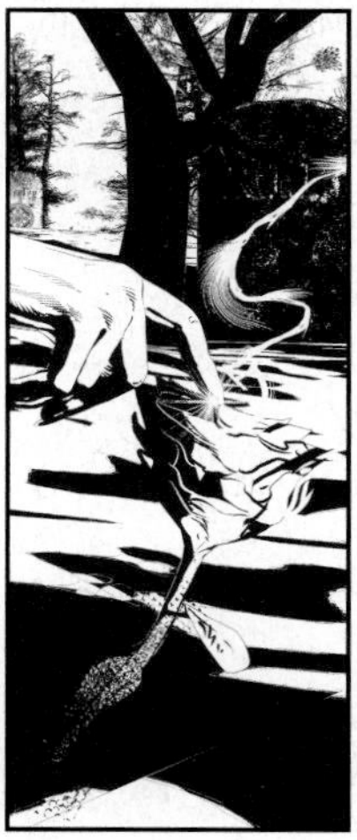

PANEL FOUR

She walks away. We don't see the flower from this angle.

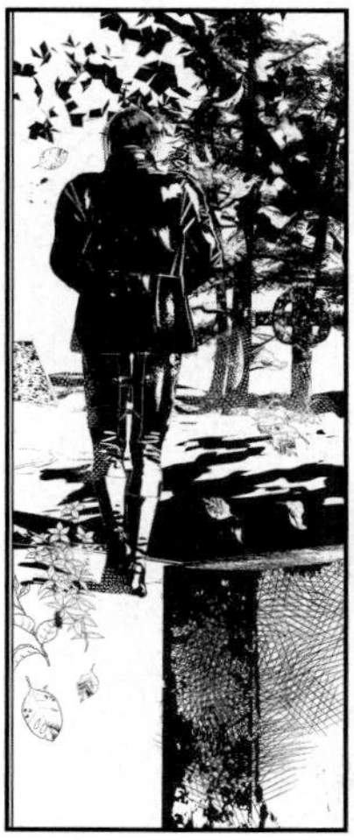

PANEL FIVE

Back on the flower, which has grown into a complete rosebush full of white flowers.

RADIO CAPTION
"Something we've never seen before."

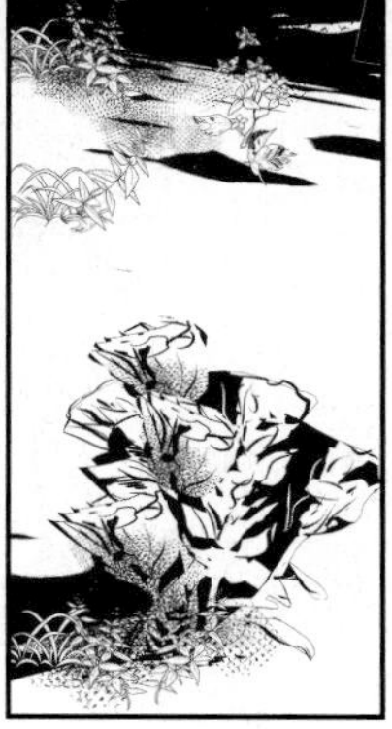

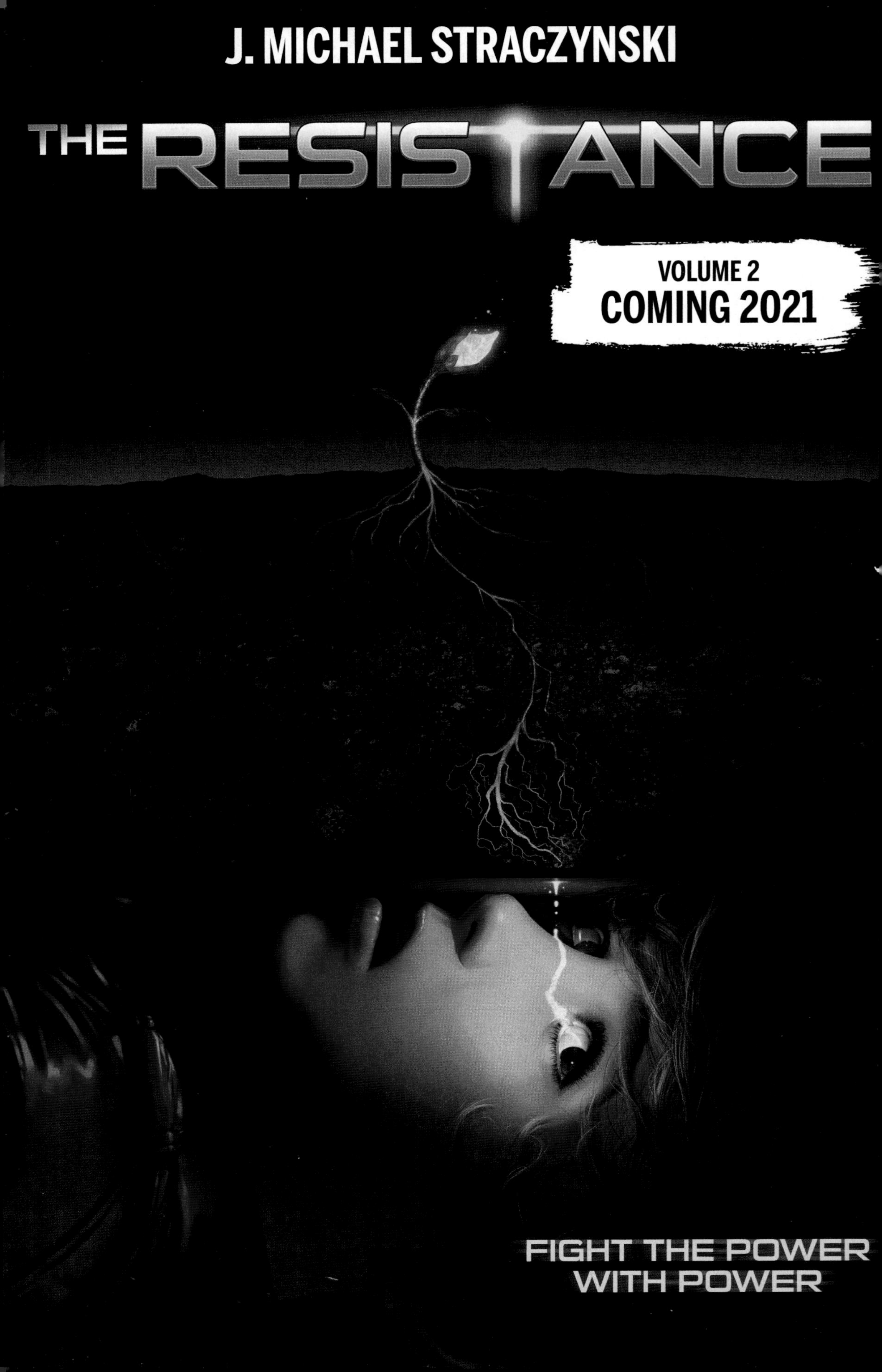
J. MICHAEL STRACZYNSKI
THE RESISTANCE
VOLUME 2
COMING 2021
FIGHT THE POWER
WITH POWER